DATE DUE		

Latin Looks

LATIN LOOKS

Images of Latinas and Latinos in the U.S. Media

edited by

Clara E. Rodríguez

Fordham University

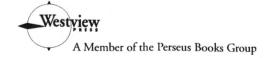

A Member of the Perseus Books Group

Copyright © 1997 by Westview Press, A Member of the Perseus Books Group

Published in 1997 in the United States of America by Westview Press, 5500 Central Avenue, Boulder,
Colorado 80301-2877, and in the United Kingdom by Westview Press, 12 Hid's Copse Road, Cumnor
Hill, Oxford OX2 9JJ

Library of Congress Cataloging-in-Publication Data
Latin looks: images of Latinas and Latinos in the U.S. media / edited
   by Clara E. Rodriguez
      p.   cm.
   Includes bibliographical references (p.   ) and index.
   ISBN 0-8133-2765-2.—ISBN 0-8133-2766-0 (pbk.)
   1. Hispanic Americans and mass media—United States.
I. Rodriguez, Clara E., 1944-   .
P94.5.H582U65   1997
305.868'073—dc21   97-1840
                                                                                      CIP

The paper used in this publication meets the requirements of the American National Standard for Per-
manence of Paper for Printed Library Materials Z39.48-1984.

PERSEUS
POD
ON DEMAND   10   9

Contents

Illustrations

Figures

Tables

PHOTO 4.3 **Myrtle Gonzalez** was the industry's first Latina star. A native Mexican Californian, she was the daughter of a Los Angeles grocer. Her first film was *Ghosts* in 1911. Between 1911 and 1917, she starred in more than forty films, many of them westerns and often portraying "vigorous outdoor heroines" (Rios-Bustamante, 1992:22; see also Reyes and Rubie, 1994:413–414). (Courtesy of The Museum of Modern Art Film Stills Archive)

PHOTO 4.4 **Beatriz Michelena** starred in her first film *Salomy Jane* in 1914. By 1919, she had starred in sixteen feature films, winning the acclaim of the major trade paper of the day, which placed her on its cover page and referred to her as the "greatest and most beautiful artist" in motion pictures (Rios-Bustamante, 1992:22). (Courtesy of The Museum of Modern Art Film Stills Archive)

PHOTO 4.5   **Mona Maris** was born in Buenos Aires to a Spanish family; she made her screen debut in England in 1926 (Reyes and Rubie, 1994:438). The publicity caption with this photo described her as an "Argentine actress, educated in Europe, who first won fame in German pictures." She starred in a number of films. This photo was taken about the time of one of her most noted films, *The Arizona Kid* (1930). (Courtesy of The Museum of Modern Art Film Stills Archive)

PHOTOS 4.6 and 4.7
Dolores Del Río has
been referred to as "the
first Latina superstar"
(Rios-Bustamante,
1988:20). Her career
spanned half a century
and included starring
roles in both silent and
sound movies. The
daughter of a banker in
Mexico, she was "discovered" by a film director and brought to Hollywood as the
female Valentino. During her career, she played a wide variety of leading roles. She
also became a top star in Mexican movies during the 1940s, made various television
appearances in the United States, and was known as the "First Lady of Mexican
Theater" (Reyes and Rubie, 1994:389–393). These photos show the cool beauty,
elegance, and glamour for which she was known, especially during the 1930s. Photo
4.6 is dated ca. 1935; Photo 4.7, 1933. (Courtesy of The Museum of Modern Art
Film Stills Archive)

PHOTOS 4.8 and 4.9
Lupe Vélez was born in San Luis
Potosi, Mexico, and educated in
a convent school in San Antonio,
Texas. Her first major role was
opposite Douglas Fairbanks in
the silent movie *The Gaucho*
(1928), in which she played
what was to be the first of a long
line of "fire-spitting vamps" (Hadley-Garcia, 1993:45). Already a star in the late
1920s, she was able to successfully make the transition to sound movies in the 1930s
because her voice was "husky and cartoon-like"—a clear asset in the comedic
characters she played. Her career skyrocketed in 1939 when she began her "Mexican
Spitfire" series. She made eight films in this series before committing suicide in 1944.
Photo 4.8 was taken in 1928 for *Lady of the Pavements*. Photo 4.9 is ca. 1931.
(Courtesy of The Museum of Modern Art Film Stills Archive)

PHOTOS 4.10 and 4.11 **Rita Hayworth** began her career as Margarita Cansino, the name given to her by her father, a noted Spanish dancer, and her Irish mother. She made twelve films with this name, often playing Mexican señoritas. Her first film was a Spanish-language short subject, but her major screen debut was in 1935 in *Dante's Inferno*. Photo 4.10 is from this period. Photo 4.11 shows her as Rita Hayworth in *Gilda* (1946). Anglicizing her name, broadening her forehead, losing weight, and dying her hair red, she went on to become "The Love Goddess," the "ethereal all-American girl," and the favorite G.I. pinup girl during the 1940s (Reyes and Rubie, 1994:418). (Courtesy of The Museum of Modern Art Film Stills Archive)

PHOTO 4.12
Olga San Juan, known as the "Puerto Rican Pepperpot," was born in Brooklyn, but her parents returned to Puerto Rico when she was three. She costarred with Fred Astaire in *Blue Skies* (1946), from which their dance "Heat Wave" remains a classic. Here she is shown in *One Touch of Venus* (1948) (Hadley-Garcia, 1993:82; Reyes and Rubie, 1994:493–494). (Courtesy of The Museum of Modern Art Film Stills Archive)

PHOTO 4.13 **María Montez** was born in Ciudad Trujillo in the Dominican Republic, but she was educated in a convent school in the Canary Islands. Because her father was a Spanish consul, she traveled and lived in South America, France, England, and Ireland. Discovered in Manhattan in 1940 by a talent scout, she became a top money-making star for Universal Films during the 1940s. She made eighteen films, the majority of them in technicolor, and she was a favorite pinup girl of servicemen during World War II. Her name became synonymous with exotic adventure epics, such as the one she posed for in this photo, *Queen of the Nile* (1945). Hadley-Garcia (1993:155) notes that, unusual for a Latin, she played authority figures

that dominated nefarious proceedings and functioned as a sex symbol in diverse nationalities. (Courtesy of The Museum of Modern Art Film Stills Archive)

PHOTOS 4.14 and 4.15
Carmen Miranda is probably the best-known Latina star. Born in Portugal and raised in Brazil, she was already a popular and well-known performer in South America before she was brought to the United States by the theatrical producer Lee Shubert in 1939. She appeared in fourteen Hollywood films and at the height of her career was the top money-making star in Hollywood. Known for her exotic, magnificent headdresses; sparkling smile; radiant personality; energized and rhythmic dancing and singing—and her platform shoes—she developed a signature style that was sometimes imitated and parodied. In Photo 4.14 she appears in her well-known attire; in Photo 4.15, in a more conventional pose, both ca. 1942. (Courtesy of The Museum of Modern Art Film Stills Archive)

PHOTO 4.16 **Katy Jurado** came to Hollywood from Mexico City in 1951. She is shown here in 1952, when she hit her Hollywood peak in *High Noon* (1952) as a strong Latina character who had been a mistress to the two leading men but was also the proprietor of a store and a saloon (Hadley-Garcia, 1933:124). Curiously, in Mexican films she "was always cast as a glamour girl or wealthy socialite and sometimes sang and danced . . . [whereas] in American films she almost always played a sultry Mexican beauty, Indian squaw, or suffering mother (Reyes and Rubie, 1994:428). In the mid-1980s, she played the mother in one of the few Latino-themed television sitcoms, *aka Pablo.* (Courtesy of The Museum of Modern Art Film Stills Archive)

PHOTOS 4.17 and 4.18
Rita Moreno, born in Humacao, Puerto Rico, and raised in New York City, was the first Latina to win an Academy Award and the first woman to have won all four coveted entertainment awards: the Oscar, Tony, Emmy, and Grammy (Katz, 1994:972). A performer since the age of seven, she made her Broadway debut at thirteen and her film debut in *The Toast of New Orleans* (1950) at eighteen. She is shown in Photo 4.17 for that film, in which she played a Cajun coquette. Photo 4.18 was taken while she was on location for the film *Untamed* (1955), a saga of pioneer days in South Africa. The publicity literature for the film described her as a "Lovely Latin bombshell" and a Latin spitfire. (Courtesy of The Museum of Modern Art Film Stills Archive)

PHOTO 4.19 **Chita Rivera** was born and raised in Washington, D.C., the third daughter of a Puerto Rican musician who played in the U.S. Navy band and a mixed Scots–Irish–Puerto Rican mother. At eleven, she won a scholarship to the Balanchine School of American Ballet. At seventeen, she was hired for the musical *Call Me Madam* and thus began her theatrical career as a singer and dancer. She played Anita in the Broadway version of *West Side Story* in 1957. Nominated for the Tony five times, she has received two, one for *The Rink* and the other for *The Kiss of the Spider Woman*. She has also received numerous other awards, including the Drama Desk Award, the Drama League Award, the Fred Astaire Award, and the Mother Hale Award. More a singer-dancer than an actress, she feels she escaped the pressures toward stereotyped portrayals that actresses like Rita Moreno experienced more intensely (Pacheco, 1993). (Courtesy of the Academy of Motion Picture Arts and Sciences)

PHOTO 4.20 **Raquel Welch** was born Raquel Tejada in Chicago. Her mother was of English descent and her father was a Bolivian-born engineer. She became an instant icon when she burst onto the movie scene in two science fiction classics, *Fantastic Voyage* and *One Million Years, B.C.* in 1966. Acknowledged as an undisputed major female star of the 1960s, she has appeared in over thirty-five films and tackled a wide variety of roles. In addition to her movie career, she made a triumphant Broadway debut in the hit musical *Woman of the Year* and has performed nationally and internationally in her own highly successful musical review. In 1996, she made her critically acclaimed debut as a continuing major character on television's *Central Park West* and is scheduled to host and narrate a six-part documentary on one hundred years of sensuality in the cinema. (Courtesy of Raquel Welch)

PHOTO 4.21
Charo was born María Rosario Pilar Martínez in Murcia, Spain. Despite having appeared in very few films, Charo received extensive exposure on television talk shows in the 1970s. Formerly the wife and singer of Xavier Cugat, she became known as the "coochie-coochie girl." Her "hot-blooded" and

"hyper" persona combined with her heavily accented, often humorous errors in English continued the comical style of Carmen Miranda and Lupe Vélez (Hadley-Garcia, 1993:200). Her cute, sexy, dizzy persona was sometimes contrasted with her skills as an accomplished classical guitarist. She appears in this photo for the film *The Concorde Airport* (1979) with her ever-present chihuahua. (Courtesy of the Academy of Motion Picture Arts and Sciences)

PHOTO 4.22
Rosie Pérez was raised in Brooklyn of Puerto Rican parentage. She studied marine biology in college and was twice "discovered" while dancing at a dance club—first by a *Soul Train* producer and then by Spike Lee, who cast her in her first major movie, *Do the Right Thing* (1989). Since then, she has had major roles in a number of

movies and was in line for an Oscar for her performance in *Fearless* (1993). In 1995, she was listed in the *Hollywood Reporter* as the most bankable Latina star (Avila, 1996:26). She has also developed her strengths in dance and has served as choreographer for other celebrities, including Diana Ross and Bobby Brown, and for the Fly Girls of TV's now defunct *In Living Color*. She is shown here in a scene from *White Men Can't Jump* (1992). (Courtesy of the Academy of Motion Picture Arts and Sciences)

PHOTO 4.23
Ramon Novarro is shown here in *The Prisoner of Zenda* (1922), in which he starred under his given name José Ramon Samaniegos. Changing his name, he went on to become a "guaranteed money-maker for MGM" (Hadley-Garcia, 1993:17), starring in such major motion pictures as *Ben Hur* (1926) and *Mata Hari* (1932) with Greta Garbo. (Courtesy of The Museum of Modern Art Film Stills Archive)

PHOTO 4.24
Antonio Moreno appears here as the wealthy owner of the world's largest department store, Mr. Cyrus T. Waltham, in the movie *It* (1927) opposite Clara Bow. Moreno, born in Spain, starred in a number of major silent films and had made at least twenty-nine such films by 1929. (Courtesy of The Museum of Modern Art Film Stills Archive)

PHOTOS 4.25 and 4.26
Gilbert Roland, shown here
ca. 1940, was born Luis
Antonio Damaso de Alsonso
in Mexico. He played a
variety of leading and
supporting roles thoughout a
long career, beginning in
1923 with silent movies and
continuing into the late
1970s. (Courtesy of The
Museum of Modern Art Film
Stills Archive)

PHOTO 4.27 **César Romero** is shown here ca. late 1940s. A descendant of the Cuban liberator Jose Martí, he played both ethnic and nonethnic roles in films and played the Cisco Kid in six adventure films in 1940 and 1941. He began acting in films in the mid-1930s, but his screen heyday occurred in the 1940s. He also had a substantial career in television in the 1960s, including as the Joker in *Batman,* and in the 1980s as the Greek billionaire on *Falcon Crest.* (Courtesy of The Museum of Modern Art Film Stills Archive)

PHOTO 4.28 **Anthony Quinn,** shown here in 1955 at the height of a long and illustrious career, which began in 1936. He was born to an Irish-Mexican father and a Mexican mother in Chihuahua, Mexico, but he was raised in Los Angeles near Hollywood. He has won two Academy Awards for Best Supporting Actor, one in 1952 for his role as Emiliano Zapata's brother in *Viva Zapata* and the other in 1956 for his portrayal of Paul Gauguin in *Lust for Life.* He has played a wide variety of character roles on screen and in the theater, written a best-selling autobiography, and developed his artistic talents as a sculptor and a painter. (Courtesy of The Museum of Modern Art Film Stills Archive)

PHOTO 4.29
Ricardo Montalban is shown here ca. 1950, just prior to the release of his film *Right Cross*. Born and raised in Mexico, he was described at this time as a romantic, dramatic screen favorite and *Life* magazine proclaimed him in 1950 to be "the new romantic star" (Reyes and Rubie, 1994:488). He has had a long and versatile career in film and television, both as a respected actor and as an advocate for Latinos in the media. He was instrumental in forming the organization Nosotros in 1969, which seeks to improve opportunities for Latinos in the media. (Courtesy of The Museum of Modern Art Film Stills Archive)

PHOTO 4.30
Fernando Lamas, shown here ca. 1950, like Ricardo Montalban made his film debut in his native country (in his case Argentina) in 1942. He starred in many films in the United States during the 1950s, usually as the romantic lead. (Courtesy of The Museum of Modern Art Film Stills Archive)

PHOTO 4.31 **José Ferrer** was born José Vicente Ferrer Otero y Cintron in Puerto Rico. In contrast to many of the other major Latino stars of the 1950s, he did not play the usual romantic leading men. He was the first Latino to win an Oscar, for Best Actor in *Cyrano de Bergerac* (1950). (Courtesy of The Museum of Modern Art Film Stills Archive)

PHOTO 4.32 **Xavier Cugat,** like Carmen Miranda, was an important feature of Latin musicals during the 1940s. The Cuban bandleader is shown here with his orchestra and Lina Romay, his lead singer during this era. She was the Brooklyn-born daughter of a Mexican diplomat. (Courtesy of The Museum of Modern Art Film Stills Archive)

PHOTO 4.33   **Desi Arnaz,** born Desiderio Alberto Arnaz y de Acha III in Santiago,
Cuba, began his screen career in 1940 in *Too Many Girls*. He married Lucille Ball,
who starred in the film, in that same year. He and his wife formed the highly
profitable and innovative Desilu Productions in 1948. This company created and
produced not just the *I Love Lucy* show—for which they both became famous—but
many others as well. The idea of casting a "Latin" as the husband to an "All-
American" girl was originally opposed on the grounds that the public wouldn't go for
it. Ball, especially, persisted in the proposal and the couple went on to star in one of
the most successful and long-lasting (1951–1957) situation comedies on television.
Arnaz is shown here in *Forever Darling* (1956). (Courtesy of The Museum of
Modern Art Film Stills Archive)

PHOTO 4.34 **Edward James Olmos** is probably the best-known Chicano actor today. His role as the taciturn but morally steadfast Lt. Castillo in television's *Miami Vice* brought him a greater level of national recognition than his previous, highly praised roles (Newman, 1992). Known for his support of social causes as well as the intensity and depth of his acting, he was born in Los Angeles and began his career in 1975 with a small part in *Aloha Bobby and Rose*. He has gone on to major roles in a variety of well-received movies. He also directed and starred in *American Me* (1992). He is shown here with Jaime Escalante, whose life he played in *Stand and Deliver* (1988). (Courtesy of The Museum of Modern Art Film Stills Archive)

PHOTO 4.35 **Raul Julia** was born Raul Rafael Carlos Julia y Arcelay in San Juan, Puerto Rico, in 1948 and died of a stroke in New York in 1994. A talented actor with a well-established career in serious theater, he began his film career in *The Tempest* (1982), a modern version of the Shakespearean play. He went on to make over twenty-seven films. Despite his acclaimed dramatic ability in films such as *Romero* (1989), *The Penitent* (1988), and *The Kiss of the Spider Woman* (1985), and the wide breadth of his characterizations, he is perhaps best known for his role as Gomez in *The Addams Family* movies. He is shown here as Gomez in *Addams Family Values* (1993). (Courtesy of the Academy of Motion Picture Arts and Sciences)

PHOTO 4.36 **Antonio Banderas**, born in 1960 in Málaga, Spain, appeared in numerous Spanish films and was a member of Spain's National Theater for a number of years before making his U.S. debut in *The Mambo Kings* (1992). His heart-throb image was enhanced in a number of major movies, for example, *House of the Spirits* (1993), *Philadelphia* (1993), and *Assassins* (1994). He is shown here in a scene from *Desperado* (1995). (Courtesy of the Academy of Motion Picture Arts and Sciences)

PHOTO 4.37 **Andy García** was born in 1956 in Havana, Cuba, and raised in Miami Beach. His debut in English-language films came in 1985 when he appeared in *The Mean Season*. Since then, he has gone on to play a variety of roles in numerous major films, receive an Oscar nomination for Best Supporting Actor in *The Godfather Part III* (1990), and be listed by the *Hollywood Reporter* as the top Latino star in 1995. He is shown here in *Jennifer 8* (1992). (Courtesy of the Academy of Motion Picture Arts and Sciences)

PHOTO 4.38 **Jimmy Smits** was born in 1955 in New York; his mother was Puerto Rican and his father was from Suriname. Although he lived in various parts of New York and Puerto Rico, he spent most of his youth in Brooklyn, where he was both a football and drama star. He went on to receive a master's in fine arts and became well known for both television and film work. He first came to national attention as the sensitive but tough Latino attorney Victor Sifuentes on *L.A. Law* and then as *N.Y.P.D. Blue*'s sexy leading man. He won accolades for his recent performance in *Mi Familia/My Family* (1995). Known for his intense and dramatic acting in films, he is shown here in a scene from *The Old Gringo* (1989). (Courtesy of the Academy of Motion Picture Arts and Sciences)

Introduction

What are Latin looks? At first "blush," it seems that there is a Latin or Latino look that everyone recognizes. This person is slightly tan, with dark hair and eyes. Upon further thought, we find other factors that contribute to the "Latin look," for example, Spanish usage, accented English, occupation, education, residence, relationship to Anglos,[1] self-identification, and identification by others. But does this image accurately reflect Latinos and their history in U.S. media? The more I reflect on these questions, the more I would say that—as the authors of many of the chapters in this volume argue—Latin looks are to a considerable extent determined by political, economic, and historical contexts, and the images are often at variance with current and past Latino realities.

Victoria Medina, founder and president of The Studio, an organization in New York City established to help Latinos in the business of acting, illustrated the difference between realities and images in an anecdote (personal communication, March 22, 1995). When a casting call went out for an actress to play a Latina part, three "genuine" Latinas showed up. One was fair-skinned, blond, and tall. Another was tan and of medium build and had dark hair and eyes. The third had darker skin and was of African descent. These three genuine Latinas represented the heterogenous reality of Latinos in the United States. This is the reality that surfaces when a casting call goes out with the generic term *Latina* attached. Yet, those who present Latinos on the screen seek certain images. By the same token, those who satisfy "Latino" images are not viewed as appropriate for other (nonethnic) parts. Victoria Medina's conclusion? She believes it is unfair to specify one Latino look. Instead, the right person should be cast for each particular role.

In 1995, *The Hollywood Reporter,* in a survey of Hollywood's most bankable stars, listed Rosie Pérez as the second most popular Hispanic star (Andy García was the first) (Avila, 1996:26). Among my undergraduate students at Fordham University in New York City, Pérez is without a doubt the best-known and most frequently identified Latina actress in Hollywood today. But her name invariably elicits extreme reactions especially from Latina students. One response is that she is an "embarrassment to her race." In other words, her image, the way she projects herself, her manner of speech and dress, and her general style are viewed as embarrassing to other Latinos. (Some Latinos are concerned that all Latinas will be judged by the image Pérez projects.) Other Latinos feel there is nothing wrong with Pérez's image: It is a tough one that should be put out there. Latinas should be respected as tough.

A third group maintains that Pérez's image is a commodity in demand in today's media market. These students argue it's "not her problem." She has perfected and personally gained success with this image that the public wants. In essence, the problem is not Pérez but the expectations that society has for Latinas. We might then ask: Did Pérez develop and market her image or was this role imposed on her (that is, was it the only one that would play)? Then the question becomes who determines this image—the audience? the media power brokers? the filmmakers? And, finally, why is this the major Latina image?

Regardless of the diverse reactions to Rosie Pérez, no one person can represent the Latino culture(s). Just as no one assumes that Roseanne Arnold represents all working-class White women, we cannot assume or expect that Rosie Pérez and the characters she plays represent all Latinas. Pérez's image has a right to exist. The problem remains that few other Latina images are available today. Latina looks have become very narrowly and often negatively depicted. As will be seen in later chapters of the volume, this situation has not always prevailed—and can, in the future, be corrected.

Another problem is that too often in today's media the strengths of Latina women are projected as negatives. For example, their commitment to home and children translates to the television image of an impoverished mother with twelve children. Allegiance to family is recast as stupidly protecting a drug-addicted, crime-ridden brother. Latinas' strength and creativity in the face of adversity are converted to illicit activities, often prostitution—always unsuccessfully and always in poverty. Latinas' sensuality and spirited love of life become unbounded promiscuity. Love of music and dance is projected as substituting for brains. A resolute desire to raise healthy children independent of macho, controlling, and abusive men is translated as dependent women on welfare. The responsibility Latinas take for helping others and taking care of them is made equivalent to a faceless maid, who does not think and has limited speech.[2] The strength of Latinas in the face of drugs and crime becomes the Latina victim. The ability to overcome cultural boundaries and engage in intercultural dialogue becomes either a slut screwing a White man or a victim.

All these images are simple and one dimensional and show the Latina as passive, dependent, and with an unreserved sexual appetite. Whether portrayed as a spitfire, a prostitute, or, more rarely, a secretary, she is always dependent on men. She is easy, promiscuous, and weak. She never gets the man in the end, although she often sleeps with him along the way. She is, as in the refrain of the satirical play *Beautiful Señoritas* (Prida, 1991), "always ready for amor" (love). Whether in Spanish-language *novelas* (soap operas) or recent films, she is *caliente* (hot), waiting for the All-American man to save her from her misery.

As the chapters in this book show, historically, Latinas have been portrayed as either frilly *señoritas* or volcanic temptresses, more recently with thick accents and aggressive sexual appetites. As in the case of women in general, lack of sexual control is their undoing and the reason they find themselves in their dilemmas. They are sexual beings who generally seem unable to resolve any issue or reach their goals without somehow having sex with a man. In essence, they are passive, feeble, unintelligent, and dependent. Occasionally, there is a strong woman, but she is eventually subdued by a "real" man.[3] (Basinger, 1993; Butler Flora, 1973; Fregoso, 1993; López, 1991) Where are the *abuelas* (grandmothers), teachers, sisters, students, school crossing guards, secretaries, professors, lawyers, judges, and corporate trainees? Where are the undistinguished but nonetheless complex and interesting women who are not stereotypes? As Blanca Vásquez (1990) and other Latinas have asked, "Where am I" on these screens? Also, where are my sisters, my mother, my friends, the Latinas I know and respect? Why are the images consistently poor, why are alternative images absent?

Similar questions can be raised about the images of male Latinos, for they are similarly, and all too often, narrowly and negatively cast. Most recently, there appears to be a return to the association of Latino males (as opposed to Latinas) with the Latin lover image, with major Latino actors such as Antonio Banderas, Andy García, and Jimmy Smits often mentioned in this context. Although this phenomenon may be viewed by some as representing a positive image, some scholars argue that the Latin lover was generally the Latin loser—an "effete, asexual, comedic figure," who always lost the girl when she met a Yankee (Woll, 1980:24)—or "one-dimensional" (Garcia Berumen, 1995:9). Early Latin lovers may also have been seen by audiences as Mediterranean rather than Latin American (Hadley-Garcia, 1993; Woll, 1980). Moreover, even though a number of major leading men (and leading ladies, for that matter) played Latin lovers in early films, the majority of characters and movies emphasized a negative, "greaser" view of Latinos (Hadley-Garcia, 1993; Woll, 1980).

A related question is whether the use of European prototypes for such leading roles was (and still is) a disservice to the larger, more heterogenous Latino population. By so consistently excluding and depreciating the wide diversity of Latin looks, Latino images were split into two polarities, the rich European types and the poor, often unidentified indigenous or African-descended masses. The issues inherent in this question are also raised in the following questions.

Issues and Trends

Would Hispanic images be improved if only Latinos played Latino characters? Should Latinos play only Latino roles?

For Victoria Medina, the point is not who plays what but "to maintain the integrity of the Latino characters" and to do something that is good—not always a portrayal of victimization (personal communication, March 22, 1995). Others argue that Medina's goal is hopelessly idealistic. Certainly, the best actor for any particular role should play that role. But until an ideal world is achieved, there will be pressure for Latino actors to play Latino parts. Furthermore, this pressure helps Latino actors get started and usually improves the validity of the characters' portrayal.

To what extent can Latino actors—or the best actors for the part—be hired so long as movies are cast according to "profit power"?

There is a notion that no matter what happens in the film, the movie will sell if certain stars are in it. *The House of the Spirits, The Perez Family,* and *Evita* all had Latino settings and Latino characters but no Latinas in major roles. The lackluster performance of the first two films at the box office raises the question of whether star casting does truly produce profits. The critics' unenthusiastic response to these same films casts further doubt on whether such an approach produces a better picture. As of this writing, it is still too early to say whether the choice of Madonna to star in *Evita* will result in the monetary success anticipated. However, the initial fever that accompanied the holiday release of the film seems to have cooled with the publicity surrounding the lack of Oscar or Screen Actors Guild Award nominations for the movie.

But the bottom line is that casting choices depend on the director and many directors don't quite get the story when it comes to Latino themes.[4] In effect, the Latin looks or images produced reflect not the reality of Latinos but commercial considerations, the perceived prejudices of audiences, the residence and isolation of image makers far from Latino communities, the sociological development of Hollywood, the ideology of consensus (or, herd mentality), connections to political and social currents (for example, wars), and the responses of filmmakers to political and social pressures on the industry.[5] (Woll and Miller, 1987:3–21)

Why concern ourselves with Latino images or looks at all?

Assimilationists find an inherent divisiveness in addressing "difference" or "ethnicity" in the media.[6] In essesse, they ask, why do we need to look at Latino images at all? Why do "Latinos" insist on being Latinos? Why don't Latinos forget about all that ancestry stuff and just say they are "American"? Or if Latinos have to bring in the business of being Hispanic, why don't they just say they are Americans of Hispanic descent? Latinos could also just attach the term "American" to their national origin as others do, for example, Irish Americans, German Americans, and African Americans. "Latinos" come predominantly from "the Americas" so this solution seems obvious.

But this line of argument seems irrelevant to the actual history of Latinos in the United States. With greater time in the United States, Latinos have become clearer about being both Latinos and Americans—not one or the other, but both.[7] Increasingly, for many U.S.-born Latinos, to say that one is Latino (or Puerto Rican, Ecuadorian, and so on) implies that they are also American. They are Latinos from the United States. Inherent in this definition are issues of rights and entitlement—legitimate claims to cultural heritages and to political, economic, and social rights as citizens of the United States.

Latinos who are U.S. citizens, whether or not they speak with an accent, are often met with the query, "So, what are you?" Because generally "American" does not suffice for those who have "Latino looks," this book on Latin looks is necessary. For if the

United States is to fulfill its promise, then Latinos—along with all other groups— need to be presented fairly, honestly, and accurately. Only then can we all relate as equals. What gives the question of "Latin looks" greater significance is the increasing number of Latinos in the United States. Although estimates differ on when—in the year 2000 or the year 2030—Latinos will become the largest minority group in the United States, no one disputes that the event will happen. And whenever it happens, it appears that Latinos will maintain strong identification as Latinos (Massey, 1994).

An Overview of the Book

The chapters in this book provide some of the best analytical, empirical, and historical perspectives available to address these questions, together with the best writing on the changing (and the unchanging) Latino images in feature films, television, and the news. The emphasis is on English-language television and films produced in the United States between 1900 and 1994—almost the full span of the twentieth century.[8] The book includes both social science and literary analyses, many now difficult to find. Particular emphasis is given to representations of class, gender, color, race, and the political relationship between the United States and Latin America. The readings are thought provoking and should enable readers to view widely available films or television programs through new lenses that expand conventional interpretations. To maintain the temporal contexts within which the pieces were originally written, most of the chapters have not been altered. Thus, for example, some projects described as in process may have been completed.

This book is, on the one hand, about how Latinos are portrayed in movies, television, and other media. On the other hand, it is a book about the history of race and ethnicity in the United States as projected in the media. Its ultimate goal is to develop and strengthen analytical skills and fostering in readers a critical eye when viewing the media. We live in a media-oriented society, and because media often serve an entertainment function, we may be lulled into passively accepting the images projected as mirrors of real life and of people (Wilson and Gutiérrez, 1995). It is important for future media development and for our own quality of life that we constantly question and are cognizant of media image manipulation and the role of the media in modern society. The concluding section of the book, "Strategies for Change," is intended to help readers develop critical and analytical viewing skills and also to pursue effective strategies for change.

There are five major points made in this book.

1. Hispanics are underrepresented and misrepresented in the media.

That Hispanics are underrepresented and misrepresented in the media is supported by current and extensive historical and empirical research. Underrepresentation in itself leads to misrepresentations of Hispanics, and negative perceptions of the "ethnic

Other" cause many ethnic others to question their identity and experience difficulty defining themselves. Teenagers' acute awareness of the negativity of contemporary Hispanic images on television was documented in a study by Lichter and Lichter (1988:12) of 1,217 adolescents in the Howard Beach section of Brooklyn, New York. Although they found that the Black, Italian American, Asian American, Jewish, and Hispanic students tended to complain about negative portrayals of their own group on television, the strongest complaints came from the Hispanic students. Moreover, whereas the Howard Beach teenagers surveyed were rarely joined in their feelings by those outside their ethnic group, in the case of Hispanics, both group members and nonmembers agreed that television treated a particular ethnic group worse than it really was. Thus, for all these teens, how Latinos looked on television was not only *not* representative, it was also worse than the actuality. (See Chapters 1 to 3.)

2. Latino images in Hollywood films have become more negative with time.

By developing a historical perspective on Latinos in the media, we can contrast the past with more contemporary views in which strengths have been projected as negatives and narrow casting has been the rule. But this does not mean that the images have been unchanging. Nor does it mean that there is total agreement on exactly what these images have been (see on this point, Chapter 6 by Berg). Last, it does not mean that only Latinos had negative images (see especially Chapters 1 to 3).

3. The similarities in the portrayals of Chicanos, Puerto Ricans, and other Latino groups—and how these have changed over time—far outweigh the differences.

Although this book is about Latino images, the underlying issue is the construction and projection of images that reflect and reinforce inequality. In this regard, particular attention is given to the similarities (as opposed to the differences) between Chicano, Puerto Rican, and other Latino films and images.

The book's title *Latin Looks* is purposely chosen to underscore the tendency to view Latinos as if they all looked the same. It also highlights the common experience that many Latinos have had in the United States, although many perceive their experience as singularly applicable to their group. Thomas Gómez (1905–1971), one of the earlier Latino actors, indirectly spoke to this common experience when he said: "After the war, I was treated with more respect, and people stopped using words like 'Spic,' at least openly" (Hadley-Garcia, 1993:91). On reading this statement, I was surprised that this was a term that had been employed at that time. I had assumed that the term had been invented with the migration of Puerto Ricans to New York in the 1950s. Thus, a major point of this book is to ask what are "Latin looks," who creates them, why are they perennial, and why do issues concerning Latin looks continue to surface? (Implicit in these questions is the issue of whether Latin looks belong only to Latinos, that is, whether only Latinos can play Latinos.)

4. The quality of Hollywood's presentation of Latinos has fluctuated with the larger political and economic relationships that the United States has had with Latin America.

As has been true for other countries and other groups, the images of Latinos often reflect the fears and the political, social, and economic conditions of a period. In examining the role of history in creating current images and stereotypes and providing models for subsequent paradigms and stereotypes, the authors of the chapters in this book also point to the role of stereotypes in controlling "the Other," for example, in rationalizing racism and legitimizing or justifying imperialism and domination. The authors thus leave us with the awareness that we must always ask questions about how political and economic factors influence how groups come to occupy or leave the position of negativized "Other" in the media (see especially the chapters in Part II).

5. Fighting the currents, alternative filmmakers have sought to deconstruct media images of Latinos and construct new images and spaces that are "by, for, and about" the Latino community (Fregoso, 1993).

The chapters in Part III show how the movies produced by alternative filmmakers represent a creative response from the Latino community to issues of exclusion, discrimination, and stereotyping. In reflecting on these efforts, we can begin to examine how we can continue to create alternative images and integrate more Latinos into the media and yet avoid creating and perpetuating stereotypes—both old and new.

Related to the focus on alternative images, Part IV provides viewers with materials with which they can improve their critical and analytical skills. Thought questions on the readings are included in this section, together with a listing and description of concrete, practical steps that can be taken to change the current situation of underrepresentation and misrepresentation of Latinos in the media.

Changing and Unchanging Images

Many of the authors of the chapters in this volume share the perspective that Latino images in Hollywood films have tended to be negative. This does not mean that the images have been unchanging. Nor does it mean that there is total agreement on exactly what these images have been (see on this point, Chapter 6 by Berg). Last, it does not mean that only Latinos had negative images. All groups that differed in some way from the White, middle-class, Anglo-Saxon male ideal have been placed at various times in the position of negativized "Other" (Friedman, 1991; Wilson and Gutiérrez, 1985, 1995; Woll and Miller, 1987). "Our movie classics preached an assimilationist, often racist and sexist, philosophy," and our top stars did not reflect the nation's actual ethnic or racial makeup, but rather "an anti-ethnic image of America" (Friedman, 1991:2, 7; Jarvie, 1991).[9]

Different ethnic and minority groups are sometimes seen to share interchangeable stereotypes. Hall (1981), for example, writes about the universal images fashioned for all people of color and anyone else in the "Other" category. Hall's image categories of the "slave figure," the "native," and the "clown/entertainer" bear a marked resemblance to, for example, Keller's (1985, 1994) Latino categories of "Cantina girl," "spitfire," and "buffoon."

Yet, Hollywood's relationship to each group has been unique, with a separate complex history and specificity (López, 1991). Indeed, López (1991:404) takes issue with what she calls the fairly standard thinking of ethnic studies of the cinema, in which it is argued that regardless of whether characters were "Indian, black, Hispanic, or Jewish, Hollywood represented ethnics and minorities as stereotypes that circulated easily and repeatedly from film to film." She feels the images were in fact more nuanced. One very important distinction described in this book is the bifurcated approach taken early toward Latinos but not duplicated in other groups. This resulted in Latino actors and characters being divided according to their perceived color and class, with European types becoming major actors, whereas darker, less-European types played *bandidos* and Hispanic or "native" extras (Cortés, 1991:23ff; Hadley-Garcia, 1993; Ríos-Bustamante, 1992).

Hollywood's history with each group has also been in part a reflection of larger political and economic relationships between the United States and other countries (see Chapters 5, 8, 9, 11, 12, 13, and 15). Political and economic factors have clearly influenced how groups came to occupy or leave the position of negativized "Other" in the media. Examples often cited are the negative characterizations of the Germans and Japanese in films made during the world wars and subsequent more positive images at war's end when economic and political relations improved. Less well known are changes in the images of Latinos resulting from changing political conditions, geopolitical considerations, market factors, and protests from Latin America.

Scholars generally agree that the images—although not necessarily the employment—of Latinos improved during both world wars (Hadley-Garcia, 1993; Keller, 1985, 1994; López, 1991; Noriega, 1992; Reyes and Rubie, 1994; Richard, 1993).[10] There is also agreement on the impetus for this change. The motivation was simple: It was important to keep the hemisphere united against the Axis threat. There were also economic concerns: With large portions of the European economy closed to U.S. films, the Latin American market assumed greater importance. The push to develop an Allied hemispheric strategy worked, for eventually all of the Latin American nations declared war on the Axis, and Mexico and Brazil even sent combat forces to support the Allies. Also, with the exception of Argentina, which still showed German newsreels, all other countries replaced European products with North American products. The change was swift and reflects the extent to which political and economic structures have (or can) influence cinematic images.

The Possibilities for Change

As mentioned earlier, an overriding purpose of this volume is to make readers critically aware of the images of Latinos in U.S. television, news coverage, and film throughout the twentieth century. This ability to be critical is extremely important vis-à-vis media where the images created sometimes come to substitute for reality and where, in particular, our understanding of the history of "the ethnic Other" is filtered through film images.

An example can be seen in the 1990 movie *A Show of Force*. It is described in what is rapidly becoming the major film resource on CD-ROM, the Film Index International (1993–1995), as "a film of a true story of an American journalist" who uncovered a major political scandal in Puerto Rico. In fact, it was three Puerto Rican reporters from the *San Juan Star* (Carmen Jovet, Manuel Suárez, and Tomás Stella) who uncovered this political scandal, which was dubbed the Puerto Rican Watergate (Canel, 1990). According to the Brazilian director, Bruno Barreto, a North American (that is, U.S. or Canadian) character was needed to dramatize the cultural antagonism between the two cultures in Puerto Rico. Whatever the merits of this argument, the movie is inaccurately presented as a true story in a major source used by researchers and the public.

My hope is that greater awareness will lead to positive change. That change is possible is evident from the fact that Latino and African American images have changed over time (see Chapters 1 and 3). One model of change is represented by events of the 1960s. The riots, together with subsequent investigations, contributed to civil rights legislation and affirmative action policies to improve representation. These changes were accompanied by changes in public opinion. A second approach is to take a proactive stance, for example, in filmmaking, to develop independent, alternative images—as described by the authors of the chapters in Part III of this volume.

A third example is found in the Production Code Administration (PCA) in which, with the advent of World War II, government and industry joined forces to ensure that nothing would be allowed on the screen that might "offend the sensibilities of our Latin American" allies (Richard, 1993:xvii). The role of the PCA was pivotal. Although in its early years the PCA could only suggest that insults be eliminated, by 1934 it could literally prevent a film from being exhibited in the United States. Richard (1993) describes in detail the process of change in the movie industry between 1935 and 1955.[11] His analysis of PCA files shows that the PCA used its power extensively both to eliminate negative images and to introduce positive images of Latinos and Latin America. Positive images of Latin Americans that did not alter the plot were inserted into movies through a character, for example, commenting on his "most memorable memories" of Mexico or on meeting "the most wonderful girl in Mexico" (Richard, 1993:xxxiii). Alternatively, a conga dance or Latin music might be included even when there was no other Latin theme in the movie.[12]

Other variables contributed to the effective shift in images during this period. The appointment of Nelson A. Rockefeller in 1940 as head of the newly created congressionally funded Office for Coordination of Commercial and Cultural Relations Between the American Republics helped.[13] The Rockefeller family had extensive economic interests in Latin America. Rockefeller's appointment of John Hay Whitney to head the Motion Picture Division of this agency also helped. "Jocko" Whitney was wealthy, "well known and well liked among Hollywood's aristocracy" (Richard, 1993:xxvii). Whitney developed a nonprofit, privately controlled California corporation that included the major heads of the movie industry, the guilds, the agents, and the specialists in all phases of motion picture operation. This, too, facilitated change.

The government and nongovernment agencies all worked in close cooperation, with the PCA as "watchdog," to ensure that Latin American images were positive (Richard, 1993:xxvi). A Cuban-raised Latin American specialist, Addison Durland, was hired as part of the PCA staff in 1941 and took on a pivotal role in correcting major errors in Latin image projection, for example, the view of Brazil as a Spanish-speaking country (Richard, 1993:xxiii).[14] These changes, with all their limitations, and politically motivated though they may have been, illustrate how image change has occurred. Additional models are needed.

The Book's Approach

This book is eclectic and interdisciplinary. As noted earlier, it is in one sense a media book about how Latinos are portrayed in movies, television, and other media. In another sense, it is also about the history of race and ethnicity in the United States. The book differs from more impressionistic or reflectionist books in that it gives considerable attention to empirical and historical research. (This is important when talking about "images," which are by their nature highly subjective and impressionistic.) The focus on how images of a people are presented brings the book into the humanities, through the realms of esthetics and the visual arts. By highlighting issues of identity and cultural representations, the book intersects with psychology, sociology, and anthropology. In a concern with political culture and representation, and the ways political and economic forces interplay with cultural ones, it relates to political science and political economics. Yet, for all its social science content and methodology, it avoids the jargon of the various social science disciplines.

The authors of the chapters in this book do not avoid the critical questions or controversial issues often raised in postmodernist discourse on film. Policy implications and recommendations are specifically addressed. Although most of the recommendations concern Latinos in the media, many also apply to other groups as well. My intention is that by focusing on Latino images, the images of other groups, as well as the relationships of all these groups to each other, will be better understood.

The book is not meant to be passively absorbed, but read actively and interactively. The material in the final section is meant to help the reader and the student of film and media to develop and strengthen analytical skills and a critical eye. These new skills, plus the insights derived from individual chapters, can be applied to numerous movies available at video stores and libraries and to material from syndicated television shows. These skills can also be applied to new television shows and movies as they are presented. My hope is that as more people become aware of past biases and injustices, things will begin to change and we will see improvement in the validity and honesty with which Latinos and others are portrayed.

NOTES

1. In this book, I use the terms *White* and *Anglo* to refer to non-Hispanic White Americans. I use *Black* and *African American* to refer to non-Hispanic Black Americans. The terms *Hispanic* and *Latino* are used interchangeably.

2. More in-depth views of the lives and thoughts of Latina domestics can be found in Romero (1992) and Chavez (1992).

3. Very different views of Latinas in the United States can be found in literature written by Latinas; see, for example, Acosta-Bélen (1979, 1986); Alvarez (1991); Anzaldúa (1987); Elsasser, MacKenzie, and Tixier y Vigil (1980); Esteves (1990); Gomez, Moraga, and Ruíz (1983); Hardy-Fanta (1993); Mohr (1986); Ortiz Cofer (1990); Sánchez-Korrol (1994, 1996).

4. A recent series of interviews by Ed Morales with Latino journalists and others in the media echoed this sentiment. Morales summarized what seemed to be a "universal concern" that "the people who run the media are out of touch with a group that is rapidly becoming the country's largest minority" (Morales, 1996:25).

5. The images produced also vary depending on who is perceiving these images. In essence, the position of "the Other" changes, depending on the reference point. Latinos may perceive images of Latinos differently than non-Latinos. Of concern then are the biases of the filmmakers and what the audience sees (Cowan, 1991:353–359; Woll and Miller, 1987:3–21).

6. See Friedman (1991:1–10) for a critique of these and other arguments.

7. See Nieto (1992) for a discussion of how generally in the United States these concepts or categories have been seen to be mutually exclusive and how through multicultural education people can come to see how individuals could be Black, Hispanic, and American at the same time, instead of just one of these.

8. The book does not cover films produced in other countries or Spanish-language films produced in the United States. The book also is not concerned with images developed in music, literature, or magazines—all extremely important sources of images. Although readings could have been included to discuss these areas, it was my sense that this would make the scope of the volume too broad and the focus less clear.

9. At least one scholar argues that the experience of Latinos has been better than that of other groups because Clause 10 of the Production Code of the movie industry—a set of principles that the film industry agreed to abide by—required that neither foreign nationals nor the history of their countries be defamed (Richard, 1993:xvii). The Production Code Administration (also known as the Hays office) censored and removed the harshest of negative Hispanic stereo-

types. This was not a service "performed for North American Blacks, all Orientals, Arabs, or indigenous Indian tribes" (Richard, 1993:xvii). Richard (1993:xxviii) contends, "Within a larger context, it should be emphasized that absolutely no other racial or ethnic minority ever enjoyed that guardianship in Hollywood's long history. Aside from various religious organizations during the war years no one was afforded more (government and industry sanctioned) on-screen censorial protection than Hispanics and Latin America as a whole." Thus, in some of the films produced during the "Good Neighbor" era of the 1930s and 1940s, it became possible for the Latino to get the Anglo girl; this was not even conceivable for Blacks, Indians, or Asians.

10. This "Good Neighbor" period, 1935–1955, has been variously referred to as the "golden moment" or the "break" (López, 1991:406). But López (1991) argues that the outcome was just the same old images of subordination and negative otherness repackaged into new cinematic bottles.

11. Richard's (1993:x–xi) analysis is based on his examination of Production Code Administration files 1935–1955 and a review of over 2,100 films.

12. Given that travel to Latin America was not common, these images were accepted (in a fashion similar to that described in Chapter 1) as realistic reflections of the land to the south of the United States. In addition, people learned not about Latin America in these movies, but what its proper relationship should be to the United States (Richard, 1993:xxv).

13. This agency subsequently came to be known as the Office of the Coordinator of Inter American Affairs (CIAA) and then (when Rockefeller left) as the Office of Inter American Affairs (Richard, 1993:xxvii).

14. There is general agreement in the literature on the improvement of Latin images during wartime, but less consensus on the roles played by all involved in the shift or the exact length of the "good times" period. Richard (1993:xff), for example, argues that the best period of Latino images was 1935–1955, and that the PCA was in the main responsible for these more positive images. He also maintains that this period coincided with that of the censorial PCA's greatest power. After reviewing PCA files between 1935 and 1955, Richard (1993:xx) argues that the agency insisted on the removal of what was then considered offensive Hispanic imagery.

But Keller (1994) contends that the Production Code did not affect Hispanic images much until the war years. As Keller (1994:116) sees it, "in practical terms, little attenuation of the image of Hispanics resulted from the code until the establishment of the Good Neighbor policy of the FDR administration, and subsequently, the wartime creation of the Office for Coordination of Inter-American Affairs." Keller (1994:111–116) also argues that the code tended to hurt U.S. citizens or residents who were not White. The code specifically forbade portrayal of miscegenation, that is, sexual relations between Blacks and Whites.

He also argues that other major factors affected Latino images during the 1930s–1950s, for example, the conglomeration of the film industry, whereby eight vertically integrated and managed studios controlled the industry and applied a standard Hollywood formula that tended to exclude Latinos. This conglomeration consolidated production, distribution, and exhibition of Hollywood films (Keller, 1994:112). Keller also notes that protests in Latin America against U.S. films (Mexico banned films by certain companies in 1922) and the initiation and subsequent abandonment of Spanish-language production also contributed to the improvement of Latino images in film (Keller, 1994:111).

PART ONE

Latinos on Television and in the News: Absent or Misrepresented

The authors of the three chapters in this section—all excerpted from longer works—discuss Latino images in the news and television. These chapters have a dual focus: the lack of Latino representation and the misrepresentation of Latino events, characters, and culture. The National Council of La Raza (NCLR) in Chapter 1 and Lichter and Amundson in Chapter 3 use an empirical approach. Their work represents the most systematic, rigorous, and comprehensive examination of Latinos in the media to date. NCLR reviews research on the numbers of Latinos in the media and on their portrayals. Lichter and Amundson examine the portrayal of Hispanic characters on television over time, using the scientific method of content analysis. Their chapter concludes with an update covering the 1994–1995 season. Chapter 2, by Quiroga, is a first-person account, written in 1993 by a veteran Hispanic journalist in Boston, combining analyses of case studies and personal experiences. Together, the three chapters emphasize the impact of underrepresentation and negative portrayals on Latinos, on non-Latinos, and on public policy. Many of the findings discussed in these chapters parallel those in the subsequent section on Latinos and film.

"Not Enuf of It and It's Mostly Bad—and Shrinking"

NCLR finds an all-too-familiar picture of underrepresentation and negative portrayals. NCLR's disturbing conclusions in Chapter 1 are that Latinos are almost invisible in both the entertainment and news media, leaving the nation's second-largest minority "out of the picture." Moreover, when Latinos do appear, they are consistently portrayed more negatively than other racial and ethnic groups. These two problems, underrepresentation and negative portrayals, have been persistent themes in films, in television, and in the news. Study after study reveals the chronic condition of Latino underrepresentation, but even more alarming is the finding that underrepresentation has worsened with time. Beginning with the examination by the National Advisory Commission on Civil Disorders (the Kerner Commission, 1968) of television characters during the 1960s, Hispanics have consistently been the least likely to appear in television entertainment programs. Moreover, the proportion of Hispanic characters has actually declined from 3 percent to 1 percent between the 1950s and the 1980s (NCLR, 1994:2). During this same period, the number and proportion of Hispanics in the United States increased dramatically, and the representation of African Americans on television increased substantially. The representation of African Americans fluctuated from season to season (from 6 percent to 16 percent), but Hispanics remained within 1 percent of the ten-season average each year. This lack of variation suggests that over the past thirty years, Latinos have been consistently underrepresented. Recent data indicate that despite greater numbers of Latinos in the United States, Latino representation on television has actually declined. Employment statistics from the Screen Actors Guild show a similarly dismal picture of severe and persistent underrepresentation (Screen Actors Guild, 1995).

This is a sad and unacceptable state of affairs. But it is not hopeless. After the Kerner Commission shamed Hollywood for ignoring African Americans, the movie and TV industries committed themselves to add more diversity and better reflect the social realities of the United States. These industries did change—a lot and fast. Although there were and still are problems in their depictions, as Lichter and Amundson chronicle in Chapter 3, African Americans began appearing in movies and on TV in increasing numbers and in better roles. Important progress has been made, showing how fast change can occur when the commitment is there. Now, as the twentieth century ends, Hollywood and TV need to review their commitment to diversity and include previously slighted and ignored groups.

A portion of the NCLR study not excerpted here documents an even lower representation of Hispanic characters on Saturday morning programs—a time slot that tends to be targeted to children. Here, too, there have been no major year-to-year fluctuations. The effect of this underrepresentation on Latino and non-Latino children has yet to be investigated, but UCLA psychologist Gordon Berry's review of research done on children suggests, "Children's beliefs and feelings about [isolated] minority groups frequently are influenced by the way they are portrayed on television" (NCLR, 1994:19). Others have observed that Latino cartoon portrayals are among the most offensive representations of Hispanics on television (NCLR, 1994:7). These findings raise important questions about long-term effects. For example, does the relative invisibility of Latino characters or the negative portrayal of Latino characters affect the educational achievement or dropout rates of Hispanics? This is an important area for further research.

Hispanics and the News

As a recent article in the official publication of the Directors Guild of America indicated, the underrepresentation of women and other minorities has a net negative impact on the television and film industry: "Not only does this deny the industry the use of a host of strong creative talent, it also limits the ability to produce a good product. That in turn will ultimately cost the studios and networks money" (Petersen, 1995:16). Although Hispanics made up 9 percent of the total U.S. population in 1990, they only received 3 percent of roles (NCLR, 1994:3).

This same underrepresentation holds for Latinos in the news—both on and off camera. Latinos hold few "gatekeeper" positions in network news operations and they are underrepresented as correspondents and anchors. In a recent content analysis of news stories presented on three major broadcast television networks (ABC, CBS, and NBC) during 1995, researchers found that only 1 percent of the news stories focused on Latinos and issues related to Latinos. This is equivalent to 121 stories out of approximately 12,000 stories per year (Carveth and Alverio, 1996:2, 5).[1] Of these stories, the vast majority (85 percent) fell into four "problem" categories: crime (19 percent), immigration (21.5 percent), affirmative action (22.3 percent), and welfare (8 percent).[2] Moreover, in contrast to other issues, for which there may be a number of experts or network-paid consultants, "It was rare to see an expert on Hispanic issues" and when experts or commentators were employed, they tended to be "white state and federal government officials" (Carveth and Alverio, 1996:10). In addition—and also in contrast to coverage of other news stories—Latinos appeared on camera in only about half of the stories covering Latinos. Thus, in half of the stories about Latinos, Latinos were missing. These absences from network news led the study authors to conclude that Latinos are "symbolically annihilated" in network news (Carveth and Alverio, 1996:2). The significance of these findings is heightened by the fact that most Latinos receive their news from the English-language media.[3]

All three chapters in this section highlight how news coverage tends to present Latinos as "problem people." Although rarely covered, when Hispanics are shown they are portrayed as having problems or being a problem (to Anglo society). (This applies to some other minority groups as well.) Latinos tend to be viewed in terms of the problems or difficulties they pose for Anglo society, and their own cultural activity and creativity are largely overlooked. During the 1970s, coverage often focused inordinate attention on the more bizarre or unusual elements of minority communities, such as gangs, illegal immigration, and interracial violence. Although these were undoubtedly legitimate stories, one might reasonably ask, where are the counterbalancing stories? Without stories to offset this pattern, the image that is projected is that "they" (Latinos) have problems and they present problems to others.[4]

The focus also tends to be on Latinos as "objects" not "subjects" of the news. Thus, commentary on Latino themes is generally provided by non-Hispanics. Latinos, who have an authoritative or legitimate perspective to share, are not included. Alternatively, persons with Hispanic surnames who share little with the Latino communities in thought, identification, or involvement are sometimes hired to represent essentially de-ethnicized points of view. Thus, we have, on the Public Broadcasting System,

Linda Chavez and Richard Rodríguez. These are individuals who in their writings have made clear the distance they feel from Spanish-speaking communities, issues, and identities. They are also individuals whose views have been strongly criticized by many Hispanic organizations as not representative of most Hispanics.

The Effects of Exclusion

On a more subtle level, the virtual absence of Latino "newsmakers" in broadcast news undermines the creditability and prestige of Hispanics seeking to influence public policy (NCLR, p. 24). This situation is aggravated by the media's tendency to cite non-Hispanics more frequently even in news coverage of stories with predominantly Latino themes. The subtext then is, "Hispanic issues rarely matter and even when they do, Hispanics' perspectives on these issues don't matter much" (NCLR, p. 24). Yet, as Quiroga notes in Chapter 2, some of today's most pressing national issues have a disproportionate impact on Hispanics, such as welfare reform, crime, national health insurance, job creation, substance abuse, immigration, and AIDS. Yet, "When the National press covers these issues Hispanics are seldom heard from. Their opinions are rarely sought" (NCLR, p. 24).

As Quiroga makes clear, this situation is also impractical. Given the large numbers of Hispanics in the United States, as a society we cannot afford to have newsrooms where no one speaks Spanish. Quiroga's description of the *Washington Post*'s awkward handling of the 1991 Latino riots in Washington, D.C., underscores this.

The exclusion or invisibility of the Hispanic community in the media is well illustrated in Quiroga's description of the coverage of the Rodney King incident. From the media coverage, as Quiroga puts it in Chapter 2, "Viewers would be pressed to describe the violence as something other than the rage of blacks against whites and Korean bystanders." Yet, one of the four "White" officers charged was of Latino descent.[5] In addition, according to Quiroga, Hispanics accounted for half of the 8,700 people arrested citywide during and after the riots; in fact, the Los Angeles Police Department arrested *more* Hispanics (4,307) than Blacks (3,083). Nineteen Hispanics also died during the civil disorders—just three short of the number of Black fatalities. Last, the Los Angeles mobs ravaged about as many Hispanic businesses as Korean-owned ones. Yet, the Rodney King incident was projected by the media to be (and is still generally recalled as) an essentially Black-White or Black–Asian American issue.[6]

Negative Portrayals and Stereotypes

Both the NCLR study and Lichter and Amundson document that those token Hispanic characters that *do* appear tend to be stick figures in secondary or stereotypical roles, with few lines and minimal contribution to the story plots. Moreover, Hispanic characters are portrayed more negatively than others. Common stereotypes are lazy and lower class, "failures," "criminals," "not to be taken seriously," and devious and "untrustworthy."[7]

The results of Lichter and Amundson's study are especially disquieting. This study is no haphazard, impressionistic view of Latino images. Its findings are based on considerable data and its methodology is scientific and sound. The authors conclude, "Hispanics are nearly invisible or confined to stereotypical roles" (Lichter and Amundson, 1994:8). This problem exists despite changes, such as cable, new program genres,[8] and greater risk-taking in programming. Lichter and Amundson also conclude that portrayals of minorities have not altered and that Latinos and Blacks are still more likely to be portrayed as working class or poor than Whites.

The Impact

The findings discussed above are in and of themselves disturbing, and they become even more distressing with the realization that these stereotypes have prevailed in entertainment programming for decades. The situation becomes alarming when we realize that media stereotypes have substantial influence on perceptions of—and opportunities available to—Hispanics. For example, we know that the media can have a powerful role in shaping attitudes, reinforcing preexisting stereotypes, and reducing stereotypes. We also know that—as the American Psychological Association has stated—"The less real-world information viewers have about a social group, the more apt they are to accept the television image of that group" (NCLR, 1994:19; see also Wilson and Gutiérrez, 1995:50–53). Finally, we know from recent demographic research that Hispanics (and particularly Hispanic children) are increasingly segregated from non-Hispanics. If we put these factors together, we have the makings of a rather unpleasant stew—a boiling pot rather than a "melting pot."

The NCLR analysis of public opinion research data shows that non-Hispanics are largely ignorant of the condition of Hispanic Americans; they have extremely negative views of Hispanics, views that are often wildly inconsistent with the facts; and the public perceptions of Hispanics are remarkably similar to stereotypical media portrayals of Latinos. These views are held of all Hispanics, not just the newly arrived or the older U.S.-born Hispanics. A 1989 survey of fifty-eight different ethnic groups by the American Jewish Committee found that all of the Hispanic groups— these included Mexicans, Guatemalans, Nicaraguans, Puerto Ricans, and Cubans— were ranked forty-ninth or lower in "perceived social standing." Only Gypsies were ranked below Mexicans and Puerto Ricans. Indeed, "Wysians," a fictitious group, ranked above all of the Latino groups in the survey (NCLR, 1994:22).

Implications

A number of important implications follow from the analyses discussed here. NCLR argues in Chapter 2 that the underrepresentation and negative portrayals of Latinos in the media result in increased discrimination and undermine beneficial public policy. If the few Hispanic characters in the media are found disproportionately in the less successful, more evil, negative, and stereotypical roles, then the media may be contributing to prejudice and discrimination against Latinos by reinforcing derogatory stereotypes. If Latinos and Latino themes and perspectives are underrepresented, then it is unlikely that Latino issues will even reach the policy arena. Neither the non-Hispanic public nor policymakers will understand the need to address widespread employment or housing discrimination against Latinos if the media fails to project these as serious problems. In essence, if Latinos are not there articulating their needs, their situation must be O.K.

According to NCLR, this leads to an ironic situation in which "The very phenomenon that stimulates discriminatory behavior—the absence and stereotypical portrayals of Latinos—tends to undermine public support for policy interventions to address such discrimination" (1994:24). Furthermore, "the failure to balance these negative portrayals with positive Latino role models or accurate information about the condition of Hispanics, promotes opinions about Hispanics that are inconsistent with the facts" (1994:22).

NCLR also maintains that negative media portrayals also tend to undercut support for corrective policies by supporting the perspective that those who are disadvantaged in U.S. society have only themselves to blame. In other words, if a group is negatively depicted (as evil or unsuccessful), then it must be so in real life. In the case of Hispanics, little in the media shows the opposite and the non-Hispanic public has few, if any, real-life opportunities to see otherwise or to experience the opposite of these portrayals. The conclusion becomes if Hispanics have problems in real life that require corrective policies, they are not deserving and such policies would not be effective. On this point, in Chapter 1 NCLR quotes the media scholar Erna Smith: "Recent studies suggest a link between news coverage and the modern racist, who believes discrimination is a thing of the past, and that any problems . . . non-Whites face in American society are of their own making."

Equal Opportunity and Individual Responsibility

There is a tension in the discourse about Latino images. On the one hand, it is argued that media biases and stereotypes reduce opportunities for Latinos. If we accept this view, are we letting the individual off the hook? Are we abrogating individual responsibility? Isn't it up to the individual to succeed in society? On the other hand, it is argued that the negative and sparse portrayals of Latinos reflect the sad reality of Latino life in the United States. If we accept this view, are we not deflating the motivation of young Latinos to succeed in U.S. society? Clearly (and this should go without saying), all individuals need to take responsibility for themselves and for those for whom they are responsible. The question is what can we, as a society, do to ensure that opportunities are equal? What can we do to eliminate barriers? Individuals should not have to fight against negative stereotypes and portrayals. That is not what is envisioned in a society that provides equal opportunity to all.

Recommendations

The issues raised by the chapters in this section are further addressed in the final chapter of the book, "What We Can Do." One can add to or quibble with the specific recommendations listed. But what is most important is that the issues be addressed. They must be addressed, first, because these are issues of equity. The United States is a country premised on equal opportunity for all, and this must be ensured in all areas; opportunities cannot be greater for some groups and less for others. Second, these issues must be addressed because Hispanics are an increasingly larger proportion of the U.S. population, accounting for nearly one-fifth of all new workers (Fullerton, 1995). Thus, it is in the interest of all Americans to address these issues, for improvement in Latinos' "social and economic condition is critical to the country's well-being" (Brichetto, quoted in Quiroga, 1995:15).

It is also important to conduct research in this area. The news has a major influence on public opinion on policy issues, and we need to know more about the hows and whys of its operation. We need to study exactly how media portrayals of Latinos shape viewers' attitudes toward Latinos and Latino issues, so that we can determine how best to improve portrayals in this area and counter negative impacts. In particular, it is important to study how these portrayals affect Latino children and teenagers.

NOTES

1. The researchers also found that most of these stories originated from the West Coast and the Southwest. Other areas with significant Latino populations, such as New York, Miami, and Chicago, produced few stories (Carveth and Alverio, 1996:2).

2. Another 15.7 percent of the stories were on Selena, a rising Chicana singer who was murdered during the year of the study, and the trial of her murderer (Carveth and Alverio, 1996:6).

3. A 1996 study by the Southwest Voter Research Institute of over 1,400 registered Latino voters found that the majority receive their news from the English-language media, especially television (Torres, 1996). In addition, analysis of the Nielsen Hispanic Television Index for

1993–1994 and a special tabulation of its National Audience Demographics led Nielsen Media Research to estimate that 60 percent of all Latinos watch television in English ("Special Reports: Latino Viewing of Network TV 1993/94," 1994:1).

4. Even in local area studies, we see echoes of the earlier history of non-Whites' exclusion and misrepresentation (NCLR, 1994). In areas where Hispanics represent substantial portions of the population, for example, San Antonio, they tend to be absent from the news pages that cover business, lifestyle, obituaries, marriages, births, and civil rights.

5. As Quiroga makes clear in Chapter 2, only one article in the *Los Angeles Times* noted this, reporting that he was routinely "teased about his Latino heritage by white friends in high school." In all other articles in the *Los Angeles Times* and in other papers, he was routinely referred to as one of the "whites" who assaulted King.

6. In contrast, the Washington, D.C., Mount Pleasant riots in May 1991 occurred in a neighborhood that was not predominantly Latino, yet the coverage of the event portrayed this area as predominantly Latino. As Melita Garza (1992) of the National Association of Hispanic Journalists indicated, although many newspapers referred to the area as a predominantly Hispanic neighborhood, U.S. census data indicated it was 35 percent Black, 35 percent White, and 27 percent Hispanic, mostly Salvadoran. Moreover, a CNN reporter tried to link the violence among the Salvadorans with a uniquely Mexican American celebration, Cinco de Mayo, because it occurred on the same day. In both Los Angeles and Washington, D.C., there appears to have been a major gap between the press and Latinos in the neighborhood.

7. As NCLR indicates in Chapter 1, "One common media stereotype is that Hispanics are poor, of low socioeconomic status and lazy." Accompanying these stereotypes is the likelihood that Hispanic characters are more likely to be criminal, patronized, or untrustworthy. Hispanic characters are twice as likely as White, and three times as likely as Black characters to be shown on television committing a crime.

8. Examples of new program genres are *In Living Color* and reality-based crime shows such as *NYPD*.

1

Out of the Picture: Hispanics in the Media

National Council of La Raza

Overview

The "mass media"—an almost undefinable mix of television news and entertainment, feature films, and print materials of all kinds—constitutes an enormous "socializing force" in today's society. The media wields power that shapes Americans' attitudes toward each other and the world. Unfortunately, the media's portrayal of Latinos[1]—who constitute at least nine percent of the 1990 U.S. population and are projected to become the largest minority in the country early in the next century—has been largely unscrutinized by the press, the federal government, or other independent groups. Given the growing importance of the Latino population, and recent policy debates about the effects of violence in the media on society, it is appropriate that the media's treatment of Hispanics be carefully studied and assessed.

Until very recently, relatively little research has been conducted on the treatment of Hispanics in the media. However, the number of such studies is growing, and existing research has produced remarkably consistent findings. These studies, described in the following section of this report, reveal that:

Hispanics are almost invisible in both the entertainment and news media.

Hispanics are virtually absent as characters in the entertainment media and as correspondents and anchors in news media.

When Hispanics do appear, they are consistently and uniformly portrayed more negatively than other race and ethnic groups.

Latinos are more likely than other groups to receive portrayal in the media that reinforces crude and demeaning cultural stereotypes. Positive media portrayals of Latinos are also uncommon.

Although most of the research described and analyzed below refers to the television medium, similar studies covering feature films and print media are also included where appropriate. As this report demonstrates, to the millions of Americans whose principal views of Hispanic Americans are shaped by what they see on the television screen, the nation's second largest ethnic minority is essentially "out of the picture."

Absence of Hispanic Portrayals in the Media

Entertainment

In the late 1960s and early 1970s, spurred by the findings of the Kerner Commission that criticized the role of the media in the race riots of the 1960s, a number of researchers began to systematically study media portrayals of minorities. Most of these studies focused on African Americans and women; almost none included Hispanics. In the late 1970s, a few studies began to examine portrayals of Latinos. These studies found that, while both Blacks and Hispanics were underrepresented among television entertainment characters, Hispanics were the least likely to appear in these programs.

For example, the Annenberg School of Communications' Cultural Indicators Project found that between 1969 and 1978 only 2.5% of prime time television characters were Hispanic compared to 8.5% who were African American.[2] A follow-up Annenberg study of the 1977–1979 television seasons found the proportion of weekend Black characters (6.5%) and Hispanic characters (1%) significantly smaller than those on prime time.[3]

Similarly, in a three-season (1975–1978) study of fictional commercial television series characters, researchers at Michigan State University concluded that "Hispanic Americans are significantly underrepresented in the TV population." Out of a total of 3,549 characters, the study found only 53 Latinos—or 1.5% of the total population of TV characters—with speaking roles. Hispanic American females were especially scarce and no Hispanics appeared on Saturday morning shows. The study showed that in a typical week of watching television (total of 21 hours), the average viewer would only see five or six Hispanic American characters.[4] In a decade-long (1971–1980) study of television's portrayal of minorities and women in drama and comedy drama, Brigham Young University researchers concluded that "the relatively powerless 'other' minorities [including Hispanics] have become virtually excluded" from such programming.[5]

While the number of African Americans on television has increased in recent years, Latinos are still largely absent from the screen. The emerging research in the 1970s provided "ammunition" to groups seeking to increase the number of minorities on television. As a result, the number of African Americans on television grew dramatically in the 1980s. By the 1990s, according to one study, the percentage of

African American characters seen on television exceeded their percentage of the population.[6] However, recent studies document that the number of Latinos on television and in film remains persistently small.

The Center for Media and Public Affairs, a Washington, D.C.–based public interest research organization, has monitored the proportion of Hispanic characters on TV over the years. In *Watching America*, an analysis of programming from 1955 to 1986, the Center revealed that Hispanics hovered around the two percentage point mark of television characters throughout the 30-year period. Even more disturbing was the Center's finding that the trend was going in the wrong direction. For example, the Center found that the proportion of Hispanics on television had actually *decreased* from about three percent in the 1950s to around one percent in the 1980s.[7] (See Figure 1.1.)

According to more recent studies, this negative trend continued through the late 1980s and early 1990s. For example, in a 1992 study, Pitzer College researchers surveyed a week of network television programming during the fall of 1992. Out of 569 characters appearing in speaking parts on ABC, CBS, NBC, and Fox, Latinos accounted for just 1.6% or 9 of the 569 characters.[8] Another study covering a week of network, Public Broadcasting Service (PBS), and selected cable programming in the spring of 1992 concluded that "Hispanic characters are particularly absent from commercial entertainment television," and that Latinos and other ethnic minorities "are practically excluded as actors, actresses, or even caricatures in mainstream commercial programs."[9]

The absence of Latinos in prime time—when TV viewing is at its peak—is even worse than in the aggregate. In a 1993 study of minorities and women in television from 1982 to 1992, the Annenberg School found that Latinos averaged only 1.1% of prime-time characters over the ten years of the study, compared to 10.8% for African Americans. Moreover, while the percentages for African Americans have fluctuated over the ten seasons from 6% to 16%, Hispanics were within 1% of the 10-season average each year,[10] suggesting that underrepresentation of Latinos on television was a chronic, essentially permanent condition over this decade.

The Annenberg report further noted that "people of color" make up less than five percent of the Saturday morning program population. African Americans averaged 2.9% during the 10-year period, although they reached 6.9% by the 1991–92 season. However, Hispanics are seen, on the average, only once every two weeks (0.5 percent). The report concluded that "despite changes in styles, stars, and formats, prime-time network dramatic television presents a remarkably stable cast,"[11] confirming the notion that the absence of Latino portrayals on Saturday morning programming during any single chronological time period cannot be attributed to year-to-year variation.

Another method of assessing the presence of Hispanics "on-screen" is to measure the proportion of total roles—regardless of whether such roles portray an identifiably ethnic character—which are held by Latino actors. A 1993 study by the Screen

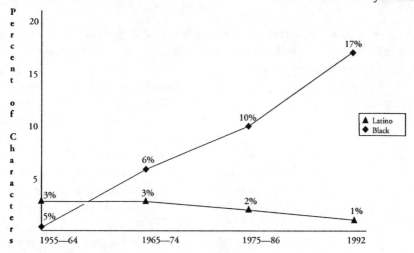

FIGURE 1.1   TV Ethnic Portrayals over Time
SOURCE: Center for Media and Public Affairs

Actors Guild (SAG) and the American Federation of Television and Radio Artists
(AFTRA) documented highly disturbing employment patterns covering all SAG-
sanctioned dramatic TV productions including episodic series, mini-series, and
movies made for television.

According to the SAG/AFTRA study, Whites receive 82% of all roles (Whites constitute 76% of the U.S. population), and Blacks hold 13% of roles (approximately the
same as their proportion of the general population). Asian/Pacifics and American Indians are underrepresented by one percentage point. However, Hispanics, who constitute at least nine percent of the population, receive only three percent of on-screen
roles; in other words, Latinos are underrepresented in on-screen television roles by a
full six percentage points.[12] These data demonstrate that, in order to reach parity, Hispanic employment on-screen would have to increase immediately by 300%!

Overall, the available data conclusively demonstrate that, by every standard, Hispanics have been severely and chronically underrepresented in TV entertainment
programming for nearly 40 years. Moreover, Latinos do not appear to have shared in
the gains made by African Americans and women in recent years with respect to increased representation as characters on television entertainment programs.

News

Television viewers are presented with fewer news and public affairs programs than
entertainment shows; similarly, the reading of news-oriented print materials occupies a shrinking percentage of the typical American's recreational or leisure time.
Notwithstanding these trends, the extent to which ethnic minorities are portrayed in

news and public affairs programs on television and in print is of vital interest to society. News programs by definition are supposed to portray reality, while much of the other media is fictional in nature. Newspapers and television's public affairs programming help shape public opinion on policy issues—and may have an even greater effect on views of policy makers. Finally, the nation's "Fourth Estate," which enjoys unique protections under the Constitution, has a correspondingly unique ethical responsibility to assure equitable, accurate portrayals of all minority groups in its news coverage. Although there has been relatively little research on this issue, available data strongly suggest that the mainstream news media has failed to assure such equitable coverage.

As with television entertainment portrayals, coverage of issues with Latino themes is extremely rare in the broadcast news media. The 1983 Project CASA study found that only 18% of television stories and 17% of radio stories qualified as Hispanic-focused. Moreover, the vast majority of these stories focused on crime and other "hard" news; less than 14% of television and 4% of radio stories dealt with minority issues.[13]

Inadequate broadcast news coverage of Hispanics is particularly obvious when measured by the number and proportion of Latinos who appear on-screen as correspondents, anchors, and other "newsmakers." For example, Hispanics historically have been severely underrepresented as on-screen correspondents in the broadcast news media. The landmark U.S. Commission on Civil Rights study, *Window Dressing on the Set: Women and Minorities in Television*, found *no Hispanics*, male or female, among the 85 TV network correspondents in 1976.[14]

Nearly two decades later, it appears that the situation has improved only marginally. A 1992 *Vista* magazine article reported on a study which found that, of all the television stories on network newscasts in 1989, 91% were filed by White reporters, 5% by Black reporters, 3% by Asian reporters, and only 1% by Hispanic reporters.[15] The 1993 Annenberg study found that Latinos make 1.5% of television network "news deliverers," i.e., correspondents and anchors, a percentage lower than any other group studied. By contrast, African Americans are 14.2 percent of news deliverers.[16]

The print media do not appear to fare much better. While comprehensive, longitudinal research in this area is particularly scarce, anecdotal evidence strongly suggests that major newspapers frequently fail to adequately present Hispanic perspectives in their coverage of the news. One early study of three daily newspapers in San Antonio, a city which at that time was almost half Hispanic, found that Hispanics were underrepresented in all categories of news coverage when compared with Whites of similar socioeconomic status. The researcher noted:

> The results of the study are similar to the findings of studies of media treatment of other minority groups. They indicate that the newspaper image of Mexican Americans in San Antonio is inaccurate. Mexican Americans are not explicitly labeled, directly stereotyped, or otherwise discriminated against. They are neglected. At almost all occupational and income levels they are underrepresented in the news.[17]

A 1983 Project CASA study examined local daily newspapers over a two-week period in six southwestern cities in which Hispanics represented 20% to 65% of the population. The authors concluded that:

> Primary Hispanic coverage (Hispanics as the focus of the story) was well below population proportions. . . . As for Spanish surname citations in newspaper bulletins, if Mexican Americans are born, wed, and die in numbers equivalent to their presence in the population, the newspapers don't report it. Such citations of Mexican Americans appear less than half as often as Hispanic population proportions would predict.[18]

Latinos also appear to be underrepresented in newspaper coverage of civil rights issues. For example, an NCLR analysis of 626 articles on civil rights issues—an area in which one might expect Latinos to be significantly overrepresented—in the *New York Times* and the *Washington Post* from January 1989 through November 1990 revealed that only 50, or 7.9%, even mentioned Hispanics.[19]

Even when print news coverage includes Latinos, it appears that this coverage is inadequate. Specifically, such coverage appears to focus on Latinos as "objects" of the news to be commented on by others, rather than as "subjects" of the news who have an authoritative or legitimate perspective to share. One 1980 study of six southwestern newspapers, for example, found that only one-third of the sources cited in stories relating to Hispanics were themselves Hispanic.[20] A more recent analysis revealed that about one-half of identifiable sources cited in Hispanic-related broadcast news stories had Spanish surnames.[21]

The Annenberg School also examined the proportion of Hispanics on major network news that are either delivering the news, making news, or cited as sources or authorities. According to the study, Latinos make up 1.5% of all newsmakers, only 0.3% of news deliverers, and were not cited at all as sources, spokespersons, or authorities—by far the lowest proportion of any other group.[22]

Based on the available data, it appears that Hispanics are seriously underrepresented as on-air correspondents and personalities in the broadcast news media, and perhaps in the print media as well. Moreover, even when Latinos appear in the news, they do so very infrequently as experts, authorities, or newsmakers.

Negative Portrayals

Entertainment

Not only are Hispanics severely underrepresented in entertainment programming, those that do appear in such programs tend to be portrayed negatively. These negative portrayals fall into two broad categories. The first category involves general "good vs. evil" or "successful vs. unsuccessful" roles. On the one hand, Latinos are less likely than other groups to be cast in positive roles; on the other hand, Hispanics are more likely than other groups to be portrayed negatively. The second category involves characterizations that are stereotypical—often crudely and blatantly so.

Although the first study to systematically examine Hispanic television portrayals was not published until 1980, an impressive body of evidence has emerged in recent years. Using a standard research technique known as "content analysis," a number of scholars have documented the extent to which television entertainment programming tends to portray Hispanics negatively; these studies are described below.

One major study by Robert and Linda Lichter of the Center for Media and Public Affairs analyzed a sample of 620 fictional entertainment programs involving 7,639 individual characters with speaking roles from the 1955 through 1986 seasons. The study, published in 1989, found that only 32% of Hispanics on television from 1955–1986 were portrayed positively, compared to 40% of Whites and 44% of Blacks. By contrast, 41% of Hispanics were portrayed negatively, compared to 31% of Whites and only 24% of Blacks.[23] Subtracting the percentage of negative characters from that of positive characters produced overall measurements of "+20" for Blacks, "+9" for Whites, and "–9" for Hispanics.[24]

Similar findings were reported in a 1993 study by the Annenberg School of Communications covering the 1982–92 period, which grouped characters into simple "hero" vs. "villain" categories. According to the Annenberg report, although positively valued ("good") characters outnumber evil ("bad") by a factor of between two and three to one overall, foreign, young, and Latino/Hispanic men were found to have the least favorable "hero/villain" ratios.[25] Citing its 20-year-old database of 21,000 total characters on television, the Annenberg School has found that for every 100 "good" White characters, there were 39 villains, yet for every 100 Hispanic "good" characters, there were 75 villains.[26]

Not only are Hispanics portrayed negatively in a traditional "good vs. evil" sense, they frequently appear on television as stereotypes and caricatures. In the Michigan State University study covering fictional programming over three TV seasons, Greenberg and Baptista-Fernandez found that "[Hispanic characters are mostly] males, of dark complexion, with dark hair, most often with heavy accents. Women are absent and insignificant."[27] Based on this research, the authors concluded that, when cast, Hispanics tend to wind up in stereotypical roles, "usually as crooks, cops, or comics."[28]

Similarly, a 1992 University of Texas study examined a week of programming on the networks, PBS, and selected cable outlets. After noting the severe underrepresentation of Hispanics, the study concluded, "If they [Hispanics] appear, they are mostly token or stereotypical characters in secondary roles with few lines or with minimal contributions to the story plots."[29]

One scholar found cartoon portrayals targeted at children to be particularly offensive. In a 1983 study, for example, Barcus observed that:

Cartoon comedy programs contain the most blatant ethnic stereotypes. These programs
. . . frequently provide cruel stereotypes of ethnic minorities. And cartoon comedies
alone amount to nearly one-half of all program time in children's TV.[30]

One common media stereotype is that Hispanics are poor, of low socioeconomic
status, and lazy. The Michigan State study noted that "half [of Hispanic characters]
are lazy, and very few show much concern for their futures. Most have had very little
education, and their jobs reflect that fact."[31] The Lichters' analysis revealed similar
results; according to the Center for Media and Public Affairs, Hispanics on TV in
the 1955–86 period were nearly twice as likely as Whites to be of "low socioeconomic status," half as likely to be a "professional or executive," and 50% more likely
to be portrayed as an "unskilled laborer."[32] (See Figure 1.2.)

More recent studies suggest that portrayals of Hispanics as poor or lazy have not
improved significantly since the 1955–86 period. The Pitzer College study, which
examined a week of TV network programming in 1992, showed that 75% of [His-
panic] characters studied were in the lower socioeconomic status category vs. 24% of
Blacks and 17% of Whites. According to the study's authors, "In general, African
Americans are portrayed positively on prime-time TV. . . . Latinos were more likely
described as powerless and stupid."[33] Given these research findings, it is not surprising that one researcher has concluded that Hispanics and other minorities "have replaced Blacks in the lower social classes on television."[34]

A second common stereotype casts Hispanics as "failures"; the two major studies
in the field both confirm the media's tendency to equate Latino characters with a
lack of success. According to the Center for Media and Public Affairs, the "failure"
rate of Hispanics was more than double that of Blacks and 50% higher than that of
Whites during the 1955–86 period.[35] This high failure rate was compounded by a
low success rate of Hispanic characters; according to the Lichters' research, Latino
characters were less likely to have succeeded in achieving their objectives than either
Whites or Blacks.[36] Similarly, the Annenberg study covering the 1982–92 period
found that, in terms of "outcome," Latino/Hispanic and Asian/Pacific American
characters have higher relative failure rates than other groups.[37]

Another variant of this theme involves portrayals of Hispanics as people who do
not have to be taken seriously. According to the Pitzer College study of the 1992 season, fully 44% of Latinos on TV were "condescended to or patronized" on screen,
compared to 30% of Blacks and only 21% of Whites.[38] Yet another variation of the
stereotype portrays Hispanics as untrustworthy. Over the 1955–86 period, the
Lichters' research found that 20% of Hispanic characters were "deceivers or trick-
sters," compared to 13% of White characters and 12% of Black characters.[39]

Perhaps no issue has been more explosive—and exploited—in recent years than
crime; in fact some political analysts have attributed the outcome of a recent Presi-

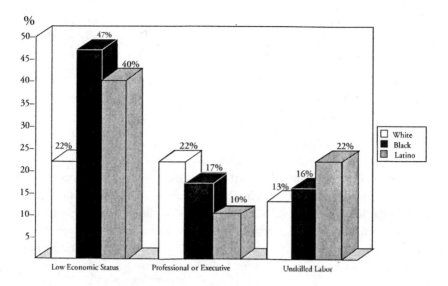

FIGURE 1.2 Traits of TV Characters, 1955–1986, by Social Background
SOURCE: Center for Media and Public Affairs

dential election in part to a single series of television advertisements. In this context, portrayals of Hispanics as criminals are particularly damaging. The Center for Media and Public Affairs study found that Hispanic characters were twice as likely as Whites, and three times as likely as Blacks, to commit a television crime. Fully 22% of Hispanic characters portrayed on TV during the 1955–86 period were criminals, compared to 11% of Whites and only 7% of Blacks. The report noted that "despite being outnumbered three to one, Hispanic characters have committed more violent crimes than Blacks" on television.[40]

In sum, Hispanics in television entertainment programs are both more likely to be portrayed negatively and less likely to be portrayed positively than any other group. In addition, TV portrayals tend to reinforce derogatory stereotypes of Latinos as people who are poor, of low status, lazy, deceptive, and criminals.

News

Hispanics appear to have been portrayed negatively in the "objective" news media as well. One of the first studies conducted on Latino portrayals in the news media was a 1969 analysis of Puerto Ricans in the *New York Times* and *New York Post*, which revealed that the English-language dailies showed little interest in Puerto Ricans, who were referred to with negative attributes and covered primarily in terms of their social disadvantages and problems. The authors found that three-fourths of a total of 64 stories dealing with Puerto Ricans centered on intergroup relations and that 85 percent of these were "problem-oriented" stories. The authors concluded that:

> Puerto Ricans are discussed and reported in the English-language press primarily in the context of the problems or difficulties that they pose for Anglo society, whereas their cultural activity and creativity is by and large overlooked.[41]

Hispanics, like other minorities, are highly susceptible to stereotyping by the news media. Journalism scholars Felix Gutierrez and Clint C. Wilson have observed that the coverage of minority issues during the 1970s often focused inordinate attention on the more bizarre or unusual elements of minority communities, such as youth gangs, illegal immigration, or interracial violence. While these are legitimate news topics, the emphasis on such coverage and the near absence of other news stories or dramatic themes involving minorities resulted in a new stereotype of racial minorities as "problem people," groups either beset by problems or causing them for the larger society.[42]

Although there is a paucity of comprehensive survey research in this area, some empirical research has been carried out which verifies the characterization of Hispanics in the news as "problem people." For example, in a 1989 study of the *Albuquerque Journal* and *San Antonio Express-News*, researchers found that although:

> Hispanics and Hispanic issues are present in the newspaper newshole in proportion to their presence in the population . . . ; [However], Hispanics were much too prominently reported as "problem people," for example, in judicial and crime news and news of riots.[43]

A 1990 San Francisco State University study of local news coverage in the Bay Area found that:

> People of color, Latinos in particular, were most frequently depicted in crime stories. Conversely, no Latinos were depicted in lifestyle stories, no Asians in business, and no people of color of any stripe in obituaries.

The author, Professor Erna Smith, notes that "the results echo every study of press coverage of non-whites dating back to the 1950s."[44]

The Annenberg study of TV programming over the 1982–92 period found that women make news as government officials and business persons combined 9.9 times as much as in crime-related stories; the ratio for men is 8.2, and for Latinos 5.0. In other words, according to the Annenberg researchers, for one woman in crime news there are 2.6 in business news; for one man in crime news there are 1.7 in business news; but for each Latino in crime news there is only one in business news.[45]

Based on these types of studies, Wilson and Gutierrez concluded that in recent years mainstream press reporting has:

emphasized ethnic minorities on "welfare" who live in crime-infested neighborhoods; lack educational opportunity, job skills, and basic language skills; and in the circumstance of Latinos and Southeast Asians, are probably not legitimate U.S. citizens.[46]

These negative portrayals are exacerbated by the fact that they are rarely counterbalanced by Hispanics who appear in more positive settings in the news. As documented above, Latinos are severely underrepresented as spokespersons, expert authorities, or "newsmakers." Thus, rather than helping to overcome the negative image of Latinos fostered by entertainment programming, the news media appear to reinforce this image through often stereotypical news coverage.

A Contemporary View

Overview

In order to collect the most complete and recent data available, the National Council of La Raza recently commissioned a special analysis of two groups of programs aired during the 1992–93 television season. The first set of programs analyzed consists of a sample of network fictional programming; this is essentially an update of the sample included in the Center's long-term study covering the 1955–86 period. The second set of programs examines two genres that are increasingly popular but rarely analyzed—reality-based shows and first-run syndicated series. The sample was assessed both from the perspective of the extent to which Hispanics appeared in such programming, as well as the types of roles portrayed by Hispanic characters. Summary findings of this special analysis are reported below.[47]

Network Fictional Programming

Perhaps the most striking single finding is how little has changed for Latinos in network entertainment in recent years. At a time when Black representation on television nearly *tripled*—from 6% over the 1955–86 period to 17% in 1992–93—Hispanic portrayals *dropped* from 2% to 1%, according to the Center's study.

From an historical perspective, Black characters were actually less prevalent than Hispanic characters in the 1950s and early 1960s. From 1965 to 1974, Blacks outnumbered Hispanics on television by a two to one margin (6% vs. 3%). However, this gap widened in the 1970s and 1980s, as the Black-to-Hispanic ratio of TV characters grew to more than three to one. By the 1992–93 season, the ratio was a staggering 17 Black characters for every Hispanic character on television.[48]

Hispanics also continue to be portrayed in a negative manner on network TV. For example, Latino characters were more likely than either Whites or Blacks to be por-

trayed as being of low socioeconomic status. At the opposite end of the economic ladder, while almost as many African Americans as Whites are portrayed as being
wealthy (16% and 18%, respectively), the proportion of wealthy Hispanics has fallen
over the years until none remained in the sample by the 1975–86 period; this lack of
Latino representation among the wealthy continued during the 1992–93 period. The
one piece of good news revealed by the study is that the proportion of Hispanic characters in professional occupations (25%) equalled that of Blacks (24%), although
both minority groups continued to fare less well than Whites (33%) in this respect.

This partial advance notwithstanding, negative portrayals of Hispanics in the
1992–93 season were considerably higher than those of other groups; Latinos were
twice as likely as Whites and three times as likely as Blacks to be portrayed in negative roles (18% vs. 8% and 6%, respectively).

Hispanics also continued to portray criminals more frequently than other groups.
During the 1992–93 season, Latino characters were four times more likely to commit
a crime than were either Whites or Blacks (16% for Latinos vs. 4% for both Whites
and Blacks). Similarly, 9% of Hispanic TV characters engaged in violent behavior—
more than double the proportion of Whites and Blacks (4% and 3%, respectively).

Syndicated and Reality-Based Programming

Among the fastest-growing and most popular program genres on television are so-
called "reality-based" shows, e.g., *Cops*, and first-run syndicated series, e.g., *Star Trek:
The Next Generation*. While such programs may well offer TV viewers greater diversity in some respects, the Center's analysis revealed that, if anything, these shows
paint an even more negative portrayal of Latinos than network fare.

For example, out of a total of 472 total characters analyzed from a sample of syndicated series, only six or 1% were Hispanics. Although this figure is so low that it
limits the researcher's ability to draw statistically reliable inferences, three of the six
Hispanic characters were portrayed negatively and two engaged in criminal activity.
For comparison purposes, out of the overall sample only about one of five characters
was portrayed negatively.

Reality-based shows in the 1992–93 season were notable for containing a relatively high proportion of Latino characters; unfortunately, nearly half of these characters were criminals. According to the Center's data, Hispanics accounted for eight
percent of the characters in these programs. However, a stunning 45% of Latinos
portrayed on these shows committed crimes, compared to 10% of the Whites who
were shown. Lichter and Amundson conclude that:

> These findings reflect the topical focus of these programs, most of which are real-life
> cops and robbers shows. For the most part, our study found, they show Whites enforc-
> ing the laws and minorities breaking them.[49]

Measured by both the number and proportion of characters, or the quality of roles portrayed, Hispanics on TV network shows appear to have made little progress since the 1950s. In the context of the 1990s, this absence of progress is quite remarkable; it has taken place at a time when Hispanics are among the fastest-growing population groups in the U.S., when rapid demographic change is focusing increasing attention on multicultural themes and issues, and against a backdrop of significant improvement in the proportion and quality of portrayals of African Americans and perhaps other minorities as well. As the Center concluded, "Steppin' Fetchit may be a distant memory, but 'Jose Jimenez' seems alive and well."

NOTES

Excerpted and reprinted by permission of the publisher from *Out of the Picture: Hispanics in the Media*, State of Hispanic America, August, 1994. (Washington, D.C.: National Council of La Raza, 1994).

1. The term "Hispanic" is used by the U.S. Bureau of the Census to identify persons of Mexican American, Puerto Rican, Cuban, Central and South American, and Spanish descent. Throughout this report, it is used interchangeably with the term "Latino."

2. Gerbner, George, and Nancy Signorelli, *Women and Minorities in Television Drama, 1969–1978*. Philadelphia, PA: Annenberg School of Communication, University of Pennsylvania, 1979.

3. Greenberg, Bradley S., and Jeffrey E. Brand, *Minorities and the Mass Media: 1970s to 1990s*, in Bryant, Jennings, and Dolf Zillman, *Media Effects: Advances in Theory and Research*. Hillsdale, NJ: Lawrence Erlbaum Publishers, 1994. For comparison purposes, according to the 1980 Census, Hispanics constituted about 6.4%, and Blacks constituted about 8%, of the total U.S. population.

4. Greenberg, Bradley S., and Pilar Baptista-Fernandez, "Hispanic-Americans: The New Minority on Television," in Greenberg, Bradley S., *Life on Television: Content Analyses of U.S. TV Drama*. Norwood, NJ: Ablex Publishing Corporation, 1980.

5. Seggar, John F., Jeffrey K. Hafen, and Helen Hannonen-Gladden, "Television's Portrayals of Minorities and Comedy Drama, 1971–80," *Journal of Broadcasting*, Vol. 25, no. 3, Summer 1981.

6. Lichter, S. Robert, Linda S. Lichter, and Stanley Rothman, *Watching America*. New York: Prentice Hall Press, 1991.

7. *Ibid.*

8. Nardi, Peter M., *The Issue of Diversity on Prime-Time Television*. Claremont, CA: Pitzer College, 1993.

9. Subervi-Velez, Federico A., and Susan Colsant, "The Televised Worlds of Latino Children," in Berry, Gordon L., and Joy Keiko Asamen, eds., *Children and Television: Images in a Changing Sociocultural World*. Newbury Park, CA: Sage Publications, 1993.

10. Gerbner, George, *Women and Minorities on Television: A Study in Casting and Fate* (a report to the Screen Actors Guild and the American Federation of Radio and Television Artists). Philadelphia, PA: Annenberg School of Communication, University of Pennsylvania, 1993.

11. *Ibid.*

12. Screen Actors Guild, *Employment in Entertainment: The Search for Diversity.* Hollywood, CA: Screen Actors Guild, Inc., 1993.

13. Heeter, Carrie, Bradley S. Greenberg, Bradley E. Mendelson, Judee K. Burgoon, Michael Burgoon, and Felipe Korzenny, "Cross Media Coverage of Local Hispanic American News," *Journal of Broadcasting,* Vol. 27, no. 4, Fall 1983.

14. United States Commission on Civil Rights, *Window Dressing on the Set: Women and Minorities in Television.* Washington, D.C.: U.S. Government Printing Office, 1977.

15. "Minorities in the News," *Vista Magazine,* 1992.

16. *Women and Minorities on Television: A Study in Casting and Fate, op. cit.*

17. Lee, Sylvia Anne, "Image of Mexican Americans in San Antonio Newspapers: A Content Analysis," unpublished Masters Thesis, University of Texas at Austin, 1973, quoted in Gutierrez, Felix, "Making News-Media Coverage of Chicanos," *Agenda,* Vol. 8, no. 6, November/December 1978.

18. Greenberg, Bradley, Carrie Heeter, Judee K. Burgoon, Michael Burgoon, and Felipe Korzenny, "Local Newspaper Coverage of Mexican Americans," *Journalism Quarterly,* Vol. 60, no. 4, 1983.

19. Internal NCLR analysis previously cited in Claire Gonzales, *The Empty Promise: The EEOC and Hispanics.* Washington, D.C.: National Council of La Raza, 1993. Of some note is the fact that a significant proportion of the articles mentioning Hispanics centered on a single event—a speech by then-President George Bush to the NCLR Annual Conference in July 1990 that focused in part on the pending Civil Rights Act of 1990.

20. Greenberg, Bradley, Michael Burgoon, Judee Burgoon, and Felipe Korzenny, *Mexican Americans and the Mass Media.* Norwood, NJ: Ablex Publishers, 1983.

21. *Minorities and Women on Television: A Study in Casting and Fate, op. cit.*

22. *Ibid.*

23. *Watching America, op. cit.*

24. *Ibid.*

25. *Women and Minorities on Television: A Study in Casting and Fate, op. cit.*

26. Interview with Dr. George Gerbner, Annenberg School of Communications, University of Pennsylvania, July 1994.

27. *Life on Television: Content Analyses of U.S. TV Drama, op. cit.*

28. *Ibid.*

29. "The Televised Worlds of Latino Children," *op. cit.*

30. *Images of Life on Children's Television, op. cit.*

31. *Life on Television: Content Analyses of U.S. TV Drama, op. cit.*

32. *Watching America, op. cit.*

33. *The Issue of Diversity on Prime-Time Television, op. cit.*

34. *Images of Life on Children's Television, op. cit.*

35. *Watching America, op. cit.*

36. *Ibid.*

37. *Women and Minorities on Television: A Study in Casting and Fate, op. cit.*

38. *The Issue of Diversity on Prime-Time Television, op. cit.*

39. *Watching America, op. cit.*

40. *Ibid.*

41. Fishman, Joshua, and Heriberto Casiano, "Puerto Ricans in Our Press," *Modern Language Journal,* Vol. 53, March 1969, cited in *Mexican Americans and the Mass Media, op. cit.*

42. Wilson, Clint, and Felix Gutierrez, *Minorities and Media.* Beverly Hills, CA: Sage Publications, 1985.

43. Turk, J. V., J. Richard, R. L. Bryson, Jr., and S. M. Johnson, "Hispanic Americans in the News in Two Southwestern Cities," *Journalism Quarterly,* Vol. 66, no. 1, 1989.

44. Smith, Erna, "The Color of News," in Hazen, Don, ed., *Inside the L.A. Riots.* New York: Institute for Alternative Journalism, 1992.

45. *Minorities and Women on Television: A Study in Casting and Fate, op. cit.*

46. *Minorities and Media, op. cit.*

47. All data in this section, unless otherwise noted, come from S. Robert Lichter and Daniel R. Amundson, *A Tale of Two Minorities: Black and Hispanic Characters in TV Entertainment.* Washington, D.C.: Center for Media and Public Affairs and National Council of La Raza, forthcoming 1994.

48. Lichter and Amundson note, however, that Black characters on television are not uniformly distributed. Most Black characters are concentrated on a handful of shows; in 1992, for example, 10 series accounted for nearly two-thirds of all Black characters.

49. The authors note that the reality-based format was the only one in which African Americans fared worse than Hispanics. According to the Lichter analysis, 50% of all Black characters, compared to 45% of all Latino characters, committed crimes in reality-based TV programs.

2

Hispanic Voices: Is the Press Listening?

Jorge Quiroga

A Cross Burns in Charlestown

Twenty-three year old Marisol Abreu peered out her living-room window and could hardly believe her eyes. There, in the front courtyard to her apartment a five-foot wooden cross had been set on fire.

"They make me feel like I don't have the right to live here," she said. None of the racial slurs, the hateful stares she'd endured during the time she'd lived in Charlestown hurt as much or seemed as threatening "as the powerful symbol of the burning cross, which is usually associated with the Ku Klux Klan."[1]

That hardened symbol of hate was hardly anonymous. At 7:30 P.M. a crowd of a hundred white teenagers shamelessly gathered around the burning cross. Insults, taunts and racial slurs were directed at Abreu and other Hispanic residents in the public housing projects where she and her three-year-old daughter lived. No, this wasn't the 1950's in the deep South, nor was it the 1970's when court ordered bussing stirred deep racial animosity in many Northern cities. This ugly scene took place in 1993, on a raw damp October evening in Boston, a city with its share of un-healed racial scars.

How the city's newspapers and TV news covered this troubling episode reveals much about the media's detached relationship with Hispanics in the city and the pro-found degree to which Hispanic leaders perceive themselves alienated by the press.

No Hispanics in the Rolodex

In Boston, the cross-burning incident capped a night of violence following the stab-bing of three white youths by a Hispanic teenager as retaliation for alleged harass-ment. Several hundred angry white residents chased the 18-year-old Hispanic suspect into a friend's apartment in the Bunker Hill Projects in Charlestown. As dumpsters were set ablaze, the mob screamed obscenities and racial slurs. Dozens of police were summoned to the rescue. Under heavy security the Hispanic youth was arrested and whisked out of the building into a police vehicle.

The next morning *The Boston Globe* wrote of a brewing racial confrontation, "Police speculated that the stabbing came after some youths had slashed the tires of three cars believed to be owned by the suspect and his friends. White youths are believed to be responsible for the tire slashing."[2] Press accounts dealt with the facts and the racial framework of the violence and the changing demographics in Charlestown's public housing. Once residents in the 1,111 unit complex were all white. Today they are 62 percent white, 17 percent Hispanic, 11 percent black and 9 percent Asian.

No one would excuse the bloody alleged attack of the Hispanic suspect or the frenzied reaction by the white mob. But had this "race riot" involved black victims and a burning cross or Jews and Nazi anti-semitic graffiti, the press in Boston would have certainly contacted community leaders. The spontaneous reaction from those groups would have also been more fervent.

Curiously, while two Hispanic eyewitnesses were interviewed reporters did not seek out opinions from Hispanic leaders. It seemed as if there were no Hispanic names in the newsroom rolodex. Reporters who felt the need to speak to Hispanic leaders were satisfied with simply interviewing the Hispanic director of the Boston Housing Authority, David Cortiella.

"Any community that is undergoing transition—where new neighbors are moving in—will have difficulties," Cortiella told *The Boston Herald* as he inspected the projects the next day.[3] Speaking to a WCVB reporter Cortiella warned, "Don't make it more than what it is. This is kids fighting kids."[4]

That "spin" came from Cortiella the city official looking to calm a volatile situation. Later, Cortiella expressed dismay that other Hispanic voices were not sought out by the press. "If this had been a black/white incident, the *Globe* and the *Herald* would have certainly flipped through their rolodexes and invited reaction from a whole range of black community leaders and politicians," he said.[5]

Cortiella says when he didn't read any interviews with other Hispanic leaders in the city he called the *Globe* reporter covering the story and complained. "I even had to give him the names of three Hispanic leaders, but it was me giving him leads trying to help him write the story."[6]

The story Cortiella wanted was not written. Subsequent reports did not include Hispanics in Boston representing a larger constituency. It was a missed opportunity to build bridges between the press and Hispanics.

Equally damning was the passivity of Hispanic leaders themselves. Their silence was so deafening that a week later, it forced the *Globe's* Efrain Hernandez Jr., one of a handful of Hispanic reporters in the city, to write an analysis of it.

"For many in the city's Hispanic community, the lack of public outrage by Hispanic activists since the cross burning and other racial unrest in Charlestown has itself been an outrage. Some residents saw a lost opportunity to highlight the complex barriers faced by Hispanics in the city because, at least in public, activists remained largely silent."[7]

Hernandez later explained why so many remained so silent, "Latino leaders were hesitant to get involved because they felt the Hispanic kids were no innocent bystanders, that they were partly to blame for the violence that first night. Some activists felt they had to be careful. They were frustrated about the cross burning. They really did not know what to do. It shows people are intimidated by the media."[8]

When it comes to meaningful coverage of Hispanics in the United States, the American press chooses a passive role. The reasons and consequences have created a dysfunctional dynamic distancing the press and Hispanics from each other. At times Hispanic leaders and organizations have been indecisive in responding to specific events. Sometimes when they do react they demonstrate a lack of sophistication and knowledge about using the media. The press, likewise, has often shown a broad lack of understanding and awareness of Hispanics even in the aftermath of a confrontation thick with racial overtones, like the Charlestown melee and cross burning. Once again, reporters and editors opted to talk about Hispanics rather than to talk to them.

Maybe it seems simpler not to commit time and effort to understand a group that defies easy definition. What is a Hispanic after all? The answer varies.

Nearly 10 percent of the nation's population of 250 million is Hispanic. Although you can find Hispanics in every state, the majority or nearly nine of every ten, live in just ten states: New Mexico, California, Texas, Arizona, Colorado, New York, Florida, Nevada, and New Jersey.

Mexican Americans form the largest group accounting for 60 percent of the nation's Hispanic population. Puerto Ricans are the second largest group representing 12 percent of all Hispanics, followed by Cuban Americans at 5 percent. The remaining fourth, or 23 percent, come from the Dominican Republic and the Spanish-speaking countries of Central and South America.

About one-third or 36 percent of all Hispanics are foreign born.[9] Others are multi-generation Americans and still others have ancestors whose residences predate the nation's birth. About 64 percent of the Hispanic population was born in the United States.[10] Yet, influenced by the continued influx of immigrants, Spanish is the nation's second language, spoken at home by over 17 million people. Among native born Hispanics the use of English increases with each generation. Among the native born, 62 percent of Mexican Americans, 50 percent of Puerto Ricans and 31 percent of Cubans speak English predominantly or exclusively at home.[11]

Felix Gutiérrez, a fourth-generation Californian and former journalism professor, expresses a common sentiment among many Mexican Americans when he says, "My great-grandparents didn't cross the border. The border crossed them."[12]

For many it is also hard to understand the diversity within a series of groups who hold nationality above ethnicity. Dr. Rodolfo de la Garza, a prominent Hispanic political scientist and researcher writes, "Mexicans, Puerto Ricans and Cubans have little interaction with each other, most do not recognize that they have much in common culturally, and they do not profess strong affection for each other."[13]

Some even see the term Hispanic itself as a forced label. Richard Rodriguez writes in his book *Days of Obligation*, "Hispanic is not a racial or cultural or geographic or linguistic or economic description. It is a bureaucratic integer. A complete political fiction." But the reality is that the dictionary definition of Hispanic—as someone pertaining to Spain and its language, people and culture—no longer applies in the United States. Today the term Hispanic, along with its colloquial synonym, Latino, refers to people whose origins are traced to Spanish speaking countries of Latin America.[14]

Acknowledging the bureaucratic birth of the term Hispanic in the 1980 census, many see that within the context of an Anglo-Saxon majority in America, Hispanics through a common language and a similar history do have more in common with each other regardless of national origin.

"A group consciousness is emerging despite our differences," says Raul Yzaguirre, executive director of the National Council of La Raza, the nation's largest Hispanic civil rights advocacy group. "It is all contextual," he adds. "We are talking about these things as though they were in opposition when in fact we are talking about a set of concentric circles."[15]

From Puerto Ricans in Boston, Salvadorans in Washington, D.C., to Mexicans in Los Angeles, from Chileans in Chicago to Cubans in Miami, from every country in Latin America, black, white, Indian, Mestizos, Hispanics, now account for one of every ten Americans. They are not a single monolithic community but rather a series of communities as in concentric circles. It is a distinction lost on the mainstream press.

"I do not attribute a maliciousness or an agenda on the part of the networks to 'dis' Hispanics. I really think there is a genuine pervasive and overwhelming ignorance on the part of the networks toward this community," says Lisa Navarrate, a spokesperson at La Raza's headquarters in Washington, D.C.[16]

Navarrate resists blaming the mainstream media for pernicious racism. "When you talk to the networks they think Hispanics are immigrants, recent arrivals, that we just got here yesterday and that most of us are here illegally. There are all kinds of myths and stereotypes that they take as the Gospel truth. When in reality two-thirds of the vast majority of Hispanics (Mexican Americans) were born in this country. Their roots go back to before the English got here. But we can say that till we are blue in the face and it doesn't quite resonate," Navarrate says.[17]

That is certainly the perception among dozens of Latinos interviewed for this report. From different countries of origin, foreign-born or U.S.-born, Spanish- or English-language dominant, from the East Coast or from the West, liberals or conservatives, Democrats or Republicans there is one consensus: Hispanics are ill-served by the American press.

"There is a lack of understanding as to who Latinos are. The press is still very much driven by the black/white equation. They tend to see us in that context. How are we like blacks and how do we differ from blacks? The census tells them we exist but they don't understand us in our own right," says Felix Gutiérrez.[18]

Louis DeSipio believes the way the press fails to cover contrasts among Hispanics creates a stereotype among Anglos (a loose term for English-speaking American-born whites of European descent). "They get periodic statistics from the Census Bureau that say things are terrible. Or they give a picture that is accurate for just one person," says DeSipio.[19]

From census reports, publishers and editors learn that Hispanics are the fastest-growing ethnic group in the United States. If census projections hold true, entering the 21st century Hispanics will become the country's largest minority group, surpassing blacks. Due to immigration and high birth rates the Hispanic population grew over seven times as fast as the rest of the nation's population during the 1980's. (Hispanics increased by 53 percent, in contrast to growth rates of 6 percent for whites and 13 percent for non-Hispanic blacks.)[20]

Other snapshots show that Hispanics are the least educated, the poorest, and least likely to be covered by health insurance. Hispanic children are twice as likely to be living in poverty as non-Hispanic children.[21]

A growing population, extensions to the Voting Rights Act to specific language minorities, and court challenges to district boundaries, during the 1970's and 1980's had considerable political impact. In the Southwest, for example, de la Garza and DeSipio write that, "By freeing the Mexican American vote, the parties—particularly the Democrats in the Southwestern states—have become dependent upon Mexican American votes for victory."[22] In New York, Hispanic elected representation to city, state and Congress doubled from 11 to 22 between 1986 and the November elections of 1992. Hispanic representation to the 103rd session of Congress increased 60 percent. The 7 new Hispanic seats expanded the Congressional Hispanic Caucus to 17 members, still only a paltry 3 percent of the 535 seats in the House of Representatives.

The Hispanic political potential continues to be undermined by weak voter participation. Even a record-setting 5 million Hispanic voter registrations in 1992 reported by the Southwest Voter Registration Project appears to be little more than treading water.[23] Voter registrations by definition include only voting age U.S. citizens. Expand the base to include the influx of new immigrants, along with the younger, poorer and less educated traits of Hispanics as a whole, and there is in fact little proportionate progress in voter participation. Rodolfo de la Garza and Louis DeSipio studied the effects of the Voting Rights Act on Hispanics. They conclude that, "Despite significant improvements in eliminating structural barriers to participation and in electing Latinos to office, however, Latino registration and voting rates nationally have not increased beyond pre-1975 levels."[24]

Hispanic political influence is further diminished by the very nature of Hispanics who are elected. In Washington, members of the Hispanic Congressional Caucus represent the full political spectrum—liberals, moderates and conservatives. Fourteen members are Democrats and three are Republicans. Unlike the Black Congressional Caucus, Hispanics on Capitol Hill rarely vote as a single block. Some of today's most pressing national needs, welfare reform, crime, national health insurance, jobs creation, substance abuse, immigration and AIDS, have a disproportionate impact on Hispanics, but when the Washington press covers these issues Hispanics are seldom heard from. George Condon, Washington bureau chief for Copley News Service and the president of the White House Press Corps Association, does not mince words when he says, "The press seeks opinions from those it perceives to have influence, and in Washington Hispanics are not there yet."[25]

Quantitative data provided by the U.S. Census has outpaced qualitative data available about this group. We know how many there are, how much they earn, where they live, their occupations, their legal status, the language they prefer, but we know much less about their opinions, feelings and values. Dr. de la Garza says, "The nation's knowledge about this group has lagged behind its interest in it, and this knowledge gap has become fertile ground for claims and counterclaims about Hispanics—who they are and what their presence portends for the nation."[26] Lacking substantive facts and/or interest, the press continues to pay minimal attention.

When Dr. DeSipio looked at the largest-circulation daily newspapers in forty major cities in the United States over a six-month period, he found that, "Overall, approximately 60 percent of the paper/days reviewed had no coverage at all. . . . Of the remaining 49 percent, the average paper contained 1.6 articles. . . . In other words one would see two articles over about a three-day period."[27]

The population in each of these forty cities was at least 10 percent Hispanic. The sampling included at least 90 percent of the Cuban, Puerto Rican or Mexican origin populations.

"I was surprised. I actually thought that was low. I thought that because so many papers served cities with large Latino communities, you'd find more written about Latinos," says DeSipio.[28]

The stories written about Hispanics tended to be local. DeSipio found no "national" Hispanic coverage. Among the papers that do have coverage, few cover the same stories. This finding suggests the absence of explicitly Latino issues that editors uniformly recognize as meeting their papers' criterion for "national" news.[29]

The relatively little coverage Hispanics do receive usually fits the typical definition of "news."

Emily Rooney, executive producer of World News Tonight with Peter Jennings, is more blunt, saying, "Most news is about conflict."[30]

David Shaw of *The Los Angeles Times* wrote, "News, as defined by the people who write, edit, publish and broadcast it, is about the unusual, the aberrant—about triumphs and tragedies, underachievers and overachievers, it's about the extremes of life, not 'normal everyday' life."[31]

"It is only when the majority culture perceives the black cat is crossing its path that anybody says anything about Latinos," says Ray Suarez, host of National Public Radio's "Talk of the Nation."[32] The former Chicago reporter watches national and local press coverage of Hispanics from his unique vantage point as the only Hispanic host of a national radio show. "I am in pretty exclusive company."[33]

Suarez says the conflict-driven nature of hard news offers rare opportunities for the public to see Hispanics in a fuller context, "It's either to highlight pathologies, drug sales, gang violence, school drop out rates or to do a Margaret Mead turn on that night's 'Evening News,' by going over to the other side of town and to see what those Mexicans are like."[34]

That is not the case for whites or Anglos who are routinely represented in many different types of news accounts. San Francisco State University journalism professor Erna Smith examined how the mainstream media covered different ethnic groups in the Bay Area.

"Whites were sources for all types of stories but this was not true for people of color. People of color were more likely than whites to be news sources of crime stories and as a group were cited more frequently in these crime stories."[35]

The degree of one-sided coverage varies between newspapers and TV news. The Bay Area may have a 15 percent Hispanic population, yet Smith writes, "On television . . . 12 percent of the Latinos were sources of crime compared with 14 percent for whites. In newspapers 60 percent of Latinos were sources of crime stories compared with 18 percent of the whites."[36]

The emphasis on news about Hispanic crime carries over from region to region. In San Antonio, Texas, Thomas Larralde looked at specific news coverage on KMOL-TV.

"Hispanics were overrepresented in crime stories and were generally portrayed as criminals, or victims. Thirty-one percent of Hispanic stories were crime related, while 21 percent portrayed Hispanics as victims of natural misfortunes. Within these stories Hispanics were rarely interviewed," Larralde writes.[37]

Of all natural misfortunes afflicting Hispanics poverty may be the worst. Nationally, more than a fourth or 29 percent of Hispanics live below federal poverty levels. The 3.1 percent increase in Hispanic poverty between 1991 and 1993 is the highest among any ethnic group in the nation. As Hispanic poverty rises, income drops. Per capita income for Hispanics in 1992 was almost half that of whites (whites—$15,981, blacks—$9,296, Hispanics—$8,874).[38]

Curiously this emphasis by the press on Hispanic criminality and poverty does not temper an overriding impulse to overlook Hispanics. It is as if they possessed some unnatural quality of transparency to be noticed but not seen with certainty.

Symmetry of Exclusion

The most racially charged incident of the decade provides an excellent example of the media looking through the Hispanic community. The police beating in Los Angeles in 1991 of 25-year-old black motorist Rodney King, and the subsequent riots in the Spring of 1992 were described by a Special Committee of the California State Assembly as the "worst multi-ethnic conflict in United States history."

Yet the image left from the news coverage of the riots was not really multi-ethnic. After viewing the police beating of King, the subsequent beating of the white truck driver Reginald Denny, and many other videotaped acts of arson and vandalism during the riots, viewers would be hard pressed to describe the violence as something other than the rage of blacks against whites and Korean bystanders.

A careful look shows that was hardly the case at all. Hispanics experienced a symmetry of exclusion from beginning to end in the press coverage. They were excluded as perpetrators, victims and as a community affected by the melee.

The first subtle omission by the press was a failure to consistently report that one of the four "white" officers charged in the beating of 25-year-old Rodney King was of Latino descent. Only one early article in *The Los Angeles Times* noted that as a youth, Officer Theodore Briseno was routinely, "teased about his Latino heritage by white friends in high school."[39]

Peter Skerry, a noted scholar on Mexican Americans writes of this omission, "Yet in its news columns and editorials the *Times* has—with this notable exception—consistently referred to Briseno as one of 'the whites' who assaulted King. Indeed, in the continuing furor over this incident Briseno's ethnic background has been almost universally overlooked."[40]

Neglecting to identify one of the officers as an Hispanic, the media framed the conflict from the outset in the familiar black/white American paradigm of racial conflict. This pattern persisted almost a year later, when the L.A. riots erupted following the acquittal of the four "white" police officers by a Simi Valley jury.

On April 29, 1992, TV cameras zoomed in at the intersection of Florence and Normandie Streets in South Central L.A., the epicenter of the riots. From the minute the TV crews went "live" with the images of black rioters venting their anger against their unsuspecting victims, to the trial in October 1993 of the two black suspects accused of beating white trucker Reginald Denny, the perception created by the media belies the facts. The press overlooked substantial evidence that the riot was a "class rebellion as well as a race revolt."[41] Selective reporting and preconceived notions in the press coverage left Hispanics on the cutting room floor.

"The problem with the race-tells-all explanation is that it overlooks the central, perhaps even dominant role that Hispanics played in the violence and suffering. According to the Los Angeles Police Department, Hispanics accounted for half of the 8,700 people arrested city-wide during and after the riots; in fact, the L.A.P.D. arrested *more* Hispanics (4,307) than blacks (3,083). Nineteen Hispanics also died during the civil disorders, just three short of the number of black fatalities. And while newscasts featured embittered standoffs between blacks and Korean shop owners, the L.A. mobs ravaged about as many Hispanic businesses as Korean-owned ones."[42]

TV news accounts projected a one-sided picture into living rooms around the world. Looking carefully at how the press framed the story reveals how little journalists knew about the city's neighborhoods and the complexity of urban tension that existed.

Being familiar with the coverage of minorities in the press from her research in San Francisco, Erna Smith decided to examine local and national TV news of the L.A. riots beginning April 29, 1992. Her study included a Korean-language news program and the nation's number one Spanish-language TV network, Univision.

"There were significant differences in the coverage on different stations. The network news coverage framed the story more in terms of blacks and whites than did the local stations in Los Angeles. . . . Blacks and whites were the central focus of 96 percent of the network news reports compared to 80 percent of the stories aired on stations in Los Angeles. . . . Conversely, Latinos and Koreans were the central focus of 4 percent of the stories aired on the networks and 18 percent of the stories aired on the Los Angeles stations," writes Smith.[43]

The visual images and the framing of these news stories contrast with the actual participants and the ethnic diversity of the affected neighborhoods. The areas of Los Angeles most decimated by the riots were heavily populated by Hispanics: Koreatown (80 percent), Pico Union (70 percent) and South Central Los Angeles (45 percent).[44] Those numbers, according to Smith, correspond with the arrest totals which showed Hispanics, "comprised half the rioters arrested in the City of Los Angeles and possibly 30 to 40 percent of the store owners whose businesses were destroyed by the violence."[45]

But in TV news the L.A. riots had a vastly different face. It was not Hispanic. Smith found that, "Latinos only comprised 17 percent of the residents and 10 percent of the store owners interviewed in the coverage."[46]

The Tomas Rivera Center in Claremont, California, also conducted a comprehensive study of the L.A. riots and the aftermath. This project specifically tracks the Hispanic presence in the 14 most highly damaged neighborhoods (including Koreatown, Pico Union and South Central Los Angeles). In this broader geographical area Hispanics still accounted for 49 percent of the residents.[47] Analyzing the most highly damaged neighborhoods helps trace the roots of Hispanic omission in news accounts.

East L.A. is the city's largest and best-known Hispanic neighborhood. Because it was largely untouched by the violence, there was an initial assumption that, "Latinos scarcely participated in and were mostly unaffected by the unrest."[48]

The result is that Hispanics in the newly emerging barrios that were in the eye of the storm were seen but unheard in the news coverage. The framework created by this type of reporting was a double-edged sword. On one side, lack of prominence spared Hispanics public and official condemnation. On the other side, the failure to be visible initially kept Hispanics out of the round table of negotiations after the riots.

As city, state and federal agencies began work to rebuild South Central Los Angeles, the initial effort mirrored the black/white framework of the coverage. None of the three commissioners who initially headed the "Rebuild L.A. Committee" was Hispanic.

The oversight became so glaring it forced a group of Hispanic business and social leaders to stage a rally outside of City Hall. They complained that Hispanics were being shortchanged in riot aid. "Joe Sánchez, president of the Mexican-American Grocers Assn., said he remains convinced that African-American organizations have received disproportionate attention and post-riot aid because they have stronger ties to City Hall and because the news media often paint riots in a black-versus-white or black-versus-Korean conflict, in which Latinos were primarily looters instead of victims."[49]

"We were left out of the reconstruction even in South Central L.A. which is nearly 50 percent Latino. It has grown to be a divisive issue. People still see the area as black and resources still go predominantly to Afro-Americans. There is a real lack of comprehension of the demographic changes in these areas," says Magdalena Duran, spokesperson for the La Raza office in Los Angeles.[50] After one year a Latino was finally added to the commission.

"When groups started to coalesce and develop strategies (to address the damage and destruction from the riots) the general feeling was that Latinos were not represented to the degree one would expect among groups like Rebuild L.A.," says Barbara Cox, an editor for the Tomas Rivera Center in Los Angeles.[51]

So how is it possible that with a predilection to see Hispanics in stories of criminality and poverty, the press could have left Hispanics out of the L.A. riots story? How could there be no voice given to Hispanics in Los Angeles even when they were in the throes of a riot?

One Hispanic observer said part of the problem is that historically Hispanics have been slow to mobilize and demand public attention. "When you abuse a Mexican he leaves the room because he doesn't want to be where he's not wanted. We've got to wake up the system . . . we're going to bug everybody. We're here, and that ain't going to change," said Fernando Oaxaca, the owner of an L.A. public relations company.[52]

The pattern of exclusion also reflects the reporters and news executives listening in the newsroom and the fact that too few of them are Hispanics who know this community and its language.

Does Anybody Speak Spanish
in the Newsroom?

It was a typical afternoon in *The Washington Post* newsroom, May 5, 1991, as reporters and editors worked toward deadline. At the assignment desk, the police radios came alive with calls for backup in the Mt. Pleasant neighborhood of D.C. Soon, radio reports told of a major confrontation between police and Hispanic residents. Apparently a cop had shot an Hispanic immigrant and people were angry.

"At the *Post* people started to gather around TV monitors when the local stations cut in with live reports from the scene," says Greg Brock, Front Page Editor, "Then someone in the newsroom suddenly asked, 'Think we should send somebody down there?'"

Brock says there was no reporter in the city room who spoke Spanish, so the editors called the International Desk and borrowed a Spanish-speaking correspondent who was sent to the disturbance.

The Washington Post, which prides itself on its national and international reporting, was now covering a local disturbance in its own backyard as a foreign war. The scene is hardly surprising to one of the few Hispanics who worked at the *Post* before 1991.

"When I left the *Post* in 1989 I was one of only two Latino reporters and the other one did not speak Spanish," says Zita Arocha, a staff reporter from 1985 to 1989.[53]

Prior to her stint at the *Post*, Arocha reported for *The Tampa Times*, *The Miami Herald* and *The Miami News*. In Washington she specialized in immigration and Hispanic affairs. Arocha says before she left the paper she warned her Anglo editors that tensions between the city's burgeoning Hispanic community and the police department were near the breaking point.

"I spelled it out for my editors that the Latino community was a time bomb for the city and that the *Post* did not have the resources to cover it."[54]

Two years later the lid blew off. The violence began after Daniel Gomez, a Salvadoran immigrant, was shot by a black female officer trying to arrest him for disorderly conduct. Police say Gomez had been drinking and lunged at the police officer with a knife.

"What began as a largely Hispanic disturbance on May 5 in Mount Pleasant, grew on May 6 into a free-for-all that spilled over into adjoining neighborhoods. At its peak 1,000 police in riot gear were involved and up to 600 black, Hispanic and white youths were engaged in running battles with the police. As of May 8, some 160 adults and juveniles had been arrested. Thirteen police officers had been injured, and six police cars, a handful of businesses, stores, and a city bus were set afire. While the shooting of 30-year-old Daniel Gomez set off the violence, Hispanics claim the eruption was the result of a history of mistreatment and neglect by police and the city administration."[55]

"The news organizations in general missed the boat on covering the Latino community and didn't take the opportunity to cover it adequately before the riot so that there was no anticipation on the part of the greater community that this could happen," said Milagros Jardine, a radio reporter for WMAL who covered the Mt. Pleasant riot.[56]

Jardine was one of several dozen journalists, city officials and community leaders who met almost two months after the riots to review how well the city's news organizations responded. There was general agreement that the media had missed the circumstances of the community's rage prior to the event and in its wake.

"Once the reporters got there I think they started generalizing and started taking in lots of theories and sort of projecting what they thought had happened rather than really listening to what the people in the community were telling them had happened. If there is a fault to be placed, it's the fact that the big news organizations have ignored this [Hispanic] community and for some reason don't see it in their best interest, don't see it as an interesting, exciting, stimulating story to cover," Jardine said.[57]

The Capital's Hispanic population exploded during the 1980's with the arrival of thousands of Central Americans fleeing political unrest. The biggest influx came from El Salvador.

Despite Hispanic growth the city's politics and demographics remain overwhelmingly black oriented. Apparently there were few reporters who had a working knowledge of the city's newest immigrant groups. Reports during the three-day melee included gross exaggerations, rumors and misinformation.

TV news reports, during live-shots from the scene, provided the most glaring unsubstantiated misinformation. "Some Anglo journalists went so far as to suggest a link between rioters and Central American leftist guerrillas, reporting that the reason the protestors were so successful in burning police vehicles and doing so much damage was because they had prior training and connections to guerrilla movements somewhere in a foreign land," said Clavel Sánchez of National Public Radio.[58]

Hispanic reporters blamed the misrepresentations of the Mt. Pleasant neighborhood on the lack of Hispanic staff in the city's major media outlets.

"I think it became very self evident to each of the media organizations just how out of touch they were with this particular community," assessed Carlos Sánchez, a reporter at *The Washington Post* who was later assigned to cover the disturbances.[59] Even Sánchez's boss could not disagree.

"Our coverage prior to the disturbances in Mt. Pleasant was inadequate," said Milton Coleman, the *Post's* Metro Editor. "I think our coverage got much better the day that Carlos Sánchez was assigned to do this full time. Having reporters who were culturally in tune with the community, or who spoke Spanish became a necessity."[60]

Coleman said that the *Post* was able to recruit as many as six or seven Spanish-speaking staff to cover the story. "Not all of them were Latino. Many of them were Anglos," Coleman recalled.[61] The *Post* only had two Hispanic reporters at the time. Today, 12 Hispanics work in the newsroom; they make up 2.2 percent of the staff.[62]

The employment picture for Hispanics in the news media 25 years after the Kerner Commission Report remains bleak despite recent gains.

Hispanics argue that more Hispanic journalists in newsrooms minimize distortions, exaggerations, and misrepresentations of their Hispanic communities because they understand the vast differences and commonalities among them.

"Employment is a vehicle toward coverage. The end result of diversifying the newsroom is supposed to be coverage and content, what is coming off the TV screen or pages of the newspaper. If you do not have Latinos working in the newsroom you are not going to be able to influence the coverage," says Felix Gutiérrez, a former journalism professor now working at the Freedom Forum.[63]

Hispanic employment in America's newsrooms remains a thorny issue. Underrepresentation remains substantial despite modest gains. Even in markets with a substantial Hispanic presence, Hispanic employment in the newsroom remains low. You wouldn't expect many Hispanics at *The Wichita Eagle* or *The Richmond Times Dispatch*. Yet in New York City, which is 25 percent Hispanic, *The New York Times'* newsroom staff is 3.6 percent Hispanic. Los Angeles is 40 percent Hispanic, yet *The Los Angeles Times'* news staff is 6.46 percent Hispanic. Locally or nationally, underrepresentation of Hispanics is broad. The U.S. is nearly 10 percent Hispanic yet only 4 percent of the news staff at the top 57 daily newspapers in the country is Hispanic.[64]

"That is nothing to write home about. The increases should be much higher than that considering the fact that there have been recruitment programs for nearly a dozen years," says Zita Arocha, now a free-lance journalist who conducts an annual survey and report on the status of Hispanics for the National Association of Hispanic Journalists. She says the typical excuse offered by news managers that able Hispanic reporters are hard to find does not hold true any more, "We have many young Latino journalists working in smaller markets who are ready and good enough to get up to the next rung in medium and large market newspapers. All they need is the opportunity."[65]

Hispanic news managers, the decision makers in the newsroom, are an even rarer breed. Only 2.3 percent of news managers in the top 57 newspapers are Hispanic.[66]

On the broadcast side of news the raw numbers imply Hispanics have made slightly better gains.

"The minority share of the newsroom work force edged to a new high in television last year, but moved backward a bit in radio. Hispanics made substantial gains. The Hispanic share of all TV news personnel went up from 3 percent in 1990 to 5 percent in 1991 and 6 percent in 1992," writes University of Missouri journalism professor Vernon Stone after reviewing employment records from 411 TV stations and 296 commercial radio stations for the Radio and Television News Directors Foundation.[67]

Yet Hispanic journalists analyze the same numbers and see in them more than meets the eye. Aggregate industry totals are misleading.

"Before you go out and buy another TV set, consider the fact that the network news still doesn't look like America, and neither does its prime-time programming," writes Zita Arocha.[68] "The University of Missouri study finds the proportion of Latino employees still smaller among television stations affiliated with the three major networks—ABC, NBC, and CBS—than among 'other' stations sending up Spanish-speaking fare generated by Univision and Telemundo."[69]

Arocha says, "The statistics do not break out differences between English- and Spanish-language TV but it is my gut feeling that a great part of the aggregate increase is due to the recent boom in Spanish-language TV."[70]

"Most of us are the only one in the newsroom," says Diane Alverio, a TV reporter in Hartford, Connecticut. "And the people in the newsroom making decisions, what stories, what angle and how to cover them are not Hispanic."[71] Hispanic reporters tell stories that have a familiar ring to other minorities.[72] They say that pushing aggressively for Hispanic coverage beyond crime and welfare is like putting on a "sombrero" in the newsroom that delegates the reporter to the so-called "taco beat."

"The hardest part is striking a sense of balance in your work. You do not want to neglect the community you care about, but you also have to show that you can cover anything if you are given the opportunity," says *The Boston Globe*'s Efrain Hernandez Jr.[73]

In most markets where Hispanics have yet to make substantial economic and political gains Hispanic reporters say the balance they are forced to strike tilts away from Hispanic coverage.

"If you are one of those rare Latinos in a newsroom you will also have to make a career decision. You know that to rise in the system you do the front page stories or the lead stories in the broadcast and that Latino stories are not going to get that play," says NPR's Ray Suarez. He says many Hispanic reporters choose professional survival. "So there you are; one of the only people on the inside who can pitch for a different look at the news, and if you do that and become perceived as an ethnic novelty act, you limit your own future opportunities. So you either whitewash yourself to get ahead or you become an advocate inside the newsroom and become marginalized."[74]

"They are struggling to be mainstream," observes Rita Elizondo, executive director of the Congressional Hispanic Caucus Institute.[75] At the Institute it is Elizondo's job to convince reporters to write stories that have a specific Hispanic interest, and to include Hispanic opinion in reporting about the U.S. Congress. It is never an easy job, but often Hispanic reporters make it even harder to do.

"They are finally at *The Washington Post* or they are finally at NBC, and they are struggling so hard to be part of the team and the mainstream that they rarely venture out into covering Latino issues because they don't want to be tagged Latino. It is very disappointing because we certainly don't get the coverage from the non-minority reporters."[76]

Without a concerted advocacy inside and outside the newsroom for more complete coverage of Hispanics, the impression and myths perpetuated are of a people lumped together as a monolith despite vast differences, a people unwilling and unable to help themselves.

"Indicative of that national mood is a 1990 national poll that found that compared to Jews, blacks, Asians and southern whites, Americans perceive Latinos as second only to blacks in terms of being lazy rather than hard-working and living off welfare rather than being self-supporting. The survey also reports that Hispanics are seen as the nation's least patriotic group."[77]

The low opinion of Hispanics makes perfect sense. Most people base their feelings about minorities from what they read or watch on TV.

Hispanic Magazine looked at all stories published by *The Chicago Tribune, The Los Angeles Times, The San Antonio Light* and *The Washington Post* during a week in August, 1992. Despite the fact that all the cities serviced by these major dailies have sizable Hispanic communities, the authors, "had to look carefully in each paper to find any story positive or negative, about or including Latinos. When Hispanics were mentioned in news articles they were more likely to be found in a crime story as the perpetrator, victim or police officer."[78] The survey found a distinct absence of Hispanic political priorities and opinion, either from grass roots or mainstream political leaders.

In another survey, Unabridged Communications of Arlington, Virginia, reviewed 4,000 articles published in seven major newspapers and three newsmagazines during July and August, 1992. Unabridged Communications notes that, "There was no coverage devoted to Latino political priorities," and that the stories, "failed to reflect positive contributions Latinos are making to society." The study's author concludes, "If you only had the articles that I culled over these two months you would not have a feel for who the [Hispanic] leadership was or what the needs of this particular community of interests were."[79]

Newspapers provide slightly better coverage of the political priorities among Hispanics. DeSipio's survey found that of those stories with Latino-relevant political content, 30 percent dealt with electoral politics. But even this figure obscures an underlying indifference. "In one of the largest categories, electoral politics, mention of Latinos was limited to the inclusion of a Latino surname in 41 percent of the coded articles."[80]

The overwhelming number of articles made reference to Hispanics in a political context without interviewing Hispanics.

That pattern can be detected even in cases where Latino political importance is widely recognized.

Getting the Story to Page One

It was a slow newsday in Boston. Massachusetts Governor William Weld had scheduled a morning press conference to introduce Deborah Ramírez, a Northeastern University Law Professor, as the chairperson of the newly appointed Hispanic-American Advisory Commission. The group was formed to examine the status of Hispanics in the state and make recommendations to improve their economic conditions.

When it came her turn to speak on that April morning 1993, Ramírez remembers looking out across the packed conference room. Present were Hispanic judges, business people, government officials, educators, along with regulars of the State House press pool. "I looked up," Ramírez recalls, "and I noticed that the old press hands at the State House, the political reporters, were not taking any notes."[81]

From her carefully prepared text, Ramírez a former assistant U.S. Prosecutor who was hired by Weld when he was U.S. Attorney, spoke with passion about the plight of the state's Hispanics. Preliminary findings gave cause for extreme concern: Hispanics had surpassed blacks as the largest minority in the state; Massachusetts, not generally regarded as a Hispanic hub, had in fact the tenth-largest concentration of Hispanics in the country; Hispanics in Massachusetts suffered the highest Hispanic poverty rate in the nation. Ramírez said the purpose of the Commission was to find much needed ways to help Hispanics help themselves.

That evening only one TV station carried a brief voice-over on the news. The next morning not a word was printed about the Commission and its mandate in either of the city's two dailies, *The Boston Globe* and *The Boston Herald*. Ramírez was flabbergasted. "What do you do when the problem is that no one will cover you? The story only got reported in the Hispanic press. But in the English-language press, which is where we have to get our story out, there was absolutely nothing."[82]

Angry and disappointed Ramírez phoned *The Boston Globe* to complain. She says she was assured an article had been written and it would be published. It was printed several days later. But the article had been buried, literally and symbolically, in the back pages of the Saturday edition next to the obituaries. The headline read, "New panel leader cites roots."[83] The article highlighted Ramírez's graduation from Harvard Law School and "her promise to her mother never to forget her roots."[84]

The "Rose Grows in Spanish Harlem" angle was not the emphasis Ramírez had hoped for. "The focus was on me personally and my story. It's as if this was a piece for the feature section. They didn't cover it as if this was a real news story," Ramírez says.[85]

The Hispanic-American Advisory Commission scheduled four hearings across the state in the Spring and Summer of 1993. Planning efforts netted events that were well attended. Hundreds of residents were offered an opportunity to talk about the dire conditions faced by Massachusetts Hispanics. Problems were discussed in detail. Solutions centered around jobs and economic opportunity. Through it all, press coverage remained sporadic. Newspapers in smaller cities and towns tended to play up the hearings while the Boston press continued to ignore or bury the story.

Ramírez realized then that time was running out. The final report and recommendations were due to the Governor in September. An important story was no story at all if it did not get on the front page. In Massachusetts that meant the front page of *The Boston Globe*.

"It is not as if the newspapers were not covering us at all. I couldn't quite say that. But it is the bad placement of the stories, the weak emphasis given and the misleading captions that diluted our efforts," says Ramírez.

What became apparent to Deborah Ramírez and the 28-member commission would seem obvious to professional lobbyists and public relations specialists. Yet it is one that many grassroots, community-based or voluntary organizations miss. They are so busy working on "the cause," that little time and effort is given to getting the message out. The fact of the matter is that today the voices heard in the media are often individuals or groups who understand how to lobby or work the media. They know how the game is played.

Ramírez had to make her case not with the reporters who had covered the hearings, but with their editors who decided story placement and emphasis. A week before the final report was due, Ramírez persisted and was able to schedule a meeting with the *Globe* senior editorial staff. Using the skills of an experienced prosecutor she argued for better coverage, showing that the findings were substantive. "I presented the group with a copy of the report and the executive summary," says Ramírez, recalling how she was able to seal the agreement, "I offered them an exclusive on the story if they covered the Commission's final presentation to Governor Weld."[86]

Two days before the final press conference, a front page story article appeared in *The Boston Globe*. The headline read, "Report on State's Hispanics Seeks Services, Business Aid."[87] The article covered various recommendations for economic and social empowerment, emphasizing a proposed economic center to provide assistance for small businesses. Ramírez had succeeded.

After Gov. Weld received the report, another article appeared with the headline, "Weld vows to fund business center for state's Hispanic community."[88] Various commission members were quoted outlining the commission's findings, cautioning that the document was only as good as its implementation. Deborah Ramírez got what she wanted, the Governor going on record in Boston's paper of record promising to help Hispanics. "Our administration will use any recommendations in this report to call to action to empower Hispanics in Massachusetts and to break down cultural, economic and racial barriers" Weld said.[89]

"Going into the final weeks of the commission's work I realized that 80 percent of what we were going to accomplish for the Hispanic community would come from getting our story in the *Globe*," says Ramírez. "When it hit the front page of the *Globe* everyone started calling. Congressman Joe Kennedy's office called, the Bank of Boston called, I even heard from the U.S. Attorney designate saying that he wanted to be responsive to the needs of the Latino community."[90]

Without the front page coverage in *The Boston Globe*, the issues raised by the Commission might never have been noticed by the public or policy makers.

Ramírez, for one, believes the prominent coverage may have prompted such swift action by the Governor.

Conclusions

Public policy decisions are influenced by the quality and quantity of media coverage. Whether it is riots, a cross burning, a mayoral election or a commission's findings on the status of Hispanics, governmental response may be framed by media reporting. Hispanic political development occurs apart from news coverage and sometimes despite the negative or slanted reporting. When there is an increase in Hispanic political clout, the press—being a reactive medium—reflects it in both the quantity and quality of the reporting.

NOTES

Originally prepared as Discussion Paper D-18 for The Joan Shorenstein Center, Harvard University, John F. Kennedy School of Government, January 1995. Excerpted by permission of the author and reprinted by permission of The Joan Shorenstein Center.

1. Rakowsky, Judy, and Dowdy, Zachary R., "Burning Cross Placed Outside Hispanic Home," *Boston Globe*, October 21, 1993.

2. Dowdy, Zachary R., and Lakshmanan, Indira A.R., "Melee Follows Stabbing, Arrests in Charlestown," *Boston Globe*, October 20, 1993.

3. *Boston Herald*, October 21, 1993.

4. WCVB-TV, Boston, NewsCenter Five at 6, October 21, 1993.

5. Interview, November 2, 1993.

6. Interview, November 16, 1993.

7. Hernandez Jr., Efrain, "Hispanic Activists Decry Silence on Cross Burning," *Boston Globe*, October 28, 1993.

8. Interview, November 17, 1993.

9. *Ibid.*

10. *Hispanic Americans Today*, U.S. Department of Commerce, Bureau of the Census, 1993.

11. De la Garza, Rodolfo, DeSipio, Louis, Garcia, P. Chris, and Falcon, Angelo, *Latino Voices: Mexican, Puerto Rican and Cuban Perspectives on American Politics*, Westview Press, Boulder, 1992.

12. Interview, October 21, 1992.

13. De la Garza et al., p 14.

14. De la Garza et al. report, in their 1992 survey of Latino political attitudes, little preference among survey participants for the pan-ethnic terms Latino or Hispanic. They write, "More respondents prefer to be called 'American'" (p. 13). National-origin terms such as Mexican, Puerto Rican or Cuban are the preferred identity choice among respondents.

15. "Who Is Latino," *Talk of the Nation*, National Public Radio, Washington, D.C., October 11, 1993.

16. Interview, October 20, 1993.

17. *Ibid.*

18. Interview, October 21, 1993.

19. Interview, September 19, 1993.

20. *Hispanic Americans Today.*

21. *Ibid.*

22. De la Garza, Rodolfo, and Louis DeSipio, "Save the Baby, Change the Bathwater, and Scrub the Tub: Latino Electoral Participation After Seventeen Years of Voting Rights Coverage," *Texas Law Review,* June 1993, p. 1494.

23. The 5 million in 1992 is an increase from 4.4 million Hispanics registered to vote in 1988.

24. De la Garza and DeSipio, p. 1501.

25. Seminar, Shorenstein Center, September 28, 1993.

26. De la Garza et al., p 2.

27. DeSipio, Louis, and James Henson, "Newspaper Coverage of Latino Issues in Forty Cities," Delivered at the meetings of the South-West Political Science Association, Fort Worth, Texas, March 28–31, 1990.

28. Interview, November 11, 1993.

29. DeSipio and Henson.

30. Interview, October 20, 1993.

31. Shaw, David, "Minorities in the Press," *Los Angeles Times,* 1990.

32. Interview, October 14, 1993.

33. *Ibid.*

34. *Ibid.*

35. Smith, Erna, *What Color Is the News?* San Francisco State University, December 1991, p. 4.

36. *Ibid.,* p. 5.

37. Larralde, Thomas, "News Coverage of Hispanics," Policy Analysis Exercise, Harvard University, Kennedy School of Government, April 13, 1993.

38. "Latino Poverty Rises, Income Drops," *Hispanic Link Weekly Reports,* October 11, 1993 (from U.S. Census Bureau data released October 4, 1993).

39. Skerry, Peter, *Mexican Americans: The Ambivalent Minority,* The Free Press, New York, 1993, p. 9.

40. *Ibid.*

41. Tharp, Mike, and David Whitman, with Betsy Streisand, "Hispanics' Tale of Two Cities," *U.S. News and World Report,* May 25, 1992, p. 40.

42. *Ibid.,* p. 40.

43. *Transmitting Race: The Los Angeles Riot in TV News,* Shorenstein Center Research Paper R-11, May 1994.

44. "When the Subject Turned to Race; How Was It Covered?" presented by Erna Smith at the National Press Club, October 22, 1993.

45. *Ibid.*

46. *Ibid.*

47. Pastor Jr., Manuel, *Latinos and the Los Angeles Uprising: The Economic Context,* The Tomas Rivera Center, Claremont, California, 1993.

48. *Ibid.,* p. 6.

49. Baker, Bob, "Latinos Shortchanged in Riot Aid, Group Says," *Los Angeles Times,* September 15, 1992.

50. Interview, November 8, 1993.

51. Interview, November 10,1993.

52. *Ibid.*

53. Interview, November 2, 1993.

54. *Ibid.*

55. *Hispanic Link Weekly Report,* Vol. 9, no. 19, May 13, 1991.

56. Transcript from conference at the National Press Club, Washington, D.C., sponsored by Hispanic News Media Association of Washington, D.C., June 20, 1991.

57. *Ibid.*

58. *Ibid.*

59. *Ibid.*

60. *Ibid.*

61. *Ibid.*

62. Arocha, Zita, and Roberto Moreno, *Hispanics in the News Media: No Room at the Top,* National Association of Hispanic Journalists, Washington, D.C., 1993.

63. Interview, October 21, 1991.

64. Arocha and Moreno, p. 1.

65. Interview, November 8, 1993.

66. Arocha and Moreno, p. 1.

67. Stone, Vernon, "Good News, Bad News," *Communicator,* August 1993.

68. Arocha and Moreno, p. 31.

69. *Ibid.*

70. Interview, November 4, 1993.

71. Interview, November 8, 1993.

72. See *Muted Voices: Frustration and Fear in the Newsroom* (An analytical look at obstacles to the advancement of African American journalists), National Association of Black Journalists Task Force Report, August 1993.

73. Interview, November 17, 1993.

74. Interview, October 14, 1993.

75. Interview, October 20, 1993.

76. *Ibid.*

77. Smith, Tom, "Ethnic Survey," GSS Tropical Report Number 19, National Research Center, 1990, cited in de la Garza et al., *Latino Voices,* p. 2.

78. "Bad News," *Hispanic Magazine,* November 1992.

79. "Media Notes," *Hispanic Link Weekly Report,* October 1992.

80. DeSipio and Henson.

81. Interview, October 13, 1993.

82. *Ibid.*

83. Locy, Toni, "New Panel Leader Cites Roots," *Boston Globe*, April 10, 1993, p. 19.

84. *Ibid.*

85. Interview, October 13, 1993.

86. Interview, September 29, 1993.

87. Hernandez Jr., Efrain, "Report on State's Hispanics Seeks Services, Business Aid," *Boston Globe*, September 20, 1993, p. 1.

88. Hernandez Jr., Efrain, "Weld Vows to Fund Business Center for the State's Hispanic Community," *Boston Globe*, September 23, 1993.

89. *Ibid.*

90. Interview, September 29, 1993.

3

Distorted Reality: Hispanic Characters in TV Entertainment

S. Robert Lichter and Daniel R. Amundson

The Past as Prologue

It takes diff'rent strokes to move the world.
—*"Diff'rent Strokes" Theme Song*

When Kingfish uttered his last "Holy Mackerel, Andy!" in 1953, it marked the end of television's most controversial depiction of blacks. Ironically, the departure of "Amos 'n' Andy" also signaled the end of a brief period of ethnic diversity that would not reappear in prime time for two decades. Several of the earliest family sitcoms were transplanted radio shows set in America's black or white ethnic subcultures. "The Goldbergs" followed the lives of a Jewish immigrant family in New York for twenty years on radio before switching to the new medium in 1949. It featured Gertrude Berg as Molly Goldberg, everyone's favorite Jewish mother. An even more successful series that premiered the same year was "Mama," which chronicled a Norwegian immigrant family in turn-of-the-century San Francisco. Theme music by Grieg added to the "ethnic" atmosphere, as did accents that made Aunt "Yenny" into a popular character. These white ethnic shows were soon joined by the all-black "Amos 'n' Andy" as well as "Beulah," which starred the black maid of a white middle-class family.

All these shows relied on stereotypical dialogue and behavior for much of their humor. But social standards were changing, and the new medium created its own demands and perceptions. For example, not only Amos and Andy but even Beulah had been portrayed on radio by white males. When the popular radio show "Life with

Luigi" made the switch to TV in 1952, Italian American groups protested its stereo-typed portrayal of Italian immigrants. Black groups were equally outraged over "Amos 'n' Andy," which had been an institution on radio since 1929. As the program evolved, it centered on the schemes of George "Kingfish" Stevens, who combined the soul of Sgt. Bilko with the fate of Ralph Kramden. A small-time con man with big plans that never panned out, he became an immensely popular, lovable loser. His schemes usually pulled in the ingenuous cabbie Andy and the slow-moving janitor Lightnin'.

From Kingfish's fractured syntax ("I'se regusted") to Lightnin's shuffle and falsetto "yazzuh," the series drew on overtly racial stereotypes. The NAACP blasted the por-trayal of blacks as "inferior, lazy, dumb, and dishonest," and urged a boycott of Blatz beer, the sponsor. The pressure from civil rights groups probably helped bring the series to a premature end, since it attracted sizeable audiences throughout its two year run.

*   *   *

While controversy surrounded "Amos and Andy," little debate attended television's earliest and most high profile Latino portrayal. From 1950 through 1956, Ziv pro-ductions sold 156 episodes of "The Cisco Kid" in syndication to individual stations across the country. Resplendent in his heavily embroidered black costume, Cisco rode across the southwest righting wrongs and rescuing damsels in distress. He was accom-panied by his portly sidekick, Pancho, who served as a comic foil. Pancho was loyal and brave, but his English was every bit as fractured as the Kingfish's. Further, al-though Cisco and Pancho were positive and even heroic characters, they were often outnumbered by evil and frequently criminal Latino adversaries. In its simplistic pre-sentation that combined positive and negative ethnic stereotypes, "Cisco" set the tone for the "Zorro" series that would follow it on ABC from 1957 through 1959. Thus, these early high-profile representations of Latinos proved a mixed bag, as television's conventions of the day were applied to both network and syndicated fare.

The All-White World

"Cisco" and "Zorro," which were aimed at children, outlasted the first generation of ethnic sitcoms for general audiences. By the 1954 season "Mama" was the only sur-vivor of this once-thriving genre. Thus, by the time our study period began, TV's first era of ethnic humor had already come and gone. The urban ethnic sitcoms were replaced by homogeneous suburban settings. There was nothing Irish about the life of Chester Riley, nothing Scandinavian about Jim and Margaret Anderson. The new family shows were all-American, which meant vaguely northern European and carefully noncontroversial. The few remaining ethnics were mostly relegated to minor roles or single episodes.

Just how homogeneous was this electronic neighborhood? From 1955 through 1964, our coders could identify only one character in ten as anything other than northern European on the basis of name, language, or appearance. Such a small slice of the pie got cut up very quickly, and many groups got only crumbs. Just one character in fifty was Hispanic, fewer than one in a hundred was Asian, and only one in two hundred was black.

*   *   *

Hispanics had virtually no starring roles. For most Hispanic characters, life consisted of lounging in the dusty square of a sleepy Latin town, waiting for the stars to come on stage. Occasionally Hispanics would show up as outlaws in the Old West, but even then mostly as members of someone else's gang. Their comic roles were epitomized by Pepino Garcia, a farmhand for "The Real McCoys," who functioned mainly as a target of Grandpa Amos McCoy's tirades. Pepino and "The Real McCoys" were replaced in 1963 by Jose Jimenez in the "Bill Dana Show."

Like their black colleagues, a few stars stood out in a sea of marginal and insignificant roles. A notable exception was Cuban band leader Ricky Ricardo in "I Love Lucy," played by Desi Arnaz. As the co-star of one of the most popular shows on TV (and co-owner of Desilu Productions, along with wife Lucille Ball), Arnaz was a prominent figure in Hollywood. When exasperated by Lucy's schemes and misadventures, Ricky added a comic touch with displays of "Latin" temper and lapses into Spanish. "I Love Lucy" made its mark on television comedy and TV production in general, but it did little for Hispanic characters. The same could be said of another early show with a Hispanic setting, which nonetheless cast Anglos in the major roles. Guy Williams played Don Diego, alias Zorro, the masked champion of the poor and oppressed in old Los Angeles. Their oppressors were evil, greedy Spanish governors and landowners. In one episode Annette Funicello, fresh from the Mickey Mouse Club, showed up as the singing senorita Anita Cabrillo. Despite its "Hispanic" characters, the show was not a generous portrayal of either the people or the culture.

The departure of "Amos and Andy" and "Beulah" all but eliminated black stars. Jack Benny's valet Rochester was one of the few major roles still held by a black in the late 1950s. Black characters didn't even show up in the backgrounds of early shows. Urban settings might feature a black delivery man, porter, or waiter, but black professionals and businessmen were virtually nonexistent. Some westerns like "Rawhide" and "Have Gun, Will Travel" presented a few black cowboys riding the range with their white counterparts. Aside from such occasional and insignificant roles, black characters were simply not a part of the early prime time world.

The Return of Race

In the mid-1960s, the portrayal of ethnic and racial minorities underwent major changes. The proportion of non–northern European roles doubled over the next decade. Before 1965, all racial and ethnic groups to the south or east of England, France, and Germany had scrambled for the one role in ten available to them. Now nonwhite characters alone could count on better than one role in ten. From the first to the second decade in our study [1955–1975], the proportion of English characters was cut in half, while Hispanics became half again as numerous and the proportion of Asians doubled. Blacks were the biggest winners, gaining a dramatic fourteen-fold increase in what had been virtually an all-white landscape.

The invisibility of Hispanics during this period remained more than metaphorical. They were simply not part of television's new ethnic "relevance." Latinos had few continuing prime time roles of any sort during the late 1960s, and certainly no major star parts like Bill Cosby's Alexander Scott. In fact, most Latinos who were cast during this period showed up in episodes of international espionage series that used Central and South American locales. "I Spy" had many episodes set in Mexico, bringing the agents into contact with some positive and many more negative Hispanic characters. In other espionage shows, such as "Mission Impossible," the action often centered on a fictitious Central American country, which was inevitably run by a jack-booted junta that could only be stopped by the enlightened Anglo-led team from north of the border.

One of the few exceptions to this pattern was the western "High Chaparral." Rancher John Cannon had settled in the Arizona territory to found a cattle empire. When his first wife is killed by Apaches, John married Victoria Montoya, the daughter of a wealthy Mexican rancher. The marriage was as much a business move as a romance, since it united the two families. Once tied by marriage, Don Montoya helped John build his herds and produce good breeding stock. Together the two families fought off Apaches and other marauders. Culture clashes between the two families occurred, but usually as a minor part of the plot. Unlike most Mexicans shown in previous westerns, the Montoyas were rich, powerful, sophisticated, and benevolent. In most episodes, Victoria attempted to civilize her more rustic husband and establish a proper home on the range. To be sure, this series still presented semiliterate Hispanic ranchhands, but these portrayals were overshadowed by the Montoyas.

The other exception was the short-lived social relevancy series "Man and the City." This series presented more contemporary problems of Latinos in an unnamed southwestern city. The show was notable for frequently asserting the dignity and rights of Latinos. For example, in a 1971 segment, a cop is killed in the city's barrio. The police department pulls out all the stops to catch the killers, imposing a curfew and holding suspects incommunicado without legal counsel. All the suspects are Hispanics from the barrio who have little connection to the case. The mayor is forced to intervene and remind the police chief that the city has laws. He demands that all suspects, including minority groups, be given their full rights. The police are reluctant, believing this will impede their investigation. The mayor insists and the police obey his order. They eventually capture a key suspect who helps them catch the killers. There is no indication that racial tensions in the city have ended, merely that one violent episode is over. The groups involved have not learned to like each other; nor are they presented as peacefully coexisting. The point here is that all people have rights and deserve to be treated with dignity and equality. This seems to be the only series that attempted to derive socially relevant plotlines from the barrio.

Not only did the proportion of black characters jump to 7 percent between 1965 and 1975, but the range and quality of roles expanded even more dramatically. In adventure series like "I Spy" and "Mission: Impossible," blacks moved into their first starring roles in over a decade. Not only were these roles more prominent, they offered a new style of character. Alexander Scott of "I Spy" and Barney Collier of "Mission: Impossible" were competent, educated professionals. These men were highly successful agents whose racial backgrounds were clearly secondary to their bravery and skill. They opened the way for blacks to appear in roles that did not require the actor to be black. There was no more use of poor English, servile shuffling, or popeyed double takes for comic effect. Instead, Collier was presented as an electronics expert and Scott as a multilingual Rhodes Scholar.

The new visibility of blacks quickly moved beyond the secret agent genre. In 1968 the first of television's relevance series managed to convert a negative stereotype into a positive one by casting a young black rebel as a member of "The Mod Squad." Linc Hayes' militant credentials included an afro haircut, aviator sunglasses, and an arrest during the Watts riots. Not to worry, though. This brooding black rebel was working with the good guys on the L.A.P.D.'s undercover "youth squad," where the dirty dozen met the counterculture every Tuesday at 7:30.

While ABC was coopting the Black Panthers into the establishment, NBC looked to the black middle class for "Julia," the first black-oriented sitcom in fifteen years. As a dedicated nurse and loving mother in an integrated world, the Julia Baker character looked ahead to "The Cosby Show" rather than backward to "Amos 'n' Andy." She certainly had more in common with Claire Huxtable than with Kingfish's nagging wife, Sapphire. Unfortunately, she also lacked the vitality and wit of either Sapphire or future mother figures who would be more firmly rooted in black culture, like "Good Times'" Florida Evans.

"Julia" suffered from the dullness of being a prestige series, just as "The Mod Squad" labored under the hype that attended the relevance series. What they had in common with better-written shows like "I Spy" and "Mission Impossible" was a tendency to replace the old negative black stereotypes with new positive ones. The authors of *Watching TV* wrote with a touch of hyperbole, "They were no longer bumbling, easy-going, po' folk like Beulah, but rather articulate neo-philosophers just descended from Olympus, though still spouting streetwise jargon."[1] Having discovered that blacks didn't have to be cast as valets and janitors, white writers turned them into James Bonds and Mary Tyler Moores. Thus, as blacks suddenly began to appear on the tube after a decade's absence, they remained invisible in Ralph Ellison's sense. The frantic search for positive characters smothered individuality with good intentions.

Let a Hundred Flowers Bloom

In the early 1970s TV began to broadcast a different message about minorities. The unlikely agent of change was an equal opportunity bigot named Archie Bunker, who excoriated "spics," "jungle bunnies," "chinks," "yids," and every other minority that ever commanded an epithet. When "All in the Family" became the top-rated show within five months of its 1971 premiere, it attracted a barrage of criticism for making the tube safe for ethnic slurs. The producer of public television's "Black Journal" found it "shocking and racist."[2] Laura Hobson, who wrote "Gentlemen's Agreement," an attack on anti-Semitism, decried its attempt to sanitize bigotry, "to clean it up, deodorize it, make millions of people more comfy about indulging in it."[3] Of course, the point of the show was to poke fun at Archie and all he stood for, as the script and laugh track tried to make clear.

Norman Lear's strategy was to educate audiences by entertaining them instead of preaching at them. So he created a kind of politicized Ralph Kramden, whom audiences could like in spite of his reactionary views, not because of them. He intended that the contrast between Archie's basic decency and his unattractive rantings would prod viewers to reexamine the retrograde ideas they permitted themselves. As Lear put it, the show "holds up a mirror to our prejudices. . . . We laugh now, swallowing just the littlest bit of truth about ourselves, and it sits there for the unconscious to toss about later."[4] As a tool for improving race relations, this approach may have been too subtle for its own good. Several studies suggest that liberals watched the show to confirm their disdain for Archie's views, while conservatives identified with him despite his creator's best intentions.[5] But another legacy of the program was to pioneer a more topical and (by television's standards) realistic portrayal of ethnic relations.

An immediate consequence of "All in the Family" was to introduce the first sitcoms populated by black families since "Amos 'n' Andy." A year after demonstrating the audience appeal of a white working class milieu not portrayed successfully since "The Honeymooners," Lear and his partner Bud Yorkin transferred the setting to a black ghetto in "Sanford and Son." Unlike the integrated middle class world of TV blacks in the late 1960s, "Sanford and Son" revolved around the foibles of a junk dealer in a poor black section of Los Angeles. "Sanford" proved so popular that it soon trailed only "All in the Family" in the Nielsen ratings.

Meanwhile, in an irony Archie would not have appreciated, "All in the Family" spawned not one but two additional black family sitcoms. "The Jeffersons" featured Archie's one-time neighbor George Jefferson as an upwardly mobile businessman whose snobbishness and inverted racism made him almost a black Archie Bunker. "Good Times" was actually a second-generation spinoff. When Archie's liberal nemesis Maude got her own show in 1972, the scriptwriters gave her a quick-witted and tart-tongued black maid named Florida Evans. Two years later the popular Florida got her own show as the matriarch of a family living in a Chicago housing project. This series developed the "Sanford" technique of finding sometimes bitter humor among lower status characters trying to cope with life in the ghetto while looking for a way out of it. Scripts featured ward heelers, loan sharks, abused children, and other facets of life on the edge, in sharp contrast to the comfortable middle class world of "Julia" or the glamorous and exotic locales of "I Spy."

By this time, other producers, stimulated by Norman Lear's enormous success, were providing sitcoms that drew their characters from minority settings. "What's Happening!!" followed the adventures of three big city high school kids. "Diff'rent Strokes" created an unlikely "accidental family" in which a wealthy white man raised two black kids from Harlem in his Park Avenue apartment, without any serious clash of cultures. This trend almost never extended from the ghetto to the barrio. The one great exception was "Chico and the Man," a generation-gap sitcom that paired an ebullient young Mexican American with an aging Bunkerish Anglo garage owner. This odd couple clicked with audiences, but the show's success was cut short by the suicide of comedian Freddy Prinze (Chico) in 1977.

Like the black sitcoms, "Chico" used minority culture as a spark to enliven a middle class white world that seemed bland or enervated by comparison. Minority characters of the early 1970s prided themselves not on their similarity to mainstream culture, but on their differences from it. Assimilated characters like Alexander Scott, Barney Collier, and Julia Baker gave way to the racial pride of George Jefferson, Fred of "Sanford and Son," and Rooster on "Starsky and Hutch." Where would Fred Sanford or George Jefferson be without their jive talk and street slang? Language was just one way of stressing the differences between racial and ethnic groups.

Minority characters also picked up flaws as they took on more complete roles. Fred Sanford was domineering and could appear foolish. George Jefferson could be as stubborn and narrow-minded as his one-time next-door neighbor. By badgering the interracial couple living upstairs and labelling their daughter a "zebra," he left no doubt about his views. But the thrust of the ethnic sitcom was not to ridicule minority cultures. Instead, racial and ethnic backgrounds were used as an educational tool. The religious, cultural, and other traditions that differentiate minorities from the mainstream were now treated as beneficial rather than problematic. Removed from the confines of the melting pot, these groups offered new approaches to old problems. Television charged them with the task of teaching new ways to the often obstinate world around them. Blacks and Hispanics participated in this era of racial and cultural re-education. It was Chico Rodriguez who taught Ed Brown to relax and be more tolerant on "Chico and the Man." Benson, the sharp-tongued butler, tried to maintain order amidst the chaos of "Soap," while steering his employers onto the right track. In one episode he even saved young Billy from the clutches of a religious cult.

The most spectacularly successful effort to combine education with entertainment was a hybrid of the miniseries and "big event" genres. Indeed, "Roots" became the biggest event in television history. This adaptation of Alex Haley's best-selling novel traced the history of four generations of a black family in America, beginning with Kunta Kinte, an African tribesman sold into slavery. It ran for eight consecutive nights in January 1977. When it was over, 130 million Americans had tuned in, including 80 million who viewed the final episode. Seven of the eight episodes ranked among the all-time top ten at that point in television's history. "Roots" created a kind of national town meeting comparable to the televised moon landing or the aftermath of President Kennedy's assassination. It was blamed for several racial disturbances but credited for stimulating a productive national debate on the history of American race relations.

While blacks could look to the high-profile presentation of African American history presented by "Roots," there was no similar presentation of Hispanic history. If Anglos relied exclusively on Hollywood for information on Latino contributions to American history, their knowledge would extend little further than John Wayne's defense of "The Alamo" against the Mexican "invaders." Illustrations of Latino culture were equally rare. In fact, the only high-profile Hispanic character during this period was Chico Rodriguez. Despite its popularity, "Chico and the Man" was not known as a series that explored Latino culture or Hispanic contributions to American history and culture.

Despite occasional failures, ethnic comedies became the hottest new programming trend of the 1970s. "All in the Family" was the top-rated show for an unprecedented five straight seasons, surpassing previous megahits "I Love Lucy" and "Gunsmoke." Other top twenty regulars included "Sanford and Son," "The Jeffersons," black comic Flip Wilson's variety show, and "Chico and the Man." The ethnic wave crested during the 1974–75 season, when a remarkable six of the seven top-rated shows were ethnic sitcoms—"All in the Family," "Sanford," "Chico," "Jeffersons," "Rhoda," and "Good Times."

If the new decade offered an unaccustomed array of new roles for minorities, it contained some traps as well. Ethnic characters gained more prominent and desirable roles, but also more unflattering ones. Bumblers, buffoons, and bimbos took their place alongside heroes and sages. For example, Vinnie Barbarino and Juan Epstein were two of the uneducated underachievers on "Welcome Back Kotter." Barbarino's Italian heritage added ethnic color to his machismo image, while Epstein's ethnic background was contrived for comic effect. He was presented as Buchanan High School's only Puerto Rican Jew. "Good Times" created some negative black characters, such as insensitive building supervisors and abusive politicians. In "What's Happening," the Thomas family made do without their con man father after he walked out on them. His occasional visits home were usually in search of money for some new scheme. A steady stream of minority characters began to show up as criminals in cop shows like "Kojak," "Baretta," and "Barney Miller."

"Barney Miller" also deserves note as one of the most multicultural shows of the time. In the 1975–76 season the squad room contained Polish detective Wojohowicz, Asian American Nick Yemana, African American Harris, and Puerto Rican Chano Amenguale. While Chano was far from perfect he appeared to be a capable officer and no more eccentric than his colleagues on the squad. In the next season Chano was replaced by Detective Baptista, who was a fiery Latina, but not as significant in the squad as Chano. These characters at least served to offset the Hispanic criminals they often arrested.

The late 1970s retained a mix of ethnic heroes and fools in some of the most popular shows of the day. But ethnic characters were beginning to lose their novelty. For instance, "CHiPs" ran from 1977 through 1983 and one of the starring characters was Officer Frank Poncherello. Even though Poncherello was played by the well-known Eric Estrada, Poncherello's Hispanic heritage was all but invisible. It no longer mattered in this series that one of the leads was a Latino. During the 1979 season, three dramatic series were launched with black leads, but none came close to the ratings necessary for renewal. "Paris" starred James Earl Jones as a supercop who ran the station house during the day and taught criminology at night. "The Lazarus Syndrome" featured Louis Gossett as the chief of cardiology in a large hospital. "Harris and Company" focused on the problems of a single parent raising a family. The twist was that this black family was held together not by a matriarch but a middle-aged widower. Thus, Hollywood was at least trying to create some positive role models for black males. But no such efforts extended to Latinos. There were no network series built around a Latino family, Hispanic high school kids, or any of the other patterns found in sitcoms featuring blacks. It would be several years before the short-lived ABC series "Condo" would prominently cast Latinos as middle class characters.

Overall, the 1980s offered little that was new to racial or ethnic minority portrayals in the wake of TV's ethnic revival. These groups continued to be presented more or less as they were in the late 1970s. Despite the continuing presence of racial and ethnic diversity, however, racial themes were no longer in vogue. Integration was assumed as a backdrop, as the prime time world became less polarized. The age of pluralism had arrived, but the thrill was gone. The riots were over, the battles won, and characters got back to their other plot functions. Among these were crime and other wrongdoing. Comedies like "Taxi," "White Shadow," and "WKRP in Cincinnati" continued to present integrated casts, but ethnic characters in dramatic series were often on the dark side of the law.

Ironically, television's multicultural world of the 1980s provided an updated version of the stereotypical Hispanic banditos who populated the westerns thirty years earlier. In the fall of 1980, ABC's controversial sitcom "Soap" introduced a remake of Frito Bandito. Carlos "El Puerco" Valdez was a South American revolutionary playing a love interest of Jessica Tate. They had met when his band kidnapped her for ransom. This plan failed, but after things took a passionate turn, she became a benefactor of his revolution. "El Puerco" led a bumbling, low-budget revolution and he was not above taking time out to romance his new gringo benefactor. "El Puerco" was both Latin lover and bandito with a measure of Jerry Lewis buffoonishness thrown in. Thus, it was down this line that the Frito Bandito's sombrero had been passed—to a fatigue-wearing ne'er-do-well.

There were also more sinister turns in Latino portrayals. Crime shows like "Miami Vice," "Hill Street Blues," and "Hunter" presented Hispanic drug lords as a major nemesis. Trafficking in human misery made these characters rich enough to own cities and sometimes even small countries. They were among the nastiest criminals on TV in the 1980s. There were also petty Hispanic criminals in the slums of "Hill Street Blues" and "Cagney & Lacey." These small-time hoods, drug addicts, and pimps were less flamboyant than their big-league counterparts, but no less unsavory. Altogether, TV's latest crop of Hispanics included a cruel and vicious group of criminals.

"Miami Vice" was not only a source of criminal Hispanics—after all the squad was led by the enigmatic Lieutenant Martin Castillo and on the distaff side of the unit was detective Gina Navarro. However inconsistently, the show did attempt to show successful law-abiding Latinos mixed in with the criminal crop. For all of its flaws "Miami Vice" at least attempted to reflect the presence of Latinos in Miami. Contrast this attempt with more contemporary shows like "Baywatch," "Acapulco H.E.A.T.," and others that rarely if ever reference the Hispanic populations in their host cities.

There were occasional attempts to base shows on Hispanic casts, but all proved unsuccessful. In 1983 the Lear-wannabee sitcom "Condo" briefly pitted a bigoted WASP against his Latino next-door neighbors. The following season, the equally short-lived "A.K.A. Pablo" dealt somewhat more seriously with ethnic questions. Focusing on struggling young comic Pablo Rivera and his extended family, the series wrestled with questions about ethnic humor and the preservation of Hispanic culture. Pablo made many jokes about his family and his Mexican American heritage in his nightclub act. This frequently offended his traditionalist parents, who expected him to treat his heritage more respectfully. Despite its brief run, this series was one of the few to deal explicitly with aspects of Latino culture.

A more mixed portrayal appeared in the 1987 series "I Married Dora." In this fractured fairy tale, Dora Calderon was the housekeeper for widower Peter Farrell and his family. When faced with deportation, Dora and Peter joined in a marriage of convenience. Like many television housekeepers before her, Dora was the voice of wisdom and compassion in the household, but her own illegal status gave her role an ambiguous twist. In 1988, a series called "Trial and Error" was based on Latino characters from the barrio in East Los Angeles. The show revolved around a free-wheeling entrepreneur who ran a souvenir T-shirt company and his upwardly mobile roommate, who was a newly minted lawyer. This series had a lighter touch with less attention to Hispanic culture, but it met with the same quick demise as its predecessors.

Both "A.K.A. Pablo" and "Trial and Error" sprang from the efforts of comedian Paul Rodriguez. It is not uncommon for bankable stars to get their own television series. This is particularly true for stand-up comics, who have taken their nightclub acts into successful series like "Roseanne," "Home Improvement," "Grace Under Fire," and "Seinfeld." This approach has proven to be a very important avenue onto the screen for blacks. Several exclusively black shows currently on the air are the result of the work of a bankable star. Among those who have followed in the footsteps of Bill Cosby are Keenan Ivory Wayans of "In Living Color," Martin Lawrence of "Martin," Mark Curry of "Hangin' with Mr. Cooper," and Charles Dutton of "Roc." Unfortunately, this approach has so far been a dead end for Latinos.

Blacks fared better in the 1980s, largely escaping the criminal portrayals of other minorities. When black characters did turn to crime, they were usually small-time criminals driven by desperation. There were even times when their criminal acts were presented as social commentary. For instance, in an episode of "Hill Street Blues," a black militant occupies a housing project and takes hostages. He threatens to kill them unless the city agrees to keep the project open and fix it up. The man is frustrated and angry that weeks of negotiating led to nothing. The city simply set a new closing date and moved on. Rage and desperation drive him to act and a tense standoff ensues. In the end, he is mistakenly shot by a police sniper. Everyone is shocked by his desperate act and his tragic death.

Meanwhile, TV turned out numerous positive black role models as diverse as "The Cosby Show's" Heathcliff Huxtable, Mary Jenkins of "227," Rico Tubbs on "Miami Vice," and Bobby Hill of "Hill Street Blues." These shows suggest the diversity of major roles that were at last becoming available to blacks. "227" and "Amen" continued the sharp-tongued tradition of 1970s sitcoms, without the abrasive or objectionable images that had brought criticism. Tubbs and Hill both carried on the tradition of "salt and pepper" law enforcement teams. Hill also represented the educative function of minorities by helping to wean his partner Renko, a southerner, away from residual racist tendencies.

Of course, "Cosby" was the biggest hit of all. This series further developed the low-key humanistic colorblind approach that Bill Cosby has popularized over two decades as "I Spy's" Alexander Scott, high school teacher Chet Kincaid on "The Bill Cosby Show," and finally in a black version of "Father Knows Best." The enormous success of this venture led some critics to snipe at Cosby for playing black characters in whiteface to maximize audience appeal. Black psychiatrist Alvin Pouissant, retained by the show to review scripts for racial authenticity, notes that the criticisms come from white reporters more often than black viewers: "Sometimes it seems they want the show to be 'culturally black' . . . and sometimes it seems they would be happier to see them cussing out white people, a sort of protest sitcom. Some seem to feel that because the family is middle class with no obvious racial problems, that constitutes a denial or dismissal of the black person."[6]

Compared to the plight of TV's Hispanics, debates over whether the Huxtables are divorced from the black experience may seem a luxury, a sign that a one-time outgroup has reached a mature phase in its relationship with the Hollywood community. In 1979 organized opposition even persuaded Norman Lear to withdraw a new comedy series at the last minute. "Mister Dugan," a sitcom about a black congressman, was scheduled to premier on CBS a week after Lear arranged a special screening for the Congressional Black Caucus. The screening was a disaster, with Congressman Mickey Leland calling the lead character "a reversion to the Steppin' Fetchit syndrome."

Lear promptly pulled the show from the schedule. He remarked at the time, "We have a high social conscience, and we want to get the story right. We do not favor the short-term gain over the long-term public interest. Dropping the show was an exercise in that commitment."[7] This was an extraordinary episode in a business often excoriated for caring only about the bottom line. When the medium's most successful producer is willing to withdraw a series on the eve of its broadcast, writing off a $700,000 investment, it shows the power of social commitment in television. The only question is the strength and direction of that commitment.

Moreover, such criticism is belied by the top ten ratings obtained by such diverse families as the Sanfords, Jeffersons, and Evans, not to mention Kunta Kinte and his kin. The success of upper and lower class, matriarchal and patriarchal black family series suggests that television has gone beyond using black characters as a sign of racial diversity. It has begun to show diversity within the black community as well, at last recognizing both the cultural distinctiveness and the universal humanity of this group of Americans. Unfortunately, Hispanics have never played a significant role in television's debate over race relations. When television has explored discrimination, prejudice, or the appropriateness of inter-racial relationships, it has almost always staged them as a black versus white issue. Whatever racial tensions exist between Latinos and other groups in American society, they have very rarely made it to the small screen.

A Tale of Two Minorities

Black representation continued to increase during the 1990s, as the number of shows with all-black or mostly black casts jumped. Driven largely by the Fox network's quest for new audiences and trademark shows, these new series drew heavily on the struttin' and jivin' characters of the 1970s. Both the 1992 and 1993 seasons featured ten such series, including hits like "Hangin' With Mr. Cooper," "Family Matters," "Martin," and "Fresh Prince of Bel Air." Intense debate has ensued over the quality of these roles and portrayals, which critics disparage as latter-day minstrel show stereotypes. However, such complaints have not diminished the popularity of these shows, particularly among black audiences.

Despite continuing controversy, television's portrayal of blacks is in many ways more diverse and substantive than ever before. For instance, on Monday nights viewers could contrast the wealthy Banks family on "Fresh Prince of Bel Air" with the working class Cumberbatches in "704 Hauser Street." On Tuesday, they could see the struggles of a single mother in "South Central," followed by the stable two-parent extended family in "Roc." Then there were the Winslows, a comfortably middle class black family that was a cornerstone of Friday night viewing for years. In addition there were numerous black characters in integrated series such as "L.A. Law," "Law & Order," "Evening Shade," "Love & War," "NYPD Blue," "In the Heat of the Night," and "seaQuest DSV." African Americans were seen as lawyers, judges, police captains, and a host of other roles in these shows.

While shows that were exclusively or mainly about blacks comprised about one eighth of the prime time schedule in 1992–93, only one series in the previous three seasons was based on a Latino family or character. Moreover, that series—the short-lived "Frannie's Turn"—mainly used Hispanic traditions as a comic foil for feminist putdowns. This series revolved around the marriage of a Cuban emigré named Joseph Escobar and his wife, Frannie, an Anglo of unclear ethnic origins. Whatever ethnic and cultural differences may have existed between them were rarely played upon, since most of the plots dealt with Frannie's quest for equality. However, when aspects of heritage did come up, they frequently reflected poorly on Latinos. For instance, the first episode dealt with Frannie's discovery that Joseph has been sending money to a Cuban liberation movement while telling her to cut the household budget. At one point in the ensuing argument, she suggests sarcastically, "Who knows, maybe they'll send you the Bay of Pigs decoder ring." In the few episodes that aired, the couple's children seemed oblivious to their heritage, and no effort was made to teach them about their father's culture. Overall, this series made no greater use of ethnicity than "I Love Lucy" did almost forty years earlier.

Otherwise, Latino characters remained largely supporting players or background figures in the prime time schedule. The highest profile in 1992–93 was enjoyed by Daniel Morales, who replaced Victor Sifuentes on "L.A. Law." Most other recent Latino roles involved lower status jobs or far less airtime in low-rated series. Examples include Chuy Castillo, the cook at the "Golden Palace"; Jennifer Clemente, a very junior attorney in the U.S. Justice Department on "The Round Table"; and detective Rafael Martinez on the "Hat Squad." There was also Mahalia Sanchez, a bus station cashier in the "John Larroquette Show," rookie detective James Martinez in "NYPD Blue," and Paco Ortiz in "Nurses," none of them starring roles.

The cultural diversity within the Latino community was almost completely absent from prime time. Most Hispanic characters on television came from a "generic" background without reference to national origin or past. Television has rarely pointed out the cultural, historical, or economic differences among different groups within the Latino community. The few shows to make such distinctions, from "Miami Vice" to "Frannie's Turn," usually did so to place a particular nationality in a negative light. In "Miami Vice" differing national origins were connected with different types of illegal activities, while in "Frannie's Turn" a Cuban heritage was not a badge of honor. Sadly, the highest-profile Latino characters of the season were Eric and Lyle Menendez, whose murder trial was featured in two made-for-television movies.

An Update

As we have seen, before 1965, prime time was a nearly all-white world populated mainly by generic northern Europeans, save for the occasional black servant or Mexican bandito. Soon thereafter, the spectrum widened to embrace an array of ethnic and cultural traditions. But various minority groups shared unequally in television's new search for ethnic roots. [Editor's Note: These disparities are discussed in detail by the National Council of La Raza in Chapter 1 of this volume.]

Some of these disparities are summarized in Table 3.1. As the table makes clear, between 1955 and 1986, proportionately fewer Hispanic characters were professionals or executives and more were unskilled laborers. Fewer Hispanics had starring roles, were positively portrayed, or succeeded in attaining their goals. Indeed, according to our 1994 study,[8] the more villainous the character, the sharper the group differences that emerged. Hispanic characters were twice as likely as whites and three times as likely as blacks to commit a crime. Once TV's roster of Hispanic stereotypes solely included the grinning bandito criss-crossed with ammunition belts. More recently, as scriptwriter Ben Stein has observed, "Any time a Cuban or Colombian crosses the tube, he leaves a good thick trail of cocaine behind."[9]

In addition, because of their negative and criminal roles, Latinos stood apart from other characters in the methods they adopted to attain their goals. They were more likely than either whites or blacks to use violence and deceit. If Latinos were distinctive in the means they used to pursue their goals, they also differed in their motivations. Hispanic characters were much more likely to be driven by greed than other characters. More broadly, black characters managed to attain whatever they strove for more often than either whites or Hispanics. In fact, the failure rate among Hispanics was more than double that of blacks. Perusing these figures, it is difficult to

TABLE 3.1   Traits of TV Characters, 1955–1986

	White	*Black*	*Latino*
All Characters	89%	6%	2%
Social Background*			
Attended college	72	44	**
Lacked high school diploma	25	49	**
Low economic status	22	47	40
Professional or executive	22	17	10
Unskilled laborer	13	16	22
Plot Functions			
Starring role	17	15	8
Character succeeded	65	72	54
Character failed	23	16	34
Positive portrayal	40	44	32
Negative portrayal	31	24	41
Committed crime	11	7	22

*Characters were coded only if their backgrounds were clearly indicated by the script.
**Too few characters were coded for meaningful comparisons.

SOURCE: Based on a content analysis of 7,639 prime time characters that appeared in 620 entertainment programs between 1955 and 1986.

resist the conclusion that Hollywood has cracked open the door to black concerns while letting Hispanics serve as window dressing.

Examining character portrayals in 1992, we found that compared to both Anglos and African Americans, television's Hispanics were low in number, low in social status, and lowdown in personal character, frequently portraying violent criminals. The worst offenders were "reality" shows, whose version of reality often consisted of white cops chasing black and Hispanic robbers. Utilizing the same scientific content analysis approach, we examined the more recent 1994–95 season. We focused on a composite month of prime time entertainment programs broadcast on the four major broadcast networks and in first-run syndication. We found some welcome progress in television's portrayal of Hispanics, combined with some lingering sins of both omission and commission. (These results reflect our analysis of 5,767 characters who appeared on 528 different episodes of 139 prime time series.)

The proportion of Hispanic characters was up but still far below the proportion of Hispanic Americans in the real world. Latinos were "ghettoized" in a handful of series, few of which are still on the air, and few portrayed prosperous, well-educated, authoritative characters. The most striking and hopeful result, however, was a dramatic decline in the portrayal of Hispanics as criminals. Among the major findings:

- *Visibility.* TV's Hispanic presence doubled from 1992 levels. And these characters were more likely to play major roles when they appeared. But the rise was from only 1 to 2 percent of all characters, far below the 10 percent of Americans with Hispanic ancestry in real life. And a majority appeared in only two series, one of which has been canceled.
- *Criminality.* Hispanic characters were less likely to play villains than they were in the 1992 network prime time schedules. The drop in criminal portrayals was down 63 percent (from 16 percent of all Hispanic characters in 1992 to 6 percent in 1994). But even this level of criminality was higher than the 4 percent we found among whites and 2 percent among blacks.
- *New "Realities."* The most striking changes appeared in the cops-and-robbers "reality" shows, such as "COPS" and "America's Most Wanted." In 1992, a staggering 45 percent of all Hispanics and 50 percent of African Americans who appeared in these shows committed crimes. In 1994–95, the "crime rate" for both minorities plummeted to less than half the previous levels—down from 45 to 16 percent of Latinos and from 50 to 20 percent of blacks portrayed.

NOTES

Excerpted, updated, and reprinted by permission of the authors and publisher, the Center for Media and Public Affairs, from *Distorted Reality: Hispanic Characters in TV Entertainment* by S. Robert Lichter and Daniel R. Amundson, Washington, D.C., 1994.

1. Harry Castleman and Walter Podrazik, *Watching TV: Four Decades of American Television* (McGraw-Hill Book Co. 1982), p. 208.

2. *Ibid.,* p. 226.

3. Laura Z. Hobson, quoted in Christopher Lasch, "Archie Bunker and the Liberal Mind," *Channels,* October/November 1981, p. 34.

4. Quoted in *Watching TV,* p. 227.

5. See Richard Adler, ed., *All in the Family: A Critical Appraisal* (Praeger 1979).

6. Quoted in William Raspberry, "Cosby Show: Black or White?" *Washington Post,* November 5, 1984.

7. Quoted in *Time,* March 19, 1979, p. 85.

8. S. Robert Lichter and Daniel R. Amundson, *Distorted Reality: Hispanic Characters in TV Entertainment* (Center for Media and Public Affairs 1994).

9. Quoted in *Time,* March 19, 1979, p. 85.

PART TWO

The Silver Screen: Stories and Stereotypes

The chapters in this section illustrate the long, but often buried, history of Latino actors in film as well as the stereotypes that have accompanied this history. Chapter 4 is a visual retrospective of Latina and Latino male film stars. In addition to providing a historical view, the photos indicate that the past was very different from the present in a number of significant ways. The following chapters illustrate the similarities that exist in the historic depiction of Chicanos, Mexicans, Puerto Ricans, and other Latinos in film. They also highlight Latino stereotypes in the past and present.

As the largest and earliest Latino group in film, Chicanos/Mexicans have the longest history in film. The chapters by Noriega, Berg, and Cortés each present a different overview of this history. In Chapter 5, Noriega describes three major film periods, the "Silent Greaser" films, the social problem films (within which three subgenres are included), and the Chicano-produced films. What is perhaps most important in Noriega's perspective is his analysis of how political and economic factors influenced these periods. He argues that the social problem films projected views of Chicanos that, in turn, legitimated the system that was oppressing them.

For example, the courtroom settings of many of these films implicitly contrast the psychological deficiencies of the Mexican defendant against the success of American institutional activism. In these films, the characters are ultimately shown to have destroyed the demons within themselves. They have succeeded in redirecting their inherent violence and orienting themselves toward "making it" under U.S. capitalism, usually with the help of Anglo friends. This means they are involved in more acceptable and distant areas, such as helping their people in the barrio or fighting for their country overseas.

The focus in these social problem films is not on the systemic ways in which Chicanos are denied opportunities, but on individual actions. As Noriega states, the films put the Mexican American on trial, not the racist individuals or society that put him there. At the same time, the trial or litigation in the movie reaffirms the activist and rectifying role of the legal system. It legitimates the system and sanctions assimilation for the Mexican American—as long as he goes back to the barrio to help his people, or in other words, as long as he goes back where he came from and stays where he belongs. Although Latinas also were to stay where they belonged, the emphasis in many of these films was on the Latino man, with women having subsidiary parts.

The theme of "Why don't you go back where you came from?" appears in a number of major Latino-themed movies, including *My Man and I* (1952), *West Side Story* (1961), and *Zoot Suit* (1981). It is intensely ironic for some Latino groups, such as the Hispanos, Californios, and Tejanos of the Southwest, who were "here first." Others, such as Puerto Ricans, have been Spanish-speaking U.S. citizens for over three-quarters of a century. In the case of these groups, the United States came to them, they did not (initially) come to the United States. Moreover, the majority of Hispanics living in the United States today have been born here, so where do they go back to? Of course, if we were to ask all Americans to go back to where their ancestors came from, there would be very few people left, for with the exception of Native American Indians, we are a nation of immigrants.

Noriega maintains that in "the eighty years of discourse" that Hollywood has had with Chicanos, "Hollywood has engaged through outright stereotype, 'enlightened' segregationist and now silence—in a politics of denial." He understands the development of contemporary Chicano filmmaking as a reaction to this history and argues that Chicano filmmaking "initiated a counterdiscourse on Mexican-American citizenship, one that stressed a cultural nationalist, rather than an assimilationist identity." Noting the systemic racism, he is not surprised that "the post–Mexican-American Generation, or Chicanos, would reject 'political accommodation and assimilation,' and stress instead a politics of cultural difference."

In Chapter 6 Berg provides an overview of theories of stereotyping and of Hispanic stereotypes. This enables us to better distinguish between types and stereotypes and to better understand how stereotypes come to be and how they are sustained. He then applies his analysis of stereotypes to the images of Hispanics in four films of the 1980s.[1] Cortés, in a similar overview in Chapter 7, focuses on images of Chicanas.

Berg makes clear that projected "images" are not Chicano "identities," and that "labels" are not "self-definitions"; these are distinctions that often become confused when audiences observe Latinos and other groups of color on screen. There are a variety of images that have been used to describe Latinos (Subervi-Vélez, 1994:308). One can take, for example, the letter "V" and list a variety of terms utilized to describe Latino images, including vamps, vandals, victims, violent, villains, volatile, vixens, virgins. The letter "M" yields a series of terms applied to Latinas: "maids," "mistresses," "madonnas," and "mothers on welfare." The authors of these chapters lead one to ask: Which images are the most accurate? Which are the most prevalent today? Which are the most consistently used in the history of film and television? They also lead us to question the extent to which Latino images have been changing or unchanging.

The chapters also encourage us to ask what counterimages have been developed. Cortés, in asking, "How do we identify 'Chicanas' in films?" leads us to consider the context-dependent nature of "Latin looks." His search for Chicana images in film illuminates the extent to which Latin looks are generic and the extent to which Latinos or Chicanos require identifying cues, such as references by others to nationality or culture, locale, accent, or physical type, so that specific types of Latinos can be identified. In raising these questions, these chapters show that Latin looks on U.S. screens have been highly pan-Latino in nature. And they make us aware of the differences (and lack of difference) in the representation of diverse Latino communities.

Chapters 8 and 9 focus specifically on Puerto Ricans, the oldest and largest Latino group in the northeastern United States. In Chapter 8, Richie Pérez, a former member of the Young Lords, examines changing Puerto Rican images in feature films. He argues that the image of Puerto Ricans in films has changed dramatically over time and that this change coincided with a period of greater social, political, and militant activity among Puerto Ricans in the United States. In earlier films, such as *West Side Story,* Puerto Ricans were portrayed as potentially (although somewhat problematically) assimilable, but this view changed in the late 1960s and 1970s. During this period of activist Puerto Rican politics, the only Puerto Rican characters to be found on screen were those audiences—Latino and non-Latino alike—would prefer to annihilate, that is, drug dealers, prostitutes, pimps, and gunmen.

In Pérez's chapter, the reader will find similarities between the images of Puerto Ricans and the images described by Noriega, Berg, and Cortés of Mexicans and Chicanos. Just as Noriega argues that Mexicans were portrayed as unable to overcome their "internal demons" and deal effectively with their "social problems," so too Pérez argues that Puerto Ricans were portrayed as social misfits and personally inadequate victims. Pérez finds the dominant images of Puerto Ricans in films made between 1949 and 1961 to be urban ghetto dwellers and juvenile delinquents. He also argues that *West Side Story* (released in 1961) established definitively these images and perpetuated the stereotype of Puerto Rican males as knife-carrying gang members who could solve their problems only through violence. These same images find their counterparts in the social problem films discussed by Noriega. As we will see in Chapter 11 in the next section, in the same way that Noriega describes Chicano dissatisfaction with media images as an impetus to the development of an alternative Chicano cinema, so too discontent with the images described by Pérez motivated Puerto Rican filmmakers to create alternative images.

Women

In Chapter 8, Pérez describes how *West Side Story* exemplified and established in the public mind a dualistic image of Puerto Rican women as (1) Madonna—the innocent, passive, virginal Maria; or (2) Whore—the hot-blooded, fiery, sexy Anita. This same duality can be seen in the Mexican and other Latina images described by Berg and Cortés. This image of the Latina as a "hot-blooded tamale" harks back to the Mexican spitfire image of Lupe Vélez in the 1930s, Carmen Miranda during the 1940s and 1950s, Charo in the 1970s and 1980s, and currently to the 1990s' own Rosie Pérez. The image of the virtuous Virgin Maria also has antecedents among earlier Latina leading ladies, for example, Dolores Del Río and María Montez.

The images of all women (Latinas and non-Latinas) have tended to be dualistic. Women have historically been portrayed as one-dimensional "good girls" and "bad girls" and as extensions of and subordinate to men (Basinger, 1993). The Maria and Anita dichotomy has generic antecedents in prostitutes and princesses. What makes Latina images different is that there are so few images, that they are so narrow, and that lately they are so consistently negative and lower class. To a degree, this may reflect a general perception of the position of Hispanics in U.S. society. However, one may well ask where are the everyday women, the non-crack-addicted mothers who also populate all levels of the Latino communities and who are, in fact, more prevalent in Latino communities than prostitutes, junkies, transvestites, and welfare and child abusers? Where are the women who are neither madonnas nor spitfires? They are absent. Moreover, why does the Latina spitfire still survive in the films of today while the "good" Latina señorita has grown rare indeed?

Anglos and Latinos

Another pattern found in Latino films is in the portrayal of Anglos/Whites in relation to Latinos. Both Noriega and Pérez refer to the "American savior," or "urban missionaries," who save Latinos. In such films, White teachers, doctors, nuns, and priests go into a ghetto or urban area to "save" Latino residents. According to Pérez, in most cases, the savior is initially rejected, often raped, and always assaulted and denigrated before at least some Latinos get "saved," "see the light," or "come around." Pérez notes that this perspective fits in well with President Lyndon Johnson's War on Poverty perspective. The "gringo/White savior" image appeared early on in films, for example, in the silent movie *El Americano* (1919) with Douglas Fairbanks, Sr. Keller (1985:33ff) and Hadley-Garcia (1993:70) also find that antedating urban or ghetto backdrops, "Anglo good samaritans" were common in early westerns, including those with Hopalong Cassidy, Gene Autry, the Lone Ranger, Roy Rogers, and Tex Ritter. Here, the Anglo cowboy often fought bad Mexicans in defense of good Mexicans—because the Mexicans couldn't help themselves.

According to Pérez, the urban cowboy genre developed in the 1970s continued this "White savior" thrust. The cowboy only moved from the wide open spaces of the West to the crime-ridden, dirty, dangerous streets of the urban United States. Along with this geographic shift came a shift in the depiction of villains. The villains were now even more deserving of quick annihilation. In the past, they may have been faceless *bandidos,* but now they were morally undesirable junkies and criminals who were also the main cause of crime, fear, and other upsets to peace. The urban cowboy focused on crime and killed the people who would commit crime, the Latinos. *Death Wish* (1974) is a good example of this.

West Side Story (1961) and "Otherness"

In Chapter 9, Alberto Sandoval Sánchez presents an excellent critical analysis of the first major film (and play) on Latinos in the Northeast, *West Side Story.* Despite the popularity of this film when it was made and the continuing appeal of the play for high school and college drama production, little has been written on how the subjects of the story, Puerto Ricans, view it. Sandoval Sánchez examines the images portrayed and the symbols used to convey the underlying story. After beginning on a personal note, he deconstructs the film. On one level, it is a love story. On a deeper level, he argues, the film is the beginning of an explicit discourse of discrimination and prejudice toward immigrant Latinos. (This is similar to Noriega's analysis about the immigrant narrative in Chapter 5.)

Recounting the history of the making of *West Side Story,* Sandoval Sánchez argues that the film projects a series of binary oppositions about class: the West Side versus the East Side of New York, the Spics ("the Sharks") versus the White Anglo-Saxons ("the Jets"). He also maintains that the film focuses on "stories"—as the title indicates—and ignores "histories." Thus, the "troublesome" political and economic history between the United States and Puerto Rico is ignored, particularly its relationship to the migration of Puerto Ricans to New York. The long history of Puerto Ricans on the West Side and in New York (since the nineteenth century) is overlooked. And, last, the long and rich immigrant history of the West Side is not part of the film. Essentially, Sandoval Sánchez views the film as providing an early and important medium within which the confrontation of Anglos/Whites with foreign Latino "Others" is depicted.

Contemporary Films

In contemporary films (those made after 1980), we find the same invisibility and marginality for Latinos as in television and the news. We also find an increasing association of Latinos with crime. Of the "All-Time Top 50 American Movies" listed in the *World Almanac and Book of Facts* (1996), even in those movies set in areas with substantial proportions of Latino residents, Latino themes are absent and Latinos are almost invisible.

For example, in New York City, Latinos have constituted a substantial proportion of the total population for over forty years and were conservatively estimated to constitute 24.3% of the total population in 1990.[2] Yet, movies set in New York, such as *Ghostbusters* (1984), *Home Alone 2* (1992), *Fatal Attraction* (1987), and *Santa Claus* (1994) lack any substantial Latino component; others with substantial or important scenes in New York City are similarly unrepresentative of the actual demographics of the city, for example, *Three Men and a Baby* (1987) and *Indiana Jones and the Last Crusade* (1989). *Crocodile Dundee* (1986) includes only the stock stick figure stereotype, "Rosita," the maid with the thick Spanish accent. *Ghost* (1990) also incorporates some Latinos who spoke briefly—a repellent villain and a confused spiritualist-seeker.[3]

The films set in Los Angeles are similarly devoid of significant Latino representation, for example, *E. T., The Extra-Terrestrial* (1982), *Mrs. Doubtfire* (1993), *Top Gun* (1986), *Rain Man* (1989), *Lethal Weapon 2* (1989), and *Lethal Weapon 3* (1992). If an occasional Hispanic character appears in California films, he or she is inevitably a waiter, maid, bellhop, or valet as in *Beverly Hills Cop* (1984) or a criminal as, for example, in *Beverly Hills Cop II* (1987). Even the hero in the all-American favorite *Forrest Gump* (1993) did not encounter any Latinos in all his exploits and travels, and his experience in Vietnam did not expose him to any Latinos despite the vast numbers of Latinos who served in this war.

Terminator 2 (1991) did include a minor Latino character. True to the *bandido* stereotype, he smuggled weapons and drank tequila. This film also introduced the English-accented phrases "Hasta la vista, baby" and "No problema" to the alien Terminator, who was as puzzled as this viewer was with regard to their relevance.[4] *Pretty Woman* (1990) also had two Latino characters: an unredeemable, drug-addicted prostitute and her pimp–drug dealer friend.

In essence, when we examine the major movies of the past two decades, we are (at best) reminded of what Quiroga refers to as that curious attribute of being noted, not quite completely ignored but not fully seen or counted. We see Asians and African Americans in these films, for example, in *Forrest Gump* (1993) and *Rambo: First Blood Part 2* (1985), but Hispanics are few and far between, and when they are visible, they are in marginal roles, with menial or negative positions.

Images connecting crime and Latinos are of long standing in Hollywood films. Such images were dramatically and strongly personified in major movies such as *West Side Story* (1961) and *Zoot Suit* (1981). In the 1980s and 1990s, the Latino crime and violence images increased in number and intensity. Chapter 10 is focused on images of Latinos and crime in films of the 1980s and 1990s. I review seven recent popular films in which Latino characters are central to the plot, *Scarface* (1983), *Carlito's Way* (1993), *The Specialist* (1994), *American Me* (1992), *Mi Vida Loca* (1994), *The Mambo Kings* (1992), and *El Mariachi* (1993).

NOTES

1. These films are *La Bamba* (1987), *Born in East L.A.* (1987), *Stand and Deliver,* (1988), and *The Milagro Beanfield War,* (1988). In all of them, Latinos had an important say in the creation of Latino images.

2. Los Angeles is currently one-third Hispanic; California as a whole, 25.8 percent Hispanic. Note that these are 1990 decennial census estimates and do not include the undocumented or Hispanic estimates of the undercount.

3. It is interesting that the Latino actor-comedian, Rick Aviles, who played this villain, was originally rejected because he was seen as being too "clean-cut." He was hired after growing a two-weeks' beard and acquiring a long-haired wig (Domínguez, 1995:15).

4. See Hill (1993, 1995), who argues that the use in film of what she calls "junk Spanish" terms is fundamentally distancing—it serves to distance the utterer from the voice and to denigrate the source of that voice. In so doing, use of these terms subtly reasserts Anglo dominance.

4

Visual Retrospective: Latino Film Stars

Clara E. Rodríguez

The photos in this chapter give us an idea of the long, but often buried, history of Latinos in film. Although there are important similarities between the history of past Latina stars and that of their male counterparts, there are also important differences. The photos also indicate that this past was very different from the present in a number of significant ways. Just how different was this past from the present situation of Latinos in film? To some degree, this depends on whether we are speaking of the history of Latina stars or Latino male stars.

In the case of women, some differences between the past and the present are striking. First, there were leading Latina stars in major movies. Second, they had clearly identifiable Hispanic names. Third, they played diverse roles and were cast in a variety of social positions. Today, it is difficult to find such equivalents. The early dichotomy between rich, valuable, and virginal *señoritas* and the spitfires or "catineras of easy virtue" (Garcia Berumen, 1995:11) has been reduced to a single more negative view of the spitfire. We see in the histories of the Latina stars pictured here the struggles of subsequent actresses against what became the predominant spitfire stereotype. We also see in these photos the development of highly successful but "invisible" Latina stars, that is, actresses whose Spanish origin was generally not known by the public.

The early dichotomy between spitfire and señorita is most strongly seen in the characters played by Dolores Del Río and Lupe Vélez. Dolores Del Río, the first Latina superstar, early established herself in varied popular and often aristocratic roles, whereas Lupe Vélez, another major star of the same era, was early associated with comedies and the "hot tamale" image (Hadley-Garcia, 1993:30–31). Contemporary writers unfortunately often measure Vélez against Del Río and find Vélez wanting. Moreover, they derive the current, rather negative, Latina spitfire image from Vélez's earlier spitfire character. As a result, Vélez is often not recognized for her real comedic abilities or her highly successful movies. Her "Carmelita" character in these movies was a spitfire, but she was also the star, the protagonist. Carmelita was spunky, funny, and smart, often outwitting others and getting the guy in the end. This is in sharp contrast to recent spitfires, marginal characters who never get the guy. These are easy, supersexed, or violent and vulgar Latinas who fume and fornicate without humor, without substance, and without much intelligence.

The early Latina actresses struggled against the spitfire image. Rita Moreno, for example, in the early 1950s was quickly tagged by the studio as a "Latin spitfire." She went on to make fourteen films in eleven years but took many of the roles in these films out of economic necessity. She said she played all these roles the same way: "barefoot with my nostrils flaring" (Reyes and Rubie, 1994:452). She was dubbed by the press "Rita the Cheetah." Struggling against the spitfire stereotype, she stayed off the screen for eight years after her Oscar-winning role in *West Side Story* when the only roles she was offered were "the conventional Rosita and Pepita type roles and she refused to demean her talent any longer" (Reyes and Rubie, 1994:453). Instead, she expanded her talents into other arenas, such as theater, clubs, and television. As evidenced by the professional acknowledgment she has subsequently received, Moreno's struggle against the spitfire image was ultimately successful. She has played a wide variety of roles and racial or ethnic types beyond the Latina spitfire, including an Irishwoman in *The Miracle Worker,* a Greek Cherokee in *The Sign in Sidney Burstein's Window,* a Hungarian in *She Loves Me,* a midwestern WASP in *Gantry* on Broadway, and a Slavic hooker on TV's *The Rockford Files.*

These struggles still continue for Latinas in film. But there are also hopeful signs as we witness the inroads that talented actresses such as Jennifer López, Lauren Vélez, Sonia Braga, Elizabeth Peña, Trini Alvarado, Daphne Zuñiga, and Lisa Vidal are making in movies today.

Turning to Latino male images, we see some important historical similarities to women. As was the case with early Latina actresses, major movies featured leading Latino male stars with distinguishable Spanish surnames who played a fairly wide variety of characters across the spectrum of the social structure. Like Latina images, Latino male images have changed over time, but in different ways. As noted in the introduction, actors who personified the Latin lover image figured prominently in early films and today can be found again—albeit less conspicuously—in the "perceived personas" of Antonio Banderas, Andy García, and Jimmy Smits.[1] The *bandidos* that populated early westerns became urban *bandido* equivalents when films about Latinos were increasingly set against inner-city backdrops.

As with Latinas, a bifurcated approach was taken, with the Latino villains being poorer and darker in coloration and the Latin lovers being upper class and conforming physically to European prototypes. The photo of Antonio Moreno (one of the earliest Latin lovers) and a gaucho extra on the set of the 1926 film *The Temptress* illustrates this duality (see Photo 4.1).[2] As for more contemporary Latin lovers, it appears that although the actors continue in the main to embody European prototypes, the Latino characters they play are less legitimately wealthy and upper class than in the earlier period of film and the urban versions of the *bandido* characters continue to be abhorrent.

PHOTO 4.1   **Antonio Moreno and Gaucho** between scenes in the production of *The Temptress* (1926) at the MGM studios; Greta Garbo also starred in this film. The caption on the back of this photo reads in part: "Here's a new one—a South American cigarette holder and ash duster. Antonio Moreno tries it out between scenes . . . Clever, these South Americans! (Courtesy of The Museum of Modern Art Film Stills Archive)

Another correspondence between female and male images involves the development of clearly identified, central, and continuing "Hispanic" characters. Both Carmen Miranda and Lupe Vélez were identified with a recognizable and continuing character that was clearly identified as "Latina." Similarly, Latino male characters have been central to at least three major TV and film series. But Latinos did not always play this central character. One such series was *Zorro*. Described by Hadley-Garcia (1993) as a Latino Robin Hood tale set in old California, the story was originally written in 1919 as a magazine story, then as film script for Douglas Fairbanks, Sr., who played the first Zorro in 1920.[3] In none of the subsequent film and television versions have Latino actors played the central character.

The Cisco Kid is another series with a Latino hero as the central character. Based on O. Henry's 1907 short story "The Caballero's Way," the character the Cisco Kid was a positive role model. He was nonviolent; he never killed or threatened anyone; he "did good deeds, didn't outstay his welcome, had a sense of humor, and if at times he flirted with white women, marriage was out of the question" (Hadley-Garcia,

PHOTO 4.2   The Cisco Kid. A number of actors played the Cisco Kid, but it was perhaps **Duncan Renaldo** who came to be most closely identified with the character because he played the role on the 156 episodes that aired on television between 1950 and 1954. (Courtesy of The Museum of Modern Art Film Stills Archive)

1993:102). Before 1939, Warner Baxter (who was Hollywood's top-paid actor, but who was not Hispanic) played the Cisco Kid in three films (Hadley-Garcia, 1993:57). César Romero, Duncan Renaldo, and Gilbert Roland played the role during the 1940s, Duncan Renaldo (see Photo 4.2) in the 156 episodes that aired on television between 1950 and 1954. Last, there is the long-running television program *I Love Lucy* in which Desi Arnaz played the major male lead, Ricky Ricardo.

In summary, in the past there were more leading—and recognizably Spanish-surnamed—stars in major movies and they portrayed a wider variety of roles and statuses than appears to be the case today. But a bifurcated approach characterized casting, in which only those Latino stars who were viewed as European prototypes had leading roles. Those who were darker in coloration played extras or were not individually identifiable. (Ironically—as has been the case for other groups—when a character with darker pigmentation was called for, brownface makeup was applied.) In addition, the majority of Latino images, and the majority of Latinos, were still not displayed in positive terms.

There were, however, continuing Hispanic characters for both men and women— something that is again absent today. Many of these characters tended to fit the classic stereotypes of spitfire and clown (Carmen Miranda, Lupe Vélez, and Ricky Ricardo) or of Latin lover and *caballero* (Dolores Del Río's classy *señorita* persona, the Cisco Kid, Zorro, and the various incarnations of Latin lovers). Finally, the variety of Latina images, in particular, diminished over time and roles became more narrowly cast and marginal. For men, Latin lovers are common and popular again; however, many are not as legitimately wealthy or powerful as they were in earlier days.

NOTES

1. See Jarvie (1991), who distinguishes between the "real" and "perceived" ethnicity of actors as well as of the roles the star plays on screen. In this case, "perceived persona" refers to the ethnicity and role type embodied by the actor.

2. As Cortés (1991:23) has noted: Indianized or Africanized Latinos were colored; Europeanized ones were White (usually labeled as "Spanish" to differentiate them from colored "Mexicans"). For screen Latinos, physical appearance and stated (or implied) ancestry became the racial dividing line. Within the interracial love plot convention, "Spanish" Latinos played White, whereas "Mexicans" usually functioned as colored, thereby permitting the screen coexistence of the Latin lover (White) and the lecherous Latino greaser (colored).

3. The first *Zorro* film (1920) illustrates the class-color-culture divisions projected. Set in early-nineteenth-century California, the film depicts Zorro as the Robin Hood of the time, fighting the evil, "oppressive" governor, who is making "good" rich people poorer and victimizing and oppressing the "natives" (words in quotes are from the film). Although Zorro fights in the name of the poor natives, clearly he is protecting the status quo in which "good" rich people—*caballeros*—coexist symbiotically with the "natives." His mask conceals the fact that he is, in reality, one of these *caballeros*.

The film credits do not list any actors with Spanish surnames, suggesting there were few if any Latinos involved in this production. Perhaps in part for this reason, and perhaps because "brownface" was apparently not used in this film, color of skin does not appear to be used to distinguish class levels; instead, clothes serve to mark the divisions. The Spanish Californians are dressed in clothing reminiscent of Spanish bullfighters and Gypsies. The natives are dressed in garments reminiscent of Geronimo and Cochise in later westerns; these natives often assume a "cowering Indian" stance. Less prominent natives wear robelike garments, as in Roman times. The natives are portrayed as poor, the *caballeros* as rich. The *caballero* class clearly harks back to Spain; a number of Spanish cultural symbols in the film remind the viewer of the strictly Spanish ancestry and connections of this group. For example, Zorro has just recently returned from studying in Spain. Thus, the *caballeros* are European, whereas the "natives" are Indian, non-Western, nonmodern. This portrayal is consistent with Richard's (1993:xxxi) observation that "During silent screen days the terms 'Indian' and 'Mexican' were frequently used interchangeably."

5

Citizen Chicano: The Trials and Titillations of Ethnicity in the American Cinema, 1935–1962

Chon Noriega

Between 1935 and 1962, at least ten social-problem films addressed the issue of the "place" of the Mexican American in the United States.[1] With the exception of two gang-exploitation films—*Boulevard Nights* and *Walk Proud* (both 1979)—these remained the only feature-length films to be "about" Mexican Americans or Chicanos until the emergence of Chicano-produced feature films in the late 1970s.

These films were produced at a significant moment in the development of an American as well as an ethnic-American national identity. In these social-problem films, the political, socioeconomic, and psychological issues related to race and ethnicity operate at the manifest level of the narrative rather than as the "political unconscious." In the end, these films must still resolve these social contradictions and situate the Mexican American within normative gender roles, social spaces, and institutional parameters.

Before I turn to the films themselves, it is necessary to sketch in the contours of the period between the Depression and the election of John F. Kennedy, a period Chicano scholars have identified as the Mexican-American Generation.[2] Within Chicano historiography, the period is framed on either side by the border conflict era (1848–1929) and the Chicano Movement (1963–75).

It is between 1929 and 1941, as Richard Garcia argues, that the "Mexican-American mind" emerged. By 1930, border conflict had dismantled the remnants of the old Mexican political and economic system. Mexicanos, including a new wave of immigrants, had provided cheap labor for the agricultural and industrial transformation of the midwest and southwest, particularly during World War I and the 1920s. In the 1930s, the simultaneous rise of a middle class with its own organizations, such as the League of United Latin American Citizens, and a sharp decline in immigration fostered a "new zeitgeist of Mexican-Americanism, . . . a cohesive collective cluster of ideas that permeated the extensive Mexican communities throughout the Southwest."[3]

Participation in World War II provided additional cause for patriotic Americanism, as well as a liberal reformist politics aimed at securing the rights of citizenship. Between 1930 and 1963, Mexican Americans, while still raised in the cultures of both Mexico and the United States, felt that "political accommodation and assimilation were the only path toward equal status in a racist society."[4]

The progressive nature of the Mexican-American political stance becomes apparent when we consider the concurrent national policies and actions toward Mexican Americans and Mexicans. In fact, the Mexican-American Generation starts at the same moment in which the United States, between 1929 and 1934, "repatriated" some 400,000 Mexicans, including Mexican Americans and legal immigrants, in order to cut welfare payments during the Depression.[5] Under these pressures, immigration in the 1930s dropped to less than 5 percent of the peak level set in the 1920s.[6]

In 1942, with U.S. entry into World War II, repatriation contributed to a labor shortage. In addition to the 400,000 "Mexicans" deported, upward of 500,000 Mexican-American men had enlisted or been drafted into service, while 120,000 Japanese Americans had been interned as "security risks." As a result, the Bracero Program was negotiated with Mexico, which agreed to provide the United States with unskilled laborers on a short-term basis in order to harvest its labor-intensive crops. In what would become a "ratchet effect," the increased migration under the Bracero Program gave rise to a neonativism, so that Operation Wetback was implemented in order to locate and deport "illegal aliens" or "wetbacks." Between 1952 and 1956, some 2.9 million Mexicans and Mexican Americans were deported. Once again, these actions threatened the cheap agricultural labor force, and Congress extended the Bracero Program, which continued until 1964.[7]

Under both repatriation and Operation Wetback, a significant number of Mexican Americans (including U.S.-born children of immigrants) were deported, while the Bracero Program brought in an unskilled, foreign work force intended to return to Mexico. The denial of citizenship operated along both class and political lines as a means to return industrial-sector jobs to Anglo Americans, support agribusiness, and deport Mexican-American political activists and labor leaders.[8] It is within this context that Mexican-American organizations advocated assimilation and integration, and—in the late 1950s—moved into national politics.[9]

In contrast to the politics (or denial) of Mexican-American citizenship, schools—often segregated—and the YMCA, among other social institutions, sought to assimilate Mexican-American youths to the "American way of life."[10] But, "until the advent of the Sleepy Lagoon case [in Los Angeles, 1942]," Mauricio Mazón notes, "Mexican-American youth had not been the focus of either widespread police or journalistic investigation."[11] The incident, on August 1, 1942, in which a Mexican-American youth was found dead after a party (perhaps run over by a hit-and-run driver), resulted in the arrest and conviction of twenty-two Mexican-American youths for criminal conspiracy, assault, and murder. The next summer, in an event reported extensively in the press as a military offensive, Anglo servicemen in "taxicab brigades" entered the barrio in search of *pachucos* or zoot-suiters. The servicemen, in what Mazón calls a "ritual of role reversal," stripped the Mexican-American youths of their zoot suits and shaved their hair, "aggressively mimicking and reenacting their own experience in basic training."[12] On October 4, 1944, two years after the Sleepy Lagoon case, the convictions were reversed on appeal for lack of evidence, and the judge was cited for bias and violation of the defendants' constitutional rights.[13]

Despite the court reversal and the psychological rationale for the zoot-suit riots, the institutional response to these events—press coverage, popular culture, police and FBI investigations—established both the inherent "criminality" of Mexican-American youths and the role of the state as surrogate "parent."[14] The trial also maintained the need for an "external guiding intelligence"—whether Nazi, *sinarquista*, or Communist—since "Mexicans" were understood to be at once prone to violence and yet unable to defend themselves. In this manner, the Sleepy Lagoon Defense Committee—which included Hollywood activists such as Orson Welles, Anthony Quinn, and Rita Hayworth (the latter two of Hispanic descent)—was viewed as a foreign-inspired conspiracy rather than as "one of the more enduring coalitions between Mexicans, Jews, Blacks, and Anglos in American history."[15]

Between 1934 and 1968, the Production Code Administration (PCA), or Hays Office, served as the self-regulatory, institutional link between Hollywood films and the moral and political status quo. Prior censorship gave the PCA a significant role in shaping film texts, from initial treatment to final shooting script to final cut. The withholding of the PCA seal of approval could severely limit a completed film's distribution.[16] While the PCA did not mandate film production, it did define and monitor the outer limits of ideological expression and, in conjunction with the House Un-American Activities Committee (HUAC), ensured an almost nonexistent distribution for two of the more progressive (and the only independent) films about Mexican Americans: *Salt of the Earth,* based on a recent, successful miners strike in New Mexico, and *The Lawless,* about the bigotry and mass hysteria of a small town toward a Mexican-American youth falsely accused of murder and attempted rape.[17]

In its evaluation of social-problem films about Mexican Americans, the PCA often based its changes on the anticipated reaction of the Mexican government and people. PCA director Joseph Breen's letter to Dore Schary, producer of *My Man and I,* is typical: "We would like to urge that you get proper technical advice from the

Mexican angle to make certain that there are not details in the script that might be offensive to that nation."[18] In *My Man and I*, Mexican-born Chu Chu Ramirez (Ricardo Montalban) has just become an American citizen, whereupon he encounters anti-Mexican slurs and actions that test his patriotic optimism. In all other films, phrases such as "you Mexican jerk!," "damn Mexicans," and "greaser fighter" were flagged by the PCA and removed.[19] In April 1955, Breen's replacement, Geoffrey Shurlock, went so far as to flag "one aspect of *Giant* which has nothing to do with the Code": errors in the Spanish-language dialogue. In particular, he pointed to the phrases "Bien venudo" and "Perdonome," and cited the film's "rather touchy subject matter" as an impetus for correcting the errors.[20] While *Giant* is often remembered as, among other things, James Dean's last film, its plot centers on racist Texan patriarch Bick Benedict (Rock Hudson) and his relationship with his "Mexican" laborers and daughter-in-law.

But despite the fact that these films depicted Mexican Americans *cum* social problem, from the start the PCA positioned the central issue, or "touchy subject matter," as a "racial question" or "race distinction" that existed on an international level, between Mexico and the United States. In a letter to Jack Warner, Breen raised numerous objections to the script for *Bordertown*, including the fact that "Mexicans [*sic*] are constantly referred to as 'greasers' and other derogatory names." In *Bordertown*, Johnny Ramirez (Paul Muni) is a violent Mexican American who heads to a Mexican bordertown in order to get rich as a prohibition-era casino manager. Breen, later in his letter, placed the issue of "Mexican" representation in context:

> It presents Johnny, although an American, as a Mexican and in such a role that he becomes a murderer, gambler and crook, always trying to "go American." The whole story raises very vividly the race distinction between Mexicans and Americans, which is bound to be offensive to our Southern neighbors.[21]

One month later, Breen acknowledged Warner's assurances that the final script would not elicit Mexican protest.[22] The concern was a legitimate one for the industry, insofar as international distribution generated profits and Mexico and other Latin American countries had in the past banned studios that produced derogatory films.[23] But, in the repeated references to "our neighbors to the South," the PCA also revealed the influence of F.D.R.'s Good Neighbor Policy, whose sentiments were expressed in one of the code's twelve "particular applications": "The history, institutions, prominent people and citizenry of other nations shall be represented fairly."

The advent of World War II reinvigorated the Good Neighbor Policy and its impact on film production. In April 1941, the PCA hired a bilingual Latin American affairs expert, Addison Durland. Also, the federal Office for Coordination of Inter-American Affairs established a motion picture section, charged with the "basic job of spreading the gospel of the Americas' common stake in this struggle."[24] Together, these two agencies monitored Hollywood films and provided "technical assistance" in order to protect both international alliances and markets.[25] In the process, the representation of Mexican Americans was measured against an "external guiding intelligence," Mexico, rather than the Mexican-American community.

Likewise, the censors invoked the communist threat when the films' critique of domestic "social problems" suggested that discrimination had either institutional or popular (hence democratic) underpinnings. In a letter to Luigi Luraschi about *The Lawless,* Breen made these ideological limits clear:

> . . . certain it is that the story itself is a shocking indictment of America and its people, and, indeed, is a sad commentary on "democracy at work," which the enemies of our system of government like to point to. The shocking manner in which the several gross injustices are heaped upon the head of the confused, but innocent, young American of Mexican extraction, and the willingness of so many of the people in your story to be a part of, and to endorse, these injustices, is, we think, a damning portrayal of our American social system.
>
> The overall effect of a story of this kind made into a motion picture would be, we think, a very definite disservice to this country of ours, and to its institutions and its ideals. Our apprehensions about it is [*sic*] very deep. . . . [26]

In response to the script for *The Ring,* Breen warned: "We feel that it would not be good to infer that the police discriminate against these boys because of their nationality."[27] In *The Ring,* Tomás "Tommy Kansas" Cantanios (Lalo Rios) tries—and fails—to make it out of the East L.A. barrio as a professional boxer. While Tomás blames the "Anglos" for the limited opportunities and discrimination that he faces, in the final film version it is a police officer who makes sure that "the boys," including Tomás, are served at an all-white diner.

In the most unusual instance, PCA censors threatened to withhold the seal of approval for *Trial,* an anticommunist courtroom drama that also deals with discrimination against a Mexican-American youth falsely accused of rape. The film is able to combine these two themes, since the youth's lawyer is revealed to be a communist organizer using the case to stir up "race hatred." The script was seen as "a subtly Communist vehicle" since, in the words of the PCA, it seemed to present a "plea" against "guilt by association" and an investigating committee run by "an obnoxious Senator," while it also sought "kindness" for former, repentant communists.[28] Despite the rather obvious allusion to Senator Joseph McCarthy, the film was granted a seal of approval, even though, as censors noted, only the plea against "guilt by association" was dropped.[29] In part, the approval marked the steady decline of McCarthy's influence since the Senate had "condemned" him a year earlier, in 1954. But, as I will demonstrate later, "guilt by association" provided a conceptual and "actual" link between the communist threat, Mexican Americans, and juvenile delinquency. In *Trial,* which bears remarkable similarities to the Sleepy Lagoon case, "guilt by association" enables the narrative to resolve the inherent legal contradictions.

As with Mexican-American representation, the PCA based its censorship of material that criticized social institutions on the potential for "public hue and cry." This time, however, it was an American rather than a Mexican public. That—as Shurlock made explicit—the mere "likelihood" of public protests would lead the PCA to withhold the seal of approval[30] suggests that the popular appeal, like the communist threat, provided a convenient facade for the status quo which the code's "General Principles" upheld. In this way, the PCA diffused the challenge that the Mexican-American experience presented to American society and institutions, bifurcating it into Mexican and American components. Each component expressed, no doubt, the "enlightened" values of the time. Mexican Americans could not be called "greasers" or portrayed in a negative or inauthentic manner. Nor could social institutions be ridiculed or natural and human laws violated. And, as the censorship correspondence reveals, the PCA observed a strict concern for the social and moral impact of film, often in the name of the people. The PCA's overall strategy, however, engaged the same politics of citizenship found in the state courts and federal immigration policies, a politics of denial. On the one hand, control over Mexican-American representation was "repatriated" as a *Mexican* issue; while, on the other hand, the "racial question" or social problem was defined within institutional parameters as an *American* one.

The social-problem films operated within these ideological limits, enforced by PCA censorship. Given the nature of the social problem (broadly speaking, American citizenship), however, the narratives had to define the internal-external paradigm as a domestic rather than international one. As Arthur Pettit argues, American popular fiction and, later, film function to "localize" Mexican Americans to a specific geographical space: the southwest.[31] But, if we apply his concept more broadly, feature films "about" and "with" Mexican-American characters also "localize" or delimit them to certain genres: western-conquest, social-problem, and exploitation films. In this way, the film discourse on Mexican Americans is itself "localized" to violence (and sex), with the narrative constructed toward a judgment that determines the appropriate place for the Mexican-American character. Thus the films reinforce, in the words of Homi K. Bhabba, the "space of identification" or "fixity" for the Other, for the Mexican American.[32] It is important to note, however, that these films must give expression in one form or another to the social contradictions, ambiguities, and contestation that are the historical basis for "fixity" or "localized" discourse.

While an in-depth analysis of how these narratives situate the Mexican-American subject is well beyond the scope of this paper, I want to offer an initial elaboration on the scheme presented above with respect to genre, action, judgment, and social placement.[33] In the first instance, the social-problem films fall into three major genres: romantic melodrama (*Right Cross, My Man and I, A Medal for Benny*); courtroom drama/juvenile delinquent (*The Lawless, Trial,* and, as a precursor, *Bordertown*); and boxing film (*The Ring, Right Cross, Requiem for a Heavyweight*). *Right Cross* is almost identical to *The Ring,* except that it adds romantic melodrama to the plot and resolution. In addition, *Giant* can be classified as a modern western, while, in theme, *Giant* and *Salt of the Earth* combine if not conflate labor, racial, and gender issues.

While in general these genres provide for diverse courses of action, each of the above films has an act of violence as the "inciting incident," the incident the narrative attempts to resolve.[34] In the boxing films, of course, the inciting incident has to do with the Mexican-American boxer's temper and anger, which are shown to have been the result of an ethnic paranoia about the "gringo conspiracy." In addition, fist fights also start at least two other films: *Bordertown* and *The Lawless.* In *A Medal for Benny,* the "inciting incident" occurs off-camera but frames the entire narrative as the nature and impact of Benny Martín's absence unfolds. Martín had been a violent and criminal youth "run out of town" by the local judge, whereupon he enlisted in the service, killing "more than a hundred Japs" before he himself is killed. Beyond violence between men, often between Mexican American and Anglo American, nearly half of the films are based upon an accusation of interracial rape and/or crime of passion: *Bordertown, My Man and I, The Lawless,* and *Trial.* Thus, as the narratives explore Mexican-American citizenship with all good and earnest intent, they do so through the textual filter of the Mexican-bandit stereotype, the "greaser" who threatens to "shoot the cowboy" and "rape his woman."

The "greaser" is a product of American thought and popular culture since the 1820s, when Anglo Americans first settled in Texas, then the northernmost state of Mexico.[35] The "greaser" would continue to appear in dime westerns and, in the 1910s, in silent films. In numerous films, from *Licking the Greasers* (1910) to *Guns and Greasers* (1918), the Mexican bandit threatened death and rape, while the Anglo-American hero often ended up with a "greaser" wife, as in *Broncho Billy's Mexican Wife* (1915). These films represent an expression of the border-conflict period, anticipating the more direct and "enlightened" treatment of Mexican-American citizenship of the social-problem films. While the "greaser" was always Mexican, often he lived north of the border. And, in the treatment of the concurrent Mexican Revolution, these films initiated, indirectly, the immigration narrative,[36] with Mexican women as the sanctioned border crossers. In this manner, the "greaser" genre resolved the southwest's political unconscious, which returns or reemerges under the impetus of increased Mexican immigration and, in 1912, statehood for Arizona and New Mexico (exceptional for its Mexican majority). In addition to miscegenation with Mexican women, the films sometimes presented a redeemed or "noble greaser" who would protect Anglo Americans from other "greasers." It is in these two resolutions that we see the first Mexican-American or Chicano characters in the American cinema: for to be a "noble greaser" was to be a double outcast, neither Mexican nor American; while to be Broncho Billy's or Shorty Hamilton's (*Licking the Greasers*) or Dick Henshaw's (*Aztec Treasure*, 1914) wife meant assimilation, with neither economic power nor the right to vote.

The social-problem films did attempt to transcend the stereotypical representations of the "greaser" genre. In particular, the films produced in the 1950s reflect a significant liberal impulse from within Hollywood, one often poised against the HUAC investigations. These include: King Brothers Productions (*The Ring*), which regularly hired blacklisted personnel under pseudonyms; MGM's Dore Schary, producer of *My Man and I, Right Cross,* and *Trial,* who attempted to mediate or mitigate HUAC decrees; and Herbert Bibermann (*Salt of the Earth*), one of the "Hollywood Ten"; and blacklisted director Joseph Losey (*The Lawless*).[37] The nature of these changes, however, was a matter of degree rather than of kind: rape and murder now became a false accusation of rape and murder. While the false accusation allowed the films to play upon and expose racist expectations, it did little to expand the discourse on Mexican Americans beyond them. Thus the violent inciting incident leads to a comparable climax: judgment. In most films, judgment is the result of either a fist fight—*Right Cross, The Ring, Giant,* and *Requiem for a Heavyweight*—or a court decision—*Bordertown, The Lawless, My Man and I,* and *Trial.* In all cases, the Mexican-American protagonist loses the physical fight but wins the legal battle.[38]

In a broad sense, these two judgments or resolutions—fight and trial—mark a crucial boundary within the domain of discourse on the Mexican American, one that I have already shown to have circulated within immigration, legal, and censorship institutions: *Mexican* psychological deficiencies and *American* institutional activism. In *Right Cross* and *The Ring,* the fight ends the protagonist's career, causing his considerable anger at Anglo-American society to dissipate. These characters are revealed to have shadowboxed and to have destroyed, not a racist society, but the demons within themselves. Likewise, the young men in *Bordertown* and *A Medal for Benny* are shown to have misdirected their inherent violence toward "making it" under American capitalism and are redirected toward more acceptable and distant areas: helping one's people in the barrio or fighting for one's country overseas. While the films that are resolved in the courtroom affirm Mexican-American virtue, the fact that the narratives are predicated on Mexican-American violence, even if by false accusation, restricts the judgment. After all, it is the Mexican American on trial, and not the racist individuals or society that put him there. At the same time, the trials reaffirm the activist role of the legal system and state, often with lynch mobs as the alternative, so that racism must, in effect, be worked out through the passing of judgment upon the Mexican-American protagonist. What interests me here, however, is how in both instances the judgment functions to situate the Mexican-American characters within a social matrix of assimilation, within either barrio segregation or, in a few instances, racial integration.

For the most part, the social-problem films return the protagonist to the barrio, where he belongs. The Mexican American's efforts to enter the professional mainstream (*Bordertown*) or achieve economic parity (*A Medal for Benny, The Ring, Salt of the Earth*) are sanctioned only within the confines and reduced scale of the barrio. In *Bordertown*, Johnny Ramirez fails both as a lawyer and, having been disbarred for violent behavior, as a bordertown casino manager. In the end, he returns to the barrio, "Back where I belong . . . with my own people," framed between his *padre* and mother, between church and home, the barrio's two more traditional (read: conservative) institutions.[39] Even that, however, may not have been enough closure within the Mexican-American Generation, as the *New York Times* reviewer made clear: "The Mexican's [*sic*] feeble confessional . . . is an unconvincing and inconsistent denouement for the career of such a vigorous rebel against the *established order*."[40] Subsequent films would achieve closure through national, rather than barrio, institutions: the press, military, legal system, and, in *Salt of the Earth*, labor union.

In *A Medal for Benny* and *The Lawless*, discrimination is identified as the product of small-town provincialism. In particular, the films contrast the town's business leaders and police with more benevolent national institutions: the military in *A Medal for Benny* and the free press in *The Lawless*. Ultimately, however, this conflict is a red herring, insofar as the towns' social hierarchies remain unchallenged. The conflict is not over federalism but over the "space of identification" for the Mexican American. In *A Medal for Benny*, Joe Morales (Arturo De Cordova) at first identifies himself with the economic opportunism of the town's chamber of commerce, which intends to exploit Benny Martín's heroism. When the general and military come to town, Martín's father, Charley (J. Carroll Nash), is "given" a nice house rather than have him represent the town from his barrio shack. Likewise, earlier in the film Morales "borrows" Charley's rent money in order to invest in a boat and, when it sinks, "borrows" even more in order to purchase an expressive dress for Benny's girlfriend, Lolita Sierra (Dorothy Lamour). When Charley refuses to play along, the general, to the surprise of the town leaders, insists on going to the barrio to present the medal, since "a lot of fine Americans come out of shacks." Whereas the town leaders, in full police escort, had earlier descended upon the barrio in order to retrieve Charley, the general arrives with a full military parade in order to salute the contribution Charley made from within the barrio. At this point, Morales's identification shifts from economic opportunism (business/town) to national service (military/barrio), and he enlists, a move that rewards him with Benny's girlfriend, when and if he returns to the barrio.

The placement within an institutional paradigm, however, continued to center on the construction of an actual or symbolic family. The parentless Morales, in effect, replaces Benny Martín for Charley and Lolita, this time "run out of town" by the military rather than the police. As the "better" son, he will be allowed to return to the barrio.[41] In *The Lawless* and *Trial*, each of the accused, fatherless Mexican-

American youths acquires an Anglo-American, institutional father figure who defends him. The journalist in *The Lawless* saves Paul Rodriguez (Lalo Rios) from a lynch mob, and later uses the press to initiate a defense committee. At one point, Rodriguez tells the journalist that he reminds him of his older brother, who died in the war.[42] While the film depicts a barrio newspaper run by a woman, Sunny Garcia (Gail Russell), it is the Anglo-American journalist whose commitment and sacrifice (his press is destroyed) will save Rodriguez. And, in fact, the journalist character functions on two levels to further displace the notion that a barrio journalist could have defended the community: through an incipient romantic relationship with Garcia, and, at the end, when he commandeers her press in order to "say all the things *I've* left unsaid."[43]

In *Trial,* the paternal connection is made even more explicit in the lawyer's half-hearted insistence that Angel Chavez (Rafael Campos) behave like his client and not his son. Throughout the trial, Chavez asks questions so that he, too, can become a lawyer. These questions provide a clever exposition device that allows the film to describe "due process" and "guilt by association," with Chavez complicit, if not eager, in the way these lead to his own conviction and death sentence.

Chavez is accused of murder when he is caught at an all-white beach with his white girlfriend dead at his feet. She had just recovered from rheumatic fever, and the excitement of "making love" (kissing) resulted in a heart attack. In the course of the trial, Chavez's lawyer discovers that his own boss is a communist and is using the case to raise funds, stir up racial hatred, and martyr Chavez for the party. In the end, the jury finds Chavez guilty of murder, punishable by death. Chavez's lawyer, however, exposes his boss's affiliations and intentions to the judge, and offers an alternative judgment since Chavez is a minor.[44]

Rather than apply the letter of the Felony Murder Act, he suggests that the judge *also* apply the letter of the Juvenile Defenders Act (normally for "trivial offenses"), which allows for an "indeterminate sentence." Thus, he argues, "through its own technicalities," the law can correct its own errors. The prosecution agrees with the defense's "most ingenious theory of law," and admits that he was "sure that Angel Chavez was technically guilty . . . [but] . . . that his guilt was only technical." In essence, the two lawyers agree that Chavez is, in fact, innocent of murder, but uphold the conviction and the "harsh rules of law" that secured it. In these two references to legal "technicalities," *Trial* suggests that the law is an arbitrary construct, not rooted in a moral absolute. What does hold the legal system together, then, is the notion of "guilt by association": that in his sexual and political mis-associations, Chavez merits some form of punishment. (Meanwhile, the racist townspeople "have learned an awful lot" as mere *spectators.*) Thus the judge sentences Chavez to the State Industrial School for an indeterminate period of time, "until the principal determines that your release will serve your own best interests and those of society." In perhaps the most visceral way, the law(yer) becomes Chavez's father, and metes out the "justice" he claims the reformed townspeople now desire: his socialization by the state into the working class.

In an apparent (and isolated) shift in this dynamic, two Ricardo Montalban films—*My Man and I* and *Right Cross*—end with his character's marriage to an Anglo-American blonde. For perhaps the first time in the American cinema, the sanctioned miscegenation beetween Mexican and American involved a Mexican-American male. Upon closer examination, however, these films do not result in the Mexican American's integration into the so-called "dominant white culture." Nor do they punish and exile the Anglo-American woman to the barrio. While the Mexican American is repeatedly identified in the United States as a "racial" minority, black-and-white race dynamics at some point fail to hold. In part, Montalban's status as a second-generation Latin Lover (itself a step removed from "Mexican") and light skin color place him in the color line's gray zone. After all, while the PCA prohibited miscegenation, it defined it as sex between the *black* and *white* races. Even more crucial, while the women in both films are blondes, neither represents the dominant culture. In *My Man and I*, Shelley Winters, Hollywood's "bad girl," portrays a low-class alcoholic down on her luck; while in *Right Cross*, June Allyson, Hollywood's "girl next door," portrays an ethnic-Catholic Irish American long before it was thought one could become president. Thus the Mexican-American character can, through assimilation and miscegenation, leave the barrio behind, but still be emplaced within class and ethnic boundaries. In *Right Cross*, the Irish are shown to be the same short-tempered, devout, dispossessed, yet nostalgic nationalists as the Mexican-American characters, who—in most films—state how their ancestors once controlled the town, county, or zinc mine. Chu Chu Ramirez, in *My Man and I*, evinces the same self-sacrifice toward Winters's character that the Mexican Americans in other films do toward the barrio or war effort. In fact, his ceaseless optimism as a newly naturalized citizen reforms all the other low-life and redneck white characters, in particular Mr. and Mrs. Ames, despite the couple's various attempts to seduce, cheat, injure, and frame him for attempted murder.

While the script for *My Man and I* led Breen to recommend to MGM producer Dore Schary that he "get proper technical advice from the Mexican angle,"[45] the end product raises questions about the narrative function of Mexican-American representation in the social-problem films. On a manifest level, the social contradictions about Mexican-American citizenship are resolved, with the Mexican-American Generation repatriated, segregated, and institutionalized in the name of assimilation, the same ideal the Mexican-American Generation incorporated into its own, reformist political discourse. But in its representation of the Mexican American, most social-problem films were more concerned with not offending Mexico than with presenting an "authentic" ethnic-American portrayal. In *My Man and I, A Medal for Benny,* and *Bordertown,* the Mexican-American characters speak a pidgin English devoid of definite articles and pronouns, even though the Spanish language makes even greater use of these modifiers than does English. But perhaps the most telling sign is that every film presents Spanish-language dialogue *without* subtitles. In these respects, *Giant* is an exception: the production files reveal considerable research into authentic "Mexican" costume and villages, even though these scenes, unlike in the other films, are marginal. And while Shurlock cites errors in the Spanish-language dialogue, *Giant* alone uses that dialogue, again unsubtitled, to establish two levels of signification. Bick Benedict speaks fluent Spanish to order about his "Mexican" employees, while his new, East Coast wife does the unthinkable and asks for their names and about their health, in English. In the other films, when the characters speak Spanish, it is not supposed to function as a speech act that signifies within or has an impact upon the narrative but exists instead as an empty code for ethnicity. In short, there is no need for subtitles because nothing is said.

It is here that the narrative function of emplacement becomes visible, in the recognition of the de facto "mainstream," monolingual audience for these films. These were not, after all, the equivalent of the Hollywood "race" films. The oft-praised *Salt of the Earth* was no exception: it spoke more to the ex-Hollywood production team's blacklisting than to the New Mexico *hispano* community, which it portrays as *mexicano* with an even more improbable neoindigenous nationalism.[46] Thus the social-problem films situated the Mexican-American character for a largely Anglo-American audience. For a narrative articulation of this process, recall the townspeople *cum* spectators in *Trial*. But the significance of the audience is perhaps most evident in the relationship between sanctioned miscegenation and genre. Briefly, the two films in which Ricardo Montalban marries a blonde woman are romantic melodramas: in other words, women's films. The print ads for both films feature Montalban, without shirt, embracing the female lead. For *Right Cross*, one caption reads, "Girls!!! Would you do what June Allyson did? Have you ever loved a man so much that you'd pursue him no matter what?"[47] Perhaps more than anything, these ads construct a "space of identification" for the post–World War II working-class woman. Thus the placement of the Mexican-American protagonist within normative social or institutional parameters likewise places the female audience identified with the female lead/star. That identification is constructed in opposition to the married seductresses in *My Man and I* and *Bordertown* (classified at the time as a melodrama), who serve as the real evil forces in the films. In *Bordertown*, the single socialite who plays with Ramirez, calling him "savage," is also punished (with death) for her willful transgression of class *and* racial boundaries.

In *Giant*, like earlier westerns and "greaser" films, it is the Anglo-American man who marries the Mexican woman. It is in the western, a male-identified genre, that the Anglo-American protagonist can cross racial *and* class boundaries and take, in both cases, a step down. In the 1950s variant on American patriarchal society, after all, it is the man who determines/provides economic and class status as well as family name. *Giant*, however, provides a subtle turn on these conventions. It is not the hero, Bick Benedict, but his effeminate son, Jordan (Dennis Hopper), who marries the submissive mestiza Juana (Elsa Cardenas). Furthermore, their nearly equitable relationship produces the logical outcome that the "greaser" films point toward but can in no way envision: a mestizo-Anglo infant (and his Anglo cousin), depicted in wide-screen close-up. It is a rare moment in the American cinema on ethnicity, one that stops the narrative cold, with both hope and uncertainty.

With the exception of *Salt of the Earth* and *Giant,* the social-problem films "about" Mexican Americans center on a "Mexican" male protagonist and his place or role within American society. In contrast, *Salt of the Earth* and *Giant* employ a protofeminist critique in order to reorient class and racial hierarchies. *Giant,* however, does so on both corporeal and symbolic levels, with "miscegenation" between east (Leslie [Elizabeth Taylor]) and west (Bick) and, in the next generation, north (Jordan) and south (Juana). In this sense, the film embodies, or finds affinities with, the Latin American concept of *mestizaje,* which, in post–World War II thought, offered mestizo racial mixture as the solution to ideologies of racial purity.[48] In its familial construction of a new American culture—eastern liberalism, western capitalism, and Mexican Americanism—*Giant* also anticipates the cultural redefinition of *mestizaje* by Chicano and Anglo-American border artists.[49]

But, as I have argued, the role of women has often been the "political unconscious" in the social-problem films, so that Anglo-American and Mexican-American women become complicit in the placement of the Mexican-American protagonist within an appropriate class-defined, Protestant work ethic. In *A Medal for Benny* and *The Ring,* it is the "traditional" Mexican-American girlfriend who leads the protagonist back to the barrio, where—one way or another—he will support her. In this way, the female spectator, to the extent that she identifies with the female lead, unwittingly places herself alongside the Mexican-American male, becoming the mechanism that will keep him (and, by extension, her) within a marginal social context.

It is here, in the trials and titillations of Mexican-American citizenship, that the gender, "racial," and political discourses come together. To date, film critics and theorists who research the period between 1930 and 1960 have examined these discourses in relative isolation from each other. This is particularly so with respect to the representation of the Mexican American. To imply that the HUAC investigations, social-problem films, classical Hollywood style, and PCA censorship were distinctly *American* issues, and yet give little or no voice to the Mexican-American presence, is to engage and perpetuate the period's politics of denial toward the Mexican-American Generation.

It is perhaps worthwhile, then, to end with a word about Chicano Cinema, an alternative film practice that developed in the late 1960s within the overall project of the Chicano civil rights movement. During the movement, these filmmakers documented the concurrent social protests. In the postmovement period, but especially under the historical amnesia of the Reagan era, Chicano directors initiated a historical revisionism of the Mexican-American Generation. In feature films (*Zoot Suit* [1981] [see Photo 5.1], *La Bamba* [1987], *Break of Dawn* [1988]), documentaries (*Ballad of an Unsung Hero* [1983], *The Lemon Grove Incident* [1985]), and short dramas (*Distant Water* [1990]), filmmakers researched and reclaimed lost moments in American history.

In the initial development of Chicano Cinema as a cohesive or collective movement, writer/director/producer Jesús Salvador Treviño and others researched the unwritten history of Mexican-American and Chicano representation. *Salt of the Earth* was identified as a precursor; and when the Chicano Cinema Coalition organized in 1978, *Citizen Kane* (1945) was one of the first films its members screened and studied. Thus "classical" and Chicano-themed films became part of the filmmakers' self-conscious frame of reference. And, in fact, one can argue that the first two Chicano feature films draw upon the Hollywood social-problem film, but do so in order to invert its usual ideological thrust. *Raices de sangre* (Mexico, 1977, d. Jesús Treviño), for example, retells *Bordertown*, shifting the moral point of view from the Anglo-American to the Chicano community, thereby transforming the earlier film's enlightened segregationism into a radical separatism. In both films, the protagonist, a bordertown lawyer, reforms when he comes around to the film's moral point of view, eschews violence, and returns to the barrio. *Only Once in a Lifetime* (1978, d. Alejandro Grattan), on the other hand, uses the social-problem "drama-comedy," a hybrid used in *A Medal for Benny* and somewhat typical of American social-problem films in the 1970s. Again, the protagonist returns to the barrio, but, as in *Raices de sangre*, with an activist intent designed to confront American society on a collective rather than individual level.

In that subtle yet significant shift, these two Chicano-produced feature films initiated a counterdiscourse on Mexican-American citizenship, one that stressed a cultural-nationalist, rather than assimilationist, identity, or found traces of it in historical dramas of resistance such as *Zoot Suit* and *Break of Dawn*. For its part, Hollywood responded as it had in the past, when Mexico protested the silent "greaser" films: it simply stopped producing films "about" Mexican Americans or Chicanos. Taken together, the silent "greaser" films, the social-problem films about Mexican Americans, and the Chicano-produced feature films constitute the American cinema's explicit discourse on Chicano citizenship. Throughout the eighty years of that discourse, Hollywood has engaged—through outright stereotype, "enlightened" segregationism, and now silence—in a politics of denial. In the period between 1930 and 1960, often with the intervention of PCA censors, these films attempted to mediate Mexican-American demands for assimilation and the rights of citizenship, and resituate them around other issues related to national politics, juvenile delinquency, and changes in class-based gender roles. It is little wonder, then, that the post–Mexican-American Generation, or Chicanos, would reject "political accommodation and assimilation," and stress instead a politics of cultural difference.

PHOTO 5.1 **Edward James Olmos,** seen here in *Zoot Suit* (1981) as El Pachuco (a Mexican-American alter ego and one-man Greek chorus) welcoming the audience to a retelling of the story of the Sleepy Lagoon case and the zoot-suit riots. (Courtesy of The Museum of Modern Art Film Stills Archive)

NOTES

Reprinted by permission of the author and publisher from *Social Research,* Vol. 58, no. 2 (Summer 1991), pp. 413–428, New York, N.Y. Copyright © *Social Research,* 1991.

Archival research into the production files and censorship correspondence at the Margaret Herrick Library (Beverly Hills) and the Warner Brothers Archives (University of Southern California) was made possible through a travel grant from the Stanford Center for Chicano Research, January 1990. I also wish to thank the Turner Network Television Film Library for video dubs of *Right Cross* (1950), *My Man and I* (1952), and *Trial* (1955).

1. These films are: *Bordertown* (1935), *A Medal for Benny* (1945), *The Lawless* (1950), *Right Cross* (1950), *My Man and I* (1952), *The Ring* (1952), *Salt of the Earth* (1954), *Trial* (1955), *Giant* (1956), and *Requiem for a Heavyweight* (1962).

2. See Carlos Muñoz, Jr., "From Segregation to Melting Pot Democracy: The Mexican-American Generation," in *Youth, Identity, Power: The Chicano Movement* (London: Verso, 1989), pp. 19–46; and Mario T. Garcia, *Mexican Americans: Leadership, Ideology and Identity, 1930–1960* (New Haven: Yale University Press, 1989).

3. Richard A. Garcia, "The Mexican American Mind: A Product of the 1930s," in *History, Culture, and Society: Chicago Studies in the 1980s* (Ypsilanti, Mich.: Bilingual Press/Editorial Bilingüe, 1983), pp. 67–93.

4. Muñoz, "From Segregation," p. 49. In a similar argument, Richard A. Garcia defines Mexican-Americanism as a dualistic identity: "Mexican in culture and American in ideas and ideology" ("The Mexican American Mind," p. 84). For an account of Mexican-American response and attitudes toward Mexican immigration in this period, see Garcia, *Mexican Americans;* and John R. Chávez, *The Lost Land: The Chicano Image of the Southwest* (Albuquerque: University of New Mexico Press, 1984), pp. 85–106.

5. For an extensive historical account, see Abraham Hoffman, *Unwanted Mexican-Americans in the Great Depression* (Tucson: University of Arizona Press, 1974); and Mercedes Carreras de Velasco, *Los Mexicanos que devolvió la crisis, 1929–1932* (Mexico: Secretaria de Relaciones Exteriores, 1974).

6. Mexican immigration: 1901–10, 49,642; 1911–20, 219,004; 1921–30, 459,298; 1931–40, 22,319; 1941–50, 60,589; 1951–60, 299,811; and 1961–70, 453,937. Source: U.S. Department of Justice, *1976 Annual Report: Immigration and Naturalization Service* (Washington, D.C.: U.S. Government Printing Office, 1976), pp. 86–88; cited in Howard M. Bahr et al., *American Ethnicity* (Lexington, Mass.: D.C. Heath, 1979), p. 56.

7. For an extensive historical account, see Juan Ramon Garcia, *Operation Wetback: The Mass Deportation of Mexican Undocumented Workers in 1954* (Westport, Conn.: Greenwood Press, 1980).

8. The later political deportations fell under the rubric of the McCarran-Walter Act (U.S. Immigration and Nationality Act) of 1952. See Garcia, *Operation Wetback,* p. 198. For an earlier account, see Patricia Morgan, *Shame of a Nation: A Documented Story of Police-State Terror Against Mexican-Americans in the U.S.A.* (Los Angeles: Los Angeles Committee for Protection of the Foreign Born, 1954), in particular, pp. 38–39.

9. Muñoz, *Youth, Identity, Power,* pp. 50–51.

10. *Ibid.,* pp. 20–31.

11. Mauricio Mazón, *The Zoot-Suit Riots: The Psychology of Symbolic Annihilation* (Austin: University of Texas Press, 1984), p. 20.

12. *Ibid.*, pp. 86–87, 92.

13. Rodolfo Acuña, *Occupied America: A History of the Chicanos,* 3rd ed. (New York: Harper & Row, 1988), pp. 253–259.

14. Two significant institutional responses were the California Youth Authority and the Los Angeles Youth Project. As the director of the latter program acknowledged, "The 'zoot-suit' riots brought matters to a head" (quoted in Mazón, *Zoot-Suit Riots,* p. 101).

15. Mazón, *Zoot-Suit Riots,* pp. 23, 27.

16. The PCA began to lose power in the mid-1950s with the advent of television and the dismantling of the studio system under the "consent decrees" (which required the studios to divest themselves of distribution and exhibition holdings by 1953). Most of the social-problem films, however, were produced in the period before these changes had a significant impact on PCA censorship.

17. For an account of the rise and development of the PCA, see Marvin N. Olasky, "The Failure of Movie Industry Public Relations, 1921–1934," *Journal of Popular Film & Television* 12 (Winter 1984–85): 163–170; and Gregory D. Black, "Hollywood Censored: The Production Code Administration and the Hollywood Film Industry, 1930–1940," *Film History* 3 (1989): 167–189. While the PCA monitored some 20,000 films between 1934 and 1968, film criticism of these films often overlooks, as Lea Jacobs argues, how "censorship functioned at the level of representation, as a set of rules which governed the production of meaning" (Lea Jacobs, "Industry Self-Regulation and the Problem of Textual Determination," *The Velvet Light Trap* no. 23 [Spring 1989]: 4–15). In "'Something's Missing Here!'—Homosexuality and Film Reviews During the Production Code Era, 1934–1962," I examine the code's censorship of homosexual depictions and the reception of film reviewers: *Cinema Journal* 30 (Fall 1990): 20–41. For two recent case studies on film censorship, see Gerald Gardner, *The Censorship Papers: Movie Censorship Letters from the Hays Office, 1934 to 1968* (New York: Dodd, Mead, 1987) and Leonard J. Leff and Jerold L. Simmons, *The Dame in the Kimono: Hollywood, Censorship, and the Production Code from the 1920s to the 1960s* (New York: Grove Weidenfeld, 1990). Both books reprint "The Motion Picture Production Code." On *Salt of the Earth,* see Michael Wilson and Deborah Silverton Rosenfelt, *Salt of the Earth* (New York: Feminist Press, 1978).

18. Joseph Breen, letter to Dore Schary, M-G-M, 9 July 1952. MPAA Production Code Administration case files: *My Man and I* (1951). The Margaret Herrick Library, Beverly Hills, California.

19. These particular phrases are taken from an initial script of *The Ring.* See Joseph Breen, letter to Franklin Kin, King Bros. Productions, 19 November 1951. MPAA Production Code Administration case files: *The Ring* (1951). The Margaret Herick Library, Beverly Hills, California.

20. As cited in Finlay McDermid, memo to George Stevens and Henry Ginsberg, 13 April 1955. Warner Brothers Archives. Production Files: *Giant* (1956). Box #403. School of Cinema-Television. University of Southern California. Los Angeles, California.

21. Joseph Breen, letter to Jack Warner, Warner Brothers, 10 July 1934. Warner Brothers Archives. Production Files: *Bordertown* (1935). B-29. School of Cinema-Television. University of Southern California. Los Angeles, California.

22. Joseph Breen, letter to Jack Warner, Warner Brothers, 10 August 1934. Warner Brothers Archives. Production Files: *Bordertown* (1935). B-29. School of Cinema-Television. University of Southern California. Los Angeles, California.

23. See Allen L. Woll, *The Latin Image in American Film* (Los Angeles: UCLA Latin American Center Publications, 1977), pp. 16–22; and Helen Delpar, "Goodbye to the 'Greaser': Mexico, the MPPDA, and Derogatory Films, 1922–1926," *Journal of Popular Film & Television* 12 (1984): 34–41.

24. John Hay Whitney, Director of the Motion Pictures Section, as quoted in Woll, *Latin Image in American Film,* p. 54.

25. See Woll, *Latin Image in American Film,* ch. 4, "Hollywood's Good Neighbor Policy," pp. 53–75.

26. Joseph Breen, letter to Luigi Luraschi, Paramount Pictures, 5 October 1949. MPAA Production Code Administration case files: *The Lawless* (1949). The Margaret Herrick Library. Beverly Hills, California.

27. Joseph Breen, letter to Franklin King, 19 November 1951, cited above.

28. J.A.V. [Jack A. Vizzard], "Memo for the Files," 30 March 1955. MPAA Production Code Administration case files: *Trial* (1955). The Margaret Herrick Library. Beverly Hills, California.

29. *Ibid.,* and "Analysis of Film Content" form [same citation], which gives June 10, 1955, as date of approval.

30. Geoffrey Shurlock, letter to Dore Schary, M-G-M, 30 March 1955. MPAA Production Code Administration case files: *Trial* (1955). The Margaret Herrick Library. Beverly Hills, California.

31. Arthur C. Pettit, *Images of the Mexican American in Fiction and Film* (College Station: Texas A&M University Press, 1980), p. xv.

32. Homi K. Bhabba, "The Other Question . . . ," *Screen* 24 (November-December 1983): 18–36.

33. Charles Ramirez-Berg provides an in-depth analysis of *Bordertown,* which he argues established the ideological and narrative features for subsequent social-problem films about Mexican Americans. He places these films within a larger generic group he calls the "assimilation narrative" ("*Bordertown,* the Assimilation Narrative and the Chicano Social Problem Film," in Chon Noriega, ed., *Chicanos and Film: Essays on Chicano Representation and Resistance* [New York: Garland Publishing, forthcoming]). I am indebted to Charles Ramirez-Berg for our numerous discussions of these films.

34. In my discussion, I rely upon the concepts of practitioner-oriented script analysts for "classic" story structure. For an initial application of these concepts to recent Chicano-produced and -themed feature films, see Mario Barrera, "Story Structure in Latino Films," in Noriega, *Chicanos and Film.*

35. Arnoldo de León, *They Called Them Greasers: Anglo Attitudes Toward Mexicans in Texas, 1821–1900* (Austin: University of Texas Press, 1983).

36. For a comparative genre analysis of Mexican immigration films, see David R. Maciel, "Braceros, Mojados, and Alambristas: Mexican Immigration to the United States in Contemporary Cinema," *Hispanic Journal of Behavioral Sciences* 8 (1986): 369–385.

37. Victor S. Navasky, *Naming Names* (New York: Viking Press, 1980), pp. xxi, 83–84, 155–156, 337.

38. In *Giant,* Bick Benedict (Rock Hudson) also loses the climactic fist fight, when he at last "does the right thing" and defends his Mexican daughter-in-law.

39. Here *padre* refers to a priest, but its other meaning, father, is also significant in terms of how the ending situates Ramirez within the barrio by way of a symbolic, institutional family.

40. Emphasis mine. Andre Seenwald, "The Strand Reopens With *Bordertown,* a Picturesque Melodrama With Paul Muni and Bette Davis," *New York Times,* Jan. 24, 1935, p. 22. The reviewer may have also objected to the fact that Ramirez uses his ill-gotten wealth to endow a barrio law school.

41. Better because his opportunism tends more toward capitalism than outright robbery, although this, too, is corrected, and his future as a laborer accepted. With respect to the overall message, *A Medal for Benny* was one of many wartime "racial unity" films that were released as enlistment propaganda. The initial treatment for the film was completed March 16, 1943, and the final film released April 9, 1945.

42. Although Rodriguez's father is alive, his "defeatist withdrawal" allows the journalist to assume a father-like big-brother role. I use Peter Roffman and Jim Purdy's apt phrase in *The Hollywood Social Problem Film: Madness, Despair, and Politics from the Depression to the Fifties* (Bloomington: Indiana University Press, 1981), p. 255.

43. Emphasis added. The last scene depicts Garcia showing the journalist how to line-o-type and set the press, an act that identifies her as more skilled laborer than professional.

44. In an example of the limits of Latino representation in Hollywood, the judge, who is chosen for the case because he is "Negro" and cannot be accused of racism against Chavez, is played by Puerto Rican actor Juano Hernandez.

45. See note 18.

46. Likewise, Deborah Rosenfelt's introduction to the book *Salt of the Earth* (cited above) glosses over the powerful and not-so-uplifting women's experience that emerges in her interviews with Virginia Chacon, and which the film highly romanticizes into a "feel good" message.

47. M-G-M Press Book: *My Man and I* and *Right Cross.* School of Cinema-Television. University of Southern California. Los Angeles, California.

48. For the definitive expression of this concept, see José Vasconcelos, *La raza cósmica* (México, D.F.: Espasa-Calpe Mexicana, 1948).

49. In particular, I refer to the Border Arts Workshop/Taller de Arte Frontierzo (BAW/TAF) in San Diego/Tijuana, whose members included Isaac Artenstein, David Avalos, Phillip and Amy Brookman, Emily Hicks, and Guillermo Gómez-Peña. See, for example, the BAW/TAF publication *Broken Line/La Linea Quebrade* (San Diego); Guillermo Gómez-Peña and Jeff Kelley, eds., *The Border Art Workshop: A Documentation of Five Years of Interdisciplinary Art Projects Dealing with U.S.-Mexico Border Issues, 1984–1989* (New York: Artists Space/La Jolla: Museum of Contemporary Art, 1989); and Guillermo Gómez-Peña, "The Multicultural Paradigm: An Open Letter to the National Arts Community," *High Performance,* September 1989, pp. 18–27.

Stereotyping in Films in General and of the Hispanic in Particular

Charles Ramírez Berg

There are few—very, very few—nonstereotypical portrayals of Hispanics in Holly-wood cinema. Before *Zoot Suit* (1981), *La Bamba* (1987), and *Stand and Deliver* (1988)—all films with Hispanics in key creative positions—it is difficult to find ex-amples of Hispanic characters in mainstream Hollywood cinema who are complex and self-determining. Katy Jurado's strong portrayal of the resourceful business-woman in *High Noon* (1952), Ricardo Montalbán's intrepid Mexican government agent in *Border Incident* (1949), and Anthony Quinn's dignified, defiant vaquero in *The Ox-Bow Incident* (1943) are three rare cases where Hispanics are depicted as more than simplified caricatures in U.S. studio films. Hollywood has depicted the vast majority stereotypically.

Thus far, discussions of Hispanic stereotypes have focused on this historical fact (Keller, 1985; Treviño, 1984; Woll, 1980a, 1980b; Woll & Miller, 1987). In the main, the concept of stereotyping itself has gone unquestioned or assumed as a given. Wilson and Gutiérrez (1985) are distinctive in their presentation of a histori-cal overview of minority stereotypes in the mass media and a definition of the term "stereotype." Pettit (1980) combines incisive, although traditional, literary criticism with a broad survey of imagery of the Mexican in both literature and film. Moreover, these discussions fail to place Hispanic stereotyping within a contemporary theoreti-cal framework. Because most of the studies were products of less critically circum-spect times, this article will bring contemporary critical discourse to bear on ques-tions of stereotyping. Recognizing the need for a more precise definition of the term, Seiter (1986, pp. 14–26) has appropriately called for reevaluating and clarifying it, to grasp more firmly its several dimensions. It seems logical to begin a discussion of the portrayal of Hispanics in American film with a survey of the various meanings given to the term "stereotyping."

This article is in two parts. The first investigates various social scientific definitions of the term (sociological and psychological). It goes on to consider what might be gained in the study of stereotyping, reviewing concepts from several critical stances—psychoanalytical, ideological, feminist, and gay. The second part concentrates on Hispanic stereotypes in film. Six Hispanic historical stereotypes in Hollywood films are identified and defined. Synthesizing ideas from various approaches, a unified critical approach to the study of stereotypes in general and Hispanics in particular, is suggested. Finally, the current state of Hispanic images in Hollywood films today is discussed.

Stereotyping

Social Psychological and Common Uses of the Term

It is crucial to note that all people stereotype. In general, social psychologists agree on a value-neutral use of the term stereotype to indicate a basic cognitive process by which humans make sense of the world. Stereotyping is a psychological mechanism, having to do with the creation of categories, which allows people to manage the swirl of data presented them from the environment. This was recognized in 1922 by Lippmann (1941) when he gave new meaning to the term, "stereotyping," calling stereotypes "pictures in our heads." Some salient implications are clear from Lippmann's definition.

One is obvious: if everyone does it, stereotyping is not something only "bad" or prejudiced, ignorant, or racist people do. In itself, it is not necessarily bad, although what humans do with this process can make it so. Finally, because it is possible to turn a common categorizing mechanism into a hateful tool used by one people to segregate and ultimately dominate others, a better understanding of the stereotyping process, as it moves from a value-free to a value-laden concept, is needed. It is important to begin to fathom how a dominant group assigns selective characteristics to other people—social, cultural, political, sexual, racial, class, and ethnic *Others*—as an ethnocentric means of underscoring differences (rather than, say, merely noting that differences exist, or simply noting similarities). As Lippmann (1941) so presciently points out, the analyst must recognize three parts of the stereotyping process. The first is "the scene of the action," which means the concrete, historical "reality" that serves as the basis for the stereotype. Second, there is "the human picture of that scene," the constructed stereotype. Finally, there is "the human response to that picture working itself out upon the scene of action," what individuals do with the stereotype, how it affects their lives (p. 16). This article points the way to a fuller understanding of the dynamic interaction of these elements, particularly in the study of the media, by combining and unifying ideas of stereotyping into a coherent critical stance.

What exactly is meant by stereotyping, as most people use the term? Given a definition, it is possible to examine the process that various investigators have observed in the transformation of Others into symbols, then begin to discover the uses to which such symbols are molded.

In nonspecialized, everyday usage, a stereotype is an oversimplification. In popular criticism, for example, it may simply mean a hackneyed or stock character. Its connotation is negative. A stereotypical character is one that is a cliché, not "rounded." Similarly, as the term is commonly used and understood, stereotyping is a generalization used by one group (the in-group, *Us*) about members of another group (the out-group, *Them*), and the generalization is not a flattering one. In this case, what differentiates it from the category-making process described earlier is the addition of several crucial factors. Ethnocentric prejudice is one: the fact that the in-group transforms the out-group into simplistic symbols by selecting a few traits of the Others that pointedly accentuate differences (Wilson & Gutiérrez, 1985; Seiter, 1986). These negative-value differences form the basis for making Others inferior, thus excluding them from the in-group.

In addition, this kind of stereotyping is triggered by an all-or-nothing logic, whereby stereotypers place anyone identified as an out-group member into the stereotyped category. What is worse, the stereotypes are believed. Because they are perceived to be real, and do not exist merely as abstract concepts or cognitive categories, they are endowed with great power. Even when people have information to the contrary, they may genuinely believe that Mexican males are treacherous, lazy, simpleton buffoons, Latin lovers, or a combination of these. This ordinary type of stereotyping allows for little variation among members of the out-group. It is worthwhile here to distinguish among several key perspectives because each contributes to understanding how stereotypes can be used.

Sociological Perspectives

One sociological view is that stereotypes are pre-existing categories in culture. They are learned in the socialization process (Miller, 1982, p. 27). Again, Lippmann is far-sighted. "In the great blooming, buzzing confusion of the outer world," he writes, "we pick out what our culture has already defined for us, and we tend to perceive that which we have picked out in the form stereotyped for us by our culture" (Lippmann, 1941, p. 81). Two important features of such stereotyping are: (1) the "vicious cycle" aspect—when learned stereotypes are expressed they are reinforced and, thus, validated and perpetuated, and (2) that validation solidifies into norms that suggest how certain individuals and groups should be treated (Miller, 1982, p. 27). Stereotypes persist not only because they are category labels, but because they are implied "programs for action" (Royce, 1982, p. 158).

Another way to think of sociological stereotypes is to consider how groups use them to interact with one another (Royce, 1982, pp. 163–168). Different stereotyping scenarios can be delineated depending on the power relationship between groups, they may be stratified, oppositional, or cooperative. If the groups are stratified—holding unequal power—the dominant group creates subdominant stereotypes endowed with two sets of characteristics: harmless (with out-group members portrayed as childlike, irrational, and emotional), when they pose no threat; or dangerous (treacherous, deceitful, cunning), when they do. The six Hispanic stereotypes delineated later are products of such a stratified case.

When groups see themselves as opposed, competing for the same resources, subordinate groups may view the dominant group as cold, exploiting, cruel, and arrogant. If either group senses that the other is threatening its resources, the descriptive terminology becomes more severely derogatory: "aggressive," "brutal," "corrupt." The change is thought to be a convenient way for groups to rationalize "their own violent or ungenerous impulses" (Royce, 1982, p. 166). This is the case in the example at the end of this article, where it is argued that "Aliens" in recent science fiction films are—among other things—figures for actual historical aliens who enter U.S. borders, legally or illegally.

Finally, groups may coexist peacefully in a mutually beneficial relationship. Having to rely upon one another, one group may describe the other as strong, hard working, and/or friendly.

Psychological Perspectives

Psychologists trace stereotyping to an individual's early development (from six weeks to six months), when the child first makes the distinction between self and the world. This differentiation is accompanied by a dawning awareness of loss of control over his or her environment. In order to cope with this dwindling control, the developing child divides its psychological self into two parts: good (able to be controlled) and bad (unable to be controlled). Moreover, the child projects the qualities of the bad self onto the Other (bad world) in order to help preserve the illusion of maintaining power (Gilman, 1985, pp. 16–21).

Gilman's (1985) elaboration of object-relations theory pinpoints several characteristics of the deep structure of the psychological notion of stereotyping. First, in defining the Other, one also defines oneself. "Because the Other is the antithesis of the self," says Gilman, "the definition of the Other must incorporate the basic categories by which the self is defined" (p. 23). A second point that is helpful to the textual student of stereotypes is Gilman's contention that three basic categories of the Other are generated by the self-Other linkage: human mutability, human sexuality, and human social relationships—in Gilman's terms, illness (and death), sex, and race. Last, Gilman points out that, in social psychology, stereotypes are not rigid but fluid, and uses this to argue that texts—structured systems of representation—are ideal sites to study the continually varying patterns of stereotyping. For Gilman, "texts function as structured expressions of the inner world in our mental representation," and thus, stereotypical structures "exist within all texts, since the creation of the text is an attempt to provide an image of control." Finally, such systems of representation—whether in words or images—which construct the projections of our anxiety are necessarily reductive, resulting in the creation of stereotypes (Gilman, 1985, pp. 26–27).

Using this projection process as a model for the social construction of cultural Others (Wood, 1985, p. 199) allows us to think of stereotyping as society's denial of its own negative tendencies by assigning them to an Other. (The leap from individual development to broad social tendencies—from analysis of the psyche to analysis of a cultural phenomenon—is not inconsiderable, and is one of the problems in applying psychological and psychoanalytical theory to texts. See Gledhill, 1985, pp. 817–845.) Accordingly, a stereotype such as the Chicana halfbreed harlot, like the *bandido,* a familiar figure from American westerns, has dual significance. Clearly, it is a negative depiction of Mexican American women. But beyond that, it is a fascinating representation of what the dominant group fears—and has repressed—within its darker, "bad" self—in this case, unbridled sexuality. Similarly, the other Hispanic stereotypes described later fit into Gilman's three categories (1985, pp. 16–21). The Mexican bandit is a mentally ill psychopath, the Male Buffoon a laughable simpleton. The Halfbreed Harlot, the Female Clown, the Latin Lover, and the Dark Lady are all ways of depicting sexual Others. If, from the sociological approach, a stereotype is an inverted reflection of cultural values, from the psychological perspective, it mirrors repressed desires.

But not all projection is external. In object-relations theory there is also introjection, the process by which an individual internalizes qualities belonging to an external object (in the broadest sense, animate or inanimate, human or not) and claims them for the self (Klein, 1984; Wright, 1984, pp. 79–104). The individual projects the bad and absorbs the good—or tries to, at any rate. The very attempt shows that the subject recognizes that good and evil coexist. In Klein's view, this leaves the individual two options. The first is the "paranoid-schizoid" phase, in which the individual fears the bad and idealizes the good. The second is the "depressive" position, filled with guilt and regret. Klein theorizes that individuals oscillate back and forth between the two positions (pp. 306–343; Wright, 1984, pp. 79–104).

One way to apply object-relations theory critically is by noting that historically Hollywood films have demonstrated the oscillation between two such positions. They alternate from the first position, creating Hispanic stereotypes that project degradation and idealization, to the second position, showing their guilt for having constructed the Other so negatively. This may explain why many Anglo portrayals in Hollywood films with major, or even minor, Hispanic characters are so contradictory. A recurring pattern in these films gives the Hispanic stereotypical traits, if not a clear-cut stereotypical character, while at the same time, littering the landscape with all manner of derogatorily portrayed Anglos. *Bordertown* (1935) is a good example of this (although the same could be said of the films of Lupe Vélez and Dolores Del Río, and of a film such as *Viva Villa!* [1934], and its parody *The Gay Desperado* [1936]). In *Bordertown,* Paul Muni plays Johnny Ramírez, a hard-working but hot-tempered Mexican American who becomes materially successful in the Anglo world, but decides to return to his own people at the end of the film. The Anglos are unfaithful wives; oversexed blondes; fat, dim-witted businessmen; gangsters; and effete, upper-class snobs. There is not a positively portrayed Anglo in the entire film. The film ends with Johnny safely on his way back to the barrio, thus effectively containing the threat of the ethnic Other, but the rest of the film exposes deep cracks in the system, as is discussed in the section on ideology.

Psychoanalytical Perspectives

For the purposes of this study, a stereotype can be classified as a Freudian fetish—an idealized object that acts as a defense mechanism for the individual. For the subject, the fetish is a denial of the lack of a penis in the female and the corresponding threat of castration. Positive stereotyping is a reaction to the sexual threat posed by the social Other. What can be called positive Hispanic stereotypes operate this way. The Latin Lover and the Dark Lady incorporate the duality of the fetish. Sexually motivated, they are at the same time idealized constructs and denials. It is an idealization of sexuality that has the effect of marking an essential difference in the Other.

Lacan's reworking of Freud, via the semiotics of Saussure, links language, psychoanalysis, and socialization (see Benvenuto & Kennedy, 1986; Bowie, 1987; Gallop, 1985; Lacan, 1977; Lacan, 1978; Lemaire, 1977). To the psychological development of the individual and the corresponding creation of the Other, Lacan adds another element: the Mirror Stage, a different, later moment in child development. Occurring between six and eighteen months, Lacan describes it as a transitional phase during which the subject irreversibly passes from one realm, the Imaginary, into another, the Symbolic.

In the prelinguistic, pre-Oedipal Imaginary stage, the subject believes itself to be one with the mother. No separation is perceived between the self and the world and the subject experiences an unalloyed but illusory sense of unity. In the Mirror Stage, the subject begins to move into the Symbolic Order, roughly coincident with the Oedipal crisis and the acquisition of language. Because the passage into the Symbolic requires the acceptance of the loss of unity, the desire for the gone-and-never-to-return oneness is repressed, and the unconscious is created.

One of Lacan's key contributions to stereotyping study is his detailed explanation of the Other, not only as the self's obverse and oppositional defining force, but as the very field (the Symbolic Order, the world of language) where that definition occurs. Thus, the subject is fundamentally and inescapably linked to the Other—even dependent upon it. The subject is locked in a lifelong search for a unified self that can never be achieved. In the Symbolic Order, the subject exists between the two poles of desire (for the wholeness of the Imaginary) and lack (the sobering realization that unification will never be fulfilled). This gives the notion of the positive and negative sides of the Other an added wrinkle. The Other is simultaneously recognized by the subject as both positive (an ideal that may provide unity) and negative (an incomplete entity that can never provide unity). In the Lacanian model, the Other is (temporarily) idealized as the path back to wholeness, until what always happens does happen—the subject realizes that the Other is lacking. In terms of Hispanic stereotypes, it might be speculated that the stereotypes have persisted in cinema—since the earliest years of this century—because they fulfilled a need of the Anglos.

Several of Lacan's other ideas deserve mention. One is the treatment of the text itself as psyche, based on Lacan's famous remark that the unconscious is structured like a language. This gives the critic a rationale for analyzing the text rather than the individual (the author, character, or reader), and offers one solution to problems of applying psychoanalytical theory to texts.

Lacan's concept of the unconscious as an organized, subversive force, different from Freud's whirlpool of drives, is another important development. Theorizing the unconscious as structured, coherent, and operating out of its own logic, Lacan posits that its function is to question the subject endlessly, bringing to the conscious surface desires repressed by the subject's existence in the Symbolic. As in Freud, when the repressed returns it does so in disguise—as dreams, jokes, or memory lapses. But in Lacan, the repressed's return has a more profound implication. It reminds the individual of the endless desire for the Imaginary, and of the aching incompleteness of existence within the Symbolic. Repressed desires may come and go from the unconscious, but desire and repression are permanent. The unconscious, desire, repression, and its return are all inevitable facts of life. The subject moves from one signifier to another, endlessly, seeking completion. It can be argued that stereotyping fits into Lacan's Symbolic Order as one set of signifiers in the endless chain that the subject moves through in its endless search for the Imaginary.

One final idea from Lacan is important particularly when examining the visual medium, and that is scopic drive. Every act of seeing for Lacan is understood as the subject's desire-driven search for wholeness. As one commentator put it, "Unconscious and repression, desire and lack—this dialectical opposition is present in every visual recognition" (Wright, 1984; p. 116). The act of seeing is an act of desire, pure and simple, and is no less so whether what is observed is one's image in a mirror, others, or a Hollywood movie with its typical complement of stereotypes.

Ideological Perspectives: Marxist, Feminist, and Gay

One way to read a stereotype is as a negative mirror of dominant values. To be sure, the sloppy, greasy appearance of *el bandido* in any number of Hollywood westerns, coupled with his nearly psychotic savagery and immorality, reflects poorly on Mexicans and Mexican Americans. But this stereotype—standing in sharp contrast to the Anglo hero—has another effect: it reinforces the cleanliness, sobriety, sanity, overall decency, and moral rectitude of the WASP in the white hat. By extension, then, stereotypes identify, justify, and support mainstream (Anglo) beliefs (Lippmann, 1941, p. 95).

Stereotyping in films slips effortlessly into the existing hegemony, the subtle, naturalizing way the ruling class maintains its dominance over subordinate groups. Viewed as a tool of the dominant ideology, the creation and perpetuation of stereotypes in the movies and in the media function to maintain the status quo by representing dominant groups as "naturally" empowered and marginal groups as disenfranchised. In the case of Hispanics, their portrayal as bandits and buffoons, whores and exotic clowns, Latin Lovers and Dark Ladies marks them as symbols of ethnic exclusion. As Dyer (1984, p. 30) puts it, through stereotyping, ruling groups attempt "to fashion the whole of society according to their own world-view, value-system, sensibility and ideology." As hegemony, stereotypes possess two principal features: ethnocentrism, and the belief in inborn and unalterable psychological characteristics. Hegemony, however, is not static, but active and dynamic, "something that must be ceaselessly built and rebuilt in the face of both implicit and explicit challenges to it." The very existence of subordinated subcultures presents challenges to it.

Althusser's notion of ideology as lived experience providing a means for a subject to define itself, as a compact between an individual and the state wherein each helps to support the other, should be examined here. For, inasmuch as stereotypes create an Otherness that the dominant group uses to create and maintain its own identity, they play an integral part in such a scheme. Thus, stereotyping is one factor among many (economic, political, social) that helps shape the way a subject views the world. It is one clause, if you will, in a lengthy and complex contract between subject and state that attempts to explain, construct, and define the world and the subject's place in it.

When women's place in the dominant system is examined, it is seen that early feminism looked at women's images in the media, and formulated Woman as the male Other—female as a negative male. For example, Ellmann (1968) listed stereotypical traits commonly associated with women (formlessness, passivity, instability, confinement, piety, materiality, spirituality, irrationality, and compliancy). Feminist film and literary theory has progressed well beyond trait identification; still the pattern of representation that Ellmann outlines was a useful and necessary step. More recent work in feminism has placed Woman as an absence within patriarchal discourse: a sheer negative. Much feminist criticism has centered on the import of the gaze, from Irigaray's "specularization" to Mulvey's (1985, p. 804) three gazes connected with the cinema, to those feminist scholars who are investigating the relationship between text and viewer. For our purposes, her theories about the operations of voyeurism and fetishism are of interest. Her ideas about woman's place in the system could be applied to Hispanics, or other stereotyped out-groups for that matter, and is an excellent example of how the psychoanalytical, the ideological, and feminist approaches all intersect at this point:

> Woman . . . stands in patriarchal culture as signifier for the male other, bound by a symbolic order in which man can live out his phantasies and obsessions through linguistic command by imposing them on the silent image of woman still tied to her place as bearer of meaning, not maker of meaning. (Mulvey, 1985, p. 804)

Until they recently made headway into mainstream Hollywood filmmaking, Hispanics, too, were bearers rather than makers of meaning.

There are several ways that cinema offers the male viewer—for our purposes the Anglo male viewer—pleasure. Mulvey (1985) uses Freud's term "scopophilia" to describe how this may apply to films. For one thing, the Anglo male viewer derives pleasure from a gaze that controls the object of his gaze. For another, the cinema screen may function as a mirror and rekindle a remembrance of the mirror stage in the viewer. On the screen, as in the mirror, the spectator may simultaneously lose his ego and reinforce it. Film as a system of representation contains—as all seeing contains—an imploding contradiction. In terms of stereotyping, the Anglo gaze in movies controls the ethnic Other, but recognizes the Other as a threat that must be controlled. Similarly, ethnic Others in films may be seen as victims of the white male gaze, as well as fleeting ego builder/boosters. Film stereotypes demonstrate the same contradictory stance toward ethnics that is often applied to women—"Can't live with 'em, can't live without 'em." As Mulvey (1985) argues, such a contradiction endangers the very unity of the filmmaking apparatus as a formal, cultural, and ideological system. In such films (for example, *Bordertown,* discussed earlier) the Hollywood system of stereotyping brings cinema to the brink of collapse by showing the chinks in the Anglo armor. Like feminist and gay criticism, the analysis of ethnic stereotypes in Hollywood cinema offers the critic a potentially powerful tool for exposing the workings of a film apparatus that persists in creating exclusionary images of the Other—and of the socioeconomic system of which it is a part.

Hispanic Stereotyping

Six Hollywood Stereotypes of the Hispanic

There are six basic Hispanic stereotypes. Most Hispanic characters in film and television have usually been one or another of these six types. Sometimes the stereotypes are combined, sometimes they are altered superficially, but the core, defining characteristics remain remarkably consistent.

By isolating Hispanic stereotypes in this way it becomes possible to see how they may be understood, utilizing the various perspectives discussed above. This list opens comprehension to how stereotypes can be seen as in-group categorizations of the out-group; as symbolic formulations of the Other; as fetishes; as objects in an endless string of lifelong reminders of individual disunity; as socially constructed but psychologically necessary Others; and finally, as hegemony, concrete illustrations of all the dominant is not.

1. El Bandido

The Mexican bandit has already been mentioned. His roots go back to the villains of the silent "greaser" films and he continued to appear in many westerns. Typically, he is treacherous, shifty, and dishonest. His reactions are emotional, irrational, and usually violent; his intelligence is severely limited, resulting in flawed strategies. He is dirty and unkempt—usually displaying an unshaven face; missing teeth; and disheveled, oily hair. A modern incarnation of this type, the Latin American drug runner, shows superficial changes in the stereotype without altering its essence. He is slicker, of course, and he has traded his black hat for a white suit and his tired horse for a glitzy Porsche, yet he is still driven to satisfy base cravings—for money, power, and sexual pleasure—and routinely employs vicious and illegal means to obtain them. From the halfbreed villain in *Broncho Billy and the Greaser* (1914) to Andy Garcia's sadistic Cuban American gangster in *Eight Million Ways to Die* (1986), the Hispanic bandit is a demented, despicable creature who must be punished for his brutal behavior. Other versions of the bandit stereotype include Latin American rebel leaders, corrupt dictators, and inner-city youth gang members.

2. The Halfbreed Harlot

The corresponding female stereotype is a familiar stock figure in the American cinema, particularly in westerns. Like the bandit, she is a secondary character, and not always a halfbreed. She is lusty and hot-tempered, and her main function, as Pettit (1980) wrote in *Images of the Mexican American in Fiction and Film*, is "to provide as much sexual titillation as current censorship standards will permit." Doc Holliday's woman Chihuahua (Linda Darnell), in John Ford's *My Darling Clementine* (1946), is a classic example of this type. Without a man she is a leaf in the wind, so when Doc is out of town and Wyatt Earp (Henry Fonda) doesn't respond to her flirtations, she helps to cheat him during a poker game. The Halfbreed Harlot is a slave to her passions; her character is based on the premise that she is a nymphomaniac. In true stereotypical fashion, motivation for her actions is not given—she is a prostitute because she likes the work, not because social or economic forces have shaped her life.

3. The Male Buffoon

This is the second banana comic relief: Pancho in "The Cisco Kid"; Sgt. Garcia in Walt Disney's "Zorro"; Ricky Ricardo in "I Love Lucy"; and Leo Carrillo's characters in his many roles in 1930s films. In this case (as with the female counterpart, described next), many of the same stereotypical characteristics that are threatening in the Bandit are made targets of ridicule here. In the case of these stereotypes, comedy is a way of dealing with the Hispanic male's and the Hispanic female's stereotypically accentuated differences, a way of taming their fearful qualities. What is funny about this character is his simple-mindedness (the bumbling antics of Sgt. Garcia), his failure to master standard English ("Let's went, Cisco!"), his childish regression into emotionality (Ricky's explosions into Spanish).

4. The Female Clown

The Male Buffoon's female counterpart, the Female Clown, represents a way of neutralizing the overt sexual threat posed by the Halfbreed Harlot. The strategy is to negate the Latin female's eroticism by making her an object of comic derision. A key example is the film career of the beautiful Mexican actress Lupe Vélez, a comic star in Hollywood in the 1930s. Best known for her role as the dizzy "Mexican Spitfire" in a series of eight films, she also starred in a number of other comedies. Vélez's Mexican Spitfire was an alluring dingbat, her antics causing baroque plot complications, which were not unraveled until the last reel. Vélez's other film roles play interesting variations on the Female Clown theme. In *Palooka* (1934), for example, she is a Big City Vamp, a Latin gold digger who lures the rural prize-fighting champ, Joe Palooka (Stu Erwin), into a life of fast-lane dissipation. Once again, her emotionalism and her inability to restrain her baser instincts—indeed, she is controlled by them—conform with the common representation of Hollywood's stereotypical Hispanic woman.

Another well-known Female Clown is Carmen Miranda, with her colorful portrayals of Latin American women in many films in the 1940s. What is operative here is exaggeration, another way to elicit derisive laughter and neutralize the feminine Other. Miranda's multicolored costumes and fruit-covered hats, worn in splashy "Latin" musical numbers, were an instant parody of the folkloric costumes (and customs) of Latin America. Miranda's "Lady in the Tutti-Frutti Hat" number from Busby Berkeley's *The Gang's All Here* (1943) is a campy example of the good neighbor policy that was in the United States' and Hollywood's interest to foster during World War II. Furthermore, it was illustrative of the comic exoticism and eroticism attributed to the Hispanic Female Clown.

*   *   *

Psychologically speaking, these four negative stereotypes are projections of the "bad" self. But, as mentioned earlier, there are also positive stereotypes. What is important to remember is that although positive stereotypes emphasize traits highly regarded by the in-group, these images are still stereotypes—still overgeneralized simplifications that depict the Other as outside the acceptable. From a Lacanian perspective, they represent that moment when the subject perceives a signifier that can provide wholeness. In American movies, these positive Hispanic stereotypes have typically taken two forms: the Latin Lover and the Dark Lady.

5. The Latin Lover

This stereotype we owe to one star: Rudolph Valentino. An Italian immigrant, in 1921 he had worked his way up from minor movie parts to a starring role as the protagonist in *The Four Horsemen of the Apocalypse,* a story of the effect of World War I on young Argentinean men. In its famous tango scene, Valentino dances seductively with a woman and finishes by flinging her to the ground. With this and other roles as the dashing and magnetic male Other (in *The Sheik* [1921], *Son of the Sheik* [1926], and as the rising bullfighter in *Blood and Sand* [1922]), he began to define a new kind of screen lover and an Other way of making screen love. Since then, the Latin Lover has been a remarkably consistent screen figure, played by a number of Latin actors, from Cesar Romero, Ricardo Montalbán, Gilbert Roland, and Fernando Lamas to Gabriel Byrne's recent version in *Siesta* (1987), all maintaining the erotic combination of characteristics instituted by Valentino: suavity and sensuality, tenderness and sexual danger.

6. The Dark Lady

She is mysterious, virginal, inscrutable, aristocratic—and alluring precisely because of these characteristics. Her cool distance is what makes her so fascinating to Anglo males. She is circumspect and aloof, whereas her Anglo sister is direct and forthright; she is reserved, whereas the Anglo is boisterous; she is opaque, whereas the Anglo woman is transparent. The characters that Mexican actress Dolores Del Río played in a number of Hollywood films in the 1930s and early 1940s exemplified this stereotype well. In both *Flying Down to Rio* (1933) and *In Caliente* (1935), for example, she played the fascinating Latin woman who aroused the American leading men's amorous appetites the way no Anglo woman could. By making both the Latin Lover and the Dark Lady embodiments of sexual characteristics manifestly lacking in the Anglo, Hollywood stereotyped and marginalized by idealization.

Other Stereotypes

There are other, often-seen Hispanic stereotypes in Hollywood cinema. The Wise Old Man who speaks in the measured and resigned voice of experience is one. Another is what Pettit (1980) calls the Fat Mama, the solicitous and long-suffering mother hen. A third is the Poor Peon, the downtrodden and much put-upon common laborer or fieldhand. These are not explored here because they are not, in essence, Hispanic, but rather are rooted in stereotypes of the aged, women, and the poor.

Understanding the Stereotypes

The purpose of reviewing critical stances and outlining these stereotypes is not to reduce their study and understanding to the mere recognition of one or another of the types or their combinations. Rather, it is important to concentrate on Hollywood's pattern of attributing differential traits to a group, in this case Hispanics, and the implications of such attributions.

As Wilson and Gutiérrez (1985) have noted, minorities are typically represented as irrational, prone to violence, lacking in intellectual sophistication, oversexed, morally lax, and dirty. It is these characteristics that should be sought and examined. The fact that they usually conveniently appear as discrete stereotypes makes finding them easier, but should not obscure deeper, more fundamentally troubling issues—such as, why does stereotyping continue decade after decade, and in what ways are the stereotypes masked? The object of the game is not simply spotting stereotypes, but analyzing the system that endorses them. Once minority representations are seen and understood for what they are, the invisible architecture of the dominant-dominated "arrangement" is exposed and there is a chance for a structural "rearrangement."

The concept of hegemony must be scrutinized along the lines suggested by Ryan (1988, p. 485), who proposes that ideological analyses of films require a double reading. They need to be read as disclosing the shape of ideology, to be sure, but they also need to be seen as records of threats to ideological control and dominance. Hegemony, Ryan argues, is a box that attempts to contain resistance, to keep the ideological lid on. Hegemony is, thus, an unstable process, "a blanket thrown over a tiger" of opposition. "Ideology is not domination," Ryan (1988, p. 485) says, "it is, rather, the resistance of resistance." From such a perspective, the continued instances of ethnic stereotyping reveal hegemony at work. Over and over again, stereotyping hegemony tries to maintain ethnic differences that diminish the Other and redefine the norm. The very persistence of such imagery is revelatory of deep-seated problems within the system.

The Hispanic Image Today: Repeated,
Blended, Countered, and Distorted

By and large, Hispanic stereotypes, and the traits that define them, essentially have not changed over the decades. Rather, they exist as repetitive variations played upon too-familiar themes. There have been numerous cinematic examples of combinations of these six stereotypes, but such stereotypic blends are still one-dimensional, formulaic characters. In *Colors* (1988), for example, Maria Conchita Alonso's Mexican American woman is a mixture of the Dark Lady (in the first part of the film where she is the love interest for Sean Penn's Anglo cop) and the Harlot (when she becomes the mistress of one of the gang leaders to spite the cop and demonstrate how little he understood the realities of the barrio). Through it all, she never quite becomes a self-determining woman, but remains a two-headed stock character and Hollywood plot device—a standard feminine fixture in a well-worn formula.

More recently, though, a handful of Hispanic images are slowly breaking with the stereotypes. This is because more Hispanics have become involved behind the camera and are shaping their own imagery.

Countering the Stereotypes: A Problematic Stage

In the last ten years or so, there has been a gradual change in the images of Hispanics in U.S. films, stemming both from Hispanic filmmakers working within the industry and from a demonstrable market for films treating Hispanic themes. Hollywood and Chicano film first came together in an uneasy alliance when Universal Studios backed the production of Luis Valdez's successful stage play *Zoot Suit*. The film had a limited success, but established a Hollywood precedent upon which Valdez and other Hispanic filmmakers would build.

Beyond its merits as a film—which are not inconsiderable—*Zoot Suit* set the stage for a new era in the history of Hispanic images in Hollywood cinema. The recent explosion of films with Hispanic themes marks an important watershed, because never before had Hollywood seen so many Hispanics in key creative, decision-making positions. With Valdez's *La Bamba* (1987), Cheech Marin's *Born in East L.A.* (1987), Ramon Menendez's *Stand and Deliver* (1988), and Robert Redford and Moctesuma Esparza's *The Milagro Beanfield War* (1988), Hispanics were for the first time having a say in the creation of their images. The next question to be asked is a hard one: Do these films manage to break with dominant Hollywood stereotypes of Hispanics or do they perpetuate them?

An inspirational, "go for it" film such as *Stand and Deliver* seems to be a clear-cut case of stereotype breaking and culture affirmation. And, although far from a perfect film, so does *The Milagro Beanfield War*. If nothing else, it should be lauded for giving the Chicano characters self-actualization and a richly varied social-cultural context. As a matter of fact, *Beanfield* ends up stereotyping Anglos through its portrayals of the greedy land developer, his blonde floozy, and the villainous enforcer. Much more troublesome are films such as *Born in East L.A.*, which could easily be perceived as placing the Male Buffoon in the foreground against the backdrop of an insensitively depicted Mexico.

Even the enormously popular *La Bamba*, which was released in both English and Spanish versions and grossed over $50 million, is problematic for the viewer charting

Hispanic stereotypes. Some questions about *La Bamba* must be asked in order to demonstrate some of the complexities involved in decoding the work of an Hispanic filmmaker. First, what is the relationship in *La Bamba* between Ritchie and his heritage? There is a continuous tension in the film between Ritchie's attachment to his class, cultural, and ethnic roots on the one hand (his humble beginnings toiling in the fields, his devotion to his mother and his family, his discovery of his Indo-Hispanic lineage in Mexico) and his transformation into a nonthreatening middle-class American teenager on the other (his ignorance of Spanish, his decision to Americanize his name, his blonde Anglo girlfriend). In telling a Mexican American version of the American Dream, has Valdez given viewers a culturally watered-down hero? Is the film an "only in America story," therefore a celebration of a system that allows a poor Chicano kid to go from field laborer to rock star? Is such a story a demonstration of how quickly success follows acculturation? Or is Valdez simply making a movie, based on fact, that accurately recounts the assimilation experience in America?

In defense of the film, it could be said that it shows that Ritchie pays with his life for his blind assimilation. Furthermore, it could be asked why a movie like *La Bamba* needs to be a Mexican American story at all. Why couldn't it simply be a movie about the early days of rock 'n' roll? Does Ritchie Valens need to be portrayed as a symbol of the Chicano experience? Can't he simply be a human and shed all his cultural and ethnic baggage? Must every film by a minority filmmaker be a pointed statement about race and ethnicity? These questions show that, although the ascendance of Hispanic filmmakers—writers, directors, producers, actors, and other technicians—in Hollywood has created an unprecedented era in the history of Hispanic images in American film, it is a two-sided opportunity.

Distorted Images

Finally, one of the most disturbing turns Hispanic cinematic imagery has taken is its degeneration into an unrecognizable, nonhuman form. The general thesis of this author is that "Aliens" in recent science fiction films are a representation of real-life aliens, and the ethnic Other is disguised as an extraterrestrial. The strain felt in American society by the influx of foreign peoples to our shores, and the new immigration law results in the cinematic representation of Aliens in a host of films from *Close Encounters* (1976) and *Aliens* (1986) to *The Terminator* (1984) and many others. If the Aliens stand as representations of actual aliens, then these films are interesting examples of a sort of neonativism at work, because, by and large, the Aliens are either destroyed or sent back where they came. And, because Hispanics make up the majority of all aliens, naturalized and undocumented, by extension, this new screen image is worrisome indeed. As stated elsewhere (Berg, 1988), the implications of this sort of symbolic distortion are extremely disturbing.

Conclusion: Effects of the Stereotypes

Stereotypes have been examined as believed categories, and the effect of stereotyping on the stereotyped must be stressed. One of the saddest aspects of stereotyping is that out-group members may begin to believe and accept the stereotype. As Dyer (1984) argues, one damaging effect of stereotyping is that the in-group defines the out-group for both in-group and out-group. As a stereotype may serve in-group members by reinforcing the belief of their "natural" superiority over the typed out-group, it is thought also to work on out-group members, causing them to view themselves as they are portrayed by the in-group. Imagine what Hispanic viewers— both inside and outside the U.S. (or for that matter people of color elsewhere in the world)—think when they watch *Raiders of the Lost Ark* and see in the film's opening ten minutes the dashing Anglo hero betrayed four different times by Hispanic underlings. Couldn't this be insidious reaffirmation of a true power structure and an existing social order?

Stereotyping of Hispanics continues; we have only begun to grasp its significance.

NOTES

Reprinted by permission of the publisher from the *Howard Journal of Communications*, Vol. 2, no. 3 (Summer 1990), pp. 286–300.

REFERENCES

Benvenuto, B., & Kennedy, R. (1986). *The Works of Jacques Lacan.* New York: St. Martin's Press.

Berg, C. R. (1988, March). *Extra terrestrials and Simpson-Rodino: Science fiction's alien 'other' as Hispanic imagery.* Changing Images of the U.S. Hispanic in Film Conference, Cornell University, Ithaca, NY.

Bowie, M. (1987). *Freud, Proust and Lacan: Theory as fiction.* Cambridge: Cambridge University Press.

Dyer, R. (1984). Stereotyping. In R. Dyer (Ed.), *Gays and film* (rev. ed., p. 30). New York: Zaetrope.

Ellmann, M. (1968). *Thinking about women.* New York: Harcourt, Brace & World.

Gallop, J. (1985). *Reading Lacan.* Ithaca, NY: Cornell University Press.

Gilman, S. L. (1985). *Difference and pathology: Stereotypes of sexuality, race, and madness* (pp. 16–21). Ithaca, NY: Cornell University Press.

Gledhill, C. (1985). Recent developments in feminist criticism. In G. Mast & M. Cohen (Eds.), *Film theory and criticism: Introductory readings* (2nd ed., pp. 817–845). New York: Oxford University Press.

Keller, G. D. (1985). The image of the Chicano in Mexican, United States, and Chicano cinema: An overview. In G. D. Keller (Ed.), *Chicano cinema: Research, reviews, and resources* (pp. 13–15). Binghamton, NY: Bilingual Review/Press.

Klein, M. (1984). *Love, guilt and reparation and other works, 1921–1945* (pp. 306–343). New York: The Free Press.

Lacan, J. (1977). *Ecrits.* New York: W. W. Norton.

Lacan, J. (1978). *The four fundamental concepts of psycho-analysis.* New York: W. W. Norton.

Lemaire, A. (1977). *Jacques Lacan.* London: Routledge & Kegan Paul.

Lippmann, W. (1941). *Public opinion.* New York: Macmillan. (Original work published 1922).

Miller, A. G. (1982). Historical and contemporary perspectives on stereotyping. In A. G. Miller (Ed.), *In the eye of the beholder: Contemporary issues in stereotyping* (p. 27). New York: Praeger.

Mulvey, L. (1985). Visual pleasure and narrative cinema. In G. Mast & Cohen (Eds.), *Film theory and criticism: Introductory readings* (3rd ed., p. 804). New York: Oxford University Press.

Pettit, A. G. (1980). *Images of the Mexican American in fiction and film.* College Station, TX: Texas A & M University Press.

Royce, A. P. (1982). *Ethnic identity: Strategies of diversity* (p. 158). Bloomington, IN: Indiana University Press.

Ryan, M. (1988). The politics of film: Discourse, psychoanalysis, ideology. In C. Nelson & L. Grossberg (Eds.), *Marxism and the interpretation of culture* (p. 485). Urbana, IL: University of Illinois Press.

Seiter, E. (1986). Stereotypes and the media: A re-evaluation. *Journal of Communication, 36*(2), 14–26.

Treviño, J. S. (1984). Latin portrayals in film and television. *Jump Cut,* 30:15–16.

Wilson, C. C., & Gutiérrez, F. (1985). *Minorities in the media.* Newbury Park, CA: Sage.

Woll, A. L. (1980a). Bandits and lovers: Hispanic images in American film. In R. M. Miller (Ed.), *The kaleidoscope lens: How Hollywood views ethnic groups* (pp. 54–72). Englewood, NJ: James S. Ozer.

Woll, A. L. (1980b). *The Latin image in American film* (rev. ed.). Los Angeles, CA: UCLA Latin American Center Publications.

Woll, A. L., & Miller, R. M. (1987). *Ethnic and racial images in American film and television: Historical essays and bibliography.* New York: Garland.

Wood, R. (1985). An introduction to the American horror film. In B. Nichols (Ed.), *Movies and methods: Vol. II* (p. 199). Berkeley, CA: University of California Press.

Wright, E. (1984). *Psychoanalytic criticism: Theory and practice* (pp. 79–104). New York: Methuen.

7

Chicanas in Film: History of an Image

Carlos E. Cortés

In the 1952 western classic *High Noon,* Helen Ramírez, mistress to many and conscience to all in the film's small frontier town, lit up the screen with her strength, intelligence, and articulateness. As brilliantly portrayed by Mexican actress Katy Jurado, Ramírez established what may be the high water mark of screen portrayals of Chicanas (Mexican-American women). While it would be stretching the point to say that it has been all downhill since then, the history of screen Chicanas has seldom risen beyond a low-level roller coaster. Even within the larger context of women in films—not itself a consistently elevating story—Chicanas generally have fared less well than their Anglo or even their Black sisters.[1]

In the following pages I will briefly trace the historical development of the Chicana screen image. However, before embarking on this historical excursion, I need to address a few of the analytical issues involved in assessing ethnic media depictions in general and Chicana images in particular.

General Problems of Media Image Analysis

The process of filmic image creation involves three basic components—filmmaking, film content, and film impact. Considered within an educational framework, filmmakers function as teachers (intentionally or unintentionally), films serve as their resulting textbooks (effective or ineffective), and viewers are the learners (consciously or subconsciously). Filmmakers create films with Chicana, Mexicana, and Hispana characters. The films present these images to viewers, whether or not the filmmakers intended to contribute to the creation of a Chicana image. While not always consciously, some viewers will learn about Chicanas from those so-called entertainment films, and this learning may help create, reinforce, weaken, or eradicate their images of the Chicana.

PHOTO 7.1   **High Noon.** The romantic triangle between Katy Jurado, as Helen Ramírez, Gary Cooper, and Grace Kelly is clearly illustrated in this scene from *High Noon*. According to Cortés, Ramírez is a woman of ill-repute, who nonetheless maintains her independence, strength of will, dignity, and ability to act decisively and is the person who best understands the moral and ethical conflicts facing the western town. (Courtesy of The Museum of Modern Art Film Stills Archive)

(Viewers' images encompass knowledge about, perceptions of, misinformation concerning, attitudes toward, and understanding and misunderstanding of Chicanas.)

In media research, these three facets of image creation generally involve distinct forms of analysis: control analysis—examinations of the factors that influence a film and the process of making films; content analysis—examination of the completed films, the textbooks in creating images; and impact analysis—examination of the actual influence of the films on the images that develop in the minds of viewers.

Most historical studies of ethnic images in films have emphasized content analysis, for good reason. The evidence is relatively concrete—celluloid documents which can be studied directly, if they have not yet disintegrated (the fate of about half of all pre-1950 U.S. films). Some scholars have engaged in control analysis, studying the actions of individual filmmakers or the social forces that have contributed to the continuing or changing filmic portrayals of ethnic groups. Here the evidence ranges from studio archives to personal collections, from journalistic accounts to interviews, from autobiographies to cultural histories.

Comparatively few scholars have conducted impact analysis—how motion pictures have affected the way Americans learn of, think about, feel toward, and even respond to persons of different ethnic backgrounds. In terms of social significance, this may be the most important area of image analysis. Yet, from a historical perspective, it is the most difficult area to assess.

Social and behavioral scientists have developed research methods which purport to measure media impact on viewers by directly studying the viewers themselves in somewhat controlled situations. Those who have directly assessed the impact of ethnic portrayals in films (and television) have demonstrated that these entertainment-coated textbooks really do teach, although we cannot predict with certainty what any specific individual will learn. For example, in a pioneering study during the 1930s, Ruth C. Peterson and L. L. Thurstone discovered that the viewing of the classic silent film *The Birth of a Nation* (1915), which included derogatory depictions of Blacks, increased student prejudice toward Black Americans.[2] Irwin C. Rosen found that the anti-anti-Semitic film *Gentlemen's Agreement* (1947) improved student attitudes toward Jews, even though most of the tested students stated that the film *had not* changed their attitudes.[3] More recently, psychologist Bradley S. Greenberg reported that 40 percent of the white children he was studying believed that television accurately portrayed Blacks, even when these shows contrasted with their own personal experiences with Blacks.[4]

Such studies have revealed the powerful impact of media ethnic depictions by examining viewers available to scholars under controlled conditions at a certain time and place. But pity the poor historian. We who deal in the past, short of receiving a time capsule helping hand from H. G. Wells, have no way of directly studying the reactions of past viewers in any broad, rigorous, or historically continuous manner. We cannot, for example, ascertain the precise impact of the "greaser" films of the 1910s, although these films undoubtedly had an impact, in light of the entire body of research on the effect of media on ethnic image formation. At best, we can find fragmentary evidence of that impact on observed audiences, tested groups, and selected individuals, such as film reviewers and columnists.[5] Therefore, we can only reconstruct the history of the images being projected (and the factors contributing to their creation) through content analysis and then hypothesize how those film images are likely to have affected viewers' images.

Content Analysis of Chicana Images

Such analytical problems plague any scholar dealing with the history of film images. In the case of the Chicana, the problems become even more complex in both analyzing content and hypothesizing impact.

The first problem confronting the would-be analyst of Chicana depictions is ascertaining just exactly who on screen is a Chicana.[6] Sometimes no problem exists. In films like *Boulevard Nights* (1979) and *Walk Proud* (1979), which focus on Mexican-American barrios, we can assume that the young ladies with the Spanish surnames are most likely Chicanas. But it is not always that easy. Take three types of character-defining problem areas—Chicanas and American Indians, Chicanas and Mexicans (Mexican women), and Chicanas and other United States Latinas.

How about American Indians, such as Pearl Chávez in the 1946 epic *Duel in the Sun?* She is often referred to disparagingly as a "half-breed," but what exactly is her background? Does she have some Mexican ancestry, which might make her classifiable both as a Native American and as a Chicana?

How about the aforementioned Helen Ramírez and the host of other border Mexicans? Are they Mexican Americans (by birth or by naturalization) or are they Mexicans temporarily living in the United States? In Helen Ramírez' case, as in many western films, this is not an important distinction, due to the fluidity of border life. In some cases, the analytical distinction between Chicanas and Mexicanas simply cannot be made because the film fails to provide sufficient evidence. However, in the many films about Mexico *per se*, such as *Viva Zapata!* (1952), *Vera Cruz* (1954), and *The Professionals* (1966), it would be silly to classify the Mexican female characters as Chicanas.

How about differentiating Chicanas from other United States Latinas? In some films with Spanish-surnamed characters, the specific national origin is either identified or suggested by context. Generally, the filmic rule goes as follows: if it's Los Angeles, she must be Chicana; in New York, consider her Puerto Rican; in Miami, clearly Cubana. Simple, obvious, but, in truth, misleading considering the growing intra-Hispanic diversity in each of these cities. When you get to Chicago, Detroit, or Kansas City, you might as well toss a dart at a map of Latin America when it comes to using surnames or physical appearance as a method for trying to ascertain if a specific character is a Chicana. In many films, particularly those set in a contemporary urban context, Hispanic national origin is fuzzy or unspecified.

In short, the simple process of identifying who is a Chicana and who is not has its gray areas. But does all this really matter? Yes, if your concern is merely content analysis and you seek the precision of separable, distinct categories. No, if your concern is impact analysis or, speaking historically, assessing the potential impact of films on the viewing public. When it comes to Chicanas, viewer learning may result not only from the distinct depictions of Chicanas, but also from more general film depictions—of women, of ethnic women, of male and female Mexican Americans and Mexicans, and of Latinos and Latinas in general.

The Assessing of Potential Impact

Casual moviegoers or TV watchers do not concern themselves with the fine categorical issues of content analysis. They usually want to be entertained, distracted, absorbed, stimulated, or diverted.[7] It is the rare viewer indeed who consciously attempts to intellectually separate Chicanas from Mexicanas, other Latinas, or Spanish-surnamed American Indian women. For this reason—the fact that film depictions simply wash over and incidentally influence the image formation of most viewers—the broader themes of Mexicana and Latina portrayals become particularly significant for the assessment of the potential impact of films in creating a Chicana image.

This process applies not just to Chicanas and other United States Latinas. Think of the films you have seen that have characters with Eastern European surnames. When viewing these films, did you constantly attempt to distinguish Polish Americans from Slovakian Americans from Serbian Americans from Hungarian Americans from Romanian Americans from White Russian Americans? If you did, then you are truly an exception. It is more likely that this diversity of Eastern European–American portrayals has left an undifferentiated image of people with "odd" surnames, heavy accents, boisterous weddings, factory coveralls, bowling bags, and torn T-shirts in its wake.[8]

While in content analysis we can analytically separate the Black African image in Tarzan movies (or other movies set in Africa) from Black American images in films set in the United States, such a separation loses its validity in assessing the potential impact of these films on viewers' perceptions of American Blacks.[9] The same applies to Asians and Asian Americans in film. They are usually separable for purposes of content analysis, but are inseparable for purposes of assessment of potential impact.[10]

Finally, despite its teaching power, film does not operate alone. It functions as part of the total media curriculum, which includes such other components as television, newspapers, magazines, radio, and books. Moreover, the media provide only one element of the total educational process of a society. In our nation, in fact in all nations, two parallel curricula exist. In addition to the school curriculum, there operates the societal curriculum, that massive ongoing informal curriculum of family, peer groups, neighborhoods, churches, organizations, occupations, and other socializing forces that "educate" all of us throughout our lives.[11]

The mass media, of course, comprise a powerful element of that societal curriculum. Because films have influenced social perception—accurate or inaccurate, for better or for worse—the study of ethnic film images and their teaching potential rises above an ivory tower exercise in content analysis and becomes a scholarly issue of societal importance. With these observations in mind, let us turn to a brief overview of the history of the filmic treatment of Chicanas (as well as Mexicanas and other Latinas).[12] As we proceed, we must keep in mind that we cannot specify with precision the degree or nature of these films' impact, but we can be certain that an impact has occurred.

For purposes of periodization, the filmic depiction of Chicanas can be divided into four general eras. During the silent era, roughly from the turn of the century until about 1930, Chicanas usually served as passive adjuncts to the main action of films. During the second era, from about 1930 to the end of World War II, Chicana and other United States Latina characters began to move into center screen, but with limited diversity and little depth of characterization. In the third era, running from 1945 through the 1960s, although the number of Chicana film characters remained severely limited, they more often emerged as real people, sometimes with depth and power. Beginning around 1970, Chicanas and other United States Latinas entered a fourth phase, one in which they appeared more often, but were usually depicted merely as Spanish-surnamed assimilated Americans. Whether that phase is still continuing or whether we have entered a new phase of depictions, only future historical retrospect will clarify.[13]

Chicanas and Mexicanas as Film Adjuncts (1900-1930)

During the first three decades of motion pictures in the United States, Chicana characters—for that matter, Mexicanas and other Latinas in both the United States and Latin America—did not fare well, generally having little importance on the silver screen. In part, this resulted from the film marginality of Latinos, both men and women. In part, it resulted from the film marginality of women. And in part, it resulted from the special function that Chicanas served when they did appear in films.

During the early years of motion pictures, Mexican Americans in general took a real beating. Film titles reflected a widespread Hollywood stance toward the use of Mexican Americans, especially men, as film characters—*The Greaser's Gauntlet* (1908), *Tony the Greaser* (1911), *Broncho Billy and the Greaser* (1914), *The Greaser's Revenge* (1914), and *The Girl and the Greaser* (1915). And these were just the titles! As one scholar has pointed out, in the early days of U.S. motion pictures, the Mexican American served as a "convenient villain," particularly in westerns.[14] But lest this lead to the misunderstanding that Mexican Americans were singularly victimized, it must be pointed out that during this same era films were being made with such titles as *A Nigger in the Woodpile* (1904), *That Chink at Golden Gulch* (1910), and *Coon Town Suffragettes* (1914). Minorities in general, then, were acceptable movie targets as despicable villains, helpless incompetents, or society's clowns.

During the 1920s, Latin America, which had become an expanding market for U.S. motion pictures, began to protest the filmic degrading of Latinos. Many Latin American nations spoke out against negative stereotyping, particularly the villainous depiction of Latino men. Several governments went so far as to ban U.S. films that presented such derogatory depictions of Latinos.[15]

To a degree this strategy worked. Hollywood took steps, albeit insufficient and often misdirected ones, to clean up its Latino act. After *Guns and Greasers* (1918), greasers disappeared from film titles, though not from films. Not wanting to totally bury Latino villains, who had proven to be great box office attractions in the United States, but also not wanting to jeopardize the growing Latin American market, studios came up with a variety of strategies. One ploy was to invent fictional countries, so that governments could not point to these movies as dealing with specific Latin American nations; for example, the nation of Costa Roja in *The Dove* (1928). A second strategy: in films set in Latin America, be sure to include good Latinos (usually light-skinned Spanish types) along with the traditional bad Latinos (usually dark-skinned mestizos or Indian types).

What about Mexican-American women during the early silent era? There were Mexicana villains too, as in *The Red Girl* (1908). But, for the most part, the Chicana role was more benign than that of Chicanos, reflecting to a degree the interethnic sexual double standard that became a criterion for movies. This double standard held that filmic interethnic sexual relations between whites and non-whites was bad. Should it occur, it must end in failure, preferably tragedy. That informal guideline became explicit in the 1930 Motion Picture Production Code, better known as the Hays Code, that dominated U.S.-made films from the early 1930s until the mid-1950s (although not officially buried until 1966). The code read, in part, "*Miscegenation* (sex relationship between the white and black races) is forbidden."[16]

The application of this filmic taboo to white-Black, white-Asian, and white-Indian love relationships was reasonably clear and consistent. However, where Latinos were involved, the diverse, racially mixed nature of Latino ethnicity created both complications and special options. So, the Latino variant went like this:

It was not permissible for greasers—dark-skinned Mexican or other Latino men—to have successful love affairs with Anglo women. (Throughout this article, the term "Anglo" is used generically, not ethnically, to refer to all white Americans of non-Hispanic European ancestry.) The unrestrained lust of swarthy Latinos and the threat this implied for Anglo womanhood commonly established a film menace from which Anglo heroes could rescue their damsels. Since as every good Hollywooder knew, Mexican gentlemen prefer blondes, or, for that matter, any Anglo woman over Mexican women, this threat became both logical and repetitive in the western genre, which made up a large proportion of silent films. One of the grand ironies of interethnic movie history is that the so-called "Latin lovers" were seldom Latin American characters, but instead they were usually Italian or Spanish. Mexican immigrant film star Ramón Novarro, the archetype Latin lover, rarely played a Latin American.[17]

However, things changed when genders were reversed. While Mexican men could not win the hand of Anglo women (although a few light-skinned Spanish-type men did), Anglo men could be successful with Mexican women. A giant step for interethnic democracy? Not quite.

In most of these cases, the Mexican women turned out to be relatively light skinned (black hair was acceptable), somewhat cultured (for a Latina), and usually of good Spanish or at least elite Latino background. Not just any Mexican woman would do for an Anglo hero, only classy light-skinned Mexicanas; dark-skinned ones need not apply. What would become a traditional Latina niche was reserved for dark Mexicanas—prostitution or, at least, flexible virtue, usually blended with a suitably fiery temper (what Puerto Rican actress Rita Moreno has called the "Yonkee Peeg" school of acting).[18]

Moreover, in keeping with the filmic pattern of asserting Anglo ethnic superiority, the Anglo hero usually won the light-skinned Mexican woman from a dark-skinned Mexican man, your standard, useful-but-disposable Indianized Mexican greaser. Films like *The Mexican's Revenge* (1909), *His Mexican Bride* (1909), *The Mexican's Jealousy* (1910), *Carmenita the Faithful* (1911), and *The Aztec Treasure* (1914) carried through this theme. Sometimes, out of love for Anglos, Mexicanas even turned against their own families, as in *His Mexican Sweetheart* (1912) and *Chiquita, the Dancer* (1912). This interethnic double standard was also extended to other parts of Latin America, such as to Panama in *The Ne'er Do-Well* (1923), further south to Argentina in *Argentine Love* (1924), and even to fictitious South American nations like Paragonia in *The Americano* (1916). Film Chicanas, Mexicanas, and other Latinas, then, served mainly as passive sexual goals to be sought by active Anglo heroes and as living proof of Anglo superiority over Latino men.

Sensuality and Frivolity (1930-1945)

The 1932 Presidential election of Franklin D. Roosevelt led to the establishment of the Latin American Good Neighbor policy, in which Hollywood was to play a role. Moreover, social disruption in Europe, culminating in World War II, deprived Hollywood of a major film market, increased the economic significance of Latin American audiences, and made Hollywood more sensitive to Latin American reactions. Once the United States entered the war, Latin America's strategic importance prompted the U.S. government to encourage Hollywood to be an even better neighbor.

A few examples of these changes illustrate this policy. MGM obtained Mexican government script approval for *Viva Villa!* (1934), although one would never know this from viewing the violent, ludicrously macho final product. The U.S. Office of the Coordinator of Inter-American Affairs, under Director Nelson Rockefeller, stressed the need for U.S. motion pictures to help solidify the Americas in the common struggle against the Axis powers. The Hays Office, Hollywood's official self-censor, appointed a Latin American expert to help Hollywood avoid filmic blunders which might offend Latin Americans.[19]

There were some positive results. Such 1930s films as *Juárez* (1939), despite its historical inaccuracies, and *Bordertown* (1935), despite its patronizing view of Chicanos, at least reflected efforts to provide a more serious examination of Latinos (although in *Bordertown*, Johnny Ramírez' love affair with an Anglo woman predictably ends in the mandatory tragedy). Later, in films made during World War II, Latinos fought and died alongside their Anglo comrades. In fact, Hollywood's wartime "affirmative action" policy resulted in assigning a variety of recognizable ethnic characters, often including a Latino, to each filmic military unit in order to demonstrate all-American togetherness. Of course, not all ethnics made it. Blacks, for example, were almost totally segregated from World War II–era war movies (as they were segregated within the real-life military services), not to be admitted into filmdom's version of World War II until later in such films as *Home of the Brave* (1949), *The Dirty Dozen* (1967), and *Force 10 from Navarone* (1978). In the surge of World War II–spawned anti-prejudice films, a Chicano actually won an Anglo girl in the exceptional *A Medal for Benny* (1945).

So much for Mexican Americans and Latinos in general. How did these developments affect the depiction of Chicanas? Here there was both good and bad news. The good news was that Latinas, particularly Mexicanas, achieved a more extensive screen presence. The bad news was that this greater quantitative presence did not translate into either diversity or depth of portrayals.

Two characteristics stood out in most front-line film depictions of Latinas in the 1930s and early 1940s—frivolity and sensuality. Those characteristics are personified by the three leading identifiably Latina actresses of that period—Carmen Miranda, Dolores Del Río, and Lupe Vélez.[20] (I am omitting from consideration those Latina actresses with non-Hispanic professional names, who therefore were not readily identifiable as Latinas by their mere presence. For example, audiences did not view Rita Hayworth as Margarita Cansino, thereby enabling this Hispanic actress to essay a much greater variety of screen roles and identities. The same applies today to such Latina-background actresses as Raquel Welch, Catherine Bach, and Linda Carter, who played the title role in the 1983 television docudrama *Rita Hayworth—The Love Goddess*.)

The high-voltage Brazilian actress Carmen Miranda personified frivolity. Whether dancing the samba with a bizarre headdress, belting out a hotly rhythmed Latin song, or speaking heavily accented lines, Carmen Miranda seldom had the opportunity to escape from frivolity. Her assigned role was to entertain. Prohibited from more than scratching the surface of her characters, she became a prisoner of screen superficiality. Yet the very popularity of this talented entertainer combined with the severe limitations on her roles to guarantee that her repetitive depictions would make a substantial contribution to the corpus of Latina film imagery. Chalk one up for Latina frivolity.

At the opposite end of the spectrum stood Mexican actress Dolores Del Río. No frivolity here. Her claim to screen fame was sensuality, a special kind of cool sensuality, consistently restrained and ladylike (as that term was used in those days). Yet, while quite distinct from the types of parts played by Carmen Miranda, Dolores Del Río's Latina characters had one trait in common with those of her Brazilian counterpart—superficiality. Notice, I am stressing the superficiality of the characters they played, not the superficiality of the actresses. On those rare occasions when she was given the opportunity to create a full-scale woman, as in *What Price Glory?* (1926) where she played the French heroine, Dolores Del Río proved that she could etch a vivid screen portrait . . . particularly when she was not playing a Latina. Her dilemma as an actress was that she seldom received such opportunities in her three dozen U.S. films. Leaving Hollywood in 1943, partially from frustration at being stereotyped, she returned to Mexico, where she won four Ariels, the Mexican Academy Award. Chalk one up for Latina sensuality.

Striding down the middle between those two types of characters came Mexican actress Lupe Vélez. At first she was one of Hollywood's leading all-purpose ethnics, playing, in her own words, "Chinese, Eskimos, Japs, squaws, Hindus, Swedes, Malays, and Javanese."[21] Ultimately she became known as the Mexican Spitfire, a sobriquet she earned from her 1939 film of the same name as well as its numerous sequels. The recipe for her various Latina screen characters, both as the Spitfire and in such other films as *The Girl from Mexico* (1939), combined a pint of frivolity and a quart of sensuality—the hot, explosive type, contrasting with Dolores Del Río's cool, restrained version. Chalk one up for both sensuality and frivolity.

Quantitative gains in Latina portrayals, then, were not paralleled by serious qualitative gains, particularly in the areas of diversity and depth. The major exception was the occasional Dolores Del Río portrayal. Yet even here the breakthroughs were breakthroughs with reservations. While a few of Dolores Del Río's characters had depth, they had that depth *as women*, not as people. I hope that distinction is not too fine. Her depth generally came in what are stereotypically considered to be women's characteristics, like emotionality, warmth, and sensitivity. Her characters seldom had more than a touch of such pan-gender human characteristics as courage, intelligence, determination, and decisiveness. While throughout film history, these "human" characteristics have usually been reserved for male characters, during this very era they were often exhibited by Anglo women on screen. At times, Katharine

Hepburn, Bette Davis, Joan Crawford, Rosalind Russell, Lauren Bacall, and other Anglo actresses were portraying women who proved they could compete with men in strength, intelligence, quick-wittedness, and nimble tonguedness—for that matter, in such films as *Pat and Mike,* even on the athletic field.[22]

But seldom Dolores Del Río and Lupe Vélez, and certainly not Carmen Miranda. After all, they were Latinas. Their strengths, if they had any, were decidedly female. They had reached the limit of the era's Latina film image.

Chicanas as Real People (1945-1970)

But a new age was dawning. The mid-1940s ushered in the golden age (so to speak) of Chicana depictions. While that gold fell far short of 20 karats, it was still no iron pyrite. The traditional simpleminded, fiery, frivolous, and sensual señoritas continued to grace the screen, but now they had some powerful soul sisters.

Out of the west, literally, rose strong, intelligent, resolute, active Mexican-American women. Their destinies and screen futures were inextricably linked to the fortunes of that particular film genre, the American western. In numerous westerns over the next three decades, Mexican-American female characters made a mark, not only as women, but also as people. In contrast, by the 1950s, Anglo female characters had entered into a period of decline, as the rise of the family film helped put screen women back in their place . . . the home.[23] At the same time, the Mexican bandito returned in all of his swarthy treachery and savagery in films such as *Treasure of the Sierra Madre* (1943), *Ride Vaquero!* (1953), and *The Magnificent Seven* (1960).

There was one catch, of course. Most of these strong Chicana characters were prostitutes, kept women, or at least ladies of questionable (for that era) virtue. From Chihuahua (Linda Darnell) in *My Darling Clementine* (1946) to Claire Quintana (Lena Horne) in *Death of a Gunfighter* (1969), the Chicana prostitute became a regular feature of the American western.[24]

Moreover, occasionally there appeared similarly strong, similarly intelligent Chicanas who were not prostitutes: Juana Villalobos, the proud nurse with the fortitude to withstand vicious Texas racism in *Giant* (1956); the strong, stoic, deeply religious mother of Leo Mimosa, who was buried alive in a southern New Mexico cave in Billy Wilder's stunning *The Big Carnival* (1951); a one-two punch of Katy Jurado as Karl Malden's wife and Pina Pellicer as Marlon Brando's girlfriend, both sterling portrayals of intelligent Mexicanas, in *One-Eyed Jacks* (1961). Ironically, one of the most memorable Chicana portrayals of that era became buried for two decades in the boycotted classic, *Salt of the Earth* (1953). In this film, Esperanza Quintero (powerfully played by Mexican actress Rosaura Revueltas) and her comparably brave and resolute Chicana compatriots lead the way to a labor victory against a New Mexico mining company by going on the picket line when their striking husbands are barred by court injunction.

For my money, however, the high point of Chicana portrayals in this or possibly in any era came in 1952 with Katy Jurado's memorable Helen Ramírez in Stanley Kramer's magnificent western, *High Noon*. More than a full-scale woman, Ramírez attains nearly totemic proportions in this incisive tale of a town going through the traumatic change from wild west to pre-modern west. As the serially kept woman, first of outlaw boss Frank Miller (now returning from prison to seek revenge on the town sheriff), then sheriff Will Kane (Gary Cooper in an award-winning performance), and finally of Kane's ambitious but mentally flabby deputy (Lloyd Bridges), Ramírez stands at the center of the film's multiple moral dilemmas.

None better than she recognize and understand the changes occurring and the inevitable impact on their town. None pinpoint and elucidate more articulately than she the many issues surfacing with the prospective return of the revenge-crazed Miller. None analyze the strengths and weaknesses of the film's major protagonists more incisively than she. In the fullest sense of the word, Helen Ramírez is a survivor. A Mexicana in a town where Mexican ancestry is a stigma, a woman of ill repute in a town that shrouds its duplicitous morality beneath the cross of the local church, a lone woman in a town where women's identities depend on their husbands—Helen Ramírez has more than three strikes against her. But she maintains her dignity, her sense of being, her independence, her capacity for analyzing passing events, for strength of will, and her ability to act decisively.

In a pivotal scene—one of the finest ever between two women in U.S. film history—she gives weak-willed, uptight, God-fearing Amy (Kane's bride, played by Grace Kelly) a succinct post-graduate education in frontier survival and female-male loyalty. She tells Amy that if she (Ramírez) were still Kane's woman, she would fight and if necessary die beside him against Miller and his outlaw gang. Ultimately, her lecture helps provoke Amy to return to the scene of the climactic shootout and, despite her Quaker scruples against violence, to shoot and kill one of the outlaws. Interestingly, despite her religious stand against killing, when Amy makes the transition from pacificist to gunslinger, she shoots the outlaw in the back, in contrast to Kane, who kills all of the other outlaws face to face, at one point even calling to the outlaws to turn around and draw against him rather than picking them off from behind. Undoubtedly, frontierswoman Ramírez would have fought head-to-head alongside Kane had she been his wife (or woman) at the time.

In this remarkable screen figure and her portrayal by a great Mexicana actress, the new possibilities and continuing limitations of the Chicana film image were dramatized. On the positive side, Helen Ramírez is a multidimensional woman *and* human being. (Amy and most of the men in *High Noon* never escape from their traditional filmic gender limitations to become full-scale human beings.) Moreover, Ramírez becomes the film's moral and ethical fulcrum and its main commentator on events. She contributes not only to plot development but also to the revelation of the film's societal implications. How sharply this contrasts with the Chicano and Mexicano banditos, who usually contributed to western plots by embodying the anti-moral element of the frontier!

On the negative side, Helen Ramírez is still a woman of ill-repute. In that sense, she joins the long line of Chicana prostitutes, mistresses, fallen women, and ladies of easy virtue—a tradition which continues to the present and has even made the transition to urban settings as, for example, in the otherwise innocuous *Grease* (1978), where John Travolta's other girlfriend, Cha Cha, is a hot, "easy" Chicana. Beyond that, Ramírez suffers the fate of almost all dark filmic Chicanas who dare to cross the color line and have Anglo boyfriends. She loses out in the end, in this case to blond, light-skinned, virginal Grace Kelly (as Travolta nearly thirty years later will dump his Chicana girlfriend in favor of blonde Olivia Newton-John).

Not all dark film Chicanas who cross the ethnic boundary line in their love relationships end up by losing their men to Anglas (Anglo women). Some get killed, like Linda Darnell in *My Darling Clementine*. Some witness the death of their Anglo husbands, as Katy Jurado does in *One-Eyed Jacks* and *Pat Garrett and Billy the Kid* (1973). Others suffer abuse from society, as the Chicana nurse does in *Giant*.

The movie warning presented with crystal clarity in film after film is vocalized in *West Side Story* (1961) in an urban Puerto Rican context, as Juanita [Anita] sings to María: "Keep to your own kind! Stick to your own kind!" Of course, María doesn't stick to her own kind. Instead she falls in love with Tony the Anglo (more precisely, Anton the Polish American) and their love affair ends in one of the standard patterns for Anglo-Latina affairs—Tony is killed. And by whom? A Puerto Rican gang punk, of course, the modern urban greaser bandito. The more things change, the more they stay the same.

What, then, was the ultimate screen image of the Chicana to emerge from nearly three decades of motion pictures? Scratch frivolity, keep sensuality, and add strength, intelligence, fortitude, and articulateness. However, whenever possible, clothe it in the skirts of ill repute.

Chicanas as Assimilated Americans (1970-?)

In terms of Chicana portrayals, two major filmic trends begun in the 1960s have had a major impact. First came the decline of the western as a popular film genre. Second came the ethnic civil rights movement, which included an all-out frontal assault on ethnic stereotyping and increased demand for a greater ethnic screen presence. How did these changes affect Chicana screen portrayals?

First they brought the virtual end of the filmic Chicana frontier prostitute. This image probably would have died of natural causes along with the general demise of the western film. In addition, however, the Chicana prostitute became a prime target of anti-stereotypic protesters, although a few Chicana loose women managed to survive, such as Cha Cha in *Grease*. Unfortunately, the decline of the western also brought an end to the era of strong Chicana western characters.

The decline of Chicana prostitutes and the virtual disappearance of strong Chicana characters did not have to be linked. Films could have, as they always could have, created strong Chicana characters other than prostitutes or mistresses. But, with few exceptions, filmmakers did not, just as they traditionally had not.

The anti-stereotyping crusade, itself a worthy movement, led to one negative, unintentional consequence. Along with the reduction of Chicana stereotyping came a reduction in Chicana typing of any kind. Thus a paradox arose. While more Chicanas and far more Latina screen characters have appeared since the late 1960s, they have usually been far less culturally Hispanic than their filmic predecessors, except for the *de rigueur* device of saying a few words in Spanish. Unable to present the Chicana characters that film audiences had grown to expect and accept, filmmakers generally stopped portraying Chicanas as culturally unique human beings.[25]

To avoid stereotyping but at the same time to carry out filmland's version of affirmative action, movies have littered the screen with Latinas who come off as little more than Spanish-surnamed Anglas. By the middle of the 1970s you could hardly have an urban bank scene without at least one identifiably Latina teller (*Dog Day Afternoon*, 1975), an office without at least one identifiably Latina secretary (*9 to 5*, 1980), a classroom scene without at least one Miss Gómez or López, or a wealthy home without a Latina maid, usually monolingually Spanish (*Bob and Carol and Ted and Alice*, 1969, and *The Changeling*, 1979). With a few notable exceptions, such as the stalwart, stoic, yet compassionate Puerto Rican Nurse Rodríguez in *Whose Life Is It Anyway?* (1981), these Latina minor figures have seldom had the opportunity to do much more than take up space, look Latin, and spout Spanish, or at least accented English.

Lest I be misunderstood, let me clarify that I am pleased with such quantitative progress, no matter how token it may be. But this plethora of Latinas in minor cultureless roles or as background atmosphere is a far cry from such culturally real Chicanas as those portrayed by Katy Jurado and Rosaura Revueltas. Give me those strong, intelligent Chicana prostitutes anytime over the current carload of Hispanic Barbie-doll characters.

But does this mean that Chicanas and other Latinas have been totally relegated to the role of filmic atmosphere or minor supporting players? Not quite. In one area, Chicanas and other Latinas have made an ongoing mark since 1970—the urban violence film.

This new Chicana image is the result of the confluence of three factors. First, along with the decline of the filmic western came the rise of the urban violence film.

Second came the breakdown and ultimate disappearance of the Hays Code, accompanied by an almost total "anything goes" acceptance of explicit sex and gratuitous violence on screen. Third came the bull market in ethnic theme films. Put all of these together and you get films about ethnic groups in the city, replete with sex and violence. And that is precisely the locus of the contemporary Chicana film image.

In a general sense, contemporary urban Latinas are found in two types of films. Obviously the Latino gang film, a natural crossroads for sex, violence, and ethnicity. However, particularly in the last five years, a new and somewhat more complex Latina role has begun to develop—the Latina as conscience to the central Anglo character, somewhat reminiscent of the strong Chicana prostitute in the filmic old west.

First, the Latino gang film. That genre began as the major province of Puerto Ricans. Back in the days when New York City was *the* American film city, a number of films began using Puerto Rican gangs either as central to the plot or at least as major background to the action. Probably the two most notable early films were *The Young Savages* (1961) and, with musical embellishment, *West Side Story* (1961).[26] Both films involved the clash between a Puerto Rican gang and an ethnically mixed Anglo gang. Both involved Latina characters. In fact, in *West Side Story*, the two main female roles are Puerto Ricans, and one is even played by a Puerto Rican (Rita Moreno, in a performance which earned her an Academy Award). Of course, *West Side Story's* ultimate message was depressingly familiar—Anglo boys, don't mess around with Latinas, because it will end in no good. And in truth, the movie does end in this way. Anglo Tony pays for his love affair with Puerto Rican María by getting blasted by her Puerto Rican betrothed, who simultaneously adds to the long "Latinos-solve-all-problems-with-violence" filmic tradition.

The emergence of Los Angeles as a rival to New York City as filmland's primary movie site, combined with the 1960s rise of national awareness of the existence of Chicanos, has led to a series of films in which Chicano gangs figure prominently. Foremost, of course, are films primarily about Chicano gangs, such as *Walk Proud* (1979) and *Zoot Suit* (1981). In other cases, Chicano gangs form an important backdrop, as in *The Big Fix* (1978), *Boulevard Nights* (1979), and *Back Roads* (1981). The latter also features Miriam Colón in a riveting role as a tough Chicana madame in a small contemporary bordertown. In addition, Chicanos sometimes belong to multiethnic gangs, as in *Assault on Precinct 13* (1976) and *Rolling Thunder* (1977).

The Big Fix is particularly illustrative in its selective use of Chicano gangs. In one critical scene, private detective Richard Dreyfuss is attempting to drag vital information out of two hitmen who have just tried to kill him. When he fails, he turns to his Chicano comrades and tells them to get the information. The message: when Anglo heroes cannot bring themselves to resort to violence, especially torture, they can turn it over to Chicanos, because they will use it. Even when they are on the side of good, then, Chicanos tend to come out painted "violent." At the same time, films continue to show that Puerto Ricans have not lost their taste for violence, as in such films as

Saturday Night Fever (1977), *Slow Dancing in the Big City* (1978), *Fort Apache, the Bronx* (1981), and *Defiance* (1980), the latter involving a multiethnic New York gang, The Souls.

Of particular note in many of these films is the presence of important Latina characters, although not usually in leading roles. After all, gang films are basically men's films. But if their characters are seldom strongly etched, at least Latinas are sometimes central to plot development.

The second new Latina film role is less obvious, but in some respects more interesting. This is the role of the urban Latina as a moral force. For the most part, most of these have been Puerto Rican roles set in the east. One of the few western-based films of this type was *The Border* (1981), involving a Mexicana's search for her kidnapped daughter. But back to the east coast, where Puerto Rican women often appear at least briefly and sometimes significantly.

In *The Buddy Holly Story* (1978), the young rock-and-roll star becomes captivated by and later marries a Puerto Rican girl, María Elena, who provides a calming influence in his turbulent life. In *Night of the Juggler* (1980), another Puerto Rican María, who works at the New York dog registration bureau, provides critical assistance and moral support for the Anglo hero who is searching for his kidnapped daughter. In John Cassavetes' enthralling *Gloria* (1980), another Latina, Jeri Dawn, is pivotal as the wife of the mob's bookkeeper, as she struggles to provide both sense and strength for her family as it awaits annihilation by the mob. That role is particularly notable, not only because it shows that not all Puerto Rican women are named María, but also because it features possibly the finest film performance by a Hispanic actress, Julie Carmen, since Rita Moreno's Juanita [Anita] in *West Side Story.*

What do these roles have in common? First, they provide a moral core to the films. In *The Border,* the Mexicana's search creates the basic plot dilemma. In *The Buddy Holly Story,* María Elena humanizes her rocketing husband. In *Night of the Juggler,* María serves as the foil through whom the Anglo policeman demonstrates his perplexities. In *Gloria,* Jeri becomes the primary figure in the film's opening minutes for establishing a mood of fear, moral ambiguity, and powerful familial ties that gives much of the impetus for the rest of the film. Even though Jeri is killed in the first half hour, she emerges as such a strong figure that Gloria has to compete with the slain mother as she tries to protect and nurture Jeri's son, left in Gloria's care just prior to the family's slaughter. So memorable was that portrait that Julie Carmen received the Venice Film Festival Golden Lion Award as best supporting actress, although she was ignored in the Academy Award selection. While Chicana roles have generally had less complexity than Puerto Rican roles in the past decade, there have still been some fine portraits. An example is the role of young Viola López in the underrated *Red Sky at Morning* (1970). Despite its gratuitous violence, this film provides one of the rare commercial film evocations of Hispano life in northern New Mexico.

Second, like the Mexican prostitutes of the 1940s and 1950s, these Latina characters provide an interethnic link. This stands in sharp contrast to most Latinos, particularly Chicano male characters, who are generally presented as being imprisoned by their ethnicity. One major exception was the Robbie Benson character in *Walk Proud*. At first, his ongoing love affair with an Anglo girl seems aberrant within U.S. film tradition. But ultimately the film pulls its punches and returns to veritable normalcy by revealing that while Robbie's mother is Mexican, his long-lost father is an Anglo. This soothing plot twist, along with the fact that the Chicano character is played by an Anglo, supposedly made the unusual Chicano male–Anglo female relationship more acceptable. On the other hand, no excuses needed to be made if Latinas had relationships with policemen, mob bookkeepers, or even rock-and-rollers. After all, Anglos had been getting together filmically with Latinas for decades, while the reverse was generally frowned on (although it was not quite so shocking as black men with white women).

Third, although these Latina characters serve critical moral functions and create interethnic film linkages, they are seldom developed as fully as some of the Chicanas of the old west. Of the film characters mentioned, only *Gloria*'s Jeri Dawn and *Red Sky at Morning*'s Viola López truly come alive as complex human beings, and Jeri only survives for thirty minutes.

Chicano and Mexican Films

So much for the depiction of Chicanas and other Latinas in mainstream American motion pictures. There are two other elements, if minor ones, in this mosaic—Chicano films and Mexican films. Sad to say, to date neither has shown a penchant for creating strong, intelligent, multidimensional Chicana characters.

The Chicano film industry is a relative infant. But when you think of the major characters in Chicano-generated films, who leaps to mind—Seguín in *Seguín* (1978), Gregorio Cortez in *The Ballad of Gregorio Cortez* (1981), and Cheech Marín's characters in the various Cheech and Chong movies. All men! Not surprisingly, all the filmmakers were men too. While the Alejandro Grattán–Moctesuma Esparza film *Only Once in a Lifetime* (1978) does provide better female roles and, perhaps not coincidentally, a gentler vision of Chicano life, the recent U.S. Latino feature film which best develops women as people may be *Después del terremoto* (1979). Not surprisingly, the author and director of this film is a woman, the Nicaraguan-American Lourdes Portillo. Considering the glass houses that Mexican-American filmmakers have created in their depictions (or lack of them) of Chicanas, Chicanos had best be very careful about throwing too many stones at Hollywood for its failings.

So too with Mexican films. Here again well-developed Chicana characters are few and far between. Some notable ones do emerge, as demonstrated by David Maciel in his paper "Chicanos in Mexican Films."[27] For example, in Alejandro Galindo's *Espaldas mojadas* (1953), a Chicana waitress named María del Consuelo helps an undocumented Mexican worker by hiding him and later moves to Mexico in reaction to discrimination in the United States. In *De sangre chicana* (1973), María Martínez, a Chicana born in San Antonio, changes her name to Mary Martin and only dates Anglos in an attempt to escape the taint of her ethnicity. Possibly the best Mexican film effort to date in creating strong, active, and thoughtful Chicana characters is *Raices de sangre* (1978), written and directed by Chicano Jesús Salvador Treviño.[28] While much research needs to be done on Chicano images in Mexican films, Maciel's pioneering study suggests that, to date, Mexico has provided little leadership in the filmic depiction of Mexican-American women.

Chicanas on Television

Finally, a word about a related component of the media curriculum, television. In a seminal study, Bradley S. Greenberg and Pilar Baptista-Fernández analyzed depictions of Latinos on fictional television series from 1975 to 1978.[29] They found that the ratio of Latino male characters to Latino female characters during those years was five to one, in contrast to the normal television ratio of three male characters to one female character. Of these Latino characters, more than 50 percent were Mexican Americans, two thirds if you also include Mexican characters. While there have been a few notable Chicano characters on television, such as Anthony Quinn's title role in the shortlived television series *The Mayor*, probably the most paradigmatic of Chicana series characters (at least prior to the *Dallas*-inspired flood of evening soap operas) was Consuelo, the nurse receptionist to Marcus Welby, M.D.

So, have Chicanas lost out again? Numerically, yes, but I would not consider this losing, in view of the way Latinos have generally been depicted on television. In their study, Greenberg and Baptista-Fernández reported that two thirds of all serious Latino roles involved the use of violence (either pro-legal violence, as in the case of policemen, or anti-legal violence, as in the case of criminals). In fact, criminal was the largest single occupation of all Chicano characters in a fictional television series! So maybe Chicanas were better off being virtually ignored.

Conclusion

And so it goes. Chicanas have never been particularly visible in U.S. motion pictures, but neither have they been totally invisible. In each era, Mexican-American women have filled special, sometimes important, genre roles.

This leads to some basic questions. Have Chicana film characters been identifiable? For the most part, yes, although there are often problems in distinguishing Chicanas from Mexicanas, other United States Latinas, and Spanish-surnamed Native Americans. Has there been a Chicana filmic image separate and distinct from Latinas in general? The answer is yes during the 1930s and 1940s when Lupe Vélez and Dolores Del Río were making their special, personal mark and during the 1940s, 1950s, and 1960s when Latinas in the old west were clearly Chicanas. But the answer is no since 1970, as the Chicana film image has essentially been subsumed within a larger urban Latina image, including Chicanas, Puerto Ricans, and other nationally indistinguishable Hispanics. Have Chicana film images run to types? Certainly, although those types have varied over time. Have these types resulted in filmic stereotypes? A cautious yes, based on the fact that within each era there has been so little diversity in Chicana roles.

Has this affected the public perception of Chicanas? I am certain of it, based on the general research documenting the impact of films on viewers' beliefs about the attitudes toward ethnic groups. However, I leave specific impact research to my social and behavioral science colleagues. Finally, how do Mexican-American women feel about the Chicana film image that has been created? Ask María, ask any of them.

NOTES

Reprinted by permission of the publisher from *Chicano Cinema: Research, Reviews, and Resources,* Keller, Gary (Ed.) (Arizona State University, Tempe, AZ: Bilingual Press/Review, 1985). Copyright © Bilingual Press/Review, 1985.

I would like to thank the Research Committee of the University of California, Riverside, Academic Senate for an intramural research grant which supported research for this article, and my colleague, Charles Wetherell, for his incisive comments on an early draft of the article.

1. For discussions of the history of women in film, see Marjorie Rosen, *Popcorn Venus. Women, Movies and the American Dream* (New York: Coward, McCann and Georghegan, 1973), and Molly Haskell, *From Reverence to Rape. The Treatment of Women in the Movies* (New York: Holt, Rinehart and Winston, 1974). However, these two books almost totally ignore the theme of Latinas in film.

2. Ruth C. Peterson and L. L. Thurstone, *Motion Pictures and the Social Attitudes of Children* (New York: Macmillan, 1933), pp. 35–38.

3. Irwin C. Rosen, "The Effect of the Motion Picture 'Gentlemen's Agreement' on Attitudes Toward Jews," *Journal of Psychology,* 26 (1948), pp. 525–36.

4. Bradley S. Greenberg, "Children's Reaction to TV Blacks," *Journalism Quarterly,* 49 (Spring 1972), pp. 5–14.

5. For example, according to *Moving Picture World,* audiences responded to *Across the Mexican Line* (1911) by hissing the Mexican villain and applauding the actions of Anglos. *Moving Picture World,* VIII (May 27, 1911), p. 1201, cited in Blaine S. Lamb, "The Convenient Vil-

lain: The Early Cinema Views the Mexican-American," *Journal of the West*, XIV, 4 (October 1975), pp. 80–81.

6. The most extensive collection of summaries of early Mexican content films is the 39-page appendix of George H. Roeder, Jr.'s "Mexicans in the Movies: The Image of Mexicans in American Films, 1894–1947" (unpublished manuscript, University of Wisconsin, Madison, 1971), cited in Arthur G. Pettit, *Images of the Mexican American in Fiction and Film*. Edited with an afterword by Dennis E. Showalter (College Station, TX: Texas A&M University Press, 1980), p. 132.

7. For a general introduction to the impact of motion pictures on American society, see Robert Sklar, *Movie-Made America: A Cultural History of American Movies* (New York: Random House, 1975).

8. See Caroline Golab, "Stellaaaaaa . . . . !!!!!!: The Slavic Stereotype in American Film," in Randall M. Miller (ed.), *The Kaleidoscopic Lens: How Hollywood Views Ethnic Groups* (Englewood, NJ: Jerome S. Ozer, 1980), pp. 135–55.

9. See James R. Nesteby, *Black Images in American Films, 1896–1954: The Interplay Between Civil Rights and Film Culture* (Washington, D.C.: University Press of America, 1982).

10. See Eugene Franklin Wong, "On Visual Media Racism: Asians in the American Motion Pictures" (Ph.D. dissertation, Graduate School of International Studies, University of Denver, 1977; Rpt. New York: Arno Press, 1978).

11. Carlos E. Cortés, "The Societal Curriculum: Implications for Multiethnic Education," in James A. Banks (ed.), *Education in the 80's: Multiethnic Education* (Washington, D.C.: National Education Association 1981), pp. 24–32.

12. For a brief overview of the history of filmic depictions of Mexican Americans (female and male) in film, see Carlos E. Cortés, "*The Greaser's Revenge* to *Boulevard Nights:* The Mass Media Curriculum on Chicanos," in National Association for Chicano Studies, *History, Culture, and Society: Chicano Studies in the 1980s* (Ypsilanti, MI: Bilingual Press, 1983), pp. 128–31.

13. The historical analysis in this article is based on the research for my book on the history of ethnicity and foreignness in U.S. motion pictures. The evidence to date substantiates these conclusions, but as I uncover new evidence (particularly as I assess more old films) I may need to revise some of these conclusions.

14. Lamb, "The Convenient Villain," pp. 75–81.

15. Allen E. Woll, *The Latin Image in American Film* (Los Angeles: Latin American Center, University of California, 1977), pp. 16–18.

16. From the 1930 Motion Picture Production Code, printed in Robert H. Stanley and Charles S. Steinberg, *The Media Environment: Mass Communications in American Society* (New York: Hastings House, 1976), p. 82.

17. A discussion of Novarro and the myth of the Latin lover can be found in Woll, *The Latin Image*, pp. 22–26.

18. Jack Hicks, "*9 to 5*'s Rita Moreno: The Cutthroats Almost Got Her," *TV Guide*, January 15, 1983, p. 28.

19. Woll, *The Latin Image*, pp. 34–35, 54–56.

20. For another discussion of these three actresses see Ibid., pp. 41–45, 67–70.

21. *Saturday Evening Post*, January 2, 1932, p. 26, cited in Woll, *The Latin Image in American Film*, p. 38.

22. Haskell, *From Reverence to Rape*, pp. 30–31, 141–42, 181–83, and 213–20; Rosen, *Popcorn Venus*, pp. 177–80, 189–91, and 206–14.

23. Rosen, *Popcorn Venus*, pp. 263–65.

24. A related analysis of Chicana mistresses can be found in Pettit, *Images of the Mexican American*, pp. 203–07.

25. Filmmaker and film professor Linda Williams argues "a simple abhorrence of stereotype is not enough" and that a distinction must be made between type and stereotype. Types, she contends, are necessary in creating a screen representation that reflects the special reality of the Chicano experience (or any other ethnic experience, for that matter). Williams correctly suggests that in struggling to cleanse films and television of stereotyping, Chicanos (as well as other ethnic groups) may cause their depictions to lose cultural uniqueness and significance. See Chapter 13 herein. An alternate position is staked out by Maurice Yacowar, who defends filmic stereotyping of ethnic minorities, arguing, "Nor need there be anything proscriptive about such a usage of a human type as an emblem in film. It is just another kind of iconography, another convention of artistic shorthand." In other words, to hell with the social consequences of image creation, if it is done for the sake of Good Art! See Maurice Yacowar, "Aspects of the Familiar: A Defense of Minority Group Stereotyping in Popular Film," *Film Literature Quarterly*, II, 2 (Spring 1974), pp. 129–39.

26. John Whitney, "Image Making in the Land of Fantasy," *Agenda, A Journal of Hispanic Issues*, VIII, 1 (January-February 1978), p. 10.

27. David Maciel, "Chicanos in Mexican Films" (unpublished paper). The most extensive study of Mexican motion pictures in English is Carl Mora's *Mexican Cinema* (Berkeley: University of California Press, 1982), which devotes some attention to depictions of Mexican Americans (see pp. 80, 88, 135–37).

28. For a more detailed evaluation of *Only Once in a Lifetime* and *Raíces de sangre*, see Elizabeth J. Ordonez, "La imagen de la mujer en el nuevo cine chicano," *Caracol*, V, 2 (October 1978), pp. 12–13.

29. Bradley S. Greenberg and Pilar Baptista-Fernández, "Hispanic-Americans—The New Minority on Television," in Bradley S. Greenberg *et al., Life on Television: Content Analysis of U.S. T.V. Drama* (Norwood, N.J.: Ablex Publishing Corporation, 1980), pp. 3–12.

From Assimilation to Annihilation: Puerto Rican Images in U.S. Films

Richie Pérez

Discrimination against Puerto Ricans by the mass media takes three main forms: *Exclusion*—the mass media refuses to acknowledge that Puerto Ricans exist. This includes the failure of the news and television documentaries to report on our reality. *Dehumanization*—when we do appear in the mass media, we are the targets of consistent negative stereotyping, which includes ridicule of our culture and language. *Job discrimination*—Puerto Ricans are blocked from working in the mass communications industry as actors, actresses, writers, producers, editors, technicians, and reporters. We are thus prevented from bringing our unique sensibilities, awareness, concerns, and creativity to the media. This situation is not unique to Puerto Ricans. In fact, we share this problem with all people of color in America.

Media exclusion, dehumanization, and discrimination are part of the cultural domination inherent in unequal power relations, and a key feature of the historical process by which people of color have been and continue to be subordinated. Cultural domination involves racist omissions, stereotypes, lies, and fantasies which distort history and weaken the consciousness, organization, and resistance of oppressed people. Recycled in various forms, these repeated distortions become part of the society's belief system, forming the dominant myths, symbols, vocabulary, and beliefs which define the consciousness of the nation.

Among whites, the cumulative effect of media exclusion, dehumanization, and discrimination is to strengthen the historically-rooted belief in white supremacy and the inferiority of people of color. Among people of color the effect is to deprive our children of positive role models, and to rob our entire people of our history, culture, sense of pride, and self-respect. Thus, these discriminatory actions in the media contribute to maintaining Puerto Ricans in a subordinate position in America and are used to undermine the Puerto Rican freedom movement.

PHOTO 8.1 **Anita and María: Spitfire and Madonna.** This photo of Anita (Rita Moreno) and María (Natalie Wood) in *West Side Story* suggests the dual images described by Pérez and others of Madonna and spitfire. (Courtesy of The Museum of Modern Art Film Stills Archive)

Racial stereotyping in the mass media has received scholarly attention from many fields. In 1954. Gordon Allport, in *The Nature of Prejudice*, discussed the role of media-projected racial stereotyping in justifying racial hostility (Allport, 1954). In 1968, African-American psychologist Alvin F. Poussaint wrote, "If the media continue, on the whole, to depict Negroes negatively and to foster white supremacy, then this will far outweigh the effects of even the best schools for Black children" (Poussaint, 1968). The negative portrayal of minorities in film, he argued, served to withdraw status from non-white peoples; and the withdrawal of status itself is a form of legitimizing white supremacy. In a *Black Scholar* article, sociologist Francis W. Alexander asks: "What better way is there to stop the exploited from getting the 'superiority of knowledge, technique and organization' than by making the exploited look funny and weak? What better way is there to keep a race down without a lot of bloodshed than by shoving sex, alcoholism and drugs on them? What better way than by stereotyping them?" (Alexander, 1976). This article will address one aspect of this complex phenomenon—the image of Puerto Ricans in American films.

Post-War America

America emerged from WWII the most powerful of the Western "democracies." At home, the war ushered in a temporary post-war period of prosperity and rapid social and economic change. During this period, the U.S. experienced dramatic population shifts. Between 1950 and 1960, the population grew by 30 million, from 150.7 million to 180 million. An explosion of births began in 1946. These "baby boomers" created a new consumer market. When they began to enter the schools in the early 1950s, their large numbers created a shortage of classrooms and teachers. There was also a significant increase in the number of teenagers working and having money to spend. The number of teenagers working while simultaneously going to school increased by 5% between 1950 and 1960.

In addition, new telecommunications technology revolutionized the mass media, making it possible to reach ever-growing audiences with the same messages. In the late 1940s, radio was still the major source of popular music. There was as yet no distinct "teenage music." In 1946, television was introduced, and 7,000 sets were sold; by 1950, 4.4 million sets had been sold.

The generation born between 1946–1964 became the largest generation in America's history. In the early 1980s, these "baby boomers" made up almost 1/3 of the nation's population. This generation created the youth culture of the 1950s and 1960s, embracing rock and roll as their music. Up until then, "race music," with its hard-driving rhythmic beat, sexually-suggestive lyrics ("little red rooster"), and references to "rocking and rolling" was confined to Black music stations at a time of widespread racism and segregation. However, by 1949, recognizing that "race music" was reaching a wider audience, including many white teenagers, *Billboard* began to call it "rhythm and blues" and to list the top sellers. In 1950, Fats Domino, Ivory Joe Hunter, Johnny Otis, and Ruth Brown all had hits on the rhythm and blues charts.

America's policy makers, professionals, religious representatives, social scientists, law enforcement personnel, and parents had difficulty understanding these changes and their cultural implications. By 1946, considerable "official" attention was being devoted to "juvenile delinquency" and the "social decay" that many officials blamed for the increase of youth crime and challenging of authority. Mainstream America gradually became gripped by panic, fearful that the whole post-war generation had "gone bad." A widespread movement developed reflecting class and race hostilities, particularly the hysteria and anger of middle-class whites at challenges to the old "family values," and the spread of "lower-class culture" in general, and "race music" in particular. These fears and others eventually were grouped and identified as the "juvenile delinquency" problem. The extent of these concerns is suggested in the following section from *A Cycle of Outrage: America's Reaction to the Juvenile Delinquent in the 1950s* (Gilbert, 1986):

To designate April 1948 as a month for local delinquency conventions, Attorney General Clark was enlisted to persuade the President to issue a proclamation. In part, it read: "I do hereby call upon the people of the United States in their homes and churches, in the schools and hospitals . . . in institutions for the care of delinquent juveniles, and in their hearts and minds to act individually and together for the prevention and control of juvenile delinquency." The Committee [the Continuing Delinquency Committee grew out of an earlier national conference] sent the proclamation, signed by Truman, to every governor, to mayors of cities over 10,000, and to all the organizations that participated in the original delinquency conference. By February about twenty states and 230 cities had expressed an interest in holding conferences. By the end of the month over 11,000 handbooks and proclamations had been distributed.

By the early 1950s, worries about "social decay" and juvenile crime had intersected with growing fears of "communist expansion" and "internal subversion." Mirroring the "anti-communist crusade," the "anti-delinquency movement" began to zero in on mass culture, especially comics, movies, and rock and roll music.

This was the climate to which Puerto Ricans migrated to the United States in large numbers. We were a young community; in 1950, the median age of Puerto Ricans was 25 as compared to 35 for the total NYC population. Only about 13% of our people were over 45, as compared to more than 33% of the total New York City population. We were poorer than other New Yorkers. We spoke a different language and were a multi-racial people. It was easy to link us, as a people, to the problems troubling America. Significantly, before our mass migration to the United States, negative stereotypes of us were already operative and for decades had conditioned North Americans to view us as "inferiors."

Media Stereotyping of Puerto Ricans

Negative images of Puerto Ricans represent written and visual expressions of white superiority and Puerto Rican inferiority. They are historically constituted. These stereotypes existed even before the mass migration of Puerto Ricans to the U.S. They developed as justifications for the American seizure of the Island and for continued colonization. Overt racism was used by members of the U.S. government to justify holding Puerto Rico in a colonial, subordinate status, treating Puerto Ricans unequally, and protecting the U.S. from race "mongrelization." Senator Vardaman, senior Senator from Mississippi, spoke from the floor of the Senate in 1916, during the debate over the status of Puerto Rico and possible citizenship for Puerto Ricans.

So far as I am personally concerned, I really think it is a misfortune for the United States to take that class of people into the body politic. They will never, no not in a thousand years, understand the genius of our Government or share our ideals of government. . . . I really had rather they would not become citizens of the United States. I think we have enough of that element in the body politic already to menace the nation with mongrelization.[1]

The idea of a hierarchy of races, with white Anglo-Saxon Protestants at the top, was widely accepted in America at the turn of the century. American expansionists later seized upon and distorted the scientific findings of Charles Darwin to support their expansionist ambitions. The "racial purity" goal embraced by American expansionists, home grown segregationists, and others (like the Nazis), was also shared by the eugenicists, scientists, and policy makers, who argued that studies had "proven" that the lower classes and non-white peoples had "inferior genes." As the eugenicists rose in prominence in the early 1900s, politicians used their claims to justify the sterilization of the "unfit" and limitations on the further immigration of "inferior peoples." By 1917, 16 states had passed sterilization laws (Weinberg, 1977).

Puerto Ricans, as a multi-racial people, were a natural target for the racial purists. Our ancestors are Tainos, Spaniards, and Africans. To America, however, we were, and still are just another form of "nigger," a "mongrel race," inferior to whites, and thus unprepared for equal participation and undeserving of equal treatment. A 1949 study, "Cultural Conflicts in the Puerto Rican Adjustment," part of a wave of American studies of the "Puerto Rican Problem," claimed that while Americans were "generally courteous to foreigners if they spoke in their native language or wore native dress," there were "general notions" in the U.S. that all Puerto Ricans were "oversexed" and indulged in "excessive promiscuity." According to the study, Americans believed "that the men carry knives and use them unrestrainedly, that all Puerto Ricans are ignorant, unintelligent and stupid because they do not speak English; that they are colossal liars, that they are very temperamental and hot-headed; that the island is infested with diseases and that Puerto Ricans are clannish."

The media itself continually reinforced and recycled these images of the Puerto Rican. A 1948 book, *New York Confidential,* had this to say: "Puerto Ricans were not born to be New Yorkers. They are mostly crude farmers, subject to congenital tropical diseases, physically unfitted for the northern climate, unskilled, uneducated, non-English-speaking, and almost impossible to assimilate and condition for healthful and useful existence in an active city of stone and steel. . . . Finding themselves unable physically, mentally, or financially to compete, they turn to guile and wile and the steel blade, the traditional weapon of the sugarcane cutter, mark of their blood and heritage" (Lait and Mortimer, 1948).

In addition to these crude racial stereotypes, other more sophisticated ones emerged in the late 1950s, categorizing Puerto Ricans as helpless and ineffective victims, who either accepted their conditions passively or who were incapable of organizing themselves to effectively challenge the status quo. Social scientists of the era, many of whom claimed to be "friends" of the Puerto Rican people, cranked out dozens of books and articles explaining Puerto Rican poverty and marginalization as a consequence of our individual and collective inadequacies and failures. New, more sophisticated ways were found to say we were inferior: our culture was "dysfunctional," our families were "demoralized," our communities were "fragmented, disunited spheres for social living." Eventually, "culture of poverty" theories that blamed those discriminated against and economically marginalized for their own condition became the dominant American social science "explanation" for the Puerto Rican situation.

Film Images of Puerto Ricans

By the 1940s, the Puerto Rican community in New York had attracted the attention of government officials, academics, journalists, and a handful of novelists. By the end of the decade, the images of the Puerto Rican popularized in newspapers, magazines, and novels were being projected onto the screen.

Film, as a medium of communication, is an extremely powerful tool. Because film is a popular art, dependent upon acceptance by large "paying audiences," it is considered to represent an important index to social thought. The use of movies as propaganda vehicles during the war was one of the examples cited by Dr. Lawrence Reddick, curator of the Schomburg Collection of Negro Literature of the New York Public Library. It was his analysis that film was particularly effective in what it said about "history, current events, and the people and places of the world." He said, "The implied associations that are indirectly suggested and repeated by the screen stories often leave residues that are more lasting than the evocative climaxes of the films" (Reddick, 1944).

The first films dealing with Puerto Ricans re-created cinematically the anti–Puerto Rican stereotypes that had come to dominate the print media. When you think of films dealing with Puerto Ricans, *West Side Story* (1961) usually comes to mind. However, there are more than a dozen Hollywood films, made between 1949 and 1980 alone, that deal with the Puerto Rican reality or in which Puerto Rican characters play a significant role. It is the *cumulative* impact of these films and the Puerto Rican images they project that we will begin to analyze.

Teenagers in the Urban Jungle

The dominant stereotype of Puerto Ricans as juvenile delinquents and young criminals was established with *City Across the River, Blackboard Jungle, Rock, Rock, Rock, Cry Tough, West Side Story, The Young Savages,* and *The Pawnbroker.* These films also established and repeated other stereotypes, including the violent-tempered but ultimately ineffective Puerto Rican man; the mental inferior; the innocent, but sensual Puerto Rican beauty; and the "loose," "hot-blooded mama." Keep in mind that the Puerto Rican mass migration to the U.S. coincided with a mass hysteria in this country about juvenile crime and a national debate about the causes of juvenile crime and the solutions. The limiting of Puerto Rican characterizations and images to crime films effectively linked the already-established images of "otherness" and "racial inferiority" with the "modern" stereotype of criminality.

City Across the River *(1949)*

Puerto Ricans made a brief appearance in the 1949 movie, *City Across the River.* This film was a cinematic adaptation of *The Amboy Dukes,* Irving Schulman's novel about juvenile delinquents in Brooklyn. One critic identified the film as a "semi-documentary with location shooting influenced by *Naked City.*[2] *City Across the River* was among the first movies that used on-location filming to establish claims of authenticity. In this movie, a group of Puerto Rican teenagers are called "spics" and are beat up by a white youth gang that objects to them using a pool room in the white gang's "turf."

Despite the elimination of most of the book's rape, drug use, and strong violence, parents and teachers' groups around the nation protested against the film, especially the scenes showing gang members making zip guns in shop class and later assaulting their teacher.

Blackboard Jungle *(1955)*

One Puerto Rican character appeared in this controversial movie about juvenile delinquency in New York's public schools. Morales (played by Raphael Campos) is a semi-retarded youth whose Spanish accent and problems in speaking English are the target of ridicule throughout the movie. He is unable to complete a sentence without cursing. (In the book it is the "f" word, but it's cleaned up in the movie.)

Based on the 1952 novel by Evan Hunter, *Blackboard Jungle* introduced Sidney Poitier and Vic Morrow to movie audiences. Their cinematic characters competed for leadership in the film. Morales was not their equal. He was a follower, just a part of the mob. He was portrayed as being so slow that he didn't even know when he was being made fun of.

The novel *Blackboard Jungle* has been called "the first important post-war book to deal with the problems of urban youth in conflict with adult values and adult control in a purely naturalistic way." As a film, *Blackboard Jungle* was one of the first and most important films to deal with mid-fifties juvenile delinquency. Film historians consider it a "serious film" and it was treated that way by critics and commentators at the time. It is considered to have established the plot lines and characterizations of many imitative films that followed.

Opposition to the film focused on its supposed depiction of "the successful defiance of delinquents who reject authority and terrorize an American high school. Their success and their power, and the ambiguous but attractive picture of their culture aimed at the heart of the Film Code and its commitment to uphold the dignity of figures and institutions of authority" (Gilbert, 1986).

The film was blasted by many educators, including the principal of a Bronx vocational school who was "disturbed by the picture's exaggeration and its probable effects upon the public attitude toward the students and teachers." When the movie was scheduled to be shown at the Venice Film Festival, U.S. Ambassador Clare Booth Luce threatened to leave Italy and "cause the greatest scandal in motion picture history." The movie was withdrawn. A *Los Angeles Times* film critic panned the movie and went so far as to say it could damage U.S. prestige abroad, "particularly if it ever fell into Communist hands." The criticisms of the movie forced MGM to add disclaimers to the end of the film, an example of which read: "To our patrons: the school and situations you have just seen are not to be found in this area! We should all be proud of the facilities provided for our youth by the schools of New Brunswick and the Middlesex County vocation and technical high school. We suggest a visit to any of the fine schools in our city and county. You will be cordially welcome" (McGee and Robertson, 1982).

Blackboard Jungle was also the first major film to use a rock and roll soundtrack, specifically Bill Haley and the Comets' "Rock Around the Clock." "Rock Around the Clock" went on to become a teenage national anthem and was the first rock record to appear on the Hit Parade for 15 weeks. With the release of the movie and riots at rock concerts, the music and juvenile delinquency became inseparable in the minds of many Americans. Many people actually believed that music caused juvenile delinquency. Screenings of *Blackboard Jungle* frequently led to teenagers dancing in the aisles to the rock and roll music. This "wild" activity, along with reports of audiences cheering the beating and humiliation of teachers confirmed the opposition's worst fears.

The movie, a box-office hit in New York City, set an attendance record in its first ten days at the Loew's State theater. Nevertheless, the movie was banned by censors in Memphis, denounced by the National Congress of Parents and Teachers, the Girl Scouts, the Daughters of the American Revolution, and the American Legion.

Rock, Rock, Rock *(1956)*

The association between Puerto Ricans, juvenile delinquency, and rock and roll continued with the success of the vocal group Frankie Lymon and the Teenagers. Consisting of three African-Americans and two Puerto Ricans, their first record, "Why Do Fools Fall in Love?" remained in the Hot Hundred for five months and sold two million copies throughout the world.

In 1956, Frankie Lymon and the Teenagers appeared in *Rock, Rock, Rock,* one of a series of rock movies that predictably featured white suburban teens fighting with their parents over attending rock and roll shows where most of the acts were Black. *Rock, Rock, Rock* marked the film debut of 13-year old Tuesday Weld, as a teenager who must raise money to buy herself a strapless gown for the big dance after her Dad takes away her allowance. At the dance, Frankie Lymon and the Teenagers try to reassure the skeptical adults that are present by singing, "I'm Not a Juvenile Delinquent."

Cry Tough *(1959)*

Based on a story by Irving Schulman (author of the book upon which *City Across the River* was based), *Cry Tough* featured John Saxon as a small-time but aspiring Puerto Rican hoodlum (whose accent changed throughout the movie). Linda Cristal played his "hot-blooded" Puerto Rican girlfriend, given to wearing skin-tight dresses and dancing "with abandon" to "exotic" Latin rhythms.

The *Motion Picture Herald* said that Saxon's popularity among teenagers was the movie's only real selling point. "Otherwise," their reviewer said, "the film will have to be sold on the basis of lurid action plus the sexy acting of Linda Cristal in the role of a tart . . . downbeat in the extreme, the backgrounds are depressing . . ."[3]

The Young Savages *(1961)*

This film was based on *A Matter of Conviction,* a novel written by Evan Hunter (author of *Blackboard Jungle,* who now writes 87th Precinct mysteries under the name Ed McBain). In the movie, a 15-year-old blind Puerto Rican is killed by an Italian street gang. As the Assistant DA (played by Burt Lancaster) investigates, he discovers that the dead youth was actually the leader of a rival Puerto Rican gang and was acting as a pimp for his sister. She is portrayed as an innocent-looking, plainly-dressed young Latina; but in reality, she is a prostitute (with her mother's knowledge).

Filmed on location in *El Barrio,* the film used actual street gang members recruited by a minister who was running an amateur theater group called "The Centurions." Striving for realism, the film is filled with anti–Puerto Rican slurs. One character states knowingly, "All spics are good with a knife." When Puerto Ricans try to use a swimming pool in East Harlem, they are physically attacked by white teenagers who say "San Juan's polluting the water."

As Burt Lancaster conducts his investigation, the audience is shown Puerto Ricans living crowded together, chickens running wild in the hallways, with young males running their families, even engaging in sex at home, separated only by a makeshift curtain from their parents in the next room—the parents' silence implying their acceptance of this situation.

Sympathy is not built for the dead youth, but rather for one of his attackers. Shelley Winters, his mother, is the only parent portrayed who shows love and a determination to hold her already-battered family together. Although she too is poor, her home appears neat and clean, in stark contrast to the disorganization and dirt in the Puerto Rican homes. Although the film is "liberal" in its analysis of youth crime, citing poverty, ignorance, racial hatred, instability and insecurity as its causes, its visual "message" lays considerable fault on the Puerto Rican family, culture, and community as well.

West Side Story *(1961)*

Perhaps the best known film in which Puerto Rican characters played a central role was *West Side Story,* released six months after *The Young Savages* in 1961. However, the two key Puerto Rican roles, that of María and her brother, Bernardo, were reserved for white performers (Natalie Wood and George Chakiris). This was consistent with the historic Broadway taboo against people of color playing central roles, even if the script called for it. This discriminatory practice has been analyzed extensively in its application to Blacks, Native Americans, and Asians.

West Side Story did depict Puerto Ricans in both family and work situations. However, it simultaneously perpetuated the stereotype of Puerto Rican males as knife-carrying gang members who could only solve their problems through violence. It also developed the images of Puerto Rican women as either innocent, passive, virginal beauties (María, the Natalie Wood character), or "hot-blooded," "fiery," spontaneous and worldly (Anita, the Rita Moreno character for which she received an Academy award). This "Madonna/whore" dichotomy had earlier been applied to Mexican women's portrayals. Early films projected one additional stereotype of Latin women: the frivolous Latina whose accent and actions were meant to be laughed at. One analysis referred to these as "roles that dehumanize Latin American women into silly, sexy performing dolls."

> The high-voltage Brazilian accent Carmen Miranda personified frivolity. Whether dancing a samba with a bizarre headdress, belting out a hotly rhymed Latin song, or speaking heavily accented lines, Carmen Miranda seldom had the opportunity to escape from frivolity. Her assigned role was to entertain. . . .
>
> At the opposite end of the spectrum stood Mexican actress Dolores Del Río. No frivolity here. Her claim to screen fame was sensuality, a special kind of cool, consistently restrained and ladylike (as that term was used in those days) (See Chapter 7 herein, pp. 129–130.).

West Side Story was nominated in 11 categories and won 10 Academy awards, including Best Picture, Best Director, Best Supporting Actor (George Chakiris), Best

Supporting Actress (Rita Moreno), Best Screenplay Based on Material from Another Medium, and Best Costume Design. Choreographer-director Jerome Robbins received [praise] for "his brilliant achievements in the art of choreography on film." It was a tremendous box office hit in 1961, surpassed only by Disney's *101 Dalmations.*

Seen by millions, *West Side Story* built on earlier images and portrayals, and cinematically "established" the definitive image of Puerto Ricans as urban ghetto dwellers, as well as reinforcing and projecting to a wider audience already existing stereotypes.

The Liberal Perspective: Urban Missionaries

The films of the early 1960s that dealt with Puerto Ricans, while limiting us to films dealing with crime and other social "problems," tended to reflect a "liberal" view of crime, delinquency, and poverty. External conditions were recognized, to varying degrees, as being causal factors. This "liberal" view of the causes of juvenile crime was summed up well in two analyses of the 1949 film, *Knock on Any Door.* The movie starred Humphrey Bogart as a liberal lawyer defending a delinquent from Chicago's slums (this was before the word "ghetto"). The young hoodlum, played by John Derek, was charged with killing a policeman. "*Knock on Any Door* (1949) took as [its] . . . hero the persecuted innocent-at heart whose delinquency and untimely death are preordained by a harsh environment and a vindictive society . . ." (Clarens, 1980).

At the end of the movie, Humphrey Bogart says, "Nick Romano is guilty . . . but so are we." Of course, he continues, society could have chosen to eliminate the conditions that caused delinquency and adult crime and then, "This boy could have been exalted instead of jailed." But society ignored the symptoms of its own failures, said the Bogart character, and created hundreds like him through "sheer neglect."

The liberal analysis of crime is based on the premise that the social evils of capitalism can be eliminated without changing the economic base and political structure which, together, routinely generate economic, political, and social inequality. The liberal perspective does not include any structural critiques of crime, impoverishment, and the routine workings of "the system." When Puerto Ricans appear in films with this perspective, we are portrayed as delinquents who are social misfits and personally-inadequate victims.

In the mid-1960s, corresponding to America's War on Poverty, this perspective was expressed cinematically in the optimistic "urban missionary" films. In films like *Up the Down Staircase* and *Change of Habit,* white teachers, doctors, nuns, and priests go into the ghetto to "save" us. In each case, the "savior" is initially rejected, often raped, always assaulted, and denigrated, before at least some of us get "saved."

Up the Down Staircase *(1967)*

Released in 1967, this film is described in Halliwell's *Film Guide* as the "problems of a schoolteacher in one of New York's tough sections. Earnest, well acted, not very likeable melodrama." Based on a popular novel by Bel Kaufman, the film opens with the camera watching students streaming past abandoned buildings and garbage-filled lots and alleys to get to "Calvin Coolidge H.S." in New York. The main Puerto Rican character is a student who doesn't talk. Reflecting the liberal perspective of the film, an older teacher comments: "They've been given up on by too many people already."

Released the same year the struggle for "community control" began in NYC, the film ignored the growing community movement for control of the schools and instead reflected the optimistic "urban missionary" view that projected well-meaning white professionals doing battle with difficult "inner city problems." As in most of the "urban missionary" films, Puerto Ricans and Blacks served primarily as background characters, embodiments of the "problems," people who did not act in their own behalf, but were acted upon by the central characters who are always white.

At the end of *Up the Down Staircase*, José Rodríguez, the student who didn't talk, finally speaks up—with new authority and self-confidence. The teacher, played by Sandy Dennis, realizes that she has made a difference and decides to stay at Calvin Coolidge High.

Change of Habit *(1969)*

A classic "urban missionary" film, *Change of Habit* starred Elvis Presley, as a doctor running a ghetto clinic, and Mary Tyler Moore as a nun sent into the ghetto to do social work and "save souls." Puerto Ricans have roles as secondary characters: a young, "sexy" teenager who coyly tries to get Presley to examine her chest; adult Puerto Rican males, who sexually harass another nun; and a troubled Puerto Rican teenage boy. "Julio" has a speech impediment and can only speak clearly when he has a knife or other sharp object in his hand. These obvious phallic symbols make him "feel strong," he says. Mary Tyler Moore befriends him, but he rewards her by eventually trying to rape her. Of course, in the end, Elvis saves the day.

Popi *(1969)*

This comedy depicted life in *El Barrio* and one father's attempt to save his children from being trapped in the slums forever. The solution he decides on is to deny their true nationality and disguise them as Cuban refugees. Alan Arkin (continuing the tradition of non–Puerto Ricans in Puerto Rican leading roles) plays the father and displays genuine love and affection for his children. Their relationship is a positive one; but the idea of denying your identity as the only way to succeed is extremely negative. It is made more so when you consider that the movie came at a time of reawakening and reaffirmation for Puerto Ricans. The movie ends with Arkin and the children unable to go through with the plan and returning to the ghetto. For all their efforts, nothing has changed.

One reviewer described *Popi* as the "adventures of a cheerful inhabitant of New York's Puerto Rican ghetto. Ethnic comedy-drama of the kind that has since found its way in abundance into American TV series. Very competently done for those who like it, e.g. Puerto Ricans."

These films operated in a liberal social context, during the days of the Great Society and the "War on Poverty," a time when people believed problems just needed to be identified and exposed, and could finally be corrected by governmental action. "Urban missionary" films could only be made in a society where a sizable portion of the population believed that social problems could be managed, without addressing the roots of the problems.

During this period, crime movies also tended to reflect the liberal perspective. Cops in films such as *Madigan* (1968) and *Bullit* (1968) were considered to be tough but "humane." One analysis classified them as "cops of the Kennedy era," and said these films generally projected the reassuring message that "decent" folks could restore order and make things work again.

These films continued in the liberal tradition, drawing on "environmental" theories, but more and more began to introduce a cinematic counterpart to the "blaming the victim" theories popularized by Oscar Lewis in *La Vida* and other social scientists (Lewis, 1966). More attention was given to personality theories which gave primacy to individual personality "defects."

The Pawnbroker *(1965)*

Rod Steiger was nominated for an Academy Award for his role as a Jewish Holocaust survivor who runs a pawnshop in *El Barrio*. In the movie, he is terrorized by Black hoodlums. His Puerto Rican assistant, "Jesús Ortiz" (played by Jaime Sánchez), is a poor, but optimistic worker who dreams of "making it." Haunted and hardened by memories of the concentration camps and unable to express his humanity or to appreciate the humanity of others, Steiger constantly belittles the naivete of his assistant. The Sánchez character is projected as the classic poor, ineffective, Puerto Rican "loser."

Angered by Steiger's constant paternalism and cynical put-downs, and goaded on by his African-American girlfriend (a "hooker"), the Sánchez character teams up with a nasty Black hoodlum (played by Brock Peters) to rip off Steiger. During the robbery, however, Sánchez dies while shielding Steiger from a bullet.

This film, shot on location in East Harlem, was not overtly political, but hinted at the growing tensions between whites, Blacks, and Puerto Ricans in NYC. Its director, Sidney Lumet (*Twelve Angry Men*—1957, *Serpico*—1973, *Dog Day Afternoon*—1975, *Prince of the City*—1981, and more recently, *Q&A*), put together a powerful drama with the liberal perspective that "we are all victims" of urban corruption and racism, a theme he has addressed in other films. However, the Puerto Rican and Black "victims" in the film were clearly subordinated to the white protagonist—even in victimization, the film projected a racial hierarchy.

The film's impact was arguably increased by the historical events which surrounded it and the impact of these events on the national consciousness. The year before, in 1964, massive voter registration drives and civil rights activity in the South led to more than 1,000 arrests, 37 Black churches bombed or damaged, and 15 people murdered (including Schwerner, Goodman, and Chaney). In New York itself, there were massive school boycotts, with ½ million Black and Puerto Rican children staying home in support of a civil rights boycott led by Rev. Milton Galamison.

That same year saw the first citywide civil rights demonstration sponsored by the Puerto Rican community when 1,800 protestors marched across the Brooklyn Bridge in March 1964. This year also signalled the beginning of the "long hot summers" with an uprising in Harlem after a white policeman shot a Black teenager.

The year *The Pawnbroker* hit the movie screens, Americans also saw television screens project images of the Selma civil rights march, urban rebellions in Watts, San Diego, and Chicago (where Puerto Ricans fought police). In NYC, racial polarization intensified with a struggle over low-income housing pitting the Jewish and Italian communities of Forest Hills, Corona, and Howard Beach against a growing civil rights movement. That confrontation became known as the "scatter-site housing controversy."

The Possession of Joel Delaney *(1972)*

In the early 1970s, building on the popular fascination with demonic possession spurred by the release of *The Exorcist* (the book), a number of movies provided cinematic variations on this theme: *Blacula* (1972), *The Possession of Joel Delaney* (1972), and *The Exorcist* (1973). In *The Possession of Joel Delaney*, we are offered a Hollywood vision of what would happen if a Puerto Rican "voodoo demon" possessed the mind and body of young, wealthy, white, Joel Delaney (played by Perry King). The movie revolves around Delaney's sister's (Shirley MacLaine) attempt to find out what has happened to him. In addition to cutting off people's heads and putting them on the shelves with the sugar and spices, the "possessed" Joel Delaney tortures his rich sister and her kids. He forces them to strip and dance naked, to eat raw fish and dog food, and to play dominoes with him at knifepoint. Perry King's terrible Spanish accent and his comical conjugating of verbs in Spanish are overshadowed only by the realization that the film really expressed the stereotypes and fears of those who made it.

A Hardening of the Image: From
Assimilation to Annihilation

By the late 60s, the portrayal of both cops and criminals changed, reflecting America's disillusionment with the "failure" of the "War on Poverty," and a growing fear of ghetto militancy and youth protest. "In the movies of the seventies, the policeman was very much his own man—judge, jury and executioner—and he lost all allegiance to the law. The criminal, too, lost human definition and became a mere target. Society lost its authority and was usually portrayed as an ineffectual, often corrupt entity" (Clarens, 1980).

This was the era of Richard Nixon, what one Puerto Rican social commentator, borrowing from poet-musician Gil Scott-Heron, labeled "Winter in America." It was a time of "law and order," the "white backlash," Vietnam, "dirty tricks" against political rivals, increased infiltration and police repression against opponents of the government, especially militant groups and their leaders, and the official burial of the "War on Poverty."

A new variation on the cops and criminals theme emerged. It has been called variously, the urban western, the street western, the urban action drama, and the violent urban thriller. These movies took the mythic cowboy hero and moved him from the wide-open spaces of the West into the crime-ridden, dirty, and dangerous streets of urban America. They focused on crime in the inner cities and offered visual and spoken statements about crime, the kind of people who commit crime, and solutions to this very contemporary problem.

Beginning in 1970, police were more openly being portrayed by Hollywood as the "thin blue line," standing between society and the savages that would destroy it. One film called them *The New Centurions,* drawing a comparison with the elite force that guarded imperial Rome's gates against the "barbarians" of that age. Films in this category included *Dirty Harry* and *The French Connection* (1971), *The New Centurions* (1972), *The Seven-Ups* and *Badge 373* (1973), *Magnum Force* and *Death Wish* (1974).

In all of these films that are set in New York, Puerto Ricans are included among the criminal villains. If as Carlos Clarens argues, "Crime films should be seen as indicators of America's changing attitude toward crime," they must also be seen as indicators of a changing attitude towards those portrayed as criminals.

As the Nixon and post-Nixon eras progressed, cinematic attitudes towards Puerto Ricans shifted away from the optimistic assimilationist view that held out the possibility of the Puerto Rican "inferior" eventually being "civilized." *Badge 373,* released in 1973, marked the beginning of this shift, and simultaneously signalled the beginning of modern Puerto Rican protest against media stereotyping. According to its distributors, Paramount Pictures, *Badge 373* was based on the "real-life" career of a former New York detective, Eddie Egan (as was *The French Connection*). In the movie, Egan is played by Robert Duvall, and Egan himself plays a minor part. The plot involves a tough police detective trying to avenge the death of his partner at the hands of heroin dealers who are in alliance with Puerto Rican "radicals."

The movie's Puerto Ricans, a vicious low-life crew, murder, peddle heroin, and prostitute their sisters (a theme first presented 14 years earlier in *The Young Savages*) in order to buy guns for a revolution in Puerto Rico. The detective is under suspension after the death of a suspect he is chasing; but as the movie progresses, the need for extra-legal violence by the police is validated by the portrayal of the inhuman Puerto Rican criminals.

The *New York Times* review of the movie said:

> All of the evil is perpetrated by Puerto Ricans, either innocent but violent revolutionaries who run around shouting "*Puerto Rico Libre*," or uninnocent, but violent nonrevolutionaries who manipulate them. Against such forces, Eddie, the hard-nosed cop has only the instincts of his personal bigotry to guide him. And invariably the instincts of his personal bigotry turn out to be right. There is absolutely nothing to praise in *Badge 373*. . . . At some level, the screenplay means to make use of racial prejudices, expressing them, but not endorsing them, and enjoying a free ride through current anxieties that ought to be worth something at the box office (Greenspun, 1973).

Controversy over this film was fueled by the fact that its screenplay had been written by Pete Hamill, at that time a well-known liberal journalist who had frequently written sympathetically about the Puerto Rican community. In addition, one of its characters, the leader of the Puerto Rican radicals, was played by Felipe Luciano, the former chairperson of the Young Lords revolutionary organization—in his pre-Hollywood days. Indeed, the radicals in the film were obviously modeled after the Young Lords and similar groups, even adopting their identifying "uniforms" of berets and field jackets for authenticity. *Badge 373* thus added to already-existing Puerto Rican media stereotypes the image of the discontented, misguided and ultimately ineffective "revolutionary."

Badge 373 criminalized the Puerto Rican independence movement. It made it appear that no law-abiding, rational Puerto Rican supported independence for Puerto Rico, only a small criminal fringe element. Interestingly, during this period, the issue of Puerto Rican independence was winning worldwide support. The same year *Badge 373* was released, the United Nations Committee on Decolonization introduced a resolution that was approved by a majority of the nations in the General Assembly, affirming "the inalienable right to independence and self-determination for the Puerto Rican people."

Two weeks after *Badge 373* opened, a demonstration was held at the home of Paramount's parent corporation, Gulf and Western. The Puerto Rican Action Coalition condemned *Badge 373* as racist because it "denigrated the Puerto Rican community" and "vividly expresses the lack of respect for the dignity of the Puerto Rican people." The protestors demanded that the movie be withdrawn from circulation and that representatives of the Puerto Rican community be allowed to review future film scripts that concerned Puerto Ricans. Paramount president, Frank Yablans, rejected the protestors' demands. However, after a series of militant demonstrations at theaters, and after a small bomb exploded in one of the theaters showing the movie, *Badge 373* was quietly withdrawn from New York. However, it has since been "recycled" as a much edited TV movie and a rental video tape.

This militant community response to anti–Puerto Rican stereotyping seems to have temporarily stopped other exploitation-minded producers, much as the anti–*Fort Apache, the Bronx* protests forced anti–Puerto Rican images off the screens for a few years in the early 1980s. However, six years after *Badge 373,* in 1979, *Boardwalk* focused on the victimization of an elderly Jewish couple (Lee Strasberg and Ruth Gordon) at the hands of a Puerto Rican youth gang in Coney Island. The movie ends with Strasberg strangling one of his young Puerto Rican tormentors to death in the Coney Island surf. A *Village Voice* review of *Boardwalk* said:

> These kids are presented as cardboard characters who rape and steal and burglarize and vandalize synagogues just because that is what they do. They have no unemployed parents, they have no rotting homes, they have no poverty, they have no failures in school, they are not turned away from jobs they seek, they have no self-esteem dragging in the gutter and they are not called spics. They are just mad dogs, hauled on the screen when the script calls for a dramatic representation of the disintegration of the neighborhood or to set up the improbable denouement, which I can't figure out why an intelligent, sensitive man like Strasberg would agree to play in the first place.
>
> But you see, the Puerto Ricans are just getting organized. They do not yet have the loud voices that are available to the blacks. So the producers let the blacks slide, this time, and stick it to the Spics, who after all can stand as a metaphor for anyone who is not white. It is slippery, vicious racism. It is somebody's racist fantasy right up there on the screen in technicolor. This movie is rotten at its core.
>
> And it stinks (Wilkins, 1979).

However, another *Village Voice* reviewer had a different reaction to *Boardwalk* and found the charge of racism "somewhat simplistic." Andrew Sarris, comfortable with the image of Puerto Ricans as the "oppressors" of Jewish people said:

> For the first time in my memory, a thoughtful Jewish character has not bothered to try to "understand" his oppressor, or to reason with him. The only answer to force is counterforce, the only remedy for the evildoer is execution. An eye for an eye. The archetypical survivors do not intend to become the archetypical victims once more. This is the ultimate "message" of *Boardwalk,* and it is not the first time that a very bad movie has brought us very significant news (Sarris, 1979).

This urban revenge theme was repeated in the 1980 film, *The Exterminator,* in which a Vietnam veteran goes after a Puerto Rican gang that mugged and left his friend paralyzed for life. The "exterminator," played by Robert Ginty, utilized hollow-point bullets filled with mercury, an industrial meat grinder, a machine gun, and an acetylene torch to dispatch the Puerto Ricans and other "urban vermin." Once again, the Puerto Rican characters were cardboard symbols; they had no personalities. They were not people as we know human beings to be; they were really the embodiment of evil and seemed to have no purpose in life except to maim, kill, and destroy.

Fort Apache, the Bronx: *The Producers, the Stars, and the "American Renewal"*

Badge 373, Boardwalk, and *The Exterminator* were the immediate predecessors of *Fort Apache, the Bronx.* On March 1, 1980, filming for the movie *Fort Apache, the Bronx* began in the South Bronx. The movie was financed by Time-Life Films, a division of Time Inc. Time Inc. is a major media conglomerate. In 1980, it ranked 137th in *Fortune's* "500 Largest Industrial Corporations." It was the leader in the category of "Publishing, Printing Industry." It owns *Time, Life, Fortune, Sports Illustrated, People,* and *Money;* Time-Life Books, Records, and Films, Little-Brown and Co.; the Book-of-the-Month Club; Time-Life Television, Video, and Multimedia; Home Box Office; Manhattan Cable TV; and Talent Associates, Ltd. Recently, it acquired Warner Brothers and is now known as Time-Warner.

Simultaneous with the release of *Fort Apache, the Bronx* in 1981, Time Inc. made publishing history by announcing that each of its magazines would simultaneously feature articles written around a single theme, "American Renewal." The messages of this "Special Project" would reach 68 million readers. The perspective of this historic single-theme series was outlined in its ads. America was suffering from a lack of national self-confidence and sense of purpose. Americans were becoming overwhelmed by the problems they see facing the nation at home and abroad. To combat defeatist notions, Time Inc. was going to run a series "to dispel the notion that nothing can be done about the crisis . . ." and to show that Americans united can solve any problem.

Fortune's contribution to the "American Renewal" series included a discussion of "The Right Way to Strive for Equality." The magazine argued that while all Americans oppose bigotry, the civil rights movement of the past had gone too far, had become too expensive, and its supporters had become too militant. It referred to affirmative action as a "numbers game of quotas." It described the inner city ghettos as "a running sore" that is an "affront to American ideas," drawing upon negative images of disease and social pathology. Bilingual education was identified as a barrier to progress and upward mobility. Finally, the article concluded that, in economic terms, discrimination was no longer of major significance, implying that the widening economic gap between whites and people of color is not rooted in institutional or individual discrimination, or structural causes. This perspective, in effect attributes the deficiencies of people of color as an alternative "explanation."

The entire series very closely mirrored the views of the Reagan administration. And many of these same views and opinions were expressed in the movie *Fort Apache, the Bronx,* where the ghetto was very vividly depicted as a "running sore." This is not to reduce the film to simply an exercise in propaganda, but rather to identify the ideological perspective of those that financed and produced it. The film was intended to make money, and in fact was part of a much larger Time Inc. plan. It was part of a three-film package that marked Time-Life Film's entrance into the film production business and was linked to their plan to produce movies that could be recycled later through "pay-tv, cable, network, public broadcasting, and station syndication on a somewhat sequential basis."

The movie's executive producer was David Susskind, a well-known film producer and talk-show host with a liberal reputation. By 1980, like many other American liberals, Susskind had come to embrace many views identified only with conservatives. He told *Daily News* gossip columnist Liz Smith he would vote for Ronald Reagan because he was disgusted with both the domestic and foreign policy of the Democrats. The movie's producer in the streets was Daniel Petrie, whose past credits included the widely-acclaimed movie version of *A Raisin in the Sun,* Lorraine Hansberry's Pulitzer Prize-winning play about a Black family made in 1961, which Susskind produced.

The stars of the movie were Paul Newman, a screen "heart-throb," long associated with social causes; and Ed Asner, television's prize-winning "Lou Grant," an actor whose name was almost synonymous with progressive causes.

Why Films Are Important to a Civil and Human Rights Movement

Commercial movies are complex productions. They are designed for a mass audience in order to make money. They are influenced by box-office reports, analysis of popular trends, developments in other popular arts (i.e., music video), and the analysis of movie workers in the "moods, values, tastes, and concerns of their surrounding society" (Sklar, 1975). In order to make their product as attractive as possible, producers and financiers try to gauge what the public wants, what the public will believe, and what the public will pay to see. This is why many media analysts view films as historical documents which can often illuminate the social attitudes and trends of a given time period.

It is important for us to keep in mind also that the technology of filmmaking and film exhibition often overshadows the content of the film. People are more amenable to turning off their critical skills when the lights go off and the movie rolls. Films are especially suited to a non-literal generation, people who don't read, and young people raised in a media environment of short, fast images without interconnected plots or analysis.

Finally, we have to take note of the fact that films are produced today with conscious plans to "recycle" and reincarnate them in other forms. For example, prior to the release of *Fort Apache, the Bronx,* a paperback "novelization" of the screenplay was published. After its release in the theaters, television rights were sold to NBC, cable rights were sold to HBO (also owned by Time Inc., whose subsidiary Time-Life films produced the movie), and the film was distributed overseas. Finally, the movie was released as a videocassette available for sales and rentals. This "recycling" is made easier by the increasing trend towards concentration and monopoly in the mass media, by the emergence of giant media conglomerates that have the interlocking means to recycle media messages over and over again.

Given these developments in the mass media, today negative stereotypes are given "eternal life" and are distributed internationally. This takes on added significance when we consider that many studies argue that when people have no direct contact, most of their learning about other ethnic groups comes from the mass media.

The widely hailed 1968 report by the National Advisory Commission on Civil Disorders (Kerner Commission) is remembered today primarily for its stark appraisal of race relations following the 1960s urban rebellions:

> This is our basic conclusion: Our nation is moving towards two societies, one black, one white—separate and unequal. . . . What white Americans have never fully understood—but what the Negro can never forget—is that white society is deeply implicated in the ghetto. White institutions created it, white institutions maintain it and white society condones it.

The Kerner Commission analyzed the mass media from the perspective that people form their opinions about race "from the multiplicity of sources that condition the public's thinking on all events." The Commission concluded that the communications media was one of the main sources of information and ideas about race relations and contributed to the totality of attitudes held by Americans on racial and other issues.

The fight against media racism is part of the overall struggle to change our conditions. It is an influential arena in which we can struggle against the promoting of white superiority and its corollary, the inferiority of people of color. This struggle can be used to attain concrete immediate gains such as the elimination or repudiation of racist stereotypes and increased employment and financial support for independent filmmakers. It can also contribute to the ongoing goal of community empowerment and the development of a collective political consciousness, organizational capability, and an effective, accountable leadership.

Today we have the responsibility to continue the struggle. Our actions in this area will be a further advancement in the direction taken by the concerned Puerto Ricans who challenged *Badge 373* in 1973 and *Fort Apache, the Bronx* in 1980. The following statement by the Committee Against Fort Apache (CAFA) provides some relevant examples of the importance of the struggle against media racism to our people's advancement:

> CAFA recognized that it was fighting not only the giant media conglomerates which financed and distributed *Fort Apache,* but also the growing right-wing sentiment in America. We were demanding respect and reaffirming the strength and beauty of our history and culture—at a time when our past gains were being eroded and we were increasingly being used as scapegoats for the nation's economic and social failures, and when many American liberals were embracing the "solutions" of the reactionary Right. Recognizing this reality, our goals were primarily educational and organizational: to educate our community about the effects of media stereotyping and show its links to the overall situation we face.
>
> The secondary focus of the boycott organized by CAFA was economic. While we realized that we did not yet have a movement that could shut this movie down nationwide, we could have some impact at the box office. *Fort Apache* made $13 million in domestic rentals, but *Variety* reported that even this was "way below expectations for the costly, controversial picture." After this, and the failure of their other two films, Time-Life Films went out of the movie business.
>
> The organizing against *Fort Apache* also contributed to the unity of Latin, Black, Asian, and white activists for social change. In addition, it helped us identify many progressive media activists, as well as people inside the establishment media, and formed important bonds of unity for future struggle. Finally this struggle helped deepen our community's understanding of the media and showed how we can deal with it effectively. It was a fighting movement which engaged the enemy on a number of fronts, added to the historical legacy of past battles, and advanced the starting point for the next struggles against media racism and for freedom (Pérez, 1985).

NOTES

Reprinted by permission of the author and publisher from *Centro Bulletin,* 2:8:(Spring, 1990):8-27.

1. Quoted in the Verbatim Record of the 1047th Meeting, Special Committee on the Situation with Regard to the Implementation of the Declaration on the Granting of Independence to Colonial Countries and Peoples, 9/2/76, United Nations A/AC.109/PV.1047, p. 51.

2. *Naked City* was a 1948 detective thriller that was considered a highly influential trendsetter because of the gritty realistic feel it achieved with on-location filming. Prior to this, movies were usually shot on studio sets.

3. Cristal, an Argentinean whose real name was Victoria Maya, began playing leads in Mexican films when she was 16.

REFERENCES

Alexander, Francis W. "Stereotyping as a Method of Exploitation in Film." *Black Scholar,* May 1976.

Allport, Gordon, *The Nature of Prejudice.* Massachusetts: Addison-Wesley Publishing Co., Inc. 1954.

Clarens, Carlos. *Crime Movies: From Griffith to the Godfather and Beyond.* New York: W. W. Norton & Company, 1980.

Cortés, Carlos E. "Chicanas in Film: History of an Image," in Gary D. Keller, Ed., *Chicano Cinema: Research, Reviews and Resources.* Binghamton, N.Y: Bilingual Review/Press, 1985.

Gilbert, James. *A Cycle of Outrage: America's Reaction to the Juvenile Delinquent in the 1950's.* New York: Oxford University Press, 1986.

Greenspun, Roger. Review. *New York Times,* July 26, 1973.

Halliwell, Leslie. *Halliwell's Film Guide* (Fourth Edition). New York: Charles Scribner's Sons, 1983.

King, Steven. Introduction. *Blackboard Jungle.* New York: Arbor House, 1984.

Lait, Jack and Mortimer, Lee. *New York Confidential.* New York: Ziff Davis Publishing Co., 1948.

Lewis, Oscar. *La Vida: A Puerto Rican Family in the Culture of Poverty—San Juan and New York.* New York: Random House, 1966.

McGee, Mark Thomas and Robertson, R. J. *The J. D. Films.* North Carolina: McFarland & Company, Inc., 1982.

National Advisory Commission on Civil Disorders. Report. New York: Bantam Books, 1968.

Pérez, Richie. "Committee Against Fort Apache: The Bronx Mobilizes Against Multinational Media" in Kahn, Douglas and Neumaier, Diane, Eds. *Cultures in Contention.* Seattle: The Real Comet Press, 1985.

Poussaint, Alvin F. "Education and Black Self-Image." *Freedomways,* vol. 8, No. 4, Fall 1968.

Reddick, Lawrence. "Of Motion Pictures, Radio, the Press and Libraries." *Journal of Negro Education,* 1944.

Sarris, Andrew. "This Blessed Plot, This Sand, This Realm, This Brighton Beach." *Village Voice,* November 26, 1979.

Sklar, Robert. *Movie-Made America: A Cultural History of American Movies.* New York: Vintage Books/Random House, 1975.

Smith, Liz. *Daily News.* October 22, 1980, p. 8.

Weinberg, Meyer. Minority Students: A Research Appraisal. Washington, D.C.: HEW, National Institute of Education, March 1977.

Wilkins, Roger. "Under the Boardwalk." *Village Voice,* November 26, 1979.

West Side Story: A Puerto Rican Reading of "America"

Alberto Sandoval Sánchez

My final prayer:
O my body, make of me always a man who questions!
—*Frantz Fanon*, Black Skin, White Masks
To my nephew and niece in the U.S.A.,
Laura and Vladimir Estrada Sandoval

After my immigration to Wisconsin in 1973 to attend college, the musical film *West Side Story* frequently was imposed upon me as a "model of/for" my Puerto Rican ethnic identity. Certainly it was a strange and foreign model for a newcomer, but not for the Anglo-Americans who actualize with my bodily presence their stereotypes of Latinos' Otherness. Over and over again, to make me feel comfortable in their family rooms and to tell me of their knowledge about Puerto Ricans, they would start their conversations with *West Side Story:* "Al, we loved *West Side Story.*" "Have you seen the movie?" "Did you like it?" On other occasions, some people even sang parodically in my ears: "Alberto, I've just met a guy named Alberto." And, how can I forget those who upon my arrival would start tapping flamenco steps and squealing: "I like to be in America! . . . Everything free in America."[1] As the years passed by I grew accustomed to their actions and reactions to my presence. I would smile and ignore the stereotype of Puerto Ricans that Hollywood promotes. Or perhaps, was I unwilling to identify with the Puerto Rican immigrants living in New York because of my own prejudices of class or race?

As it happened I moved to New York City in 1983, to the neighborhood of Hell's Kitchen which borders the area where the film takes place, better known today as Lincoln Center. I lived in the neighborhood for eight months with the New York Puerto Ricans. Given that at the time I became acquainted with New York territories

PHOTO 9.1 **West Side Story** (1961). This opening scene from *West Side Story* illustrates some of the symbolic contrasts that Sandoval Sánchez discusses, such as the oppositional stance and physical appearance of the Anglos/Whites (the Jets) and the foreign Latino "Others" (the Sharks). Note also the white and black sneakers. (Courtesy of The Museum of Modern Art Film Stills Archive)

and shared daily the socio-economic reality of Puerto Rican immigrants, I became interested in correlating and contrasting the film with the historical reality of the immigrants. At that time I had the opportunity to see the movie, which was shown at the Hollywood Theater on Eighth Avenue, between 47th and 48th Streets.

My interest on decentering, demythifying, and deconstructing ethnic, social, and racial stereotypes of Latinos inscribed in the musical film was the result of witnessing the reaction of an Anglo-American audience that applauded euphorically after the number "America." Only then did I understand the power and vitality of the musical, not just as pure entertainment, but as an iconic ideological articulation of the stereotype and identity of Puerto Rican immigrants in the U.S.A. as well as for all other Latino immigrants. I also realized at the same time that in the musical number "America" there is a political campaign in favor of assimilation. Such assimilation is pronounced by a Puerto Rican herself, Rita Moreno, whose acting was awarded with the coveted Oscar Award.

PHOTO 9.2 **María and Tony Suspended in Time.** As this clip from *West Side Story* shows, María and Tony are suspended in time and the real world fades out at the moment that María and Tony meet and fall in love. Sandoval Sánchez argues that this scene conveys the impossibility of their love in the real world and that their love can only exist in an imagined world—as the final song in the film, "Somewhere," suggests. (Courtesy of The Museum of Modern Art Film Stills Archive)

On the other hand, the audience's reception, which was manipulated by a patriotic discourse generated and transmitted through the song, led me to question and problematize up to what point the musical configures, produces, and re-produces a racist discourse of Latinos' Otherness in the U.S.A. How does the musical film project ethnic difference as a threat to the national, territorial, racial, and linguistic identity as well as to the national and imperial subjectivity of the Anglo-Americans?

From such a questioning posture, we should examine how the musical film through its music, its dances, its romantic melodrama, and its exoticism of cultural Otherness distracts from the racism in it. How does it attract, interpellate, and position ideologically the perceiving spectator—whose social construction of reality and racial differences belong to the U.S.A.—by spatially dividing the Puerto Ricans from the Anglo-Americans, Puerto Rico from the U.S.A., the West Side from the East Side, the Latino race from the Anglo-Saxon race, the Puerto Rican cultural reality from the Anglo-American one, the poor from the rich. These binary oppositions produce a political, patriotic, and mythifying discourse in which the Puerto Ricans confront the Anglo-American power as intruders in and invaders of their territory: the U.S.A.

*   *   *

West Side Story depicts a fight for urban space, a space that has already been impregnated with cultural symbols and political significations for the relations, interactions, and social actions according to the "American Way of Life." In this sense, the film projects how the Puerto Rican migration to New York City in the 40s and 50s not only usurps the order and the semiotic spatial organization of the Anglo-Americans, but how it also constitutes a threat for the assumed coherent and monolithic identity of the Anglo-American subject. I am interested in highlighting how the Puerto Rican immigration, from the margins of the ghetto, threatens to disarticulate, according to the Anglo-Americans, their socio-political system at the capitalist center of New York City.

For those who know Manhattan, the city is divided territorially, economically, racially, and ethnically. Each socio-economic group inhabits a space concretely demarcated, and even neighborhood border crossings are avoided. Specifically it has been the film *West Side Story* (1961, but staged on Broadway in 1957) that has contributed to perpetuating the image of the West Side as a site of urban, ethnic, and racial problems.

The plot of the musical film is about the hostility, hatred, and confrontations between two gangs. As the action develops, those gangs ("the Sharks are Puerto Ricans, the Jets an anthology of what is called 'American'" [137]) reveal not a mere struggle for territory but rather a socio-economic and racial confrontation. Although the Jets constitute "an anthology of the Americans," that gang consists solely of children of white European immigrants. Their actions and values already consolidate the ideological apparatus of the Anglo-American political national subjectivity, that is, the ideological program and behavior of the "All-American Boy."

Although they belong to the working class, obviously the Jets' members act according to the values, attitudes, beliefs, and ideals of the Anglo-American national subjectivity. They have an ideological and political consciousness of their nationality and imperial superiority, as shown by their competitive spirit to be "Number One." For this reason, they emblematize the ideology of the "All-American Boy," a totally white identity which does not make room for any other racial groups in the gang. In this way, the Jets define themselves in the first song, "Jet Song," in terms of their own socio-political and personal superiority, confidence, and arrogance:

I want the Jets to be Number One, to sail, to hold the sky! We're Jets! The greatest!

It should be pointed out that blacks have no representation or participation in this "anthology." Is it because they had already been confined to their own space in

Harlem? Hence the Anglo-American power confrontation is limited to the recently migrated racial minority group, the Puerto Ricans.

In its historical specificity, the space of the West Side obtains its total meaning only by reading its "not-said" space—that is, the upper East Side, present because of its topographical contiguity. The upper East Side stands as the center of Anglo-American white power, for the upper bourgeois class resides there. At the same time, the action in the West Side is referred to as a "story." In this way the title silences the dynamic, processual, and dialectical concept of history. It postulates a binary opposition marked by the presence and absence of economic, ethnic, and racial differences: West/East; Story/History; Jets/Sharks; White Anglo-Americans/Spics. In the above terms the title *West Side Story* expresses a merely superficial structure at the level of its enunciation—a story of love. However, when the title is read in metonymical relation to the center of power, an absent structure is registered under the textual surface of the story of love; that is, the film has as its deep structure an explicit discourse of discrimination and racial prejudices towards immigrant Latinos.

From a questioning perspective, I propose to examine how the East Side's absence—a geo-political absence signalled metonymically in the title—becomes present. It displaces and decenters the story of Maria and Tony's love in the West Side. Indeed, my alternative reading, by centering on the absent action on the East Side, concentrates on the ideological production of a political and racist discourse, which could be entitled "East Side History of Hatred/Racism." With this title I name the ideological discourse of the deep structures of the text. By so doing, I decenter the melodramatic and romantic title of *West Side Story.*

My alternative reading based on the binary opposition between West Side and East Side is more fully understood by considering that in 1949 the play's original title was to be *East Side Story.* The play was supposed to take place in the Lower East Side as a love story between a Jewish girl and an Italian Catholic boy. However, with Puerto Rican immigration, the idea became dated. As a result the team of writers and producers would even consider Chicano gangs in their search for some exoticism and "color." As Arthur Laurents has stated:

> My reaction was, it was *Abie's Irish Rose,* and that's why we didn't go ahead with it.
> . . . Then by some coincidence, Lenny and I were at the Beverly Hills pool, and Lenny said: "What about doing it about the Chicanos?" In New York we had the Puerto Ricans, and at that time the papers were full of stories about juvenile delinquents and gangs. We got really excited and phoned Jerry, and that started the whole thing.[2]

Bernstein was really inspired by the Chicano gangs:

> . . . and while we were talking, we noticed the *L.A. Times* had a headline of gang fights breaking out. And this was in Los Angeles with Mexicans fighting so-called Americans.

Arthur and I looked at one another and all I can say is that there are moments which are right for certain things and that moment seemed to have come.[3]

Laurents also seems to have made the following comment:

I suggested the blacks and Puerto Ricans in New York because this was the time of the appearance there of teenage gangs, and the problem of juvenile delinquency was very much in the news. It started to work.[4]

Although the team was clearly interested in juvenile delinquency, it is interesting to observe how ethnic and racial minorities replaced each other. The writers moved comfortably from Jews and Italians to Chicanos to blacks to Puerto Ricans. They were just searching for a confrontation between peoples of color and caucasian Anglo-Americans. Such script assumptions reveal a priori the attitudes and prejudices against racial minorities in the U.S.A. at different historical periods. These prejudices constitute a discourse of racism by framing the racial Other in stereotypes of delinquency, poverty, and crime. That is, indeed, how Puerto Ricans were conceived of in *West Side Story*.

*   *   *

The first scenes of the film establish the dramatic conflict: two gangs fight for social spaces, public territories, and institutions. The first to appear are the Anglo-Americans, the absolute owners of the open spaces, that is, the streets and the basketball court. The crisis surges from the fact that the Jets do not allow the settlement of the Sharks in their territory or "home" (137). As a result, the drama articulates a binary and hierarchical opposition of power relations, and this binarism establishes the dominant paradigm of the musical film: Jets/Sharks; U.S.A./Puerto Rico; Center/Periphery. Even the following binary oppositions can be read: Empire/Colony; Native/Alien; Identity/Alterity; Sameness/Difference.

This bipolarity becomes further materialized iconically in the gangs' names: Jets/Sharks. When the film starts, in the scene where the Sharks are pursuing the Jets, on a wall in the background appears the drawing of a shark with its mouth wide open, exposing its sharp teeth. Such an iconic representation emphasizes the criminal and barbaric potential of all Puerto Ricans. Such Puerto Rican barbarism is confirmed when one of the Jets pronounces,

The Sharks bite hard and . . . we must stop them now.

Clearly the bite has metonymical implications of cannibalism and of sharks' horrifying ferocity. For this reason, Sharks is used as the metaphor to denominate immigrant Latino Otherness coming from the Caribbean. The opposition of Jets vs. Sharks re-produces an ideological configuration that opposes cultural technology to nature, aerial military techniques to primitive and savage instincts, civilization to barbarity. In this context the musical film could be read as an imperialist discourse in which the colonized are represented as a threat to the process and progress of the imperialist and civilizing enterprise.

In this first scene the two gangs have contrasting physical and racial appearances. Most of the Anglo-Americans are blond, strong, dynamic, and healthy and so embody the ideologeme: "All-American Boy." On the other hand, the Puerto Ricans are black haired, dark skinned, and skinny. This first representation installs the spectator within ready-made, stereotypical models of race and socio-cultural behavior. In the scene the Puerto Ricans provoke the Anglo-Americans, and for such actions the Jets expel the Puerto Ricans from their territory. The rejection and exclusion of the racial and cultural Other is made totally explicit with a graffiti stating, "Sharks stink." Later this insult becomes monumentalized as the Jets associate the Puerto Ricans with cockroaches: when Anita, looking for Tony, enters the candy store, one of the Jets whistles "La Cucaracha."

After a rigorous examination of the scenes, one can detect that the Anglo-Americans generally establish command by speaking first and defining the Puerto Ricans in a pejorative way. Take for example the policeman's arrival at the basketball court in the first scene, and later at the candy store. In both scenes the Puerto Ricans are ordered to leave. The policeman wants to talk only to the Jets. In this way the immigrants' voice becomes silenced and marginalized. The policeman says:

> Get your friends out of here, Bernardo, and stay out! . . . Please! . . . Boy, oh, boy. . . . As if this neighborhood wasn't crummy enough.

Indeed, the original text reads:

> Boy, what you Puerto Ricans have done to this neighborhood. (138)

> All right, Bernardo, get your trash outa here. (139)

Although the policeman's statement indicates abuse of power by an agent of power, his individualization as a character does not excuse him from participating in the blatant racism in the apparatus of power. He consciously favors the expulsion of the Latinos: "I gotta put up with them and so do you" (139). It is never a matter of acceptance or integration. Even the Jets make use of a racist and discriminatory discourse in order to expel the Sharks:

> We do own [the streets]. (140)

> We fought hard for this territory and it's ours. . . . The PR's can move in right under our noses and take it away. (141)

> We're drawin' the line.

We're hangin' a sign/Says 'visitors forbidden'/And we ain't kiddin'!

Between the two gangs erupts a hostile confrontation and warlike intensity because
the Jets want to maintain their territory and socio-political order. The Other threatens to snatch away their spaces and institutions (the gymnasium, the basketball
court, the streets, and the candy store). The Jets are not willing to give up:

> We fought hard for this turf and we ain't just going to give it up. . . . These PR's are dif-
> ferent. They keep on coming like cockroaches.

Clearly the Jets judge the Puerto Rican migration to the urban center as an invasion
of cockroaches which reproduces without control and infects the territory. In order
to exterminate them, the Jets prepare for a war: the rumble. These scenes conceive of
the Puerto Ricans only in their whole criminal and barbaric potential. The Jets trans-
fer skillfully the concept of their deadly weapons to the Puerto Ricans:

> They might ask for blades, zip guns. . . . But if they say blades, I say blades.

Those in power enunciate the discourse of the Other. By using such an ideological
strategy of transference and transposition, the script, in the lines assigned to the Jets,
accentuates and perpetuates stereotypes about Latinos, their ways of doing things,
and the image of them as criminals. The Puerto Ricans are only defined in their
criminal potentiality, as carrying weapons that the Jets will have to face and to deem
equal. Indeed, when the rumble takes place, the Puerto Ricans' disposition to fight
(and to assassinate) is accentuated by the script having them arrive first at the location. In this scene when Tony tries to make peace, Bernardo refuses reconciliation.
This stereotype of Puerto Ricans' aggression and violence becomes emphasized by
their killing a Jet first. Also, it cannot be forgotten that in the prelude to the song
"America," one of the young women also jokingly defines Puerto Ricans as criminals: "You'll go back with handcuffs!" (165). In this manner an assumed criminality
of Puerto Ricans becomes stereotyped in the eyes of the Anglo-American audience.

*   *   *

The dance scene in the gymnasium is vital for visualizing the divisive frontier line
between the two gangs. Skin color, dress codes (particularly for the women), and
dance styles define the two gangs. This iconography refers to cultural dress codes, as
well as ways of dancing. In the dance the action changes its course: the hatred between the gangs seems open to the possibility of communication and living together.
This possibility arises from the physical attraction between Tony and Maria. Their
relationship will become a story of love (of course, impossible) which will predomi-
nate from then on as the principal story line.

Maria and Tony's first encounter means love at first sight. The camera captures them exchanging glances, and these glances erase ethnic and racial differences. Such an effacement is duplicated in the camera focus: the space (and gang members) surrounding Tony and Maria are blurred. This juxtaposition situates the couple's love relationship in a mental and utopic space: the newly fallen-in-love couple ignore and absent themselves from immediate reality. From then on Tony and Maria face a dilemma of trying to locate themselves in an historical, urban space which will permit and respect their interracial relationship. Undoubtedly they, and the audience, expect this relationship to result in marriage. Both of them are conscious of their ethnic and racial differences; as Maria says: "but you're not one of us . . . and I am not one of yours." Tony will express later in a song his search for such an ideal space and time:

There's a place for us, somewhere a place for us . . .
There's a time for us.
Someday a time for us . . . Somewhere/ We'll find a new way of living . . .
There's a place for us, a time and place for us.
Hold my hand and we're halfway there.
Hold my hand and I'll take you there/ Someday, somehow, somewhere!

In this way, by erasing the historical present (in the time of the movie), the plot establishes the impossibility of an interracial marriage. Romantic melodrama is a strategy of power to hide and soften the racist discourse. The film's narrative detour from warfare to love story functions as camouflage. In these terms, the system of power disassociates itself from any *consciousness* of racial prejudices and discriminations. Indeed, Tony and Maria become the scapegoats of a racist discourse because their relationship must end in a tragedy. Although their utopic interracial marriage cannot take place, the apparatus of power does not take any responsibility for it.

Instead, the blame falls on the Puerto Ricans because Chino assassinates Tony in revenge for Bernardo's death. Hence, Latinos' Otherness functions within a chain reaction of provocation: the Puerto Ricans provoke the Jets by killing one of them, Tony responds by killing Bernardo, and the chain is closed when Chino kills Tony. With this final death, a happy-ever-after outcome for Maria (and audience) is impossible. In addition, in this last scene the apparatus of power exercises its authority and control by arresting Chino; prison is the only space available for criminal immigrants. Thus, the story contains a chain reaction, a circuit of events which begins and ends with the policeman as the representative of power.

In the final scene the audience identifies with Maria, whose role is that of a mediator. The perceiving spectator dis-identifies with Chino, and although viewers may feel some compassion, clearly only Chino bears the blame for the tragedy. Nevertheless it does not cross viewers' mind that Tony is also a criminal. His crime is obscured behind Maria's love:

When love comes so strong,/ There's no right or wrong,/ Your love is your life!

Ironically, although Tony has killed her brother, she cannot stop adoring him: "Te adoro, Anton." In this scene Maria evokes *la pietá* while holding Tony's corpse in her arms. This image evokes a Christian cultural repertoire that depends on melodrama for its lachrymose manipulation. It also articulates a series of connotations about woman as submissive and suffering mother, as the mother of sorrow and solitude.

Given that Chino will be incarcerated and that Tony is dead, the film's ideological message implies the extermination of all Puerto Ricans and a desire for them to return to their place of origin. Is there no possibility for a future Puerro Rican generation in the U.S.A.? The answer is provided by the text itself as Maria sings the last song. Clearly she states that there is no place for her integration:

Hold my hand and we're halfway there/Hold my hand and I'll take you there/Someday/Somehow/Some . . .

Maria cannot mention a place for her future happiness; in this way her love remains *suspended.* She dreams about a utopia of love after life because the "where" cannot be located either in her present or her place of origin. This "would-be world" does not exist in the text, and tragedy instead of marriage is the only possible ending for the love's closure. In the tragic finale Maria remains on the threshold of "America." She is marginalized, hysterical, and hateful:

WE ALL KILLED HIM; and my brother and Riff, I, too. I CAN KILL NOW BECAUSE I HATE NOW. (223)

At the end, while holding Tony's corpse, she becomes delirious, wishing to join him in the utopic space of eternal love.

No doubt the space without socio-historical contradictions that Maria longs for is beyond the grave. There she would meet with Romeo and Juliet, the literary prototype of the bourgeois melodrama of impossible love. With the film having such a transcendental, ahistorical, and assumed universality in its ending, it erases all historicity. What it re-produces is a mythification where *West Side Story* perpetuates itself for its aesthetic, literary, and apolitical values. Take for example the following comment from film critic Stanley Kauffman:

West Side Story has been over-burdened with discussion about its comment on our society. It offers no such comment. As a sociological study, it is of no use: in fact, it is somewhat facile. What it does is to utilize certain conditions artistically—a vastly different process. Through much of the work dance and song and cinematic skill fuse into a contemporary theatrical poem.[5]

*   *   *

There is no doubt that the song "America" and its choreography constitute one of the most rhythmic, energetic, and vital hits in the history of musical comedy.⁶ Although a Puerto Rican sings it, its patriotic message is delivered by an assimilated immigrant who despises her origin and autochthonous culture for her preference of the comfort of the "American way of life." This song with Spanish rhythm and a "typical Spanish" choreography centers the spectator in the exoticism and spontaneity of Latino Otherness. Nevertheless, the lyrics make the audience concentrate on the patriotic message exposed in the political exchange between Anita and Bernardo. The song, performed by the Puerto Ricans on the roof of the building (notice how they are confined to closed spaces), pretends to be Puerto Rican self-definition or enunciation. The song's confrontation of identities takes place when the Puerto Ricans consciously take sides on issues of nationalist ethnicity and assimilation. The importance of this scene does not simply derive from its comical aspect but also lies in the fact that here the Puerto Ricans insult each other for being divided politically and ideologically between nationalists and assimilated.

This scene was a racist and defamatory articulation towards Puerto Rico in the original text. In the film version, it was revised in order to soften a negative attitude toward Puerto Rico and Puerto Rican immigrants. Indeed the song "America" in its two versions consolidates the drama's political and ideological nucleus. Although in the original version, Anita proclaims openly her total assimilation and scorns her native land and its historico-cultural reality, the cinematographic version makes use of irony when she is singing, "My heart's devotion." Immediately the line is followed by a statement of contempt: "Let it sink back in the ocean."

ORIGINAL TEXT:
Puerto Rico . . . You ugly island. . . .
Island of tropic diseases.
Always the hurricanes blowing,
Always the population growing . . .
And the money owing. And the babies crying.
And the bullets flying. (167)

CINEMATOGRAPHIC TEXT:
Puerto Rico . . . My heart's devotion . . .
Let it sink back in the ocean.
Always the hurricanes blowing,
Always the population growing,
And money owing. And the sunlight streaming.
And the natives steaming.

Anita enunciates Puerto Rican reality as an underdeveloped country with all kinds of natural disasters, socio-economic and demographic problems, and crime. Although Bernardo discredits and demythifies Anita's exaltation of the "American Dream," his comments are subordinated and silenced because of the song's patriotic pro-U.S.A. propaganda. Anita expels any dissidence against the "American Dream" in "the land of opportunity":

> If it's so nice at home, why don't you go back there? I know a boat you can get on. (167)

Furthermore, Anita echoes the dominant ideology as she advocates total assimilation according to the example of other immigrant people in the past:

> Ai! Here comes the whole commercial. The mother of Tony was born in Poland; the father still goes to night school. Tony was born in America, so that makes him an American. But us? Foreigners! (165)

In this way the myth of immigration to the U.S.A. is re-actualized; those who may not like it can leave the land of Uncle Sam. In such terms the prejudices, discrimination, and racism that Latinos face in the U.S.A. are eliminated and silenced. What the song emphasizes and expresses is the economic prosperity and the instant material gratification of immigrants. Anita voices the dominant imperial ideology in the original text:

> Automobile in America. Chromium steel in America.
> Wire-spoke wheel in America. Very big deal in America!
> I like the shores in America! Comfort is yours in America!
> Knobs on the doors in America,
> Wall-to-wall floors in America! (168)

In spite of Anita's assimilation, once she finds out that Bernardo is dead, she changes her attitude towards the Anglo-American system. Ironically Anita, the most assimilated, ends up the most ethnic by affirming her cultural difference. Such difference becomes impregnated with hatred up to the point of telling the Jets, without fear and in total challenge: "Bernardo was right. . . . If one of you was bleeding in the street, I'd walk by and spit on you" (219). From a position of pain and rage, she advises Maria to forget Tony and, "Stick to your own kind!" In this scene now it is Anita advocating racial and ethnic segregation. In this way the system of power does not experience any guilt feelings for its racial discrimination—provided that Puerto Ricans will always be Puerto Ricans, and in instances of crisis, no matter how assimilated, they will always join their own people. The threat of racial Otherness is concretized in Anita's self-conscious difference, by extension, the potential to rebellion and socio-political subversion.[7]

On the other hand, now that Anita opposes Maria and Tony's interracial marriage, the system of power exempts itself from preventing such a marriage. In the end, it is the Puerto Ricans themselves who advocate getting married with members of the same race and culture.

*   *   *

West Side Story has had international fame and success. I have demonstrated how the universal plot of a love story registers, in its historical specificity, a racist discourse. Critics elided the issue of racism and concentrated on urban problems of juvenile delinquency. The choreography was highly praised, and a critic even proposed conserving the film as a cultural monument:

> If a time-capsule is about to be buried anywhere, this film ought to be included, so that possible future generations can know how an artist of ours [Robbins] made our most congenial theatrical form to respond to some of the beauty in our time and to the humanity in some of its ugliness.[8]

This "ugliness" cannot be verbalized because it would uncover the truth: *West Side Story* discursively articulates racial discrimination in the U.S.A.

However, the racist discourse is not totally silenced within the textual surface. In one sense when Anita enters the candy store, the practice of racism flourishes openly. While stopping her, one of the Jets says: "She's too *dark* to pass." Such a declaration confirms that the struggle for territorial supremacy is truly based on racial discrimination, of a sort which often is not euphemistic. In this way, the text contains its own critique of racism, which it locates in several domains: adolescence, juvenile delinquency, agents of power, and even in the spectators' point of view.

Another moment of possible racism appears in the film version when policeman Schrank kicks the Puerto Ricans out of the candy store and proposes a deal to live together in the neighborhood:

> I get a promotion, and you Puerto Ricans get what you've been itching for . . . use of the playground, use of the gym, the streets, the candy store. So what if they do turn this whole town into a stinking pig sty. . . . What I mean is. . . . Clear out, you! I said, Clear out! . . . Oh yeah, sure, I know. It's a free country and I ain't got no right. But I got a badge. What do you got? Things are tough all over. Beat it!

There is no doubt that he has the power and the laws to protect the country from any threat, usurpation, or disorder. Although he justifies his abuse, he is applying the national law that legitimates his abusive actions. From such a hegemonic, hierarchical, and racist position, the badge gives him power and legitimization rights. The badge is the emblem that endorses his own racism and discrimination toward the racial Otherness whom he calls openly and insolently "Spics." If he has the badge, a symbol of power, superiority, and official law, all that the Puerto Ricans have is their skin.

The blanks must be filled in so that one can read explicitly the inscribed racism in the agent of power's actions: "You got the [dark] skin." It cannot be clearer: racist discourse does not disappear at all from the textual surface. Once you fill in the blanks, that discourse reappears and erupts, subverting the policeman as well as the institutions of legal justice, maximum representatives of Anglo-American power and law, in their own practices of racism.

CODA

> The colonial child was made to see the world and where he stands in it as seen
> and defined by or reflected in the culture of the language of imposition.
> —*Ngugi wa Thiong'o, Decolonising the Mind*

I do not deny it at all. After seventeen years of living in the U.S.A. my own personal experience as an ethnic minority has led me to question the U.S.A.'s cultural and political system. I, who upon my arrival was an assimilated "American" and more Anglo-American than the "Americans," as the years passed became more Puerto Rican and more Latin American in the U.S.A. This process of disassimilation and decolonization resulted in this experiential and testimonial reading of *West Side Story*: a differential, alternative, provocative, marginal, and radical reading. I do not deny that this is an ideological and political reading, but so are the ones that pretend to be neutral, like traditional scholarship in academia. My aim has been to question, to read from the margin, and to fill in the blanks with the "not-said" in order to de-center, subvert, and transgress *West Side Story*'s official ideological discourse. As a result, I have tried to demythify and rescue the racist ideology that was silenced but registered in the textual interstices. This racist discourse is clearly inscribed in institutions of cultural power like Hollywood and Broadway and their official critical response.

Finally, I rescue a quotation from Stephen Sondheim, who wrote *West Side Story*'s lyrics, when he was asked to collaborate in the musical. He declared openly that he had never met a single Puerto Rican, nor had he shared their socio-economic disadvantages:

> I can't do this show. . . . I've never been that poor and I've never even known a Puerto Rican.[9]

Then, what are the Puerto Ricans in *West Side Story*? Are they simply literary products, ideological signs, and cultural discursive stereotypes of the Anglo-American socio-political system of power? Indeed, this cinematographic figurative construction has propagated the image of Puerto Ricans in the U.S.A. and internationally up to the point of becoming the referent a priori, the "model of/for" immigrant Puerto Rican ethnicity and identity. The reading gets more complicated when the Puerto Ricans themselves identify with this pseudo-ethnic film image produced by the U.S.A.'s cultural imperial power. Those readings rather reveal the colonial condition of Puerto Ricans. Once they are interpellated by the prefabricated Hollywood image—"Made in the U.S.A."—of their ethnicity, they identify with the imperial object/image projected in the screen. The final result is their appropriating that image as their own and accepting it as the enunciation of their own socio-historical and cultural subjectivity.

Nevertheless, both Puerto Rican and Anglo-American spectators ignore that in order to achieve the perfect rivalry and hatred between the Sharks and the Jets, Robbins

made use of discriminatory practices and racist implications. Even though such practices contributed to the success of the theatrical and cinematographic productions,
they can easily be reactualized and reactivated in every single staging and screening:

> Jerry Robbins started *West Side* with a bunch of amateurs who had never played roles
> anywhere—just a bunch of kids who danced in shows. He would always call them in
> groups, "You're the Jets," and "You're the Sharks." He would put up articles about inter-
> racial street fighting all over the bulletin boards where he was rehearsing. He would en-
> courage them not to eat lunch together, but to stay in groups.[10]

And, if those practices were not enough for the staging of the musical, Maria must
also dye her skin dark in case the actress is too white to embody the Puerto Rican
race. Such an action is the result of the Anglo-American socio-cultural and political
system that conceptualizes all Puerto Ricans as a racial Other and stereotypes them
as blacks. This happened to Jossie de Guzmán who had the role of Maria in the 1980
production on Broadway. If they darkened her skin, they did not have to do it to
Debbie Allen, a black actress who played Anita, nor to Rita Moreno in the film version. De Guzmán commented with surprise:

> "Oh, my God, I am Puerto Rican—why do they have to darken my hair?" They dark-
> ened her pale skin too, and after a bit she liked that, wanting literally to "get into the
> skin of Maria."[11]

Therefore, where do the Anglo-American cultural system's practices of racism start
or end: in the rehearsals, in the theatrical production, in the screening of the film, or
in the reception of the audience and the critics?

NOTES

This article first appeared in *Jump Cut,* January, 1995, pp. 59–66. Reprinted by permission.

1. *Romeo and Juliet/West Side Story,* edited by Norris Houghton (New York: Dell Publishing
Co., 1965; 167). The movie was produced by Mirisch Pictures in 1961, and it was distributed
by United Artists. The play was staged at the Winter Garden Theater in New York City in
1957. In this essay I alternate the movie script with the theatrical text. The play was partially
revised for the film. By using both versions my goal is to make of both a single cultural, ideological, and political text which rescues the silences or censorships in the movie version. All
quotations belong to the above edition of *West Side Story;* however, when there is no page
number next to the quotation, I am using the movie dialogue directly.

2. *Broadway Song and Story,* edited by Otis L. Guernsey (New York: Dodd, Mead, 1985; 42).

3. Craig Zadan, *Sondheim & Co.* (New York: Harper and Row, 1989; 14).

4. Joan Peyser, *Bernstein: A Biography* (New York: Beech Tree Books, 1987; 257).

5. "The Asphalt Romeo and Juliet," *The New Republic* (October 23, 1961): 28.

6. Jack Delano, a photographer who has lived in Puerto Rico and published a book with photos of the island and its people, observed in his introduction about the song "America":

> But the colonialism of the ruling nation goes further, for it colors the attitudes of nearly everyone who must deal with Puerto Rico. Even in its literature, art, and aesthetics, Puerto Rico is commonly misunderstood. The musical *West Side Story* is relevant here. In the words of its most popular song, the United States is referred to as "America." But no one in Puerto Rico ever refers to the United States as "America" and no Puerto Rican ever did. All Latin peoples in the Southern Hemisphere believe that they are Americans, too. (Since they reached the New World and settled the Antilles more than a century before the first English colony was established in North America, they have a fair case.) And the melodies of Bernstein, for all their beauty, could only have been composed by someone for whom Mexican and Puerto Rican music are essentially the same—that is, "Latin." The rich and distinctive musical tradition of Puerto Rico is almost entirely absent from *West Side Story.*

Puerto Rico Mío: Four Decades of Change (Washington: Smithsonian Institution Press, 1990; 4).

7. A similar situation occurs when Bernardo says to the Jets before the rumble starts:

> More gracious living? Look, I don't go for that pretend crap you all go for in this country. Every one of you hates every one of us, and we hate you right back. I don't drink with nobody I hate, I don't shake hands with nobody I hate. (190)

It is evident that the ethnic minority defines itself in terms of hatred and violence while the Anglo-Americans never verbalize their hatred, I should say, their racism. The system of power allows for the minority to speak on its behalf; in this way, it takes no responsibility for discrimination and racial oppression.

8. S. Kauffmann, 29.

9. *Sondheim & Co.,* 14.

10. *Sondheim & Co.,* 19.

11. Nan Robertson, "Maria and Anita in *West Side Story,*" *The New York Times* (February 22, 1980): C-4.

10

Keeping It Reel?
Films of the 1980s and 1990s

Clara E. Rodríguez

Chances are you cannot recall the last time you saw a Latino in the movies who was not somehow enmeshed in violence, whether as victim, villain, or cop. Violence in movies is not the exclusive domain of Latinos. Indeed, it seems to be pervasive and is cause for great concern at all levels, from local PTAs to the U.S. Congress.[1] But the now long-standing—and growing—association in the media of particularly Latino images with violence is becoming ever more obvious. This association began with the early *bandidos* of the silent screen; took voice in the westerns of the subsequent period; moved to urban settings in the 1960s and 1970s with images of juvenile delinquents; and continues in the 1980s and 1990s with gangs, criminals, and drug lords. Although this association has always been present, it has intensified and become more predominant in recent popular films. As in society in general, males are more often associated with crime and violence than females, but as the chapters and photos in this volume indicate, in the past other images predominated at times and prominent Latino male actors were less narrowly typecast.

Some of the best-known Latino movies of the past two decades, for example, *Scarface* (1983), *Carlito's Way* (1993), *The Specialist* (1994), *American Me* (1992), *Mi Vida Loca* (1994), *El Mariachi* (1993), and *The Mambo Kings* (1992), illustrate this strong association between Latinos and crime. Set in Latino communities, these movies often had as central to their themes, or as an unspoken backdrop, crime, drugs, and violence. This was the case whether the films were written or directed by Latinos or non-Latinos.

Scarface (1983), for example, was a remake of a 1932 film in which no Hispanic characters or themes appeared (the mobsters were Italian). In the 1983 version, directed by Brian DePalma, the film is set in Miami and involves Cuban, Colombian, and Bolivian drug lords. The main character is Tony Montana (played by Al Pacino), a coke-snorting Cuban refugee with few redeeming moral scruples and a blind ambi-

180

tion to make money in the United States by whatever means necessary. In this film, it is hard to identify a single positive Latino character and practically everyone "deservedly" dies at the end. The film is punctuated by shocking scenes of violence, including an early scene in which a circular saw is used to sever the legs and arms of a reluctant informer. The main character is made to observe the butchering of his friend in a bathroom.

Carlito's Way (1993) contains similar graphic scenes of violence. It was also directed by Brian DePalma, but it was adapted from novels by Judge Edwin Torres of the New York State Supreme Court. It is set in Spanish Harlem in 1975 and also focuses on crime and drugs. The criminals are mainly Puerto Rican, but the characters include the stock blonde girlfriend and assorted petty Latinos with negative attributes. Al Pacino again plays the lead role, Carlito Brigante, a drug dealer from Spanish Harlem who has just been released from prison. Carlito intends to go straight and stay out of trouble, but his past continues to shroud his intent and his future. He becomes involved in crime, and he (also) dies in the end. Carlito is more of a victim than Tony Montana in *Scarface,* victimized by society because of his past and especially victimized by the people he most trusts and who constitute the most substantial elements in his life.

Although *Carlito's Way* might inspire a message of sympathy for Carlito the victim, there are also other more subtle messages about Latinos conveyed in the film. One is the homogeneously negative portrayal of Latinos as criminals. Except for a police official who works in the district attorney's office, the main occupation of Latinos in this film is that of gangster. Violence, guns, drugs, and sex are at the core of almost every scene—and almost all Hispanics are portrayed as involved in a life of crime. Although non-Latinos are also portrayed as negative characters in this film, the dominant images are of small-time Latinos as tough, corrupt, and streetwise deviants.

In addition, although the majority of the roles and the setting are Latino, the major roles are played by non-Latino actors. The two characters who help Carlito are also non-Latinos, his girlfriend, Gail, who calls him "Charlie," and his Jewish lawyer. The underlying message here is that for Carlito to help himself, he must distance himself from his (Latino) community and he needs the help of non-Latinos to do this. But in a curious twist, the lawyer plays a role in Carlito's return to crime. Thus, in the final analysis, nothing can help, because Carlito cannot escape his criminal past. The question, of course, is whether this underlying message is also the more general subtext of the film, that is, the image and message that young Latinos and other viewers receive. If Latinos are to help themselves, must they distance themselves from their communities and enlist the aid of non-Latinos?

The Specialist (1994) was directed by a Latino, Luis Llosa. Like *Scarface,* it is set in Miami's underworld, and although we are not explicitly told the Latinos are Cuban, the "salsa" nightclub scene; the background music by Celia Cruz, Gloria Estefan, and Jon Secada; and the reference to "our cigars" suggest the Latino characters are Cuban. Here again, most of the Latino characters are the kind that the audience would like to annihilate—or as a young Latina student of mine put it, "Everyone feels a sense of catharsis when this guy gets blown to pieces."

In all of these films, Latinos are generally negatively portrayed, with stereotypical, highly accented speech, actions, and gestures, and every major Latino role is given to a non-Latino actor. The casting of non-Latinos as Latinos leads some Latinos to feel that the Latino characters have no Latino flavor whatsoever and they find the fake accents insulting. With regard to Latinas, there are few (if any) of any substance— good or bad.

Curiously, although Latinos are overrepresented in the underworld scenes in *The Specialist*, they are nonexistent in the rest of downtown Miami. For example, Sylvester Stallone's character rides the bus and train and on neither is a single respectable Latino to be spotted. The only Latino on the bus is the proverbial knife-wielding, low-life kid, who rudely takes an older African American woman's seat and consequently is worked over by Stallone's fists.

American Me (1992) is another recent film directed by a Latino (Edward James Olmos) that also focuses exclusively on crime and Latinos. According to the director, the film was intended to give a positive message and dissuade youth from a life of crime, but some viewers feel it glorifies the life of crime simply by placing its characters on the large screen. Moreover, it presents few alternative, positive Latino images of success.

Similarly, *Mi Vida Loca* (1994) has also been criticized as not presenting any valid and positive options in its representation of a "real" picture of gang life among Latinas. Although not directed or written by a Latino, the film was based on actual life stories and used a mixture of actors and real gang members. In doing so, it shed the light of realism on girl gangs in Echo Park, California. But despite being about real people and their real problems, the film offers no real solutions. In addition, women are depicted as having no control over their lives. Thus, for some Latino viewers, it is another film with few positive images or messages.

Finally, *El Mariachi* (1993), directed by Robert Rodriguez, conveys the inevitability of violence in Chicano life. Heralded as the Latino Spike Lee, Rodriguez, a third-generation Chicano, was a graduate student in Texas when he made this film on a budget no one could believe ($7,000). Although the film was made in Spanish, it grossed over $2 million (Avila, 1996:26). The film, which is about a young man who would like to earn his living by singing as a *mariachi*—a harmless, poetic profession—is filled with intense scenes of ceaseless violence. The main character kills men as one might kill flies. In the end, nearly everyone dies, including the would-be *mariachi*'s Latina girlfriend. He lives on with a mechanical hand (he can no longer play the guitar) and appears to have become a hit man. Again, options are few at the end.

The association of crime and Latinos seems to have become routine, with the highly popular television show *Miami Vice* further cementing this association in the public mind. The emphasis given in the film *The Mambo Kings* (1992) to crime in Miami reflects this association. The book, which won a Pulitzer Prize, told the story of the exile, expatriation, and loss of Cuban refugees as reflected in the lives of two brothers. In movieland, the story became much more closely associated with crime than the book had been. Music, featured in the title of both book and film, is subsumed in the Miami crime scene.

Major films not focused on a Latino crime scene often include Latinos only in minor parts as criminals or only in a criminal context. For example, in the major box office film of 1990, *Ghost,* Willie Lopez was a Puerto Rican/Hispanic hit man. More recently, in *Pulp Fiction* (1995), a Latina cab driver, Esmeralda Villalobos, speaking to a boxer, expresses a "special interest" in what it feels like to kill a man.

A number of major Latino-themed films made during the 1980s and 1990s did not focus on crime although they may have contained elements of crime and other problems. Examples include *La Bamba* (1987), *Born in East L.A.* (1987), *Stand and Deliver* (1988), *Salsa* (1988), *House of the Spirits* (1993), *I Like It Like That* (1994), *My Family/Mi Familia* (1995), *The Perez Family* (1995), and *A Walk in the Clouds* (1995). Garcia Berumen (1995:239), assessing the prevailing Latino images between 1980 and 1990, concludes, however, that with the exception of an emerging body of Chicano/Hispanic films, images have continued racist stereotypes. Garcia Berumen argues that in the past two decades Latinos were cast only in incidental roles with negative characteristics, for example, the Puerto Rican nurse who was also a heroin addict in *Fort Apache: The Bronx* (1981), the promiscuous Mexican maid in *Down and Out in Beverly Hills* (1986), and the characters in *Ghost* (1990) and *Pulp Fiction* (1995) noted above. Alternatively, Latino characters are the enemy in xenophobic/"get even" films such as *The Kidnapping of the President* (1980), *Lone Wolf Mc-Quade* (1983), and *Red Dawn* (1984) or drug traffickers in films such as *Crocodile Dundee II* (1988), *Romancing the Stone* (1984), *Cocaine Wars* (1985), *Scarface* (1983), and *Carlito's Way* (1993). Garcia Berumen (1995:233–234) concludes,

> For Hispanic males, the stereotypes were narcotraficantes/drug dealers, criminals or bandits, gangmembers, and undocumented workers. Latinas found themselves inevitably as prostitutes and cantineras whenever a silly summer movie required a "rites of passage" scene for some cherubic Anglo teenager or when some "good ol'boy" contingent of marines wanted some sexual frolic. Television reflected a no more realistic image of American society.

Not only have Latino actors been in "sporadic display," but few films have portrayed Latinos as the majority in this hemisphere (Garcia Berumen, 1995). As we have seen, the insignificant status of Latinos is perpetuated even in those contexts where Latinos are prominent. Films set in cities with substantial numbers of Latinos have few, if any, Latinos in the story lines or even as background figures. This is also the case with major television programs, for example, *Friends* and *Seinfeld,* which are both set in New York. Even in films about Vietnam, such as *Born on the Fourth of July,* one does not become aware of the fact that "Hispanics were one-fourth of the dead in that war and that we won more medals than any other group" (Moctezuma Esparza, cited in Garcia Berumen, 1995:234). As the National Council of La Raza indicated in Chapter 1, these examples illustrate the extent to which Latinos are truly "out of the picture." The question remains whether as we approach the next millennium Latinos will continue to be obliterated in "real and reel life" (Garcia Berumen, 1995:239).

NOTES

This essay was much enriched by the varied insights of the students in my Fordham University media classes, especially, María Jones and Lydia Roca.

1. A more precise measure of the association could be obtained by examining the extent to which Latino-themed movies contain violence as compared with white-dominant or black-themed movies. This has not yet been done.

PART THREE

Creating Alternative Images:
"The Others" Present Themselves

The previous section gave us a historical sense of the presentation of "the Other" in films focusing on Latinos. In this section of the book, we look at how the Others have presented themselves and the alternative images they have created. A historical overview of films and developments in Puerto Rican cinema in New York is the subject of Chapter 11 by Jiménez. In her description, we see the outlines of a Puerto Rican vision that challenged, in very basic ways, then-accepted practices. According to Jiménez, the films produced by Puerto Rican filmmakers were intended to "expose the terrible conditions under which Puerto Ricans were forced to live." The films were also intended to challenge the assumptions under which these conditions thrived. An important message of these films was the need to re-create and rebuild the institutions and the society that had engendered the conditions. Finally, Jiménez notes how Puerto Rican filmmakers privileged poor people and highlighted the active resistance of Puerto Ricans against unjust conditions. She places in historical context the persistent Puerto Rican protests to negative media depictions and thus puts to rest the image of Puerto Ricans and other Latinos as passive, accepting, silent victims. She also describes how Puerto Rican filmmakers took up the struggle to "discover their history" and "to expose, challenge and change their reality and images." (Their situation is similar to that of the Chicano filmmakers described by Noriega in Chapter 5.)

At the forefront of efforts by "the Others" to redefine themselves is the work by Latina filmmakers. In Chapter 12, Kotz examines the new perspectives that Latinas bring to filmmaking. She also explores the institutional, structural, psychological, and aesthetic reasons why Latinas choose documentaries as their medium. Kotz clarifies the differences between these Latinas and male filmmakers, for example, in the frequent integration of fiction, documentary, biography, and autobiography in Latina films. She documents Latina contributions to filmmaking in general while also showing how in mixing genres Latinas acknowledge the complex relationships between women's external and internal realities.

185

Some Latina filmmakers have provided an outlet for previously silenced political voices. In doing so, they have articulated political agendas that take place outside of traditional power structures and attempted to mobilize and sustain popular memory in ways that overcome institutional silence and repression. But perhaps the major contribution of Kotz's chapter is in calling attention to the emerging transnational movement of women in film, reminding us of the transnational bonds that all women share.

Two remarkable examples of effective and honest presentations of the "the Other" are the now classic *Salt of the Earth* (1953) and *Alambrista!* (1976). In Chapter 13, Williams offers a perceptive analysis of positive but realistic Chicano images in these two time-honored movies. She examines why these two movies were successful and concludes that part of the reason is because they do *not* just mechanically invert object and subject, making Latinos the heros and others the villains. Rather, in honestly reflecting a community, these films directly challenge conventional and stereotypic representations of Latinos in the media. The Latinos in these films are authentic types, products of their environment and positioned between two cultures. They are produced by, and they are producers of, history. Also distinguishing these two films is the way in which they illuminate the contexts affecting the individuals, whereas in most Hollywood films the focus is on the individual.

Two modern Latino-themed movies are contrasted in film reviews in Chapter 14 by Nieves and Algarin. Both movies focus on Latinos and, in particular, Latino families. *The Perez Family* was made in traditional Hollywood fashion; *My Family/Mi Familia* was made quite differently, with great care and attention to Latino family values, nonstereotypic depictions, and a predominantly Latino cast and crew. The chapter provides a good example of contrasting images, illuminating the differences between how Latinos are presented as "Others" by persons other than themselves and how Latinos present themselves. We might also note that the film with the more honest and realistic images garnered greater revenues at the box office. Indeed, despite the fact that *The Perez Family* played at twice as many theaters, it made only half as much as *My Family/Mi Familia* in its opening week (Llano, 1995:22). At the time *My Family/Mi Familia* played, it had the highest per screen average revenues of any movie and was the sixth most popular movie (Mejías-Rentas, 1995).

It is not just in films and poetry that "the Others" present themselves. In Chapter 15, Subervi-Vélez et al. examine Hispanic-oriented media, media for which the main audience is composed of Spanish- or English-speaking Hispanics in the United States. The authors review the historical development of Hispanic-oriented media, examining Spanish- and English-language newspapers, magazines, radio, and television. It might be argued that because some Hispanic-oriented media are not owned or controlled by Latinos, they are not representative of "the Others" presenting themselves. But because the programming is produced for the Hispanic communities' consumption, the images projected in these media tend to reflect how the Latino community views or would like to view itself. At a minimum, the images cannot afford to be widely divergent from audience expectations or be extremely negative. Indeed, in many instances, the images are intentionally nonoffensive because the advertisers who underwrite the program are interested in selling their products via this medium. Programs that present a negative view of the community will not sell products.

11

From the Margin to the Center: Puerto Rican Cinema in New York

Lillian Jiménez

Without a doubt, in order to stand on our own two feet Puerto Ricans of all generations must begin by affirming our own history. It is as if we are saying—we have roots, therefore we are!

—*Bernardo Vega*[1]

For many Puerto Rican film and video makers, picking up the camera was equivalent to "picking up the gun" in defense of civil and human rights in the United States after the Civil Rights Movement. The beginning of this "coming to self" as bell hooks describes it, was the desire to expose the terrible conditions under which Puerto Ricans of this generation had been raised; challenge the assumptions under which these conditions thrived; and re-create the institutions and society that had engendered them. In this war, images were a potent weapon. Through popular culture, distorted images of spitfires and Latin lovers (oversexed and irresponsible Latinos), brutish farm workers (substandard intelligence), *bandidos* (untrustworthy), petty tyrants, welfare recipients or drug addicts (undisciplined children) had burned their place into the collective consciousness of Puerto Ricans and the broader society. In effect, the dominant ideology and its cultural machinery indicted Puerto Ricans as responsible for their own conditions. It followed that American benevolence, through its institutions, was necessary to protect them from themselves. In the late 60s and early 70s, a new generation of Puerto Ricans responded to these assumptions with, "*Fuego, fuego, fuego, los yankis quieren fuego*" (Fire, fire, fire, the yankees want fire). As Iris Morales, a Young Lord in the documentary film produced by

Newsreel in the early 70s, *El Pueblo Se Levanta,* says, "I always thought it was my parents' fault; that my parents were the ones who had made this oppression; that they had made everything so dirty . . . but then I started thinking . . ."[2] Puerto Ricans took up the struggle to discover their history and to expose, challenge and change their reality, and images were key in this life and death struggle.

Antecedents

While it has not been widely known, the first Puerto Rican migrants to the U.S. during and after WWI, were deeply concerned with their depiction in the media. By creating a wide network of civic, cultural and political organizations, these *pioneros* organized against all forms of discrimination, including the media. In 1940, *Scribner's Commentator* ran an article entitled "Welcome Paupers and Crime: Puerto Rico's Shocking Gift to the U.S.," which said ". . . all Puerto Ricans were totally lacking in moral values, which is why none of them seemed to mind wallowing in the most abject moral degradation." Though met with rebuttals and mass meetings from 40 Puerto Rican organizations, including the Asociación de Escritores y Periodistas Puertorriqueños, this article was followed in 1947, by a series of equally vitriolic articles in the *World Telegram.* This too was met with an equally vociferous demonstration and picket line that stretched for several blocks.[3]

While thousands of Puerto Ricans had migrated to the United States prior to World War II, it is not until the advent of the intensive industrialization of Puerto Rico through the Operation Bootstrap policies (late 40s–mid 50s) that hundreds of thousands of Puerto Ricans migrated to the United States in search of economic possibilities. Settling in large metropolitan areas on the East Coast like New York, New Jersey and Connecticut, they occupied low income housing readily available as Irish, Jewish and Italian immigrants moved up the economic ladder and away to the outer boroughs and suburbs. Unlike other immigrants, however, Puerto Ricans arrived in the United States as citizens and anticipated benefits from that legal status. Racially mixed, they were more tolerant of behavior and relationships deemed inappropriate in race conscious United States. Confronted by abject discrimination in spite of their citizenship and because of their racial mixture, they developed a survival strategy relying on the existing infrastructure of home town clubs, civic associations and political clubs. To achieve educational and political objectives, they created new organizations like the Puerto Rican Forum and Aspira of New York.

While these first generations of migrants paved the way through internal and external forms of resistance, their strategies were varied and fraught with contradictions. Years of ideological and political domination by Spain and then the United States had instilled the culture with political ambivalence. Some quickly seized the opportunity to remake themselves in the model of the assimilated citizen.

A New Generation

The third generation of Puerto Ricans, who reached their late teens during the volatile and empowering Civil Rights Movement, affirmed their cultural and political identity with the emergence of new community and political organizations in New York. Raised on television, propelled by ideas of empowerment and an unremitting rage against a social order that denied their existence, they repudiated the "complacent" and "accommodationist" strategies employed by mainstream Puerto Rican political leaders of the day. Having been educated in American schools, many had served as intermediaries for their family with educational, health and social service agencies. Having weathered the full fury of institutional racism, accommodation as such was the last strategy they wished to employ. Asserting their presence in militant and forceful terms, theirs was the strategy of direct confrontation. The Young Lords, The Puerto Rican Student Union, The Movimiento Pro Independencia (the precursor of The Puerto Rican Socialist Party), El Comité M.I.N.P., Resistencia Puertorriqueña and El Pueblo del Vladic in the Lower East Side, just to name a few, were engaged in re-creating the Puerto Rican community using as role models Puerto Rican labor figures like Luisa Capetillo and Juana Colón; Nationalist leaders like Don Pedro Albizu Campos and Lolita Lebrón; and international leaders like Che Guevara. Involved in local, national and international issues, they galvanized the Puerto Rican community by traveling to socialist countries, taking up the issue of Puerto Rican independence, creating support committees for Nationalist leaders imprisoned since the early 50s and worked closely with other similar groups within the Black, Asian and white communities. This generation picked up the camera in spite of and in defense of the ones they loved.

An integral component of this political ferment and awakening was cultural revitalization based on nationalism. As "cultural workers," artists of all disciplines collaborated to create new images of Puerto Ricans through the visual arts with the development of organizations such as Taller Boricua and through the poetry of figures such as Pedro Pietri and Sandra María Estévez. A distinct Puerto Rican identity, tied to the Island, rooted in the New York experience and shaped by the anti-imperialist ideology of the period, had emerged. Film and video images created by Puerto Ricans that represented the history, culture and daily reality of the majority of Puerto Ricans were missing.

Realidades

In 1972 *Realidades,* a local television series on WNET/Channel 13, was created through community pressure. It provided the focus and center for Puerto Rican involvement in the broadcast industry and later in the independent film and video field. Community activists Gilberto Gerena Valentín, Esperanza Martell, Diana Caballero, Julio Rodríguez and others formed The Puerto Rican Education and Action Media Council in 1972 to protest negative depictions of Puerto Ricans and advocate for increased employment of Puerto Ricans within the industry. Joined by pioneer filmmaker José García, they successfully pressured WNET, by taking over the studio during an evening pledge, to establish *Realidades* with discretionary station money. Humberto Cintrón, a community activist became Executive Producer. José García, who had established several community film workshops throughout the country for the National Endowment for the Arts, became Executive Producer. Retaining its local focus for two years, several important cultural and public affairs documentaries were produced and acquired, including *Angelitos Negros,* an in-studio dance piece about a *baquiné,* the African-based burial ritual of a young child; *Towards A Collective Expression,* the first documentary by Marcos Dimas about the philosophy and work of Taller Boricua, the visual arts group he co-founded; and *Los Nacionalistas,* a documentary that recaptured the history of Don Pedro Albizu Campos and the Nationalist Party of Puerto Rico. The need to fill a national void of programming for Latinos was met when *Realidades* became a national show and developed programming exchanges with KMEX, a local public broadcast station in Los Angeles. Chicano filmmaker Jesus Treviño's seminal *Yo Soy Chicano* (1972), about the political consciousness of the Chicano movement, was the first film exchange, opening a dialogue between Puerto Ricans and Chicanos. Contact was made with Sandino Films, a collective of filmmakers in Puerto Rico and *Julia De Burgos,* a film about the life and death of the revolutionary poet, by José García was the outcome. This dialogue and working relationship with Chicano directors in the West and Southwest were instrumental in the formation of the National Latino Media Coalition, which legally challenged the industry nationally. In 1974, the Corporation for Public Broadcasting funded *Realidades* as a national series and Lou De Lemos, a Dominican with experience in commercial media, took over as Series Producer.

During this period, *Realidades* served as one of the principal creative magnets within the Puerto Rican community, attracting artists from different disciplines to collaborate and brainstorm on a myriad of projects. Writers, visual artists, poets and film and video makers like Diego Echevarria, working at Channel 13 on another show, and Diego De La Texera, co-founder of Sandino Films in Puerto Rico, gravitated to the series as a creative wellspring. However, a precarious funding base, uneven programming schedule and internal problems caused the *Realidades* series to end in 1975. Initiated by a core group of activists and makers with varying levels of skill and experience given the exclusionary practices of the media industry, *Realidades* launched the careers of many producers, many of whom are still working within the broadcast, advertising and independent film industries: Raquel Ortiz, currently Executive Producer of Cultural Programming at WGBH, Boston; Larry

Varas, CBS in NY; Livia Pérez, independent producer; Felipe Borerro, sound recordist; Eulogio Ortiz, Assistant Director with McNeil Lehrer, WNET, NY; Mercedes Sabio, Program Manager, WOSU, Athens, Ohio; and Lou De Lemos, Children's Television Workshop, New York.

As a consequence of the *Realidades* series and the advocacy and litigation waged by the National Coalition against the stations, José Rivera, the National Coalition's attorney, was the first and only Puerto Rican named to the Board of Directors of the Corporation for Public Broadcasting in the late 1970s. In addition, several Latino public affairs shows were spawned at commercial stations—many of which are still in place today like NBC's *Visiones* and ABC's *Imágenes Latinas*.

The Documentarians: The Media Guerillas

Many film and video makers chose to remain independent of the corporate media structures. The earliest wave of Puerto Rican filmmaking concentrated in the documentary format because of its relative low cost, accessibility and efficacy in representing the conditions under which the majority of Puerto Ricans lived. Newsreel, an alternative media organization patterned after the Film and Photo League of the 30s, espoused the theory that anyone could "pick up the camera and shoot" to create films that empowered people. Generally influenced by the democratic underpinnings of the media movement, a small cadre of Puerto Rican documentarians slowly evolved. Profiles of three Puerto Rican documentarians illustrate the motivation and problems faced by these independent producers.

Carlos De Jesús started out as a photographer until German television asked him to direct a film on housing in New York. This collaboration spawned his first film, *The Devil is a Condition* (1972), a celebration of Latinos and Blacks fighting to improve their housing conditions throughout the city. Made with a cache of liberated film, a borrowed camera, editing facilities and lab processing provided by German television, and an otherwise no-money budget, it was presented at the Whitney Museum and garnered awards at festivals in Paris. Lacking personal resources and requiring an institutional base, he helped found *Imágenes* at New Jersey Public Television and went on to make *The Picnic* (1976), a celebration and sharing of cultural values between Puerto Rican inmates and their families in a New Jersey prison. He continued to work in Latino series within public broadcasting throughout the country because the infrastructure for independent film was in its nascent stage. He currently teaches at NYU and City College in New York, continues to work in photography and video because of difficulty obtaining funds for film projects.

Beinvenida Matías received formal training in film production at La Escuela Oficial de Cinematografía in Madrid, Spain. On her return to the United States, she worked at Young Filmmakers Foundation, a film resource center in the Lower East Side that provided free equipment to independent filmmakers. Lacking experience and knowledge about funding for film, Beni collaborated with Marci Reaven, an NYU student who shared her values and vision about documentary film as a tool for empowerment. They made *In the Heart of Loisaida* (1979), a black and white documentary about early housing take-overs in the Lower East Side of New York by their Latino tenants. It was made essentially through in-kind contributions of equipment, labor and a small grant from Adopt-A-Building, a not-for-profit housing organization. On the basis of the first film, she and co-partner Marci Reaven received governmental support to produce *Through Young People's Eyes* (1981), a color documentary about low-income Black and Latino children in Philadelphia.

While this film was a significant breakthrough for Matías because she now had greater control over her finances, she chose a "holistic" approach to independent film by working with other filmmakers and in other areas of the field. Beni worked as a sound recordist, associate producer and production assistant to survive and refine her skills. Continuing production, she co-directed *Housing Court* (1984), a documentary that explored the complex and arcane operation of the Bronx Housing Court, with Billy Sarokin on a New York State Council on the Arts grant and Sarokin's equipment. By teaming up with people who had access to equipment and common interests, she pragmatically solved her equipment problems. In addition to production work, she served on *Independent Focus,* a local WNET showcase for independent film and video, for five years. Later, she worked with Women Make Movies' *Punto De Vista Latina* exhibition program, presenting Latin American women's films in Latino communities throughout New York and co-edited a catalogue on Third World media. Seeking a more stable creative outlet, Beni secured a job at WNET/Channel 13 on the *Metroline* series as an associate producer and worked her way up to producer. Faced with the hiring fluctuations of public television, she currently freelances.

Pedro Rivera, a history student from San Juan, Puerto Rico, was referred by members of Sandino Films in Puerto Rico to Jaime Barrios, a Chilean filmmaker and co-founder of Young Filmmakers Foundation. With his interest in history, education and film, Pedro began teaching filmmaking to Latino children at the Foundation (now known as Film/Video Arts). There he met his long-time collaborator, Susan Zeig, and together with Jaime Barrios and the *Centro de Estudios Puertorriqueños* (Hunter College) embarked on the production of a historical compilation film about the impact of Operation Bootstrap on Puerto Rico. Continuing his collaboration with the *Centro* and Zeig, he completed *Plena is Work, Plena is Song* (1989), a documentary about working-class Puerto Rican culture expressed through the African-based music and singing of *plena.* Upon completion of that film, he taught in the public school system and is currently freelancing.

In addition to these three documentarians, who without personal financial resources and experience made their mark on Puerto Rican film and video on the East
Coast, there were a number of other filmmakers on the scene dealing with issues of
labor organizing; Latino music and the political status of the Island. *What Could You
Do With A Nickel* (1981), a documentary film about Black and Latino domestic
workers forming a union in the South Bronx was co-produced by the author of this
article; Carlos Ortiz completed *Machito: A Latin Jazz Legacy* (1986), a documentary
film about Frank "Machito" Grillo, the Cuban Latin jazz composer and bandleader;
Zydnia Nazario, an architect by profession, directed *The Battle of Vieques* (1986), a
documentary about naval maneuvers on the island of Vieques off the coast of Puerto
Rico, and is currently fund raising for *Linking Islands,* a documentary film about the
evolution of Puerto Rican art and politics. Another of the few formally trained filmmakers of this era, Vicente Juarbe, directed *Puerto Rico: Our Right to Decide* (1984),
a documentary film on the political status of Puerto Rico for the Methodist Church.

These documentarians were committed to illustrating the history, social issues
and culture of Puerto Ricans so long ignored by the dominant social institutions.
They were groping for a form of expression that would lend itself to the realistic depiction of the complex strategies of survival developed by Puerto Ricans in the midst
of abject racism and poverty. While some of these films suffered from low production values as people struggled with the language of the form, limited funding and
lack of experience, they more than made up for their limitations by their passionate
quest for a validating image. Possessed with an insider's knowledge of the culture and
an unswerving need to express themselves and create celluloid images that were more
reflective of the myriad experiences of Puerto Ricans in the U.S. and Puerto Rico,
their overriding contribution was to defy conventional assumptions and assert that
Puerto Ricans should occupy the center of cinematic discourse. Further, they privileged poor people, relegated to the margins of society, with validating images that reflected the variety of implicit and explicit responses to oppression. Some subjects in-
ternalized their oppression, others fought against it and yet others, determined to
survive, got around it. These multi-faceted responses to oppression gave a name and
face to the invisible "other." The poor and uneducated women in *In the Heart of Loisaida* became their own spokespersons and were elevated as community heroes for
thousands to see.

The Story Tellers

While the documentary form had its advantages, it also had its limitations. A maker
could only work with the material retrieved from the field—if subjects did not speak
about a given point, then they were forced to rely on the narrator. Hence, most of the
aforementioned films utilized narration to a greater or lesser degree. Eschewing the ebb

and flow of the interview and talking heads format, a small group of makers chose the narrative form to visualize their stories about Puerto Rican experiences. The films, for the most part, expressed the subtle and complex fabric of the internalization of racism.

Pablo Figueroa, for example, directed his first narrative piece, *We, Together,* for NBC in 1974 about the dilemma of a fifteen-year-old girl who is compelled to take the reins of the family. *We, Together* presented the interweaving nature of the family, its centrality in Puerto Rican culture and its dissolution in the face of economic and psychological hardship. Deciding to work outside the television format with its inherent formulaic limitations, Figueroa embarked on independently making *Cristina Pagan* (1976), a short narrative about a young mother who accepts the death of her child through spiritualism. Working with a core of Latino technicians at commercial equipment houses, he painstakingly made the film with free labor and his own money. Discovering film through theater, his natural affinity for fiction was realized in the narrative form and he was able to show the inner reality of oppression, while the documentarians had chosen to show its outer manifestations. Unable to secure the financial where-with-all to produce a feature film in the late 80s, he collaborated with the Committee on Hispanic Families and Children to direct *Dolores* (1988), a short narrative, shot on film but edited on video due to economic reasons, about domestic violence within the Latino community.

While Figueroa felt alone in his solitary quest to fictionalize Puerto Rican realities, Luis Soto, formerly with Sandino Films in Puerto Rico and *Oye Willie,* another Puerto Rican series produced by Lou De Lemos for PBS, was collaborating with Angela Fontañez, who started out with *Black Journal,* WNET in 1968. They made *Reflections of Our Past* (1979), a short drama that featured young people traveling back in history to discover their history and culture under a state education contract. Originally part of a series of television programs for young children on Puerto Rican history and culture, only one video was produced. Soto established his own production company making promotional films and commercials and became the first Puerto Rican to direct a film for the PBS dramatic series, American Playhouse. His *The House of Ramón Iglesias* (1982) is a feature-length film adapted from a play about an educated Puerto Rican man who reconciles his love/hate relationship with his janitor father. The film handled the self hatred faced by many people of color head on while not sacrificing the dynamic bonds of love within the family. In 1987, Maria Norman directed *The Sun and The Moon,* a narrative feature film about a Puerto Rican woman's personal odyssey into her identity.

Searching for a Mode

The most prolific maker to emerge during the late 70s was Edin Velez. Influenced by Marshall McLuhan while studying fine arts at the University of Puerto Rico, he journeyed to New York to study video at Global Village. He became involved with the early downtown video scene of the Vasulkas in Soho. Escaping the burgeoning commercial video industry to teach at Young Filmmakers Foundation, he began working on his independent productions in earnest. While he experimented with video synthesizers for a while, his first piece to receive attention was *Tule: The Kuna Indians* (1978), a representational documentary about the Kuna Indians of the San Blas Islands off Panama. His later work, *Meta Mayan II* (1981), was a visceral and evocative personal essay of his trip to Guatemala. Not wanting to become "pigeonholed as the Puerto Rican making Latino tapes," he solicited and received funding from the New York State Council on the Arts to make *The Oblique Strategist Too* (1984), about the composer Brian Eno and *As Is* (1984), a meditation on New York. In 1984, Edin, his wife and partner Ethel and the author of this paper produced *Sanctus,* the first video installation by a Puerto Rican artist at El Museo del Barrio. While living in Japan on a National Endowment for the Arts Fellowship, he directed *The Meaning of the Interval* (1987), a personal essay on Japanese culture and *Dance of Darkness* (1989), about Buto performance.

In an effort to define himself artistically and create his own cinematic language, Edin has explored other cultures and experimented with time, location and the boundaries of the frame within video art. He is currently making a videotape about Puerto Rico, the birthplace he fled in the late 60s. It is likely that the tape will represent a synthesis of his high aesthetic sensibility and all the ambivalence of a Puerto Rican living in self imposed exile.

A Grounding in Self

Missing from the compendium of Puerto Rican filmmakers are several important non–Puerto Rican contributors. Cuban-born and Puerto Rican–raised filmmaker Ana María García made *La Operación* (1982), about the massive sterilization abuse of Puerto Rican women, and is currently editing *Cocolos y roqueros,* a documentary about how race and class are played out through culture in Puerto Rico. Diego Echevarria, a Chilean-born and Puerto Rican–raised filmmaker who worked at WNET and NBC for many years, directed two independently produced documentaries: *Puerto Rico: A Colony the American Way* (1981), a short film about the political status of Puerto Rico, and *Los Sures* (1984), a beautifully crafted film about Williamsburg, a Puerto Rican community in Brooklyn, NY. *Los Sures* premiered at the New York Film Festival but was not well received by many members of the Puerto Rican community because of its focus on marginalized members of the community and omission of stable working class families from Williamsburg. Alfonso Beatto, a Brazilian cinematographer based in New York during the late 70s and early 80s, established the Latin Film Project as a support system for Latin American filmmakers. During that time, he directed *Paradise Invaded* (1977), a documentary film about the colonialization of Puerto Rico in collaboration with José García and other Puerto Rican filmmakers. *Los Dos Mundos de Angelita* (1978), a feature-length film about the dissolution of a Puerto Rican family after its arrival in New York, was directed by Jayne Morrison, a white woman from New York, and written by a Puerto Rican. It featured an all Puerto Rican cast and many Puerto Rican/Latino crew members.

National and cultural affirmation occupied the center of these cinematic propositions as film and video makers struggled to represent and legitimize the history, conditions and cultural development of their communities in the United States. While the advent of small format video technology increased the possibilities of representation, there are only a handful of emerging Puerto Rican makers currently on the scene. Frances Negrón, an Island trained anthropologist and graduate film student, collaborated with community activist Alba Martínez to create *AIDS in the Barrio* (1988), a documentary film about AIDS in the Puerto Rican community. She is currently working on *Brincando el charco,* a documentary film about the development of the many Puerto Rican communities in the U.S. Well-known Puerto Rican artists Pepón Osorio and Merian Soto, who have produced short videotapes as part of their multi-media work, are currently working on a narrative film about Puerto Rican bilingualism and biculturalism, with Cuban Ela Troyano as director and Peruvian Alfredo Bejar as producer. This project represents *Mestizaje,* a cross fertilization of genre, cultures and artistic expression. Entertainment lawyer and member of the Young Lords Party quoted in an earlier section of this paper, Iris Morales, is collaborating with Pablo Figueroa on an examination of the legacy of the Young Lords, a militant political organization created during the political heyday of the 60s. And yet another attorney, Nelson Denis, a Cuban/Puerto Rican who studied film briefly at NYU, has been struggling valiantly to secure funding for his first feature film. A few makers have opted to work in other areas of the independent media field. Yvette Nieves-Cruz studied cinema studies at NYU and directed *L.E.A.R.,* a videotape on the anti-imperialist artists league in Mexico. She no longer makes film or video and is instead a major exhibitor of Latino film/video at the Cinefestival of San Antonio, Texas. Because of the tenuous nature of the field, many have deserted it for more secure careers.

Puerto Rican cinema has grown from its infancy to toddlerhood with little guidance and parental direction. It has emerged and developed in spite of the structural obstacles inherent in denying "voice" within this society. As more makers gain experience and mastery over the forms of their choosing, they will use the medium with more precision, sophistication, flair and experimentation. There is still a striking need for Puerto Rican and Latino makers to produce and direct films and videotapes about a multiplicity of issues and concerns. Some of these concerns are directly linked to the status and conditions of the Puerto Rican and Latino communities in the U.S., yet it would be a grave loss if the makers limit themselves or are limited by cultural institutions and its gate-keepers to just those themes. As we live in a complex and changing world, our special place within the margins allows us to interpret American culture and society in a unique way. We can contribute to the contemporary cultural discourse by producing filmic texts that present the complexity, innovative and myriad experiences of our survival in an often hostile terrain. Our contributions can be to deconstruct and reconstruct the assumptions of this society by presenting other perspectives that are more dialectical in embracing the contradictory nature of life and its dynamic movement. By presenting another sense of space, rhythm, time and seeing that is multi-dimensional, pollinated by a melange of rich cultures and traditions that are ever changing. To continue our process of growth as media makers and as members of various communities, we require not only more production but more Puerto Ricans actively involved in the critique and study of formal issues of film and video. We also need a Mentor program so that more experienced filmmakers pass on their knowledge as consultants to less experienced makers about the subtleties of fund raising; negotiating contracts with crews; and producing, etc. While it is heartening that organizations like the Latino Collaborative in New York provide technical assistance to encourage and pave the way, the issue of production resources remains an ever elusive one.

The films and videotapes discussed in this article grounded a generation of Puerto Ricans who had been nurtured with the dual and contradictory impulses of a colonized people with a passion to resist. We were "never meant to survive" as Audre Lorde says in her poetry and yet we survived, fought back and created. These films and videotapes are our testament to survival. They forced us to look at ourselves, to step outside of our condition and objectify our reality, to deconstruct and then visually reconstruct it with a new vision and power extracted from that painful process. They allowed us to reflect on ourselves—the films were our passageway into ourselves. As makers, we were tormented by lack of opportunity, experience and resources. As spectators, we liked what we saw; sometimes we didn't. Many times we disagreed with the interpretation, but we could never deny that we were engaged in a life-death dialogue about our existence. Those films and videotapes gave us strength. They fed us collectively. Is that what we look like? Is that what we sound like? Is that what our neighborhoods look like? Nobody ever looked at us except as objects and here we were looking at ourselves and sometimes we recognized ourselves—the fear, the hatred, the acquiescence, the strength and our contradictions.

Those films and videotapes came out of a movement for voice. At this historical juncture, while we have found our voice, it is still new to us. Our communities are politically fractured and there is no cohesive nature to our relentlessly slow progress. Film and video, therefore, reflects the need for us to dialogue about our condition. *Dolores* and *AIDS in the Barrio* by the nature of their subjects compel us to dialogue about the nature of racism, sexism and homophobia within our culture and community. The new generation that has been raised within the United States has developed its cultural referents almost totally from popular culture because there is no organized movement within the Puerto Rican communities. We require films that celebrate our emerging cultural forms that are born of a new *mestizaje:* the reality of Latino (Caribbean, Central and Latin American) and African American, Afro Caribbean shared experiences. And films that celebrate the new forms of resistance—the overt and covert forms that they take through song, language and organizations. We need a media that represents the best of *mestizaje*—a melange of our human experience with all its complexity, beauty and insight.

NOTES

Reprinted by permission of the author and publisher from *Centro Bulletin,* 2:8(Spring 1990): 28–43. Copyright © Centro de Estudios Puertorriqueños, 1990.

1. *Memoirs of Bernardo Vega,* edited by César Andreu Iglesias; New York: Monthly Review Press, 1984, p. xii.

2. *El Pueblo Se Levanta,* 16mm documentary film distributed by Third World Newsreel.

3. *Op. cit.,* p. 231.

12

Unofficial Stories: Documentaries by Latinas and Latin American Women

Liz Kotz

The picture North Americans have of Latin American cinema—at its most militant and its most conventional—tends to be overwhelmingly male. Of all the well-known films that comprise what has become known as New Latin American Cinema,[1] only one available in the United States—Sara Gomez' *One Way or Another*—was directed by a woman. This perception persists, despite the diverse and growing body of work by Latin American women—including that by Latinas in North America—which has developed over the past 10 years. In the past two to three years in particular, the sheer quantity of work by such women and the increased opportunities to share contacts and experiences across national boundaries has led to an awareness of a movement that is changing the shape and the direction of New Latin American Cinema. However, outside a handful of features—*The Hour of the Star*, by Susana Amaral; *Patriamada*, by Tizuka Yamasaki; and *Camila*, by Maria Luisa Bemberg—this work remains all but invisible in the United States.

What little attention has been given by U.S. exhibitors and critics has focused almost exclusively on feature films. Despite some recent exceptions, entry into this sector remains limited to the "exceptional few," and the myriad short experimental and documentary films and tapes made by women have largely been generated at the margins of existing film communities—outside the government-funded film institutes and national television systems. This situation is exacerbated further by the tendency to embalm Latin American cinema in the "great directors" model of foreign cinema; witness the current popularity of the program *Dangerous Loves*, an internationally co-produced package of six films based on stories by Gabriel García Marquez. Such programs demonstrate the capabilities of relatively high-budget, studio-based filmmaking in Latin America. At the same time, independent film and videomakers throughout the continent are producing a challenging and tremendously varied array of work. And, as conditions that influence and structure independent production increasingly become international issues—the polarization of mainstream and marginal cinemas, the hegemonic influence of national and international television networks, and the rapidly increasing use of video—Latin American independent media has great relevance for independent producers in this country.

These are also the sectors within which women producers, the vast majority of whom are under the age of 40 (and thus in the early stages of their careers) work. While few have become familiar names on the international film festival circuit, they engage a series of critical issues—what it means to be a bicultural filmmaker, for instance, or what it means to be a woman in a country undergoing a twentieth-century industrial revolution—which promise to expand contemporary cinematic practices, particularly in such genres as documentary.

By examining some recent documentaries by Latin American women alongside works by Latina producers in the United States, I am not attempting to efface the differences between filmmaking in Latin America and the U.S. but instead hope to address the increasingly transnational nature of this activity. This approach reflects a changing cultural landscape, where a number of "immigrant cinemas" and "ethnic cinemas" have sprung up alongside more traditional "national cinemas" and where alliances among those who produce, distribute, and exhibit alternative media are forming across political borders and linguistic boundaries. While omitting many important areas of activity, my discussion will outline some of the shared interests evident in this work and situate it within emerging networks of women producers throughout Latin America, the U.S., and Canada.

In the past two years, a series of key events have helped to build recognition and momentum for this emerging "movement." In October 1987 Zafra A. C. in Mexico City hosted a festival of films and videos by Latin American women, the *Cocina de Imagenes* (Kitchen of Images), at the Cineteca Nacional in Mexico City.[2] As well as presenting 12 hours of work each day during the 12-day event, the festival provided a major forum and an opportunity for Latina producers to meet, become acquainted, and discuss crucial issues. Almost 100 women—over half from outside of Mexico—attended the mass one-day meeting held during the festival to explore problems and plan strategies. The simple fact that there was enough work by Latin American and Caribbean women to provide almost two weeks of programming was an eye opener for many, while the obvious range of styles, traditions, and contexts— from made-for-TV movies to activist videotapes—exploded any preconceived ideas of what constitutes "women's filmmaking." The *Cocina* also resulted in the formation of a biannual publication *Boletín Cine/Video/Mujer* (edited in Canada by film scholar Zuzana Pick[3]) and preliminary plans for another festival in 1989.

Additionally, in the past few years the Festival of New Latin American Cinema in Havana has featured events that showcase the work of women filmmakers, including screenings of major films and large public forums.[4] Although some Latin Americans have questioned the central role Cuba plays in setting international agendas for Latin American film—the Havana festival, the Foundation for New Latin American Cinema, the magazine *Cine Cubano,* and the new *Escuela Internacional de Cine y TV* are all based in Cuba—this annual gathering provides the only regular opportunity for Latin Americans to see work from other Latin American countries. Most of the other major institutions that collect and disseminate information about Latin American cinema are based in the United States, a development that poses questions about the consequences of North American institutions setting the terms of discussion for Latin American media. Regarding work by women, these institutions have become particularly powerful, because the circuits of communication and diffusion of information based in Cuba have tended to neglect the work and concerns of women producers.

In spite of the conservative programming at most film festivals and larger exhibition venues in the U.S., some active efforts are now introducing a range of nonmainstream Latin American work to audiences here. Both the San Antonio Cine Festival and New York–based National Latino Film and Video Festival reflect the explosion of independently produced work. Projects like the Democracy in Communication program of Latin American popular video organized by Karen Ranucci, X-Change TV's subtitling and distribution of Central American television programs, and the Latino and Latin American components of the satellite-distributed public access series Deep Dish TV promise to rethink the diffusion of foreign and minority media in this country. In addition, the *Punto de Vista: Latina* (Point of View: Latina) series assembled by the U.S. nonprofit distribution company Women Make Movies represents a sustained commitment to acquire and subtitle current Latin American works as well as circulate a permanent collection for educational distribution nationwide.

Last October, Cine Acción, a San Francisco–based non-profit organization of Latino and Chicano film and videomakers sponsored the Mujeres de las Americas/Women of the Americas Film and Video Festival, which I codirected. In the course of that event we presented over 60 independently-produced works by Latin American women, about one-third of which were unsubtitled and/or undistributed in the U.S. Almost a dozen filmmakers from Latin America and the East Coast met with the local film and Latino communities during the five-day event, which featured panel discussions on documentary work, Central American media, and Chicana filmmaking. In Canada, Groupe Intervention Video has developed innovative distribution programs designed for educational and feminist audiences, expanding from its original French-language base in Québec to include English-language tapes and materials for distribution throughout the country.

At both the *Cocina* and the Cine Acción festival, the preponderence of documentary work was striking; over 75 percent of the films and tapes screened at both events could be placed in this category. The historical reasons for women using documentary have frequently stemmed from greater professional opportunities in television and journalism, as opposed to the notoriously male-dominated world of feature film production. Yet the vagaries of institutional sexism don't sufficiently explain why so many women are producing documentaries, since the majority of work is made without institutional support or funding. Certainly documentary work provides an important point-of-entry for beginning film/videomakers involved in collective and community organizing. Documentary can also appeal on a psychological level: When unsure of one's identity as a filmmaker, one can be grounded by—perhaps hide behind—the demands of the subject matter. In addition, the economics of filmmaking in most countries clearly favor documentary production. In any case, documentaries in general and television journalism in particular have provided a crucial training ground for large numbers of women film and videomakers, many of whom have used this as a springboard to work in other genres.

But there is another kind of appeal that documentary media may have for women film/videomakers in Latin America—the attraction of those people who are ignored or underrepresented in the dominant media to forms that document their own reality, culture, and perceptions. While documentaries done by women in Latin America comprise a vast field with many different formal tendencies, a great deal of this work maintains a realist aesthetic and adheres to traditional documentary criteria for accuracy and authenticity, if not objectivity.

*   *   *

The New York City–Puerto Rico film/video axis has given rise to some of the most cogent analyses of U.S. neocolonialism and the complex situation of women living under regimes of internal and external colonization. Two documentary films addressing Puerto Rican issues, Ana María García's *La Operación* (The Operation) and Zydnia Nazario's *The Battle of Vieques,* trace the inseparability of private lives from the dynamics of international imperialism and hegemony. Likewise, both works address the status of Puerto Rico as a colony of the United States and analyze local Puerto Rican problems in relation to larger issues of U.S. racism and imperialism. García, a Cuban woman now living in Puerto Rico, directed the Cine Festival San Juan held this past October; she is currently producing *Los Roqueros y los Cocolos* (working title), a film about youth cultures based on rock and salsa music in Puerto Rico and the intersections of class and ethnicity encountered in these communities. Nazario, who works in New York as an architect, is developing a new film tentatively titled *Linking Islands,* which explores identity and language in the poetry and visual art of various Puerto Rican artists living on and outside the Island.

Released in 1982 and used extensively in political organizing and educational settings, *La Operación* was a founding work of Latin American women's cinema. The chilling documentary examines the practice of sterilization of Puerto Rican women—a practice so common that it is simply known as *la operación*. In doing so, it presents a ground-breaking reformulation of feminist politics of the body and reproduction. Weaving interviews and historical analysis with graphic scenes on the operating table, the film exposes the imposition of this practice on the Puerto Rican population and suggests how it was subsequently imposed on poor women of color living in the United States.

The Battle of Vieques (1986) also deals with colonialism—specifically the U.S. militarization of the small Puerto Rican island of Vieques and the subsequent destabilization of the islanders' lives and livelihoods. After the military usurped most of the land on the Island, destroying the local economy, the Viequenses took up fishing. NATO bombing raids subsequently damaged the coastal ecology and made this work too dangerous. Now, residents are faced with a choice between work in U.S.-based hi-tech and munitions industries or emigration.

Incorporating extensive archival footage, *The Battle of Vieques* describes the history of the Island, which lies southeast of the Puerto Rican mainland, as a strategic naval base that has become a gateway to U.S. military operations in the Caribbean and Central America. In the film, Nazario reveals the conflicts produced when a militaristic culture is introduced into an agricultural society. In one scene, island fishermen enact a David and Goliath struggle against U.S. warships. Elsewhere, a Puerto Rican band is shown playing "The Star Spangled Banner" at a naval ceremony; off-key and listless, the performers seem bored and uncomfortable. In interview segments, islanders argue about the expanding role of the U.S. military in their society and discuss problems of unemployment that make the Navy's presence attractive to some.

The Battle of Vieques and *La Operación* both chart the complex power relations and permeable borders between First and Third Worlds. These films represent works of an explicitly Puerto Rican immigrant cinema—works posed on the edge between two cultures, addressing both English-speaking and Spanish-speaking audiences. They also marked a shift in North American awareness of Latino filmmaking, which in the seventies had focused on the emerging Chicano cinema movement. (The San Antonio Cine Festival, for instance, originally served as a forum for Chicano film, but quickly moved to incorporate work from Latin America and other Latino cultures in the U.S.) This work—and its complex position as both an "ethnic" and "immigrant" cultural practice—engages issues of address, audience, and interlinguality in a rapidly changing context of neocolonial relations.

*   *   *

Another tendency in media made by Latin American women is the integration of documentary and fictional forms, which can be seen in fiction films that use documentary footage and techniques as well as such documentaries as *La Mirada de Myriam* (Myriam's Glance, dir. Clara Riascos/Cine Mujer, Colombia, 1986), which incorporates reenactments, flashbacks, and fictional elements, along with documentary sequences.[5] Recognizing the complex relationships between women's external and internal realities, biographical and autobiographical works like *Diario Inconcluso* (Unfinished Diary, dir. Marilu Maillet, Canada/Chile, 1983) and *Ana Mendieta: Fuego de Tierra* (Ana Mendieta: Fire of the Earth, dir. Nereyda García Ferraz and Kate Horsfield, USA, 1988) entail a multi-leveled reworking of the ways documentaries organize and present information.

A mix of documentary, autobiography, and personal diary, *Diario Inconcluso* is a sometimes ambiguous and disorienting depiction of the life of a Chilean woman living in Montreal. The film delves into the personal experience of exile and loss, employing documentary and fictional elements that depart from a realist documentary aesthetic in order to impart a visceral sense of confusion and grief. A disturbing and often painful work, *Diario Inconcluso* follows the filmmaker as she enacts the routines of her daily life: discussions with her mother, a visit with Chilean friends, an argument with her Australian husband, and her work at a television studio. Alternating between French, English, and Spanish, language becomes a battleground of identity, as the filmmaker raises a child in a country she herself can never call home.

García and Horsfield's tape *Ana Mendieta: Fuego de Tierra*, which was coproduced with Branda Miller, is a video portrait that recounts the life and work of the late Cuban-American artist. Produced to accompany a retrospective exhibition of Mendieta's sculpture and performance documents, the tape explores the politics and emotions that shaped her unusual and syncretic art. Although García and Horsfield avoid the subject of Mendieta's highly publicized and still unresolved death in 1985, they develop a complex reconstruction of memory and loss in an attempt to come to terms with Mendieta's powerful personal and artistic legacy. The video constructs a series of fragmented perceptions that follow the continuities and discontinuities in Mendieta's life: born in Cuba, sent to live in the U.S. as a child soon after the Cuban revolution, Mendieta ended up in an orphanage in the Midwest hopelessly out-of-place and separated from her family and any emigré/exile community. Photographs from her childhood and adolescence; reminiscences by family members, former teachers, and colleagues; and Mendieta's own stunning documentation of her performances and installations constitute the collage portrait. Like Maillet's film, García and Horsfield's tape suggests the collisions and disjunctures of immigrant experience, belonging to two worlds and yet not entirely at home in either. This effect is underlined in interviews with members of the arts communities in New York and Havana, who describe how Mendieta's interest in rebuilding cultural ties with Cuba reflected a deeply personal quest for connection.

An equally dense and imaginative work grappling with contemporary problems of biographical filmmaking, *La Mirada de Myriam*, by the Colombian collective Cine

Mujer,[6] explores shifts in identity—the deep changes in what it means to be a woman—in a rapidly and often chaotically industrializing country. Like their earlier film *Carmen Carrascal* (dir. Eulalia Carrizosa, 1984), *La Mirada de Myriam* portrays a poor woman who overcomes fierce obstacles to build a creative and satisfying life. At first, the film appears to be a conventional documentary about a single mother building a life as a squatter in the outskirts of Bogotá. But this initial impression is challenged and extended by dramatic re-creations of the protagonist's childhood memories and fears, including a mystical sequence in which a rural healer cures Myriam's "evil eye." The director, Clara Riascos, explains:

> *La Mirada de Myriam* was a project that was started by Myriam herself. Myriam Ramirez is in her early thirties, a single mother with three kids, who lives in an outlying *barrio* of Bogotá. She is a very sensitive woman with a very sad past who developed an inner strength and imagination that have enabled her to struggle to overcome the obstacles that had condemned her to poverty. There was a certain magical element in this. After having had a sad, very abusive childhood, she is now a protector of the kids. She started a day-care service in her neighborhood and learned how to run it herself.[7]

Although perhaps best known in the U.S. for their earlier humorous feminist short *¿Y Que Hace Su Mama?* (What Does Your Mother Do?, 1983), in *La Mirada de Myriam* Cine Mujer departs from their previous cinematic strategy, which contested women's oppression through realist representations, and develops more indirect and provocative techniques to elaborate the complexity of women's private and public lives. This approach engages traditional elements of storytelling and fantasy to explore the psychological dimensions of empowerment and transformation. Grounded in the daily concerns of poor women, the film nonetheless provides powerful analyses of social dynamics and political issues.

An alternate approach to the problem of biography—how to convey the changing and conflicting aspects of female identity—is posed by the "collective portraits" produced by Lilith Video. Lilith, a women's video collective in São Paolo, Brazil, has produced several short documentaries, including *Mulheres Negras* (Black Women, dir. Silvana Afram, 1985) about racism and racial identity in Brazil; *Beijo na Boca* (Kiss on the Mouth, dir. Jacira Melo, 1987), composed of interviews with prostitutes in São Paolo's Boca do Lixo district; and *Mulheres no Canavial* (Women in the Cane Fields, dir. Silvana Afram, 1987), which profiles various rural women who cut cane. Each of these tapes combines multiple interviews in order to represent the range of experiences, thoughts, and feelings within specific groups of marginalized women. Jacira Melo, a member of Lilith, has described the interrelation of formal experimentation with the documentary material:

> You have so much freedom with video to develop approaches and discover a rhythm that suits the material, since video has so little tradition. For example, our work *Mulheres no Canavial,* made in a rural area with women who cut cane, has a different

rhythm than projects we shot in the city. It was an attempt to make a work very close to the rhythm of these women's lives. They have a very different pace of moving, of talking, a different rhythm of expressing themselves. I think that these questions of pacing, language, and form mean a constant search for each subject.[8]

*   *   *

As Latin American women have become increasingly active in political organizing, often taking the lead in countries where traditional forms of radical protest have been coopted or eliminated through repression, several documentary films have covered the development of these movements and their efforts to articulate political agendas outside of traditional power structures. Both *We're Not Asking for the Moon* (dir. Mari Carmen de Lara, Mexico, 1986) and *Las Madres: The Mothers of the Plaza de Mayo* (dir. Susana Muñoz and Lourdes Portillo, USA, 1986) address an emerging political subject   in the first case, a new union of Mexico City seamstresses, and in the second, the mothers and grandmothers of Argentineans who were killed, imprisoned, or "disappeared" during the military dictatorship. Made to inform both local organizing and international support campaigns, these films exhibit strikingly different forms of address, although both attempt to mobilize and sustain popular memory in ways that overcome institutional silence and repression.

We're Not Asking for the Moon documents the formation of the independent seamstresses' union in the wake of the 1985 earthquake in Mexico City. Made as an organizing film, *We're Not Asking for the Moon* was originally produced for the seamstresses' union with their cooperation. Whereas most First World news organizations framed the earthquake in the clichéd and ahistorical discourses of natural disaster and human tragedy, de Lara's film examines the politics of the destruction and its aftermath by juxtaposing interviews with the seamstresses and their families with the official interpretation of events given by government spokesmen and Mexican television. As the film progresses, it engages a whole network of local "cultural knowledges" (to use the formulation by British critic Paul Willemen)[9] that allow the viewer to situate events within contemporary Mexican history. At times, this technique may hinder understanding of the film for foreign viewers unable to read the complex political landscapes and the histories they draw upon. However, the absence of an explanatory narrative functions very effectively to insert the viewer into the experiences of chaos, grief, and confusion as the magnitude of the disaster and the obstacles to the seamstresses' efforts unfold.

De Lara organizes information and material to reveal the conflicting forces and tensions that underlie the events she depicts and thus evokes a dense history of political institutions, resistance, and repression. For instance, in one segment she intermixes shots of state-sponsored May Day celebrations in the Plaza de la Constitución—an homage to the government's cooptation of the "recognized" unions—and shots of the seamstresses demonstrating and being attacked by police. This sequence juxtaposes two relationships between state power and workers' organizations, emphasizing in the process the threat that the independent women's organization poses to both traditional union hierarchies and unresponsive government bureaucracies. In addition to the specific historical meanings implicit in this sense, it provides a deft representation of relations of power in a society where many historical bases of opposition have been effectively incorporated into the centralized political structure of Mexico's largest political party, the PRI (Institutional Revolutionary Party), which has consistently repressed independent political movements.

We're Not Asking for the Moon has become an important and controversial piece in Mexico and de Lara, a graduate of the Centro Universitario de Estudios Cinematográficos (the Mexico City film school), is now working on two other projects: a collectively-produced documentary on environmental concerns and a dramatized/ re-created documentary on political prisoners and terrorism in Mexico. Her films represent some of the excellent work being done by a younger generation of filmmakers who, rather than aligning themselves with the state-sponsored film apparatus (which is currently just about bankrupt and subject to widespread state censorship), are taking important roles in Mexico's changing political landscape. In search of fresh approaches and new audiences for independent film, many of these women are working in narrative forms—for instance, the highly innovative short fiction film by María Novaro, *An Island Surrounded by Water* (1986), which employs hand-tinted images and poetic personal filmmaking devices to tell the story of a girl whose mother has left to join a guerrilla movement in the interior of the country.

Both Mari Carmen de Lara and Lourdes Portillo are concerned with how their films help to construct a popular memory—reinvoked in times of crisis. And both the mothers in Argentina and the seamstresses' union in Mexico City have used documentary films to convey information as well as to provide inspiration. Discussing specific uses of *We're Not Asking for the Moon,* de Lara states:

> We trained garment makers to be projectionists, because the main reason for the film was to help the union get more members. What's most important is for the film to have a practical application. Also, when split over some issue, recently, they sat down and watched the film and recovered their mission and unity.[10]

The tactic of engaging local "cultural knowledges" to shape an activist film, used so effectively in *We're Not Asking for the Moon,* poses a problem in works of "immigrant cinemas" like the films made by Portillo and Susana Muñoz. Muñoz, an Argentinean who lived in Israel before coming to the United States, and Portillo, who grew up in Mexico and moved to the U.S. as a teenager, live in San Francisco. Unlike the dense national consciousness embedded in de Lara's and Novaro's films, Portillo and Muñoz's collaborations *Las Madres* and their more recent *La Ofrenda* (The Offering, 1989) address a lack of shared awareness/information between filmmaker and audience and thus broach the problem of constituting an audience for immigrant cinema. In *Las Madres* the task was to make the private anguish and political struggle of the Argentinean mothers and grandmothers comprehensible to a North American and international audience that was not, when the film was produced, very familiar with the plight of the *desaparecidos* and their families. Concerning audience, Portillo explains, "The film wasn't made for the mothers but for the rest of the world. But it's had such a success that even the mothers use it now to rekindle interest."[11]

* * *

At the Cine Acción festival, Portillo reflected on her position as the maker of immigrant cinema, in contrast to most of the Latin American participants, whose work, however marginal, addresses a national audience. She discussed the problems of trying to recuperate her relationship to her own cultural heritage and of attempting to explain that culture to a foreign—Anglo-U.S.—culture. This becomes a central concern in *La Ofrenda*, which examines the observance of Day of the Dead ceremonies in Mexico and San Francisco, where the tradition had died out and was reintroduced largely by the Chicano arts community in the 1970s. What is the fate, the filmmakers seem to ask, of folk customs in a diaspora culture? Whereas the Mexican observances are imbued with spontaneity and a lack of self-consciousness about indigenous ritual celebrations, the San Francisco scenes suggest nostalgia. Unlike the Oaxacans who describe practices handed down by abuelitas and community memory, the Chicanos who speak in the film analyze their involvement in *Day of the Dead* rituals and the role it plays in their lives. The film implies that, having been lost, culture is something that must be recovered, rediscovered, taught, and explained.

This tension is reflected in the film's structure, which employs extensive narrative to explain the Mexican practices and their history to audiences in the U.S. At work recutting the voiceover as this article went to press, Muñoz and Portillo expressed frustration with the need to translate, explain, and provide basic information. Without a social and historical context, they feared that the Mexican footage would become just another set of pretty, exotic images for consumption. But too much historical background distances and potentially dilutes philosophical issues about duality and death raised in the film. Funded by the Corporation for Public Broadcasting and slated for broadcast on public television, *La Ofrenda* illustrates some of the problems entailed in making immigrant cinema for a mainstream audience: how to present immigrant/ethnic cultural practices without becoming caught in the sets of viewing conventions—"exoticism" and "education"—reserved for other cultures; how to present images of Mexico that resist incorporation into the representations of that culture already developed by mainstream media.

A very different approach to such questions is taken in the unusual found-footage documentary *From Here, From This Side* (1988), by Mexican videomaker Gloria

Ribe, which presents a powerful essay on North-South relations. Made from clips of U.S. and Mexican films and television—all "borrowed" and rephotographed—the videotape addresses the power relations between "central" and "peripheral" countries. Ribe's assemblage of overdetermined images and materials graphically demonstrates how these relations structure cultural discourses. At the same time she refuses any claim to cultural authenticity. Instead, the tape explores the places assigned by these discourses and the world that they construct.

Ribe's earlier videotape *Tepito* (1987) used conventional documentary techniques to portray a historic working-class neighborhood in Mexico City, but *From Here, From This Side* marks her growing frustration with such strategies—the attempt to "capture" reality with interviews and provide yet more information "capsules" to a TV-soaked culture. One reason Ribe cites for her choice is the considerable time and money required by "pure" documentary filmmaking and the irony of interviewing people in order to record statements that are predetermined. Speaking at the Cine Acción festival, Ribe joked, "Maybe realism is one of the biggest fictions ever created."

In part, her found-footage technique also responds to the traditional position constructed by documentary film in relation to Third World subjects. Ribe noted how, by concentrating on Third World misery, documentaries tend to reproduce a construction of the Third World as "victim." Viewing Mexican television as official and closed to dissent, she proposes her technique as a means "to change the victimness of the Third World personage. On TV, you have fragments of reality without anything making sense of them. You take them like a pill every morning—that's why they're capsules—and we overdose on these pills"[12]

Ribe's concerns and strategies resonate sharply with many First World critical practices, and her work has received considerable attention in the independent video community in the U.S., giving it a certain "crossover" status. In addition to screenings at last year's International Public Television Conference in Philadelphia and the Cine Acción festival, *From Here, From This Side* was included in the American Film Institute's 1988 National Video Festival and subsequently exhibited in San Francisco at New Langton Arts—not a venue known for its attention to Latino or Third World media.

Both *La Ofrenda* and *From Here, From This Side* suggest interesting questions about the borders of New Latin American Cinema and the appropriation and reappropriation of cultural practices, images, and discourses. Both North and South America are sites of unprecedented flows of populations and cultural practices—especially in mass media. A major influence on these developments is U.S. mass media, which saturates the film and television circuits throughout Latin America. The resulting transnational character of media technologies, techniques, and visual languages makes it increasingly difficult to demarcate the boundaries between "First World" and "Third World" media. As people from throughout Latin America and the Caribbean have immigrated to the U.S., often fleeing the repercussions of U.S.

neocolonial involvement abroad, more established communities of Chicanos, Puerto Ricans, and Cubans have been joined by growing numbers of Dominicans, Colombians, Chileans, Ecuadoreans, and Salvadorans. The traditional segregated model of U.S. Latino populations—Chicanos/Mexican-Americans in the Southwest, Puerto Ricans in the East, and a handful of Cubans in Florida—no longer accurately describes the diversity of Latin American cultures in this country and their relationships with white, African American, and Asian North American cultures.[13]

These historical experiences of immigration, dislocation, and displacement have profound implications for discussing Latin American cinema. Situated on the border between two—or more—cultures, those who make documentaries like those discussed here are often forced to formulate film languages that can address not just different audiences but divergent modes of organizing and receiving information. And a video like *From Here, From This Side,* which entails a critical view of both U.S. and Mexican cultural clichés, will be received differently on each side of the border. Likewise, a film like *Las Madres,* made to inform an international and North American audience, will function differently when shown in Argentina. Work that is oppositional in a Latin American context may not be in the U.S. and vice versa.

Although relatively little has been written in English on Latino cinema in the United States,[14] recent critical work on Latina literature offers some useful parallels. An important contribution to criticism of writing by women from diverse traditions—Chicana, Puertorriqueña, Cuban American, an immigrant/exiled Latin American—*Breaking Boundaries: Latina Writings and Critical Readings,*[15] problematizes the bilingual or interlingual text and its exclusion from both English and Latin American literary canons. Another example can be found in contemporary Black British filmmaking and related projects—in sociology, music, and media studies—concerned with the processes of dislocation, adaptation, and hybridity developed in diaspora cultures.[16]

Just as one current in Black studies has adopted the model of "cultures of Africa and the African diaspora," the American migrations of the past decade propose parallel developments in Latin American diaspora cultures. Intersecting class, national, and ethnic identities, complicated by personal experiences, reflect a contemporary history of Latin America (and the United States) in which exile, rupture, transnational migration, and bicultural identity have become relatively common.[17] With this in mind, the range of recent documentary films and tapes by Latinas and Latin American women raises a series of questions: How does the diversity of Latina media "fit" into analyses of North American and Latin American cinemas? How do critics—both First and Third World—situate this work by film/videomakers who are themselves bicultural? And how do white North American critics, such as myself, write about these emerging immigrant cinemas without reduplicating problematic relationships between Third World cultures and First World critics? The traditional method of identifying and delineating "national cinemas" may no longer be adequate for understanding transnational networks of communications—not to mention a world where the category of "national culture" is itself hotly contested.

NOTES

Reprinted from the *Centro Bulletin,* 2:8(Spring 1990): 58–69. Reprinted by permission of the author.

1. New Latin American Cinema refers to a movement of filmmaking that emerged in Latin America in the late 1950s. For an analysis of "the complex network of determinants that catalyzed the movement's emergence and later, its effort to achieve pan-Latin America unity," see Ana Lopez, "An 'Other' History: The New Latin American Cinema," *Radical History Review,* No. 41 (Fall 1988). For an examination of work by women within New Latin American Cinema, see B. Ruby Rich, "After the Revolution: The Second Coming of Latin American Cinema," *Village Voice,* February 10, 1987, pp. 23–27, and Patricia Vega, "Video Work by Women," in the exhibition catalogue *Latin American Visions,* Pat Aufderheide, ed. (Philadelphia: Neighborhood Film and Video Project, 1989).

2. Organized by a group of women filmmakers and supporters associated with the independent distribution company Zafra and headed by Mexican filmmaker Angeles Necoechea, the *Cocina* took place two weeks before the fourth annual Latin American women's "Encuentro," also held in Mexico City. For more information on the event, see Julianne Burton, "A Feast of Film-Video: Notes from the Cocina," *Cine Acción News,* Vol. 4, No. 1 (Spring 1988).

3. Available from Film Studies Department, Carleton University, Ottawa, Ontario, K1S 5B6, Canada.

4. For a report on presentations at the 1986 Havana Festival, see *La Mujer en los medios audiovisuales: Memorias del VIII Festival Internacional del Nuevo Cine Latinoamericano* (Mexico City: Coordinacion de Difusion Cultural/UNAM, 1988).

5. For example, Tizuka Yamasaki's film *Patriamada* (Brazil, 1985), which incorporates extensive documentary footage into its dramatic narrative, or Solveig Hoogesteijn's *Macu: The Policeman's Wife* (Venezuela, 1987) and Susana Amaral's *The Hour of the Star* (Brazil, 1985), which use a documentary aesthetic in the context of feature films.

6. The Cine Mujer collective, founded in 1978, consists of Sara Bright, Eulalia Carrizosa, Dora Cecilia Rameriz, Patricia Restrepo, Clara Riascos, and Luz Fanny Tobon.

7. "Entrevista con Cine Mujer," *Cinemateca: Cuadernos de Cine Colombiano,* No. 21 (March 1987), p. 17.

8. See Liz Kotz, "An Interview with Lilith Video," *The Independent,* Vol. 11, No. 7 (August/September 1988).

9. See Paul Willemen, "An Avant Garde for the Eighties," *Framework* No. 24 (Spring 1984).

10. De Lara's comments were spoken at the panel discussion New Directions in Documentary Filmmaking at the Cine Acción Festival, San Francisco, October 22, 1988.

11. Interview by the author, January 1989.

12. Ribe also participated in the New Directions panel discussion.

13. For an analysis of East Coast Latino communities, see Xavier F. Totti, "Latinos in New York," *The Portable Lower East Side,* Vol. 5, Nos. 1–2 (1988).

14. For an overview of contemporary Latino cinema, see Eduardo Diaz, in *Latin American Visions,* Pat Aufderheide, ed., op. cit.

15. Asuncion Horno-Delgado, Eliana Ortega, Nina M. Scott, and Nancy Saporta Sternbach, eds., *Breaking Boundaries* (Amherst: University of Massachusetts Press, 1989). See also, Enrique Fernandez' article on a panel discussion at the Miami Film Festival, "El Norte: Tres Amigos," *Village Voice* (February 28, 1989), p. 34.

16. For discussions of Black British cinema, see, for example, Kobena Mercer, "Recoding Narratives of Race and Nation, *The Independent,* Vol. 12, No. 1 (January/February 1989); Coco Fusco, *Young, British and Black* (Buffalo: Hallwalls, 1988); *Screen,* "The Last 'Special Issue' on Race?" Isaac Julien and Kobena Mercer, eds., Vol. 29, No. 4 (Autumn 1988); Reece Auguiste, Jim Pines, and Paul Gilroy, "Handsworth Songs: Interview with Black Audio Film Collective," *Framework* No. 34 (1988); Martina Attile and Jim Pines, "The Passion of Remembrance: Interview with Sankofa Film and Video," *Framework* No. 32/33 (1986); and Jim Pines, "Territories: An Interview with Isaac Julien," *Framework,* No. 26/27 (1985). For more general discussions of race, identity, and cultural information, see Paul Gilroy, *There Ain't No Black in the Union Jack* (London: Hutchinson/Birmingham Center for Contemporary Cultural Studies, 1987); Homi Bhabha, "The Other Question," *Screen,* Vol. 24, No. 5–6 (November/December 1983); and Paul Gilroy and Hazel Carby, eds., *The Empire Strikes Back* (London: Hutchinson/CCCS, 1982).

17. See, for example, Zuzana Pick, "Chilean Cinema in Exile," *Framework,* No. 34 (1987), and Coco Fusco, "Long Distance Filmmaking: An Interview with the Cine-Ojo Collective" in Coco Fusco, ed., *Reviewing Histories* (Buffalo: Hallwalls, 1987).

DISTRIBUTION INFORMATION

Ana Mendieta, Fuego de Tierra, Video Data Bank, Art Institute of Chicago, 16 Colombus Drive at Jackson Blvd., Chicago, IL 60603; (312) 443-3793

An Island Surrounded by Water, Black Women, Carmen Carrascal, Diario Inconcluso, From Here From This Side: Women Make Movies, 225 Lafayette St., Ste. 212, New York, NY 10012; (212) 925-0606

Batalla de Vieques, La Operación: Cinema Guild, 1697 Broadway, New York, NY 10019; (212) 246-5522

We're Not Asking for the Moon: First Run/Icarus, 200 Park Ave. S., Ste. 1319, New York, NY 10003; (212) 674-3375

Las Madres, The Mothers of the Plaza de Mayo, Direct Cinema, Box 69799, Los Angeles, CA 90069; (213) 652-8000

La Mirada de Myriam, Cine Mujer, Apartado Aereo 2758, Bogotá, Colombia 283-6593 (Due to shared rights with FOCINE, the Colombian national film production agency, Cine Mujer has not been able to release distribution rights to the film in the United States.)

13

Type and Stereotype: Chicano Images in Film

Linda Williams

The following essay grows out of my participation in and viewing of the television program *Chicano Images in Film*.[1] It is intended to raise issues that were either too complex or too controversial for discussion within the program itself but which I consider important to an understanding of the general problem of stereotypes in the media. As an Anglo I freely admit to speaking as an outsider about issues that do not directly affect me. But as a woman who teaches and makes films within the dominant culture of patriarchy I am acutely aware of the many ways this culture's representation of women in film and the other arts operates to flatten out, stereotype, or otherwise obliterate, the many truths of my existence. I share with Chicanos, and any stereotyped minority, an abhorrence of a representational system that sees my reality as "other," my truth as grotesque caricature. Women's bodies reduced to the status of sex objects for the delight of male viewers are no less stereotyped than the lazy Mexicans who serve as foils in countless westerns to flatter the intelligence and energy of the Anglo cowboy.

What I would like to suggest here, however, is first that a simple abhorrence of stereotype is not enough. The failure to understand the ideological needs served by stereotype leads to a contrary valorization of a supposedly realistic individualism that raises more problems than it solves. Second, there may be an important distinction to be drawn between type and stereotype that can help in the search for a means of representation that will more truly reflect the realities of the Chicano experience.

A given culture's sensitivity to an offensive racial or national stereotype is often a function of the loss of that culture's historical or social need for such a stereotype. It is consequently very easy—perhaps too easy—for Anglo audiences of 1980 to look back at the egregious racism of films such as *Let Katie Do It* (1915) or *Martyrs of the Alamo* (1915) and deplore the depiction of Mexicans as lazy "greasers," and "banditos," fiendish sex and dope addicts. Both of these films were produced during a period of

214

PHOTO 13.1 This photo of **Rosaura Revueltas,** the female lead of *Salt of the Earth,* illustrates the distinction Williams makes between "type" and "stereotype." Although the actress might be seen as "typical" of the "Hispano" mining community in New Mexico, she was not a stereotypically and heavily made-up, sexually enticing, spitfire. She projects a resolute strength and a timeless beauty that seems to be grounded in simplicity. (Courtesy of Paul Jarrico)

poor relations between the United States and Mexico when American producers were not concerned with selling their product to Mexican audiences. This was to change very soon: with the outbreak of World War I, and the loss of European markets, American producers soon found it advantageous to seek out markets south of the border and shift their stereotypes from the villainous greaser to the evil Hun.[2]

In both films the stereotype of the Mexican villain operates to justify what could otherwise be viewed as American theft of Mexican soil. In *Let Katie Do It* the "good" Americans are mining Mexican land, extracting gold to take back to the States. The "bad" Mexicans' attack on the mine is thus territorially justified, as is Santa Ana's attack on the Alamo in *Martyrs of the Alamo.* But in both cases the Mexicans are so ugly and rapacious, the Americans so much the embodiment of the bourgeois American values of family and property, that historically determined territorial conflicts are displaced onto very simplistic moral grounds: the fight for territory becomes the defense of family against the fiendish lust of the Mexicans.

These obvious distortions of history show how stereotypes serve historical imperatives. In times of relatively relaxed Mexican-American relations, as during the period of both world wars, the image of Mexicans and Chicanos tended to be less offensive, though no less stereotypical, variations of the "happy Latin." But in either its villified or more innocuous forms, the stereotype ignores the true richness of a culture and its people, its variety of social types and the complexity of its history. Not surprisingly, then, those who have been treated as stereotypes often attempt to remedy the situation with realistic and socially and historically accurate portrayals of the previously stereotyped group. This often amounts to a simple reversal of subject and object: the point of view shifts from that of the Anglo majority which views the Mexican or Chicano as alien "other," to that of the Mexican or Chicano who now views the Anglo as an alien.

Thus the formerly individualized subject with whom the audience identifies becomes the new object and the formerly stereotyped Chicano object becomes the new sympathetic subject. At times this reversal can be quite illuminating, especially for Anglo audiences. Robert Young's *Alambrista!*, a film about the experiences of a Mexican migrant farm worker illegally working in the United States, ironically illustrates and comments upon this process of reversal in a scene which shows its newly arrived hero undergoing an initiation into Anglo ways by his two more experienced compatriots. The two friends teach him the proper way to enter and be served a meal in a typical North American coffee shop—including the proper technique for flirting with the waitress. The lesson is illuminating for its observations on the different body language of "gringos": a smile of confidence that is not too broad, a relaxed crossing of legs, a general air of casual assurance. The lesson amounts to a parody of the public manner of the American Anglo male—itself a stereotype—contrasted to the more formally polite and overtly "macho" manner of the Mexican male.

The brilliance of this episode, and indeed of the entire film, rests in its knowing awareness of the limitations of any cultural-linguistic group's understanding of another such group. The film does not simply reverse the positions of subject and object. Instead, it continuously confronts the subjective experiences of two cultures, refusing to objectify or stereotype either but also refusing to overtly individualize them.

This refusal to individualize is, I think, a key factor in any realist art's attempt to free itself from the stigma of stereotype. Although one might think that the natural opposition to stereotype would be to individualize the kind of characters who have so often been stereotyped in the past, in fact, this very effort often ends by adopting the representational forms of the dominant Anglo culture—forms which implicitly negate any real differences between the Anglo and Chicano experience.

In other words, the realistic representation of the lives of any minority engaged in a struggle with a more dominant society needs to represent both the historical and material situation of that minority and its very real differences from the dominant society. Thus it may very well be a mistake for film artists who wish to represent Chicano reality to imitate too closely the representational forms of bourgeois Anglo culture.

A case in point is Moctezuma Esparza's 1978 film, *Only Once in a Lifetime*, a film which does everything in its power to generate audience sympathy and identification with its Chicano hero, but which does so through the most blatantly sentimental cliches of made-for-TV movies (including a graveside monologue spoken to the protagonist's dead wife and several sad conversations with an old dog). The film neatly squelches any authentic expression of cultural or class differences in the name of a supposedly universal human nature that pretends to be beyond class, culture, and history. Thus a well-meaning, sensitive film which sets out to correct the previous cliches of the Chicano experience on film ends up adopting another set of cliches typical of a certain kind of alternately cute and touching Hollywood narrative.

This adoption of the realist and sentimental representational form typical of Anglo culture runs the risk of total absorption into the supposedly universal values of that culture, thus betraying the very qualities that have made the Mexican art, film, and literature of this century so original and distinctive.

I am not suggesting that an authentic Chicano film art would necessarily imitate the mythic proportions, cultural pluralism, historical sensibility, or even the surrealism, of the best Mexican art of this century since it is obvious that Chicano culture and experience is not identical with that of Mexico. But I am suggesting that there is a powerful need for some kind of authentic form, for some culturally differentiated voice that can speak to and for Chicanos, not just about them.

At this point it may be instructive to mention two films which I believe to have at least partially succeeded in finding new forms appropriate to the content of the Chicano experience. The two films are the now classic 1953 *Salt of the Earth*, directed by the once blacklisted Herbert Biberman, and the very recent (1976) *Alambrista!* mentioned above.

*Salt of the Earth*³ has often been hailed as a landmark in the authentic depiction of both Chicano and women's lives. I do not want to repeat those praises here but I do want to add that what is so striking about this film—which concerns Chicanas' participation in a strike begun by their miner husbands in the zinc mines of New Mexico— is its formal break with what was at the time the traditional Hollywood narrative style. The film is almost entirely narrated in the voice-over of the female lead. This voice-over adds a very personal, subjective, and distinctly female reflective quality to the events depicted. Although the film has generally been accepted—at least in recent years—as an important breakthrough in the realistic portrayal of minority groups, it is important to realize that this very concept of realism is already determined by the culture that names one form of representation "true" and another "false."

In the classical Hollywood cinema of the 1930's and 1940's, realism meant highly polished performances by known actors who could imitate real people in meticulous reconstructions of the real world created on the studio sound stage. These reconstructions were carried out according to the conventional rules of storytelling, lighting, *mise-en-scène,* and editing. When Herbert Biberman set out to make *Salt of the Earth,* he broke with some of these conventions: (1) he cast the relatively unknown Mexican actress Rosaura Revueltas in the female lead, thus breaking both with the convention of casting known stars in major roles and with the accompanying convention of casting Anglo stars in non-Anglo roles; (2) he cast not only a nonactor in the role of the husband, but the actual leader of the miners' union, thus creating a mix of acting styles quite different from the uniform professionalism of the typical Hollywood product; (3) he shot much of the film on location in the actual locales in which the real events upon which the film is based had taken place.

Like the neo-realist filmmakers in Italy who could not, in the wake of World War II and its upheaval of Italian society, return to the artifice of the studio-made film, Biberman, in the light of his impelling social theme, felt that he too needed a new form—that to imitate the studio conventions would be a formal betrayal of the theme of social struggle. His break with Hollywood's conventional realism was thus in the name of a greater realism. This is not to say that his film was in some absolute way more true-to-life, less manipulated. In many ways the contrivance of a voice-over, the unusual mix of professional and nonprofessional actors, and the obvious low-budget look of the whole production, make the film appear even more manipulated, less a seamless imitation of reality. Biberman's theme called for a form that could emphasize the social and historical embeddedness of his characters even if this meant sacrificing in some of them a range of emotional expression that a cast of entirely professional actors could give it. He thus borrowed qualities from the documentary film—a form which concentrates on social conditions to the relative exclusion of drama—in order to give his film an authenticity of social context that Hollywood films about minority groups had never before achieved.

This greater authenticity of social context, combined with the limited emotional range of at least some of the actors, created a narrative form that necessarily deemphasized the classical Hollywood narrative's celebration of the individual character. The combined tactics of deemphasizing individual character, but at the same time not falling into the trap of the one-dimensional stereotype, allowed Biberman to achieve a greater integration of character and history. Neither stereotypes nor transcendent individuals, the Chicanos of *Salt of the Earth* are authentic *types,* products of their environment and their position between two cultures, produced by and producers *of* history.

Thus, even though Chicanos become the very human subjects of his story, it was not by giving them a greater individuality that Biberman overcame the dehumanizing effects of stereotype. Instead, it was through the more careful documentation of class and culture, by showing just how these determinations operate within the lives of individuals engaged in social struggle—in particular how the "legitimate" union struggle between the workers and mine owners was transformed into an unprecedented illegitimate struggle between the men and their wives—that Biberman was able to portray a social and ethnic group in the process of genuinely changing the material and social conditions of their lives.

Director Robert Young employs a similar formal strategy in *Alambrista!*—the film cited above—about a Mexican farmer who comes illegally to the States to work as a migrant farmworker. Like *Salt of the Earth,* Young's film insists on the protagonist's social type. The product of rural Mexico's agrarian, Catholic, patriarchal, and hierarchical culture, he is confused and amazed by his encounters with working-class Anglos, as well as by encounters with his more urbanized and Anglicized compatriots. Because the film begins with a subtitled depiction of the protagonist's life in rural Mexico, the point of view of this culture is firmly established. Each of his forays across the border is thus viewed, even by Anglo audiences, as a movement from social stability (if also grinding poverty) to comparative chaos.

One particularly effective scene shows the protagonist observing the loud histrionics of a revival meeting attended by his friend, the waitress. Although her religious fervor is undoubtedly sincere, we share his mounting alarm at the emotional crescendos and sexual charge of this enthusiastic form of worship. Much of the interest of the film lies in similar encounters between the two cultures, encounters which allow Anglo viewers to experience some of the strangeness of their own culture as seen through foreign eyes and which also allow Chicano viewers to experience the double vision of their situation between the two cultures. The film thus depicts the encounter of an almost feudal peasant with the modern labor system of American agribusiness and its employment of large masses of transient workers. By emphasizing each character's existence as a type produced by a particular social and economic system, *Alambrista!* avoids both the one-dimensional insults of stereotype and the Hollywood myth of an individual hero who transcends both culture and history.

The remarkable integrity and honesty of both *Alambrista!* and *Salt of the Earth* suggest that, at this particular time, it may only be through a documentary-style presentation of social and historical context, rather than through the individual triumphs of a particular character, that an authentic representation of the Chicano experience can be made. Not individual stories outside culture and history but typical stories within both are the true antidote to stereotype.

NOTES

Reprinted by permission of the publisher from *Frontiers: A Journal of Womens Studies,* 5:2(1980):14–17. Copyright © 1980, FRONTIERS Editorial Collective.

1. *Chicano Images in Film: A Symposium,* moderated by George Sandoval, KOA, Denver, Colorado, July 6, 1980. This program, a project funded by the Colorado Humanities Program, is a sixty-minute videotape which studies the treatment of Mexican Americans in Hol-

lywood films. The panelists used film excerpts spanning the silent era to contemporary directors to discuss the impact of negative type and stereotype in film; the program concludes with a discussion of positive contributions by independent filmmakers.

2. Allen L. Woll, *The Latin Image in American Film* (Los Angeles: Univ. of California Press, 1977), pp. 13–14. This does not mean that U.S.-Mexican relations improved, but only that American producers made an effort to temper the more blatantly evil Mexican stereotypes.

3. Michael Wilson's screenplay of *Salt of the Earth,* with a Commentary by Deborah Silverton Rosenfelt, is available from The Feminist Press, Old Westbury, NY (1978).

14

Two Film Reviews:
My Family/Mi Familia
and *The Perez Family*

Santiago Nieves and Frank Algarin

My Family/Mi Familia

"Fantastic! People loved it! When Latinos see this film, they go crazy!" exclaims Gregory Nava on his film, "My Family" (Mi Familia), which was released last year and is now available on video. I agree. Wherever the film is, go find it, for there are at least three major and important reasons why "My Family" is a must-see for every Latino.

For one, it marks the first time in an English-language theatrical release targeted at Latinos where every single Latino character is actually played by a Latino, not Marisa Tomei, not Lou Diamond Phillips, not Angelica Huston.

Secondly, whatever faults I may have found with the film (and they are few), the film commands a certain integrity and respect by "taking back the very thing the media's always trying to take away from us—our culture and family," as director Nava puts it. Nava also called on the talents of a terrific ensemble of professional Latino actors, who often transcended mere scripted material into that universal connection, an essential in making the film appealing to all audiences.

Thirdly, a Latino has written and directed such a film. Chicano director Gregory Nava, who says that the family is the protagonist of his film, not any one person, fought against Latinos being perceived as a poor subculture. "For the first time in a film, 'Mi Familia' puts family in the center, as it is in our culture."

Not as powerful or riveting as his film, the classic "El Norte," "My Family," written by Nava and produced by Francis Ford Coppola and his American Zoetrope studies, is the epic and sprawling story of three generations of the Sánchez family living on the perimeters of American soil during the 1940's and 50's in "what was still then" Mexico.

The film is technically and artistically a gem. The film looks rich and there is a glow to the film that adds to a sense of spirituality and warmth, love and, yes . . . family. There are scenes that resonate in the mind long after viewing, as poignant as any from Hollywood. Some people point to the scene where Maria, the mother (played by Jennifer López), after being unjustly deported to Mexico, journeys back to her home in California. In the waters of the Rio Grande she struggles to rescue her infant son when he is torn from her arms by the river.

Another scene often mentioned shows José, the father (played by Eduardo López Rojas), feeling powerless before the negative direction his son's life is taking—the same son rescued earlier by the mother. José states with apparent despair, "I don't know what to do." That one line, as delivered by Rojas, speaks to all fathers.

Spanning three generations, over a period of 60 years, was a great structural challenge for the writers. Here the film shows some unevenness, as various segments seemed somewhat disconnected. The scenes which take place in the late twenties, fifties and the eighties, for instance, are narrated by Paco (read with perfect somber reflection by Edward James Olmos), the brother who is a writer and family historian. It is mostly through Paco's eyes that the story is told. The narration is the cohesive force between stories, the connecting tissues.

The film does touch on some tough issues, including family values and socioeconomics that affect the family, such as José's work ethic and Chucho's choice to have his piece of the American pie without working like his father.

Still, there are problems with the film. Among them is the fact that many scenes are unnecessarily lengthy, as is the film. A prime example of this was how a touching scene where Jimmy Smits reconciles with his young son in the garden simply goes on too long. So did several other scenes, which made several audience members near me squirm.

Despite Nava's concern that he is fighting the way "TV and films depict Latinos as mostly dysfunctional and family-less," the end result, between the too-long emotional scenes, the glow and warmth, the pace of the film and its literal length, add up to a sappier, passive perception of family. Perhaps this would have been lessened somewhat if the director had not chosen to exclude in any real way (perhaps it was too threatening for a broader audience) the Pachuco riots of the Zoot-suit era and the whole struggle Mexicanos waged against American imperialism.

Still, the film is a must-see, not only for those three major reasons I gave before, but because of some genuinely fine ensemble performances from Jimmy Smits, Edward James Olmos, Jennifer López, Esai Morales and Benito Martínez.

However, one performance, that of Eduardo López Rojas as José, the patriarchal head of the family, is played with such poignancy and integrity, the man simply walks away with the film, and is worth the price of admission (or rental) alone.

"In the end," says Nava, "the film is about redemption. In our community, we find meaning in our lives and in our families, despite the injustices, the oppression and the poverty. We're a life affirming culture, and that's a great message for everybody."

The Perez Family

"The Perez Family," a film directed by Mira Nair and distributed by the Samuel Goldwyn company, swirled in controversy before its release, when it was learned that the film would feature two non-Latino actors playing the major Latino characters. Marisa Tomei (Dottie) and Angelica Huston (Carmela Pérez) played the two female Cuban leads. The male lead is Latino, but not Cubano.

Latino actors and activists, led by Sonia González of *Latinos for Positive Images* (LPI), which was created to get Latino actors work, got national attention by urging audiences to boycott the film. The producers immediately shot-off what they thought were damage control responses. But one comment, made by Tomei, made matters worse. She reportedly responded to charges by LPI by saying that the producers simply could not find a good enough Latino talent to compare with Tomei.

"That's a damn lie!" exploded González. "That, Tomei should know, is an old, old line that's been handed to us since the year zero. To say they couldn't find a Cubana, a Latina, is about as insulting a remark as one could make to Latino actors seeking work!"

Meanwhile, "The Perez Family" is the story of Juan Raúl Pérez (Alfred Molina), a member of Cuba's upper-class. He is in a Cuban jail, and suddenly, Castro lets him, along with thousands of Marielitos, out of Cuba, en route to the U.S. in 1980. Off Juan Raúl goes on a boat to Key West, along with other unsavory types, like Dottie (Marisa Tomei), a former prostitute.

Raúl is a mess from all those years in prison, but Dottie, who is hornier for the almighty Yankee "freedom" than she is for Raúl, nurses him back to health.

Juan Raúl is, at first, not interested in Dottie, as his dream is to find the wife he hasn't seen in two decades, Carmela (Angelica Huston). Carmela lives a semi-sedate life of a widow in Coral Gables, Florida, working at Saks. Mostly Huston appears spaced-out here, marginalizing her role to comic relief.

From the film's incongruous opening shot on a beach (which looked more like an old outtake from Fellini's "Satyricon"), "The Perez Family" is one big incongruity. And whatever is good about the film, it is consistently undermined by the obvious miscast of the two leads, whose non-Spanish-speaking pretentions (Nu Jork, Nu Jork!) render the film a campy piece of silliness. You could have gotten a hernia from all the hard work Tomei employed at "emoting passion," as, I am sure she was told, Cubanas do.

This is the obvious result of what happens when non-Latino writers, producers, directors and even actors get together to make stories about Latinos and their experience.

Now, I'm not begrudging directors or anybody else creative control, nor am I saying that only Latino directors should make films about Latinos. What I am saying is that with creative control must come a responsibility to be true to your subject, be it Cubanos or lug nuts. Director Nair's choice of Tomei exhibits a kind of monovision and reveals a certain pretentiousness. Not to mention a slap in the face to brilliant Latino talent that exists today. There is simply no excuse.

Ultimately, the answer must lie within us. It is apparent that we need to begin to own and control our own product.

Meanwhile, word of protests against "The Perez Family" must have helped in the film's early exit from theaters. When I went to see the film on a Saturday afternoon, I was one of a total of two people in the theater. While box-office receipts for "The Family" totaled over $10 billion, "The Perez Family" (whose makers hoped their film would be confused with the better "The Family") earned a paltry $2,835,000 (personal communication, *Hollywood Reporter,* 1996).

NOTES

Reprinted by permission of the author from *Flick,* Newsletter of the Latino Collaborative, Summer 1995. Copyright © Santiago Nieves, 1995.

15

Hispanic-Oriented Media

Federico Subervi-Vélez with Charles Ramírez Berg, Patricia Constantakis-Valdés, Chon Noriega, Diana I. Ríos, and Kenton T. Wilkinson

From the border newspapers of the early 1800s through today's advanced telecommunications, Latinos have had a broad range of media that both informed and entertained in their own language and cultures. In the early days, most of these media operated in Spanish. But even then, some were bilingual, and as time has passed, bilingual media and, more recently, English-language, Hispanic-oriented media have increased in number and importance.

Hispanics from various countries have created and owned a number of the media institutions that targeted Latinos as consumers. A significant portion of those institutions have been owned, in whole or in part, by non-Latino individuals or corporations, however. But no matter who owned these institutions their employment practices and their content tended to be more favorable to Latinos than other media have been. Whether the Hispanic-oriented media are print or broadcast, they continue to present the life and times of Latinos in the United States more thoroughly, appropriately, and positively.

Newspapers

The Early Years

The Spanish-language press within the national boundaries of the United States had its beginnings in 1808 in New Orleans, Louisiana, with *El Misisipí* (see Figure 15.1), a four-page commercial and trade-oriented "publication printed primarily in Spanish, but with English translations of many of the articles and almost all of the advertising" (Wilson and Gutiérrez, 1985:175). Prior to the inauguration of *El Misisipí*, dozens of Spanish-language newspapers and periodicals, founded by the Spanish conquerors and settlers and the Mexican pioneers of the times, were published in the southwest-

EL MISISIPI.

Vol. I.) MIERCOLES 12 DE OCTUBRE DE 1808. (No. 10.

Condiciones.

I. Se publicara los Miercolas y Sabados de cada semana.

II. Se pagarán OCHO PESOS al año adelantando la mitad.

III. Los avisos se publicarán en ambas lenguas ó en la que se quiera en los términos regulares.

Del Diario de New-York.

Breve noticia de lo acaecido en Madrid el Lunes 2 de Mayo de 1808 por un Ingles que se halló presente.

Jamas ha estado el público en perfecta tranquilidad desde que en mediados de Marzo se sospechó por la primera vez la intencion del Rey Cárlos IV de trasladarse à Sevilla con toda la familia Real.

La deposicion del Pricipe de la Paz el 18 : su prision el 19 con la abdicacion del Rey Cárlos y exâltacion de su hijo Fernando verificadas en el mismo dia, cuyos eventos causaron gran satisfaccion por los felices efectos que podrian producir : la llegada de las tropas francesas à Madrid : la entrega de la espada de Francisco I à Murat ; monumento que sé conservaba en la Armeria del Rey como trofeo de la batalla de Pavia : la salida del Rey para Burgos : la entrega del Principe de la Paz á la Francia ; y por último la determinacion del Rey de pasarse á las fronteras y ponerse en manos de los Franceses en Bayona, fueron circunstancias que animaron la fermentacion y la subieron por grados à tal punto, que cada momento se temia alguna formidable explosion por la junta de Gobierno de la qual habia quedado Presidente el Infante Don Antonio para aquietar los alarmas del pueblo y evitar que hiciesen algunos actos de violencia contra los Franceses.

Un parte ó correo extraordinario acostumbraba venir todas las tardes de Bayona con las noticias de las transacciones : estas jamas se publicaban en la gaceta sinó que circulaban en forma de extractos de cartas privadas de la comitiva del Rey : los primeros causaron una satisfaccion momentánea como que consistian únicamente en la descripcion de los honores hechos al Principe era forzar à Fernando à que renunciase su corona.

El parte del Sàbado 30 de Abril no llegó. Lo mismo avino al del Domingo 1° de Mayo en cuya espera estaban ansiosas millaradas de gentes en la puerta del Sol y en las calles de la cercania del Correo.

La guarnicion francesa de Madrid estuvo toda la noche sobre las armas, y al otro dia, 2 de Mayo, se levantó el Sol sobre muchos infelices destinados à no ver mas auroras. Este dia fué notable por la salida de la Reyna de Etruria y su hermano el Infante Don Francisco de Paula para Bayona.

La curiosidad llevó à muchisimos à la plaza del palacio para ser testigos de aquella escena, y muchas mugeres y familias fueron tambien para decir à Dios à sus maridos y parientes, y para lamentar su dura suerte en quedar sin ninguna prevision cierta. Quando salio à las puertas la primera carroza, creyeron muchos del populacho que el Infante Don Antonio Presidente de la Junta ó Gobernador interino iba tambien à dexarlos y con esta falsa idea comenzaron à alborotarse.

Cortaron los tirantes de la carroza y la metieron à empujones en el patio del palacio, pero asegurados de que Dn. Antonio quedaba en Madrid, dexaron que guarnecieran y que salieran. El General Murat mandó un Edecan para que se informase del caso : el populacho parecia animado à tratarlo con aspereza, pero habiendo promediado algunos oficiales espies. quedó libre y pudo volver à su Comandante.

Al irse, pues, los coches con la Reyna de Etruria y su hermano, manifestó este tal sentimiento y aun lo expresó con tan amargos gritos que enternecieron é irritaron al pueblo : entónces volvió el Edecan con una parte de las tropas francesas y comenzó la horrible y sanguinaria escena.

No es fácil atinare si los soldados franceses ó el populacho fueron los primeros agresores, pero es cierto que los franceses comenzaron à descargar su mosquetería contra los que se le oponian, y que cañan que tuvieron proporciones se presentaron armados en las calles.

Al principio tuvieron ventajas los españoles en muchas partes de la ciudad, à pesar de que no se les permitió à las tropas tomar partido por haberlas encerrado sus oficiales en los quarteles. Cayeron muchas tropas francesas, cuyas armas sirvieron al populacho que no tenia ningunas ; pero luego que comenzaron à tener efecto las disposiciones del General Murat, se decidió la preponderancia por parte de los Franceses, que hicieron salir sus tropas y formadas en columna en los campos inmediatos entraron por las diferentes puertas, acompañado cada tozo de una ó mas piezas de artilleria volante que barrian las calles à medida que avanzaban, las quales fueron colocadas en los lugares que les parecieron mas oportunos. Ademas de esto la infanteria hacia descargas en las encrucijadas sobre quantos pasaban y gustaba tirar particularmente à todas las ventanas y balcones en que veian gente.

Las gloriosas defensas de los Españoles fueron en el Almacen de la Artilleria [illegible] donde estuvo hospedado Sir Benjamin King quando estuvo de Embaxador en esta Corte, y donde yacen las reliquias de este respetable Ministro.

(Se Continuará.)

AVISO.

Dn. Juan Rodriguez, Abagado

TIENE el honor de avisar al público y à sus amigos, que desde hoy su demora y residencia ordinaria será en su habitacion à una legua poco mas de la Ciudad hacia abajo del rio y del mismo lado, entre las habitaciones del Sr. Brown Contor de rentas de los Estados y de Don Edemon Macarte ; pero que mantendrá su estudio en la ciudad en casa del Doctor Devese, calle de Maine à de los Almacenes No. 16, donde se empleara en servicio del pú[illegible] segun su profesion desde las diez de la mañana hasta las quatro de la tarde. Octubre 6. 1808

Dn. JOHN RODRIGUEZ,

Attorney at Law,

HAS the honor to inform his friends and the public in general that from this date he will reside at his plantation, better than a league below the city and on the same side of the river, between the plantation of Wm. Brown, Esq and that of Mr. Edmond Macarty; but that he will still continue to keep his office in town, in the house of Doctor Devese, No. 16, Main street, where he will execute any business in the line of his profession, from ten o'clock A. M. till four

FIGURE 15.1 *El Misisipí* (1808). Although Spanish-language newspapers had been in existence in what was then Spanish America and is today the southwestern United States, the first Latino newspaper published within the United States was *El Misisipí* (1808–1810). It was published in New Orleans, which had been acquired by the United States in 1803, and it used both English and Spanish. (Courtesy of the State Historical Society of Wisconsin)

ern territories that belonged to Mexico until the 1860s. In fact, the very first printing press in the Americas was brought to Mexico from Spain in 1535. Thus, for over four centuries, Hispanic publications have circulated in this part of the world.

Current Status

In 1991, five Spanish-language newspapers were published daily in the United States—two in New York, two in Miami, and one in Los Angeles.[1] *La Opinión* (Los Angeles) began publishing in 1926. Its publisher was Ignacio E. Lozano, Sr., a Mexican national who wanted to provide news of the homeland as well as of the new country for the growing Mexican population in southern California. From its beginning, *La Opinión* was owned and operated by Lozano and his family, who in 1926 formed Lozano Enterprises, Inc. In 1990, a 50 percent interest in Lozano Enterprises was purchased by the Times-Mirror Company. This major media conglomerate, with interests in broadcasting and cable television as well as book and magazine publishing, also publishes the *Los Angeles Times*, *Newsday* (New York), and five other newspapers nationwide.

El Diario–La Prensa (New York) originated in summer 1963 from the merger of two newspapers, *La Prensa* and *El Diario de Nueva York*. The former had been operating since 1913 under the ownership of José Campubrí, a Spaniard who kept the paper until 1957 when it was purchased by Fortune Pope. Pope, whose brother was the owner of the *National Enquirer*, was also the owner of the New York Italian paper *Il Progreso* and of WHOM-AM, which later became WJIT-AM, one of the most popular Spanish-language radio stations in New York. In 1963, Pope sold *La Prensa* to O. Roy Chalk, who had been owner of *El Diario de Nueva York* since he purchased it in 1961 from Porfirio Domenicci, a Dominican who had started *El Diario* in 1948.

With both papers under his control, Chalk, a U.S. businessman and president of Diversified Media, merged the two papers into *El Diario–La Prensa* which he directed from 1963 to 1981, when he sold it to the Gannett Company, a major media conglomerate that at the time owned a chain of ninety English-language papers. In 1989, El Diario Associates, Inc., was formed by Peter Davidson, a former Morgan Stanley specialist in newspaper industry mergers and acquisitions. This new company bought *El Diario–La Prensa* from Gannett in August of that year for an estimated $20 million (Glasheen, 1989). Carlos D. Ramírez, a Puerto Rican from New York who had been publisher of the newspaper since 1984, stayed onboard to participate as a partner of El Diario Associates, Inc.

Noticias del Mundo (New York) began publishing in 1980 by News World Communications, Inc., an organization founded in 1976 by the anti-Communist crusader Rev. Sun Myung Moon and his Unification Church International. News World Communications publishes, among others, the *Washington Times* and the *New York City Tribune*. Although now *Noticias del Mundo* functions more independently from its staunchly conservative founder, the author Veciana-Suarez has observed that the editorial stands are "decidedly conservative in international affairs and pro-Hispanic on domestic issues" (1987:21).

El Nuevo Herald (Miami) was started in 1987 as a new and improved version of *El Miami Herald,* which had been continuously published since 1976 as an insert to the *Miami Herald.* Both the Spanish-language and the English-language newspapers are owned by the Miami Herald Publishing Company, a subsidiary of the Knight-Ridder newspaper chain. In early December 1996, *El Nuevo Herald* began publishing on the World Wide Web.

Diario Las Americas (Miami) was founded in 1953 by Horacio Aguirre, a Nicaraguan lawyer who had been an editorial writer for a Panamanian newspaper. The paper is published by The Americas Publishing company, which is owned by the Aguirre family. *Diario Las Americas* remains the only Spanish-language daily owned and operated by Hispanics without partnership by Anglo corporations. The trend of Spanish-language papers being published by major English-language dailies expanded when the *Chicago Tribune* began publishing the weekly *¡Exitos!* in Miami in 1991 and in Chicago in 1993. Another trend is the distribution of independently owned and operated Spanish-language weeklies by major English-language dailies: Such is the arrangement between *La Raza* and the *Chicago Sun Times.*

Subervi-Vélez (1988) conducted an empirical study on the political content of these newspapers. Analyzing the Spanish-language daily newspapers' coverage of the 1984 presidential elections, he found that these dailies appear to be more partisan than their Anglo counterparts. He also observed that although most of the Hispanic population outside of Miami may be liberal or inclined to vote for the Democratic party, only *La Opinión* and *El Diario–La Prensa* gave relatively more support in news stories and editorials to the Democrats than to the Republicans.

Aside from these dailies, it is estimated that across the nation over 380 newspaper-type publications directed especially to the diverse Hispanic populations in the United States are produced from as frequently as twice a week to once or twice a month (Whisler, Kirk, and Nuiry, 1996). Many of these publications are the product of extraordinary efforts of individuals in their local communities. The irregular and transitory nature of their products, which often have very limited circulation, has made it difficult to develop any comprehensive and current directory of these publications.

Finally, it should be mentioned that dozens of Spanish-language newspapers from Spain and numerous Latin American countries also reach the newsstands in U.S. cities with large Hispanic populations.

Magazines and Other Periodicals

Long before the twentieth century began, a variety of publications that can be classified as Hispanic-oriented magazines had been produced in the United States. Whisler and

Nuiry (1996:28) recently compiled a directory of Hispanic media in the United States and listed a total of 230 magazines. A comprehensive directory of all such publications is still lacking, but even a cursory review of the titles shows that culturally oriented magazines have abounded, as have those with political, social, education, business, and entertainment topics. Of particular note are the following Hispanic-oriented magazines with national circulation that are produced and published in the United States. Some are bilingual publications; others are published in only Spanish or English.

Three English-language magazines that merit particular mention are *Hispanic*, *Hispanic Business*, and *Hispanic Link*. *Hispanic* published its premier issue in 1988. According to one of its promotional pages, the major focus of this "magazine for and about Hispanics" is on contemporary Hispanics and their achievements and contributions to U.S. society. *Hispanic* is owned by the Hispanic Publishing Corporation, which is based in Washington, D.C., and is a family company. Its chairman and founder is Fred Estrada, a native of Cuba; his son, Alfredo, is the current publisher.

Hispanic Business, according to its promotional material, is "the oldest established business magazine oriented toward the U.S. Hispanic market." It is published in Santa Barbara, California, by Hispanic Business, Inc., under the directorship of Jesús Chavarría, its editor and publisher. Chavarría, a Mexican American, started the magazine in 1979 as a newsletter; it turned to regular publication in 1982.

A third English-language publication is *Hispanic Link*. Although a newsletter and not a magazine per se, it is a very important and influential publication, providing a succinct summary of the major issues and events related to education, immigration, business, legislative, political, policy, and economic concerns of the Hispanic populations in the United States. *Hispanic Link* was founded by Charles A. Ericksen in February 1980 as a column service for newspapers. In 1983, it became a regular newsletter. It reaches many libraries, Hispanic organizations, corporations with major responsibilities toward Hispanics, journalists, Hispanic advocacy groups, and influential government officials working with or interested in legislation and policy issues related to Hispanic populations. Based in Washington, D.C., it publishes national news weekly and syndicates three weekly columns in English and Spanish to media throughout the United States and Latin America. It also offers internships for aspiring Latino journalists to work in the nation's capital.

The most notable bilingual magazine is *Vista*. With its headquarters in Miami, Florida, it started in 1985 as a monthly supplement insert to selected Sunday newspapers in locations with large Hispanic populations. Published by Horizon, a U.S. communications company, *Vista* is aimed at informing, educating, and entertaining Hispanic American readers with stories that focus on Hispanic role models and positive portrayals of Hispanic people and cultural identity. Recently, several new magazines have been launched with a strong appeal to Latinas and to Latinos in urban areas. These include *Latina*, *Sí*, *Urban Latino*, *FrontEra*, *Moderna*, *Latina Style*, *Latin Style*, *Latin Heat*, and *¡Que Linda!*

In addition to the publications highlighted above, dozens of Spanish-language consumer magazines cover specialized topics. Examples of these are *Buenhogar, Cosmopolitan, Geomundo, Hombre del Mundo, Harper's Bazaar en Español, Mecánica Popular,* and *Selecciones del Reader's Digest.* Some are Spanish-language editions of English-language publications. Regardless of where they are produced, be it Spain, the United States, or Latin America, these publications have as primary clients Spanish-speaking populations. A number of journals address specialized topics related to academia, professions, and organizations. And finally, numerous state and regional publications are aimed at local Hispanic and Spanish-speaking populations. All in all, the number of magazines and other periodicals available to Hispanics in the United States is extensive and diverse. No other ethnic minority population in the United States has available such an array of printed materials. The same is true regarding electronic media.

Electronic Media

As English-language Latino-oriented print media seek new markets among Hispanics across the country, Spanish-language broadcasting efforts continue to hold and expand their own territories. The number of stations, companies, and organizations related to Spanish-language radio and television in the United States has grown, as have the content options they offer. Radio, for example, not only offers *rancheras* and *salsa,* but also top 40, *mariachi, norteña,* TexMex, Mexican hits, adult contemporary, contemporary Latin hits, international hits, Spanish adult contemporary, romantic, ballads, traditional hits and oldies, folkloric, regional, *boleros,* progressive Tejano, *merengue,* and even bilingual contemporary hits. Spanish-language television is no longer just song and dance shows with some *novelas* and old movies. It is also drama, talk shows, comedy, news, investigative journalism, sports, contemporary movies, entertainment magazines, dance videos, and specials from all over the world.

All of these options have been made available through the search for new markets by both Hispanic and Anglo entrepreneurs and the growth of both the Hispanic population and its purchasing power. In fact, in some markets the Hispanic audience for selected Spanish-language radio and television stations is larger than that of many well-known English-language stations (Puig, 1991).

Radio

Spanish-language radio programs transmitted from within the boundaries of the United States began as early as the mid-1920s—almost immediately after the inauguration of commercial broadcasting. Since then, radio directed especially to the U.S. Hispanic market has grown "from an occasional voice heard on isolated stations in the Southwest and on big city multilingual stations to a multimillion dollar segment of the broadcast industry" (Gutiérrez and Schement, 1979:5).

One of the best-known pioneers of Spanish-language radio in California was Pedro J. González, about whom two films have been made, the documentary *Ballad of an Unsung Hero* (1984) and the full-length feature *Break of Dawn* (1988). According to the interviews and documents gathered by the producer of the documentary, between 1924 and 1934, González was responsible for shows such as *Los Madrugadores* (The Early Risers). This program was broadcast from 4 to 6 A.M. primarily on Los Angeles station KMPC, which thanks to its 100,000-watt power could be heard at that time all over the Southwest—even as far as Texas—thus reaching thousands of Mexican workers as they started their day. The dynamics of González's show and his progressive political stands made him a threat to the establishment, resulting in trumped-up rape charges against him in 1934. He was convicted and sentenced to six years in San Quentin prison, released in 1940, and immediately deported to Mexico. In Tijuana, he reestablished and continued his radio career, until the 1970s when he returned to retire in the United States.

By the late 1930s, numerous stations carried Spanish-language programs either full-time or part-time. In response to the market demands, in 1939 the International Broadcasting Company (IBC) was established in El Paso, Texas, to produce and sell Spanish-language programming to various stations and brokers across the country. In Texas, Raúl Cortez was one of the earliest Chicano brokers; he bought airtime from stations and sold it to Latino market advertisers. He eventually succeeded in establishing his own full-time Spanish-language station—KCOR-AM, a 1,000-kilowatt "daytime only" station in San Antonio—which went on the air in 1946. Most Hispanic brokers, however, became employees of the stations from which they bought time.

From the 1950s to the 1970s, Spanish-language radio moved away from the brokerage system in favor of the more independent, full-time stations in AM and subsequently in FM. During these transitional years, "personality radio" was at its height. Brokers and announcers who had control over their programs and commercials became popular themselves. But by the late 1960s, the format became more tightly packaged and controlled, leaving less leeway and influence to individual radio stars. One interesting note about Spanish-language broadcast stations is that almost all the announcers came from Latin America, in spite of the growth and potential talent in the Hispanic audiences in the United States (Grebler, Moore, and Guzman, 1970).

The 1991 Broadcasting Yearbook lists 185 AM and 68 FM stations transmitting full-time in Spanish. An additional 197 AM and 203 FM stations are listed as airing Spanish programs at least a few hours per week. By 1996, the United States had "461 radio stations offering a wide variety of Spanish programs" (Whisler and Nuiry, 1996:11). These statistics provide indisputable evidence that Spanish-language radio is a powerful and growing ethnic medium in the United States.

Although the numbers attest to a remarkable growth of the Hispanic-oriented radio industry, Hispanic ownership of radio stations has not followed similar patterns. According to Schement and Singleton (1981), in 1980, of the 64 primary Spanish-language radio stations identified in their study, only 25 percent were owned by Latinos. In the top ten markets (including New York, Los Angeles, Chicago, Miami, and San Antonio), Latinos owned only about 10 percent of stations.

Another important issue concerning the ownership of Hispanic-oriented radio is the trend toward concentration of stations, particularly the most profitable ones, under major corporate groups. The oldest and largest of these businesses is the Tichenor Media System, Inc., until recently a family-owned private company in Dallas, Texas. This company was started in 1940 by McHenry Tichenor, a successful Anglo newspaperman. In 1991, the Spanish Radio Network was formed in partnership with SRN Texas, Inc. (a wholly-owned subsidiary of Tichenor Media System), and Radio WADO, Inc., to purchase the Miami and New York stations.

A second group of Spanish-language stations—the largest in terms of the audience reached—is the Spanish Broadcasting Systems (SBS), started in 1983 by Raúl Alarcón, Jr. Lotus Communications owns a third group of Spanish-language radio stations; its flagstaff operation is KWKW-AM, a station that has been serving the Hispanic community in the Los Angeles area since 1942. A fourth Spanish-language radio group is Radio America, founded in 1986 when the brothers Daniel and James Villanueva, of Mexican heritage, bought station WBRG-FM in the San Francisco Bay area. In 1988, they acquired station KLOK-AM in the San Jose/San Francisco area.

A distinct group of stations belong to the nonprofit Radio Bilingüe network in California. Efforts to establish this network date to 1976 when Hugo Morales, a Harvard Law School graduate of Mexican Mixtec Indian heritage and Lupe Ortiz and Roberto Páramo, with the collaboration of a group of Mexican peasants, artists, and activists, sought to use radio to improve life and sustain the cultural identity of farmworkers in California's San Joaquin Valley (see Corwin, 1989; Downing, 1990). With the significant backing of a grant from a Catholic charity, KSIV-FM was launched in Fresno, California, in 1980. It transmits a variety of music programs plus a diversity of information related to health, education, immigration, civic action, and the arts. Supported primarily by donations from community members, businesses, and some foundations, the Radio Bilingüe network now reaches across central California. KVSJ programming is beamed twenty-four hours a day via two satellite systems that give the 400 public radio stations in the United States and Puerto Rico access to the Fresno-based KSJV programming, which is also available to commercial stations. One of the distinctive features of this network is the operational and programming support it receives from innumerable volunteers, who produce diverse music and public service offerings in English, Spanish, and bilingual programs.[2]

As this survey indicates, Spanish-language radio stations, whether owned by Hispanics or Anglos, can be heard in practically every region of the United States. In some major metropolitan cities with large concentrations of Hispanics, for example, New York, Los Angeles, Miami, Chicago, San Antonio, and Houston, Hispanics have a variety of Spanish stations to choose from, offering a range of formats and music to please almost any of the major Latin American and U.S. Hispanic traditions. Through news and other programming services, Spanish speakers in the United States also have many opportunities to maintain ties to their countries of origin, enjoy a diversity of entertainment shows, and take part in the news and cultural developments and events in the United States as well as around the Latin world. This is a dimension that truly distinguishes Latinos from previous immigrants to the United States.

Television

Just as in the case of radio, television transmissions in Spanish started almost as soon as in English. Since the 1940s, entrepreneurs have found a significant and profitable market in transmitting to the Hispanic populations in the United States. Spanish-language television has grown enormously from the early days of a few brokered hours on English-language stations in San Antonio and New York. In 1995, over $500 million in advertising was spent on Spanish-language television (Zate, 1995). Most of these television stations are affiliates of Univisión and Telemundo. Some operate independently, whereas others have corporate ties to both U.S. and Mexican media.

The first Spanish-language television station in the United States was San Antonio's KCOR-TV Channel 41, which began with some evening programs in 1955. But a few years before this and other similar stations started, a number of Spanish-language radio entrepreneurs recognized the potential of the Spanish-speaking television audiences and pioneered in the production of special TV programs. Following the pattern used in the early stages of Spanish-language radio, time was brokered for these programs in the nascent English-language stations in selected cities. One of the earliest of these Spanish-language television programs was *Buscando Estrellas* (Star Search), which began in 1951. *Buscando Estrellas* brought to Texas a variety of talent from Mexico and provided opportunities for local amateurs to present their artistic aspirations at the recording studios and to the television-viewing audiences. Between 1956 and 1961, Pepe del Rio hosted another popular Spanish-language program in San Antonio, *Cine en Español* (Movies in Spanish), which featured old movies brought from Mexico, Spain, and Argentina.

In New York, the precursors of Spanish-language television were the well-known radio personalities Don Pessante and Don Mendez. Some anecdotal evidence indicates that during the late 1940s they may have hosted the very first U.S. Hispanic-oriented television entertainment programs by brokering time on one of the English-language channels (9, 11, or 13).

More anecdotal evidence indicates that during the early 1950s *El Show Hispano* aired on the once-commercial WATV Channel 13 on weekends. This station later

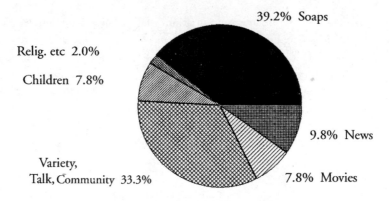

FIGURE 15.2   Programs in a Typical Week on Univisión, Fall 1993. (Excludes weekend schedule, which excludes soaps, and includes more movies, variety, and sports programs.)

became WNJU Channel 47. The program aired approximately between 1952 and 1954. It was brokered by an Anglo who also saw the potential audience and profit among the growing Hispanic populations in New York. One of the distinctive features of this show, which was co-hosted by Don Mendez and Aníbal González-Irizarry, was that in addition to its musical and comic segments, it included a fifteen-minute news section. González-Irizarry was responsible for this segment, making him probably the first Hispanic television newscaster in the early stages of this medium in the United States.[3]

During the 1960s, part-time Spanish-language programs in English-language stations also emerged in other cities with large concentrations of Hispanics, including Los Angeles, Houston, Miami, Phoenix, Tucson, and Chicago (Valenzuela, 1985:129). Such programs—sponsored primarily by a local company—were often the outcome of personal efforts of Hispanic entrepreneurs, many of whom had experiences with radio. Some stations that provided time sought alternative sources of profits or to comply with FCC requirements of public service programs to serve community needs and interests.

Between the 1960s and the end of the 1980s, the Spanish-language television industry in the United States was dominated by three networks: Spanish International Network (subsequently Univisión), Telemundo, and Galavisión. (See Figures 15.2 and 15.3, which illustrate current programming content on the two largest networks.) The potential gold mine offered by the exponential growth of the U.S. Hispanic populations was a driving force in the formation of and competition among those television ventures. This potential did not go unnoticed by the primarily English-language broadcasting and cable companies, which developed special series and cable operations to profit from Hispanics all across the United States as well as in

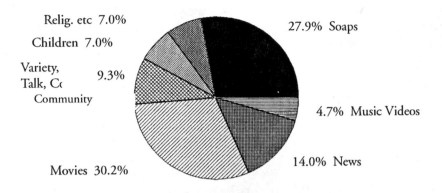

Relig. etc 7.0%

Children 7.0%

Variety, Talk, C 9.3%

Community

Movies 30.2%

27.9% Soaps

4.7% Music Videos

14.0% News

FIGURE 15.3 Programs in a Typical Week on the Telemundo Network, Fall 1993. (Excludes weekend schedule, which omits soaps and includes more movies, variety, and sports.)

Latin America. From its beginnings up to this medium's fifth decade in the United States, television continues to have substantial foreign connections in corporate structures, on-camera and off-camera personnel, and programming (Foreign Connection, 1989; Mydans, 1989).

Summary

Since the 1840s, Latinos and their life in and outside of the United States have been portrayed in predominantly limited, stereotyped, and unfavorable ways in mainstream print, film, television, and advertising (Subervi-Vélez et al., 1994). Although significant positive changes occurred through the years, the overall balance is still on the negative side, due not so much to blatant injurious stereotypes but to the absence of the full variety of Hispanics and their values. There is also serious and continuous underrepresentation in the employment of Latinos and other minorities in U.S. media industries. From the everyday selection, production, and dissemination of news to the conceptualization, creation, and production of entertainment, the proportion of Hispanics in the workforce is significantly smaller in the media than it is in society at large.

Nevertheless, Hispanic-oriented media in the United States have an extensive history developing on a par with and even sometimes ahead of general market media. This is true for print media from the 1800s to the still-emergent cable and satellite ventures. As we move into the twenty-first century, Spanish-language and English-language media directed at Hispanics in the United States, and more recently toward Latinos in Latin America, will continue to grow as such media are deemed profitable by U.S. and international companies exploring and exploiting the global communications markets. What remains to be seen and assessed is whether or not Hispanics in the United States will be at the forefront of developing and producing the new content and media affecting their lives.

NOTES

Excerpted and edited with permission of the author. "Hispanic Oriented Media" by Subervi-Vélez et al. is reprinted with permission from the publisher of the *Handbook of Hispanic Cultures in the United States: Sociology*, Felix Padilla (Ed.), Houston, TX.: Arte Publico Press, 1994, pp. 304–357.

1. In 1995, another Spanish-language daily, *El Día*, began publishing in Houston, Texas. Whisler and Nuiry's (1996) directory lists this paper with a circulation of 15,000.

2. Although some stations produce everything they broadcast, including news and commercials, many stations depend on companies called networks that produce and package programs for the Spanish-language radio market. Some networks provide news services and others provide "full-service" programming; this might include talk shows, features, music, and other formats. For additional information on this, see the original report from which this chapter was excerpted (Subervi-Vélez et al., 1994:335–350).

3. Aníbal González-Irizarry was also a well-known disc jockey and newscaster on two Spanish-language radio stations in New York (WWRL and WBNX). When he returned to Puerto Rico in 1955, he eventually became the most prominent and respected anchorman on Puerto Rican television for over twenty years on WKAQ Channel 2.

REFERENCES

The 1991 broadcasting yearbook. (1991). Washington, DC: Broadcasting Publications.

Corwin, Miles. (1989, August 20). "A voice for farm workers," *Los Angeles Times*, Part 1, pp. 3, 33.

Downing, John D. H. (1990, Spring). "Ethnic minority radio in the United States," *Howard Journal of Communications*, 2, 135–148.

Foreign Connection. (1989, April 3). "The foreign connection from Mexico to Miami," *Broadcasting*, pp. 44–46.

Glasheen, Janet. (1989, December). "Betting on print," *Hispanic Business*, pp. 42–44.

Grebler, Leo, Joan Moore, and Ralph Guzman. (1970). *The Mexican-American people*. New York: Free Press.

Gutiérrez, Félix F., and Jorge Reina Schement. (1979). *Spanish-language radio in the southwestern United States* (Monograph No. 5). University of Texas at Austin, Center for Mexican American Studies.

Mydans, Seth. (1989, August 24). "Charges of bias in Spanish-language television," *New York Times*, Sec. 4, p. 4.

Puig, Claudia. (1991, April 7). "Off the charts," *Los Angeles Times*, Calendar Section, pp. 89–90.

Schement, Jorge Reina, and Loy A. Singleton. (1981, Spring). "The onus of minority owner-ship: FCC policy and Spanish-language radio," *Journal of Communication*, 31 (2), 78–83.

Subervi-Vélez, Federico A. (1988). "Spanish-language daily newspapers and the 1984 elec-tions," *Journalism Quarterly*, 65 (3), 678–685.

Subervi-Vélez, Federico A., with Charles Ramírez Berg, Patricia Constantakis-Valdés, Chon Noriega, Diana I. Ríos, and Kenton T. Wilkinson. (1994). "Hispanic oriented media," *Handbook of Hispanic cultures in the United States: Sociology*, Felix Padilla (Ed.). Houston: Arte Publico Press, pp. 304–357.

Valenzuela, Nicholas A. (1985). *Organizational evolution of a Spanish-language television net-work: An environmental approach*, Doctoral dissertation, Stanford University.

Veciana-Suarez, Ana. (1987). *Hispanic media, USA*. Washington, D.C.: Media Institute.

Whisler, Kirk, and Octavio Nuiry. (1996). *The 1996 complete Hispanic media directory*. Arkansas City, KS: Giligand.

Wilson, Clint, Jr., and Félix F. Gutiérrez. (1985). *Minorities and the media: Diversity and the end of mass communication*. Beverly Hills, CA: Sage.

Zate, Maria. (1995, December). "A billion-dollar year for media spending," *Hispanic Business*, pp. 50, 52.

PART FOUR

Strategies for Change

This section is included to help readers become more analytical and critical in viewing Latino images in the media. The three chapters will help readers clarify and better articulate their reactions to media images, the reasons for their assessments, and the criteria they have used to arrive at these assessments. I hope that these chapters will also help readers to reflect on the readings included here and to focus on broader issues, such as the contexts within which images are shown and interpreted, how images are projected, why some characters are seen in a positive light and others in a negative light, and how stereotypes are often subtly conveyed. I also hope that these chapters will assist readers in moving to a more activist or proactive stance with regard to the issues of underrepresentation and misrepresentation of Latinos in the media.

This section contains three chapters. Chapter 16 includes (1) viewing guides, exercises, and projects; (2) a listing of recent Latino-themed films; and (3) a review of other relevant texts. Chapter 17 is intended to deepen readers' appreciation of the material provided in this volume. It contains questions for review and reflection keyed to individual chapters. Finally, Chapter 18 lists and discusses concrete, practicable steps that can be taken to change the current situation of underrepresentation and the misrepresentation of Latinos in the media.

16

Promoting Analytical and Critical Viewing

Clara E. Rodríguez

There are many ways of viewing. The material in this chapter will help readers—that is, viewers—both to become more aware of how they view films, videos, and television programs and to develop new ways of viewing. To explore the distinction between critical and uncritical viewing, ask yourself the following questions with regard to a film or TV program you have viewed:

1. Who is telling this story?
2. Given the perspective of the camera, which characters does the director want us to follow? With whom do you identify? Why?
3. Can you imagine the world of the film as seen by characters who are denied a point of view in this film? Can you develop an alternative scenario around the point(s) of view of characters who function as peripheral, almost invisible, reactors to the central characters, for example, butlers, maids, waitresses, bartenders, cab drivers, and anonymous victims?
4. Where else could the camera go?
5. Who else could tell us stories?
6. What stories have not been told yet?
7. Can you provide a socioeconomic profile of the typical hero in coming-of-age films? Can you think of an example of such a hero who is *not* a White, upper-middle-class, suburban male between fourteen and twenty-one years old? Have you observed other types of people in other situations come of age in the United States? Have you seen their stories in movies?
8. How are the answers to these questions related to who the directors, writers, producers are? to the tenor of the times? to the current fads? to the audience with the most money to spend?

These questions, which were developed by Graham (1995), help us as viewers sharpen our understanding of films, their impact, and how they elicit the reactions

240

they do. The questions also force us to examine issues of "social equity" (Candelaria, 1985).[1] Discussing your responses to the questions with a friend or in a group will begin the process of learning to see in new ways.[2]

Exercises

The exercises provided at the end of this chapter are intended to raise fundamental questions about the images of Latinos in movies, television, and other media. They can also be applied to other minority groups. The first exercise concerns film analysis and review. The second exercise is specific to television programming. It is intended to be used in conjunction with reading Chapter 3 by Lichter and Amundson, but it can also be used independently. The exercises can also serve as the basis for a film or television diary to develop viewing skills over a set period of time.

Readers can use either exercise to focus on a particular type of program, a theme, a film genre, or a period of time. For example, films can be compared along a specific dimension, such as the portrayal of indigenous women in films between 1960 and 1990 or Latinos in westerns of the 1950s and 1960s. The exercises assist viewers to develop a sharper, more comparative thrust. They also help viewers to better see similarities and differences between films and to better understand and articulate subjective reactions to visual images, especially those in film and television.

Teaching Aid

If the exercises are used in a course, they can also serve as the basis for a paper or project. A student could integrate the analysis of a film (or television program) using the exercises in this chapter, the readings in this volume, and the student's own research and reading. Alternatively, students could use the exercises to compare two films or programs, for example, with regard to character depiction or advertisers for the shows. Utilizing the exercises for a paper or thesis serves two purposes. The focus on a particular dimension, such as race, color, class, gender, or political relations with the United States, lends cohesion to the student's thinking. The exercises will also ensure the systematic data gathering, rigor in observation, comparison, and method necessary in good research.

Whether or not the viewer is in school, using the exercises a few times will make her or him a more critical consumer and reviewer of television, films, and media in general. Students and other users have commented that the exercises help "bring matters into focus," "enable the viewer to see the interaction between television and the real world," and "help to organize opinions and understanding of the stereotyping of a minority in the media." The exercises have also helped viewers to "question characters and actions" in ways they hadn't before, and they have found themselves "analyzing more in depth and observing beyond what is presented." Finally, the forms have been self-revealing, causing questioning of formerly unquestioned images. Viewers have said they were "surprised at their own perceptions" and that they were "frustrated by pop culture images after writing about the characters." Some viewers appreciate these insights, others have been disturbed by them, but few have forgotten them.

Viewing Projects

Because literature in this area is still in its emerging stage, viewers may be at a loss as to how to approach a viewing project in this field. The following is a list of possible projects:

1. Film Diary

Using Exercise 16.1, viewers might choose a particular time period and focus on a theme, dimension, or genre. For example, viewers might choose five major films of the 1940s and examine the role of Latina women in these films. Or they might ask, how was "color" associated with Latinos in these films?

2. Television Diary

This project is similar to the film diary, but relies on Exercise 16.2. It is specific to television programs, such as situation comedies, variety shows, soap operas, and so forth.

3. Biography

Viewers might choose a particular Latino actor or actress and research his or her life. They could discuss the movies made by this performer, the roles played in these movies, how the movies and the performer were viewed at the time, and how "Hispanicity" affected his or her career.

4. Latino Characterizations

Viewers might examine changes in the characterization of a particular Latino character or stereotype that appeared in various films, for example, Zorro, the Cisco Kid, the Mexican spitfire.

5. Film Reviews

Viewers might examine the reviews of a particular film and compare these to their own response to this film, utilizing either of the exercises included in this chapter.

6. Elements of Success

Viewers might examine why particular Latino-themed films have been successful (or not) at the box office. For example, note the following differentials in the box-office take of the major Latino-themed films of 1995: *A Walk in the Clouds* ($44 million), *Desperado* ($23 million), *My Family/Mi Familia* ($11 million) (Cabrera, 1996).

7. Video

Viewers might make their own video, based on their analysis. The video might be accompanied by a short written summary that explains the intent of the video.

Films

An advantage to studying film today is the wide accessibility of films in video format. The following is a list of recent films that are relevant to Latinos in the United States. Viewers can rent most of these in video stores; some can also be found in public libraries. The emphasis in this list is on films of the 1980s and 1990s. A wide variety of films are included; some are reflective of stereotypes and others purposely depart from traditional stereotypes.

American Me (1992)
and the earth did not swallow him (1995)
Ballad of Gregorio Cortez (1983)
The Believers (1987)
Blood In . . . Blood Out (also called *Bound by Honor*) (1993)
Born in East L.A. (1987)
Break of Dawn (1989)
Carlito's Way (1993)
Colors (1988)
Crossover Dreams (1985)
Desperado (1995)
El Mariachi (1993)

El Norte (1983)
Fort Apache: The Bronx (1981)
Havana (1990)
House of the Spirits (1993)
I Like It Like That (1994)
Internal Affairs (1990)
Kiss of the Spider Woman (1985)
La Bamba (1987)
La Gran Fiesta (1987)
Life with Mikey (1993)
Like Water for Chocolate (1993)
The Mambo Kings (1992)
Mambo Mouth (1990) (HBO movie)
Mi Vida Loca (1994)
The Milagro Beanfield War (1988)
My Family/Mi Familia (1995)
The Old Gringo (1989)
The Penitent (1988)
The Perez Family (1995)
The Puerto Rican Mambo (Not a Musical) (1992)
Q & A (1990)
Renegades (1989)
Romero (1989)
Rooftops (1989)
Roosters (1995)
Salsa (1988)
Scarface (1983)
Seguin (1982)
A Show of Force (1990)
The Specialist (1994)
Stand and Deliver (1988)
Steal Big, Steal Little (1995)
A Walk in the Clouds (1995)
What Happened to Santiago (1989)
Young Guns (1988)
Zoot Suit (1981)

In addition to the documentaries noted in other chapters, the following documentaries that focus on Latinos in the United States are ones that universities or libraries might own or consider purchasing.

Birthwrite: Growing Up Hispanic (1989)
Carmen Miranda: Bananas Is My Business (1995)
Chicano Park (1989)
La Ofrenda: The Days of the Dead (1989)
Latino Hollywood (1995)
Musica: The Development of Latin Music in the U. S. (1985)
Two Worlds of Angelita (1983)
Yo Soy Chicano (1972)
Yo Soy Joaquin (1969)

Also of relevance, but seldom noted, are a trio of commercial movies made by the Fania All-Stars during the early 1970s. According to Calvo Ospina (1995:65), these movies played a critical role in diffusing Latin music developed in New York to Latin America. They were the first to document the origins of the music "as an expression of Latin American social identity" (Calvo Ospina, 1995:65). These are also available in video format:

Our Latin Thing (Nuestra Cosa) (1971)
Salsa (1973)
Fania All-Stars: Live in Africa (1974)

Texts

The following works provide discussions of some of the films listed. This book owes a major debt to these and earlier works. It is not possible to list all the useful books, but a few of the best known are described here to encourage readers to use these additional resources.

One of the earliest and most often cited works is by Allen L. Woll, *The Latin Image in American Film* (UCLA Latin American Center Publications, University of California, 1977, revised edition, 1980). This is a historical view of the (un)changing image of Latinos in film. It is a classic book in this area. As its title indicates, it uses the term "Latin" for images that are today referred to as "Latino." This shift in terms reflects the change that has occurred in Latin images. The earlier term, "Lain," included both Europeans of Latin linguistic origins, such as Italians and Spanish, and Latin Americans. Thus, Gilbert Roland, who was Mexican, was also a "Latin" lover at the time—as was Rudolph Valentino. The more contemporary term "Latino" is not so encompassing and excludes Europeans who do not have Spanish origins. It is generally used to refer to those of Latin American, Spanish, or Spanish Caribbean origins in the United States.

Chon Noriega's (Ed.) *Chicanos and Film: Essays on Chicano Representation and Resistance* (New York: Garland Press, 1992) is a very good collection focused on Chicanos in film. It covers representation in the U.S. and Mexican film industries. It also deals with critical issues in Chicano cinema and presents manifestos and testimonials from those involved in Chicano cinema.

A major earlier text is Gary D. Keller's (Ed.) *Chicano Cinema: Research, Reviews and Resources* (Binghamton, NY: Bilingual Review/Press, 1985). This text also has as its focus Chicano cinema. It covers research and criticism, images of Chicanas in films, interviews with the author of *Zoot Suit,* and reviews of films. In addition, it includes lists of resources, for example, a directory of Chicano film distributors.

Rosa Linda Fregoso's *The Bronze Screen: Chicana and Chicano Film Culture* (Minneapolis: University of Minnesota Press, 1993) is a very interesting, novel, analytical view of film culture "by, for, and about Chicanas and Chicanos" (Fregoso, 1993:xv). Focusing specifically on selected films by Chicanos, Fregoso examines issues of cultural identity, gender representations, race, Chicano film culture, the use of humor, and the border as metaphor to understand cultural processes and the formation of subjectivity.

A very useful recent work is that by George Hadley-Garcia, *Hispanic Hollywood: The Latins in Motion Pictures* (New York: Carol Publishing Group, A Citadel Press book, 1993). This book is available in both English and Spanish and is written to be easily accessible to the nonacademic reader. The author builds on the work and structure of Woll's (1977) book described above. The book includes excellent and varied photographs, as well as a listing of earlier, little-known works in this area. It takes a historical approach and emphasizes the role of political and economic factors on the images represented. As in Woll (1977), the term "Latins" is used in the English subtitle (the term used in the Spanish-language version is "Latinos").

A more recent text in this area is Luis Reyes and Peter Rubie's *Hispanics in Hollywood: An Encyclopedia of Film and Television* (New York: Garland Publishing, 1994). As the title indicates, this is an encyclopedic treatment of Latinos in Hollywood. Reyes is a Hollywood publicist with a long-term interest in this area. The book includes details not noted in other works, for example, about little-known Latino actors of the 1930s. It is also filled with an extensive and impressive collection of photographs. It is an extremely useful resource.

A Guide to the Exercises

Choose a film in which there is at least one Latino character or that has a Latino theme. Think about the Latino image(s) in your film. What are they? How are they drawn? How are race, class, color, and gender used to convey these images? The following questions will facilitate your answering these questions. They are general questions that are relevant to some films and not others.

What is the character's function with regard to the plot? Is the character positive or negative? If you codify the character's function as positive, would you say his or her role is: (1) heroic, (2) charitable or altruistic, (3) friendly or helping, (4) competent, or (5) other? If negative, is the character (a) malevolent, (b) greedy or selfish, (c) foolish, (d) incompetent, or (e) other?

If the character represents a combination of functions, what are these?

Is the character victimized? Who victimizes the character? How is the character victimized?

Does the character attempt or commit a crime? What type of crime? How serious is the crime?

Does the character use controlled substances? What is used and how often is it used?

Does the character have sex? Or is the character said to have sex? If so, what kind of sex? extramarital? premarital, homosexual, other?

What are the character's goal(s)? How are these goals attained? through legal or illegal means? through sex, money, personal charm, embarrassment, other people, intelligence?

What motives does the character have for his or her actions?

What is the interaction between the characters?

How do you feel about the characters and why?

In filling out the exercises, assume that you are writing to, or talking with, a friend who has not seen this film or program. See the notes at the end of each exercise for definitions and further directions.

NOTES

1. Candelaria (1985) maintains that "social equity" should be a legitimate variable in critical reviews of films. She asserts that contrary to the usual approach taken in film criticism, films should be viewed with an eye toward how well they promote values of social equity. Speaking as a humanist, she says that one of the most important values of the humanities is that they invite, perhaps even demand, that we critically analyze those human activities that most reflect the complexity of the human condition. Thus, fields such as history, literature, linguistics, and anthropology characteristically engage in analyses that consider issues of social equity as they examine human situations. Candelaria believes this approach should be applied to the examination of movies. Such an approach would help us to better understand and appreciate the multiplicity of human experiences.

2. These questions are also useful for teachers, a film discussion group, a social issues club, or a school project or paper.

EXERCISE 16.1   Film Viewing

TYPE:	Musical	Western	Historical Drama		Comedy
	Social Problem	Drama	News	Action	Animated
	Other: _____				

TITLE: _____

Director: _____   M   F _____

Writer/Producer/Significant Others: _____

_____

_____

Date Released: _____   Length: _____   Company: _____

Setting: _____

Major Actors and Minor Latino Roles:

	Ethnicity	Color	Status[1]	Role[2]	Outcome[3]
Actor 1:					
_____	____	____	____	n/a[4]	____
Character 1:					
_____	____	____	____	____	____
A2:					
_____	____	____	____	n/a	____
C2:					
_____	____	____	____	____	____
A3:					
_____	____	____	____	n/a	____
C3:					
_____	____	____	____	____	____
A4:					
_____	____	____	____	n/a	____
C4:					
_____	____	____	____	____	____

Story:

Plot: _____

_____

_____

_____

_____

_____

_____

Gender Relations (Who gets whom):

_____

_____

_____

_____

Class Relations (Who is who):

_____

_____

_____

_____

_____

_____

_____

Race/Ethnic Group Relations (Who does/says what to whom, how and why):

_____

_____

_____

_____

_____

_____

_____

_____

Theme/Subthemes (Discuss and assess):

_____

_____

_____

_____

_____

_____

Random Reflections/Additional Comments:

_____

_____

_____

_____

_____

_____

NOTES

1. *Status Columns.* In the case of actors (i.e., A1, A2, etc.), status refers to how esteemed the actors are in their profession. In the case of the characters (i.e., C1, C2, etc.), status refers to the socioeconomic status or social position of the character in the movie (i.e., occupation, income, prestige, etc.) as viewed by other characters. In filling in these columns, use the following rating scales:

A1, A2, etc.	C1, C2, etc.
Professional Prestige:	*SES or Economic Status:*
1. High	1. Rich
2. More than medium	2. Middle class
3. Medium	3. Working class
4. Low	4. Poor
5. Unknown	5. Unknown

2. *Role.* This refers to the role played by a particular character. The question is, what is the character's role in relation to the plot? Is the character the

1. Protagonist/Star/Major character/Hero/Heroine/Lead
2. Antagonist (person causing the conflict with the lead/villain)
3. Supporting character
4. Five-line character (bit part, walk-on)
5. Extra (no lines)
6. Other

3. *Outcome.* This column refers to whether the character ultimately succeeds or fails in the film.

1. Succeeds
2. Fails
3. Mixed or unfinished
4. Other

4. *n/a.* Not applicable to actors.

EXERCISE 16.2   Television Viewing

Choose a television show with at least one Latino character (preferably one you have seen before). Use this page to describe the program and each character in the show. Then answer the questions on the following pages. (Add pages as needed.)

Name of Program: _____ Network _____ Channel _____
Date of Program: ___/___/___ M/T/W/H/F/Sa/S _____ am/pm
Length of Program: _____ Genre of Program: comedy, drama, entertainment,
news, etc. _____
Setting: _____
Producer/Director: _____
Writer(s): _____
Company: _____

Character Name: (abbreviate)	Race/Color	Sex	Educ.[1]	SES[2]	Other Charac.[3]
_____	_____	M/F	_____	_____	_____
_____	_____	M/F	_____	_____	_____
_____	_____	M/F	_____	_____	_____
_____	_____	M/F	_____	_____	_____
_____	_____	M/F	_____	_____	_____
_____	_____	M/F	_____	_____	_____
_____	_____	M/F	_____	_____	_____
_____	_____	M/F	_____	_____	_____
_____	_____	M/F	_____	_____	_____
_____	_____	M/F	_____	_____	_____
_____	_____	M/F	_____	_____	_____
_____	_____	M/F	_____	_____	_____

1. Why did you choose this show?

_____
_____
_____
_____

2. Give the plot or describe the situation in this episode.

_____
_____
_____
_____

3. Explain the positive or negative functions of the characters, in particular the Latino character. (For example, if the character was friendly, helpful, or heroic, this would be positive; if he or she displayed foolish, selfish, or malicious behavior, this would be negative.)

_____

_____

_____

_____

_____

4. Discuss the motivations for the Latino character's actions.

_____

_____

_____

_____

_____

_____

5. Describe the methods or means used by the Latino character to pursue his or her goals.

_____

_____

_____

_____

_____

6. Assess the image and role of the Latino character in this program. (Is this character negative or positive to society and to the particular group he or she represents?)

_____

_____

_____

_____

_____

7. How long has the show been on television? (Estimate)
_____ 6 wks   _____ 6 mos   _____ 1 yr   _____ 1–2 yrs   _____ > 3 yrs

8. How much airtime did the Latino character have?
_____ sec.   _____ min.

9. How much did the character speak relative to other characters?
_____ a lot   _____ some   _____ little   _____ not at all

10. Who are the advertisers on this show?

_____   _____
_____   _____
_____   _____
_____   _____
_____   _____
_____   _____

11. What is the relationship of these advertisers to the show? to the probable viewers of this show?

_____
_____
_____
_____
_____

12. Notes (Other comments):

_____
_____
_____
_____
_____
_____
_____
_____
_____
_____
_____
_____
_____
_____

NOTES

1. Use a scale of 1–5, with 5 being highest for the Education of the characters.

2. SES refers to socioeconomic status, i.e., the character's occupation, income, prestige as viewed by others in the cast. Use a scale of 1–5, with 5 being highest for the SES of the characters. For further clarification on SES, see Endnote #1 in "Film Viewing."

3. Refers to other characteristics you think are important to the character, e.g., the character is legally blind, bi-sexual, or heir to a fortune.

17

Questions and Reflections About the Readings in This Book

Clara E. Rodríguez

The following questions provide readers with an opportunity to reflect on the ideas discussed by the authors and the relationship of these ideas to readers' own perspectives or to those of other writers. The questions, which are specific to the chapters in this volume, will help readers to summarize, mentally or in writing, the major ideas in each of the chapters. These questions emphasize critical thinking and will also help readers to read, respond, evaluate, and integrate the ideas presented. Using these questions as a guide, readers can articulate a coherent synthesis of the readings, while at the same time becoming more aware of their own values and perspectives.

Chapter 1. "Out of the Picture: Hispanics in the Media," by National Council of La Raza (NCLR)

1. Friedman (1991) and Wilson and Gutiérrez (1995:73ff) have documented that many minority groups have been misrepresented and underrepresented in the media. What makes the Latino situation as NCLR describes it unique?
2. What can be done to improve the lack of representation and the misrepresentation of Latinos in the media?

Chapter 2. "Hispanic Voices: Is the Press Listening?" by Jorge Quiroga

In the four case studies Quiroga discusses, how are the following points illustrated?

1. Press indifference toward Hispanics seems more the rule than the exception.
2. Reporters and editors habitually speak about Hispanics, not to Hispanics.
3. Newsrooms regularly present Hispanics as unable or unwilling to help or speak for themselves.
4. Hispanics are not quite completely ignored, but neither are they fully seen or counted.

5. The media influence how Hispanics view themselves as well as how others perceive Hispanics.
6. Where there is a lack of Hispanic clout and input, the media encourage a homogenous view of Hispanics.
7. News operations often fail to meet the challenge posed by a changing population.
8. Poor newsroom attitudes, for example, limited knowledge about Hispanics and stereotyping, low employment of Hispanic journalists, and inconsistent efforts by Hispanics to hold the press accountable weaken the link between Hispanics and the press.

Chapter 3. *"Distorted Reality: Hispanic Characters in TV Entertainment," by S. Robert Lichter and D. R. Amundson*

1. Lichter and Amundson argue that the representation of African Americans in television has improved both in the quantity and in the diversity of characterizations. Does this change imply that it is possible to also improve the current characterizations and numbers of Latinos in the media?
2. Lichter and Amundson's analysis of television characters indicates that change has not been linear or even. For example, there was greater ethnicity in the earliest phase of television as compared with the subsequent "All-White World" phase. What are the implications of this finding for future change?
3. Do you think that the recent improvements in visibility and criminal associations noted by Lichter and Amundson are significant or too minor to merit attention?

Chapter 5. *"Citizen Chicano: The Trials and Titillations of Ethnicity in the American Cinema, 1935–1962," by Chon Noriega*

1. Noriega argues that although Chicanos were portrayed as citizens, they were actually kept at arm's distance, that is, "Otherized." What evidence does he use to support this statement?
2. How does Noriega contrast the history of Mexicans in the United States with the Hollywood films made during the 1932–1962 period? How was Chicano filmmaking a response to this history?
3. What patterns does Noriega find in the films he discusses?

Chapter 6. *"Stereotyping in Films in General and of the Hispanic in Particular," by Charles Ramírez Berg*

1. Reflect on films or television programs you have recently seen in which there were one or more Hispanic characters. Did these characters conform to the basic

Hispanic stereotypes noted by Berg? Were they modern-day, urban *bandidos* or *bandidas?* Latin lovers? male or female clowns? half-breed harlots? or inscrutable, prosperous, and virtuous dark ladies?

2. Berg argues that stereotypes are basic ways in which all people make sense of the world. What makes Latino stereotypes, or stereotypes of any group that is classified as "Other," injurious and problematic for all concerned?

3. Undocumented migrants have often been referred to in the media as illegal "aliens." Do you agree with Berg that there is a strain felt in U.S. society because of the influx of foreign peoples and that this results in cinematic representations of "aliens" in a host of films? For example, the *Star Wars* trilogy, which featured many "aliens," was filmed between 1977 and 1983. These three movies were top money makers, ranking third, seventh, and twelfth in the "All-Time Top American Movies" (*World Almanac and Book of Facts,* 1996:250).

Chapter 7. *"Chicanas in Film: History of an Image," by Carlos E. Cortés*

1. Cortés argues that the decline of the western and the rise of the civil rights movement contributed to the disappearance of some stereotypes, for example, the Chicana prostitute. Strong Chicana or Latina characters were not developed to replace them, however. Cortés maintains that although more Latina characters have appeared since the late 1960s, they have been culturally less Hispanic and less unique as human beings. They have been Spanish-surnamed "Anglas" or "Hispanic Barbie dolls." Cite examples and explain why you agree or disagree.

2. Cortés notes the development of a new role for Latinas as conscience to a central Anglo character. How different is this from the wise, but-still-doesn't-get-the-hero roles of earlier Chicanas in westerns, such as Katy Jurado in *High Noon?*

3. Some contemporary movies, such as *Pulp Fiction,* portray "difference" without apologies, as raw, in your face, and matter of fact. The assumption is that such a perspective moves viewers—as well as the characters involved in the plot—beyond the polite racism of the past. Do you agree that this more explicit approach is less racist or sexist? Why or why not?

Chapter 8. *"From Assimilation to Annihilation: Puerto Rican Images in U.S. Films," by Richie Pérez*

1. Pérez argues that Puerto Rican migration peaked at the same time that post–World War II baby boomers emerged as teenagers in the 1950s. He notes that this was also a period in which there was mass hysteria about juvenile

crime and a national debate about the causes of juvenile crime and solutions. How might the following events have affected the development of Puerto Rican media stereotypes?

a. The politically conservative, cold war climate during which the Hollywood 10 were jailed and the McCarthy hearings took place

b. The liberalization of the Production Code in 1956 whereby the ban on films depicting prostitution, drug addiction, abortion, and interracial marriage was lifted

c. The 1952 decision of the Supreme Court to grant First and Fourteenth Amendment protections (always enjoyed by the press) to the film industry

d. The financial depression in the film industry fed by the rise of television, the establishment of European quotas for U.S. films, and the attractiveness of foreign films for U.S. audiences

2. Pérez also notes the "historically constituted" nature of Puerto Rican media stereotypes and the role these stereotypes played in justifying the U.S. seizure of Puerto Rico for continued colonization. He argues that these previously established images of "Otherness" and "racial inferiority" became linked with modern media stereotypes of criminality. Is this historical political relationship addressed in any of the films reviewed by Pérez? If so, how is it addressed?

3. Pérez notes a change in the image of Puerto Ricans over time. He argues that *West Side Story* established definitive images of Puerto Ricans as urban ghetto dwellers and dichotomized images of Puerto Rican women. How are the roles of Puerto Rican women in subsequent films, such as *Fort Apache: The Bronx* different from or similar to their roles in *West Side Story?*

Chapter 9. "West Side Story: *A Puerto Rican Reading of 'America,'"* by *Alberto Sandoval Sánchez*

1. In *Black Skin, White Masks*, Frantz Fanon states that his final prayer is: "O my body, make of me always a man who questions!" How is this prayer relevant to Sandoval Sánchez's analysis of *West Side Story?* What makes this prayer relevant to film analysis today?

2. A common theme in earlier films and history textbooks was "How the West Was Won." Recently, there has been an emphasis on documenting "How the West Was Lost" and presenting the Native American Indian's perspective on the West. How is Sandoval Sánchez's analysis of *West Side Story* similar to this more recent approach?

Chapter 10. "Keeping It Reel? Films of the 1980s and 1990s,"
by Clara E. Rodríguez

1. To what extent have films that you have seen recently portrayed Latinos as involved with criminal activities?
2. Rodríguez notes that the association between Latinos and crime is found in movies made by both Latinos and non-Latinos. Why is this? What can be done to alter this association?

Chapter 11. "From the Margin to the Center:
Puerto Rican Cinema in
the United States," by Lillian Jiménez

1. During the period that Jiménez focuses on, what contextual factors contributed to the kind of films made?
2. Was the third generation the first to protest media depictions? How did the third generation protest these depictions?
3. According to Jiménez, what are the contributions of the Puerto Rican filmmakers she discusses?
4. How do you interpret the following statement by Jiménez: "Films and videotapes forced us to look at ourselves, to step outside of our condition and objectify our reality, to deconstruct and then visually reconstruct it with a new vision and power extracted from that painful process. They allowed us to reflect on ourselves—the films were our passage-way into ourselves."
5. Jiménez discusses Puerto Rican filmmakers at a particular historical juncture. How can the current generation of Puerto Rican and Latino filmmakers and television producers maintain and continue to empower their generation and the generation that follows as these earlier filmmakers did?
6. Jiménez discusses the need for Puerto Ricans to create structures to institutionalize and preserve Puerto Rican cinema. One possibility is a mentoring program. What else can be done?
7. Describe the ways in which Puerto Ricans protested through filmmaking their dehumanization and discrimination in U.S. society.
8. According to Jiménez, has U.S. oppression helped Puerto Ricans to become more aware of their identity and to seek justice?

Chapter 12. "Unofficial Stories: Documentaries by Latinas
and Latin American Women," by Liz Kotz

1. Are there particular issues covered in the documentaries that Kotz discusses that are of universal concern to all women, for example, sterilization?

2. What is the next step for Latinas who make films? Should they make commercial films? If so, where should these films be made—in the United States, Latin America, or Europe? How would they raise financial support for these projects?

3. Why are Latina filmmakers more prominent in documentary films than in feature films? What images are they able to present in these documentary films?

4. How did Latinas' increasing involvement in political issues manifest itself in the documentary films reviewed by Kotz and what is the importance of these films?

5. The documentaries Kotz discusses focus on issues such as colonialism (internal and external), racism, and gender conflicts. With regard to these issues, what is the potential of documentaries, such as *La Operación,* to empower the audiences that watch them?

6. Is the perspective of a Latina documentary filmmaker reflective of a different or broader Hispanic experience than that of a male Latino filmmaker?

7. According to Jiménez, what is to be gained by "the Other" presenting himself or herself?

Chapter 13. *"Type and Stereotype: Chicano Images in Film," by Linda Williams*

1. What distinction between "type" and "stereotype" does Williams make with regard to Latino images in films? Why is it important to distinguish between these two approaches?

2. Williams argues that individualization in a film threatens to create further stereotypes. Do you think that there is a danger that in focusing on groups, or cultures as a whole, new generalizations and stereotypes would be created and perpetuated?

3. How is Biberman able to avoid succumbing to stereotypes in his movie *Salt of the Earth?*

Chapter 14. *"Two Film Reviews:* My Family/Mi Familia *and* The Perez Family," *by Santiago Nieves and Frank Algarin*

1. What are the implications for future movies of Nieves's comparison of two Latino-themed films focused on Latino families?

2. Can only Latinos play Latino characters effectively?

Chapter 15. *"Hispanic-Oriented Media," by Federico Subervi-Vélez et al.*

1. Subervi-Vélez et al.'s historical overview documents the long and continuing history and broad range of media oriented to Latinos. These media have been both in Spanish and English. How do you think these Hispanic-oriented

media will change in the future? Will they grow or diminish as Latinos become more English dominant?

2. At present, Hispanic-oriented media are fairly separate from the mainstream media outlets. Do you think there will be greater crossover in the future? For example, will more general market corporations go into partnership with Latino-oriented media? Will they develop more programming oriented toward the Latino market? If so, how, where, and why will this occur? If not, why not?

18

What We Can Do

Clara E. Rodríguez

As the chapters in this volume make clear, Americans of Hispanic descent are truly "out of the picture." What can be done? Although it may seem that the prospects for change are dim, there *is* much that can be done, particularly if we join with others in these efforts toward change.[1] Even simple individual efforts, detailed in this chapter, that we can make as consumers of media can do much to change the current situation. That change is possible is evident from the success of other efforts at social change that appeared to be just as formidable. Who would have predicted in 1980 that no smoking legislation would permeate universities, airports, restaurants, and corporations, and that cigarette ads would be banned at some athletic events? Who could have foreseen the important role that shareholder resolutions played in corporate divestment in South Africa? Who would have thought megadevelopers like Disney and Donald Trump would have to complete environmental impact statements and mitigate environmental impacts in their projects?

Small victories are also evident in the media field. Wilson and Gutiérrez (1995) document the results of earlier successful change efforts for many various groups, including Latinos. More recent victories have also been claimed.[2] These victories have generally not been acknowledged, however. Media outlets seldom discuss (particularly in the media) their inadequacies with regard to misrepresentation and underrepresentation of Latinos or other groups in programming and staffing. Moreover, few will admit to being pressured. Thus, awareness of the victories gained is limited, and many victories claimed as successes by advocacy groups such as the National Hispanic Media Coalition (NHMC) or smaller, more local groups such as Latinos for Positive Images (LPI)[3] are denied by their targets.[4] But the reality is that such efforts do have a substantial effect, particularly on those who invest in the ventures that are objected to, including corporate sponsors, investors, and producers.

Clearly, problems remain to be confronted. This is an area in which artistic freedom is often sacrosanct, and the line between its defense and discrimination or exclusion is blurry at best. This is also a period of escalating costs for media productions and cutbacks in government funding for the arts. Finally, freedom of speech is a long-standing and fundamental right in the United States. Nonetheless, changes are possible and are, to a degree, necessitated by domestic demographic changes; by the increasingly global economy; and by a growing awareness of the media monopoly, with its racial and ethnic exclusivity and hegemonic character.[5] Balance, accuracy, and fairness do not have to be at odds with artistic freedom, cost efficiency, or freedom of the press.

Change at the industry level is unlikely to come about because "It is the right thing to do," however, but rather because, as activists in this area have pointed out, "The money is on the table." In other words, it would be foolish for the industry to leave the money on the table and not recognize the strengths of the Hispanic community as a viable consumer population or the profitability and benefits that can come from changing the current clichés to present a more realistic and multidimensional picture of the United States. As both the Newspaper Association of America (NAA) and the American Society of Newspaper Editors (ASNE) have noted, hiring minorities is a business imperative (Boyd, 1995; Caughey, 1995). It makes good business sense to accurately reflect and cover communities of color and other diversity dimensions, such as age, gender, political beliefs, and religion.[6] The rapid increase in minorities, present and projected, has provided a wake-up call for many to consider the advantages that may accrue from diversification.

Much can be done, and a clear sense of what has to be done can facilitate the task. With regard to Latinos, we need to increase employment of Hispanics in all media, especially in print and broadcast newsrooms. The fact that 21 percent of journalists taking their first newspaper job are minorities, as are 37 percent of newspaper interns, is encouraging.[7] We also need to counter the lack of importance and urgency that often accompanies current coverage of Hispanic news. Moreover, we need to include Hispanics in more stories, not just those that are specific to the Hispanic community. This is not a quick and easy task. As NCLR (1994) has pointed out, ensuring accurate, sensitive, and proportional entertainment portrayals and news coverage requires a multifaceted, comprehensive, and long-term program.

In the following section, I focus on what individuals, businesses, political leaders, and community-based or nongovernmental organizations can do. The following two sections detail many of the recommendations made by NCLR on what the government and the media industry itself can do.

What Can You as an Individual Do?

As an individual, you can register complaints. With whom? With the Mass Media Bureau of the Federal Communications Commission (FCC), local radio or television station managers, news directors, producers, specific journalists or newscasters, and your representatives in Congress and members of the Telecommunications and

Finance subcommittee of the Commerce committee in the U.S. House of Representatives. To register either a positive or a negative comment about a film, write to the Head of Production at the studio that released the film. (The studio's logo and name are usually included in the beginning credits of a film and on advertising posters.) Addresses of major studios are available from media advocacy groups, such as Latinos for Positive Images, in library reference books, and on the Internet.

Letter-writing or telephone efforts can be enhanced if you organize a group to replicate your endeavors. You can develop letter-writing campaigns to any of the persons and agencies mentioned above. Such efforts are also amplified when you write to the companies that sponsor a show.[8] The addresses of advertising companies and their clients are available in the advertisers "Red Book" (*The Standard Directory of Advertisers,* annual), which is available in most libraries; lists of station managers are available from media advocacy organizations. Most people underestimate the significance of letters and phone calls. They doubt that one person can have any influence. Yet, given how few letters are received (particularly in this area), each letter or phone call is seen to represent many viewers. This is particularly true of letters to sponsors. Also, the absence of critical feedback is often interpreted as indicative of either support or neutrality—in the same way that "no news" is "good news," "no feedback" is interpreted as "no problem."

If individuals can learn more about the nature of the press and the entertainment media and how they function, national political and social interest groups can organize a national and local press and media strategy, give it high priority, and make it a consistent and ongoing effort. These change efforts should include the Spanish-speaking media. Student groups, local community organizations, Hispanic-owned businesses, Latino elected and appointed officials, and other Hispanic leaders can expand their advocacy agendas to include a media focus. Specifically, individuals and such groups can

- *Encourage responsible corporations to give advertising support* only to those programs and entities that ensure equitable and accurate Hispanic portrayals and employment.
- *Conduct and publicize new research* on portrayals of Hispanics and on the effects these media portrayals have on public opinion and on Hispanic self-perceptions. Areas to examine include feature films, broadcast and print news coverage, advertising, radio, and television.
- *Make sure that advocacy efforts are aggressive and consistent* so that there is both broad and continuing public awareness of the problem as well as effective continuing implementation of solutions.

Certain sectors could become more involved in media advocacy. Latino and other government officials can use their power to promote more accurate Hispanic media portrayals. Hispanic-owned firms, as well as their non-Latino vendors and customers, can exercise considerable clout with the media through their advertising expenditures. There already exists a large, long-term, and profitable Spanish-language media industry—this, in fact, distinguishes Latinos from other racial and ethnic groups in the United States. Hispanic-owned firms and the Spanish-language media can become more active in supporting new and creative media efforts and encouraging the community's support of such ventures. In addition, they can investigate ways in which investing in worthy Latino projects can be more profitable, perhaps by appealing to the general market.

To move beyond pretty ideas on paper to action, we must realize that because we are part of the system, we have the power to influence change. It is our individual responsibility as consumers to write, to boycott, to make known our opinions, to make our voice heard.

What Can Government Do?

For a democracy to function well, all citizens must be provided with equality of opportunity and equal protection under the law. A democratic government must thus intervene where necessary to ensure that no segment of its citizenry is underrepresented or misrepresented. In the following section, I present and discuss several ways that citizens and their government can address some of the inequities surrounding Latinos and the media.

- *Adopt Legislation.* Congress can consider additional legislation to address use of negative and stereotypical portrayals of Hispanics by the media and the underrepresentation of Latinos in the media. In the same way that federal law requires that bank loans be made in the same areas from which deposits are drawn, legislation could be passed to require that program content and employment patterns of radio and television stations reflect the demographic makeup of their broadcast areas.
- *Conduct Public Hearings.* Congress and state and local legislatures can call public attention to these issues by holding public hearings.
- *Revise, Strengthen, and Enforce Regulatory Standards.* The agency most directly involved with the media, the Federal Communications Commission (FCC), can revise, strengthen, and enforce its regulatory standards so that a "100 percent of parity" standard is used to measure equal employment opportunity compliance rather than the current "50 percent of parity" guideline. As NCLR (1994:37) has noted, "To do otherwise is tantamount to a Commission endorsement of employment policies and practices that lead to underrepresentation of Hispanics and other minorities."
- *Impose Penalties.* The FCC can deny station license renewals or impose fines and other penalties on licensees found to have violated equal opportunity guidelines.

- *Use Current Data.* Given the rapid Hispanic population growth, the FCC can use updated demographic data from the census and other sources to hold licensees to the highest possible standard.
- *Perform Comprehensive Research and Follow-Up.* The U.S. Commission on Civil Rights can conduct a comprehensive study of media portrayals of minorities and women, with a special focus on Hispanics and other previously neglected groups. It can institute vigorous oversight and enforcement measures and support positive programming efforts.
- *Revise EEOC Priorities.* The Equal Employment Opportunity Commission can place a higher priority on the media. It can also carry out hearings on Hispanic employment in the entertainment and news industry. Moreover, it can conduct investigations and where appropriate pursue litigation against media entities under its jurisdiction.
- *Increase Efforts from The Corporation for Public Broadcasting.* The Corporation for Public Broadcasting (CPB) can aggressively seek out, produce, and promote high-quality Hispanic programming. Because CPB is a quasi-federal agency that receives public funding, it has a special obligation to provide programming that fairly and accurately portrays all groups in U.S. society.
- *Increase Funding for Hispanic Programming.* Although the National Endowment for the Arts and the National Endowment for the Humanities have recently experienced major cutbacks in their budgets, Hispanic-focused projects could be given support through enhanced outreach efforts so that a wider group of applicants can apply for the programs and special competitions.
- *Focus Federal Funding on Hispanic Issues.* The federal government can increase the proportion of research funding allocated to Hispanic-oriented media research. As NCLR (1994) has pointed out, few federally funded studies are focused principally, much less exclusively, on Hispanics. NCLR (1994) recommended that such federally supported, media-related research be required to include Hispanic samples and emphases, consistent with the growing proportion of the population that is Latino.

What Can the News and Entertainment Industry Do?

Many in the media industry are aware of and involved in addressing the dual problem of misrepresentation and underrepresentation of Latinos. Indeed, several trade associations have prepared reports on Latinos and other minorities in the media. But not enough has been done to correct the deficiencies documented in these reports and highlighted in this book. The media industry needs to do much more to increase the numbers and positions of Latino employees and to increase and improve the roles they play. Here, I offer a number of specific suggestions.

- *Adopt Content Standards.* NCLR (1994) noted that all sectors of the media industry should adopt voluntary standards and codes of ethics that conform to guidelines set forth by UCLA Professor Gordon Berry (1993) concerning the portrayal of racial, ethnic, and gender groups. In considering such standards, consistent with the need for artistic freedom and the protections of the First Amendment, the media industry should ask itself the following questions. (These are also questions you might ask yourself when determining whether particular programs or films are unfairly representing Latinos.)

    Does program content

    - portray various ethnic groups (both males and females) evenly in society, including depictions of historical, cultural, and current events?
    - portray various ethnic groups (both genders) evenly in their contributions to the arts and sciences?
    - show a diversity of professional and vocational roles and careers within ethnic groups (each gender)?
    - define or limit occupational aspirations in terms of ethnicity (gender)?
    - portray ethnic groups (both genders) throughout the range of socioeconomic conditions and lifestyle situations?
    - portray both traditional and nontraditional activities being performed by characters, regardless of ethnicity and gender?
    - portray active, creative, and problem-solving roles proportionally among various ethnic groups (males and females)?
    - use dialogue between various characters that is free of stereotypic language, demeaning labels, and race-related (gender-related) retorts?
    - portray emotional reactions such as fear, anger, aggression, excitement, love, and concern regardless of ethnicity (gender)?
    - stereotype personality traits based on ethnicity (gender)?

- *Disseminate a Set of Principles or a Code of Ethics.* All sectors of the news and entertainment industry can voluntarily adopt—and widely disseminate—a set of principles or code of ethics that commits the industry to promoting equitable, accurate, and sensitive portrayals of Latinos and other minorities. These principles can be disseminated not just to media watchdog organizations, civil rights organizations, and community groups; they can also be incorporated in the annual performance standards and reviews that industry entities conduct in the normal course of business.
- *Develop Training and Career Paths.* A key void for the Latino community in the entertainment industry is a dearth of persons in decision-making positions who have the ability to "green-light" projects. To begin to expand the pool of

Hispanic players, the industry can develop and support film school scholarship programs, entry-level career-track development efforts, and on-the-job training programs. Attention must be given to how to develop substantive and meaningful training programs for promising Hispanic actors, producers, writers, and directors so that tokenism can be avoided.

- *Increase Latino Employment and Promotions.* Each segment of the media can immediately prepare and adopt specific plans and strategies to ensure parity in Hispanic employment and promotions for all occupational categories within a reasonable period. These plans and strategies can be prepared in conjunction with major media trade associations, such as the National Association of Broadcasters, the Motion Picture Association of America, the National Cable Television Association, and the Association of Newspaper Publishers.
- *Make Greater Use of Caucus Research and Expertise.* For many years, industry trade associations, for example, the Screen Actors Guild, the Directors Guild of America, and the National Association of Hispanic Journalists, have produced reports concerning the situation of minorities in the media. These reports have not received the attention they deserve and their recommendations have not been heeded. This is unfortunate. The management side of the entertainment industry can increase cooperative efforts with, and use the expertise and resources of, these groups to improve the situation of Hispanics in media.
- *Enforce Diversity Clauses.* Diversity clauses in standard collective bargaining agreements can be more vigorously enforced. In all collective bargaining agreements signed by production companies or advertisers with the Screen Actors Guild (SAG), for example, the company agrees to "realistically portray the American scene" in its full diversity, and "to provide all qualified performers with equal access to auditions and casting" (Screen Actors Guild, 1993:1). As part of that contractual agreement, the production company voluntarily provides SAG with data on the age, ethnicity, and gender of performers hired. These data are helpful in identifying problems, but violations of the diversity clauses themselves are rarely acted on. Legal steps can be taken to impose civil penalties and other sanctions against violators of these diversity clauses.
- *Develop Latino-Focused Programming Material.* Production studios and independent producers can aggressively seek out promising Latino-focused programming material.
- *Support Independent and Community-Based Projects.* The industry can provide increased support for Hispanic independent and community-based entertainment projects. Much of the entertainment industry's most innovative and creative efforts, especially from women and African Americans, originates

with the independent and community-level arts and entertainment communities. The industry can support similar Latino community-based efforts, including theaters and production companies, to help develop and nurture creative talent. In addition, the major film festivals can seek out more minority entrants, especially from Latinos and other underrepresented groups.

- *Conduct Periodic Self-Assessments.* Each segment of the news industry can conduct a periodic self-assessment of its coverage of the Hispanic community. Self-assessments can include commissioning content analyses of its news coverage by independent organizations or scholars, organizing community forums and symposia to obtain input from the Latino community, and determining the extent to which Hispanic perspectives are included in stories on "non-Hispanic" themes, such as the economy, business, and the arts.
- *Create Internal Monitoring Mechanisms.* The news industry can develop more effective internal mechanisms for monitoring the comprehensiveness and the accuracy of its news coverage. For example, it can

  - retain and disseminate to all editors and reporters lists of trustworthy Latino sources or technical experts on Hispanic issues;
  - make an affirmative effort to include Hispanic views on "mainstream" stories, as well as invest resources in special series and features on Hispanic themes;
  - hire or retain distinguished Hispanic scholars, perhaps on a rotating basis, to fill an ombudsman role to monitor and comment on the organization's coverage of Latino issues.

We can do all this and much more. Change is dependent on will—this is true both on the individual level as well as at more institutional and organizational levels.[9]

NOTES

1. Most of the recommended actions in this section have been adapted from NCLR (1994) and Quiroga (1995).

2. These victories have involved staff dismissals and the retraction of statements that defamed Latinos. Some examples include campaigns against Howard Stern, *Chicago Tribune* columnist Mike Royko, and Jeff Katz, a Sacramento DJ, for their "insulting and lewd" comments (Richmond, 1996; "When a Newspaper Touches a Nerve," 1996:12); the allegations of the Spanish-language journalist Armando Montañer concerning Latinas and welfare; as well as the successful boycott against *The Perez Family.*

3. Latinos for Positive Images (LPI) came into being in New York City through mobilizing a boycott in 1995 in response to the lack of Latino casting in the film *The Perez Family.* The organization continues to hold forums to share and disseminate information to proactively combat negative and unfair images and to support endeavors that fairly and constructively

project Latinos and the issues facing the Latino community. LPI seeks to promote a progressive agenda for all people and to support Latino artists and opportunities in the media. The organization also seeks to mobilize the Latino community to use its economic power to demand and obtain better and more representation in the media.

4. For example, NHMC conducted a two-year campaign in which it targeted ABC and its affiliates and examined their compliance with FCC regulations. This national media watchdog group claimed success in getting ABC to follow through on promises to put more Latinos in prime time when ABC scheduled a new sitcom (*Common Law*) featuring a Hispanic lawyer for the fall 1996 season. But according to Alex Nogales, NHMC president, ABC refused to "publicly acknowledge its previous shortcomings or give the advocacy groups credit" (Braxton, 1996).

5. See "The National Entertainment State" (1996) for details on the increasing corporate concentration of the media industry and reactions to this concentration.

6. As was noted in a recent survey by ASNE of twelve newspaper editors, in the news business, minority reporters are journalistic assets and their absence handicaps employers (also see case studies by Quiroga, Chapter 2, this volume). Another editor in this survey noted, "Unless you have a newsroom that reflects the community, you will not have a journalistically strong newsroom"; a third editor stated, "We have an obligation to non-minorities to help them see the world the way others see it" (Caughey, 1995:18).

7. These figures are based on a 1996 minority employment survey that included 66 percent of U.S. daily newspapers. The survey also found that 11.02 percent of professional newsroom employees were Asian American, Black, Hispanic, or Native American. This was up from 4 percent in 1978, when annual surveys were begun (ASNE, 1996).

8. One successful example that is often cited is the campaign that targeted sponsors of Howard Stern's talk show. Letter writing and an economic boycott were organized to protest Stern's negative comments after the death of the Tex-Mex singer Selena. A number of firms pulled out as sponsors of the show (Torres, 1995).

9. With will and organization, much can be done to create climates for change within different arenas, including radio, TV, film, and individual living rooms. One model for change is that utilized by the Non-Traditional Casting Project in New York, which brings together people in a position to influence change and provides a neutral agent who facilitates an agenda for change. The agenda includes the implementation of nontraditional casting, increasing diversity both on and off the sets, and showing others how this agenda is part of a win-win strategy for all.

References

Acosta-Belén, E. (Ed.). (1979). *The Puerto Rican Woman* (1st ed.). New York: Praeger.

Acosta-Belén, E. (Ed.). (1986). *The Puerto Rican Woman* (2nd ed.). New York: Praeger.

Alma Gomez, Cherrie Moraga, and Vicki Ruíz. (1983). *Cuentos.* New York: Kitchen Table Press.

Alvarez, Julia. (1991). *How the Garcia Girls Lost Their Accent.* Chapel Hill, NC: Algonquin Books of Chapel Hill.

American Society of Newspaper Editors. (1996). *Annual Employment Survey.* Reston, VA: Author.

Anzaldúa, Gloria. (1987). *Borderlands/La Frontera: The New Mestiza.* San Francisco: Spinsters/Aunt Lute.

Avila, Alex. (1996, April). "The 25 Most Powerful Hispanics in Hollywood," *Hispanic,* pp. 20–28.

Basinger, Jeanine. (1993). *A Woman's View: How Hollywood Spoke to Women, 1930–1960.* New York: Knopf.

Berry, Gordon L. (1993). "Multicultural Portrayals on Television as a Social Psychological Issue," in *Children and Television Images: Images in a Changing Sociocultural World,* Gordon L. Berry and Joy Keiko Asamen (Eds.). Newbury Park, CA: Sage.

Boyd, William M. II. (1995, September). "Diversity is a Bottom-Line Issue," *The American Editor,* p. 21.

Braxton, Greg. (1996, May 22). "Latino-Based Sitcom Seen as Partial Win," *Los Angeles Times,* pp. F1, F7.

Butler Flora, Cornelia. (1973). "The Passive Female and Social Change: A Cross-Cultural Comparison of Women's Magazine Fiction," in *Female and Male in Latin America: Essays,* Ann M. Pescatello (Ed.). Pittsburgh: University of Pittsburgh Press, pp. 60–83.

Cabrera, Katarina. (1996). "1995 Film Retrospective," *frontera: the next generation, 1*(1), 38.

Calvo Ospina, Hernando. (1995). *Salsa: Havana Heat, Bronx Beat.* New York: Monthly Review Press.

Candelaria, Cordelia. (1985). "Social Equity in Film Criticism," in *Chicano Cinema: Research, Reviews and Resources,* Gary D. Keller (Ed.). Binghamton, NY: Bilingual Review/Press, pp. 64–70.

Canel, Fausto. (1990, Winter). "Y Que Pasa Hollywood?" *Mas,* p. 10.

Carveth, Rod, and Diane Alverio. (1996). *Network Brownout: The Portrayal of Latinos in Network Television News* (Report prepared for the National Association of Hispanic Journalists). Washington, DC: National Association of Hispanic Journalists.

Caughey, Bernard. (1995, September). "Editors Discuss Affirmative Action," *The American Editor,* pp. 17–18.

Chavez, Denise. (1992). "Chata," in *Iguana Dreams: New Latino Fiction,* Delia Poey and Virgil Suarez (Eds.). New York: HarperPerennial, pp. 43–53.

Cortés, Carlos E. (1991). "Hollywood Interracial Love: Social Taboo as Screen Titillation," in *Beyond the Stars II: Plot Conventions in American Popular Film*, Paul Loukides and Linda K. Fuller (Eds.). Bowling Green, OH: Bowling Green State University Popular Press.

Domínguez, Robert. (1995, January 15). "H'wood 'Nix' to Hispanix in Flix," *Daily News*, p. 15.

Elsasser, Nan, Kyle MacKenzie, and Yvonne Tixier y Vigil. (1980). *Las Mujeres: Conversations with the Hispanic Community*. Old Westbury: Feminist Press.

Esteves, Sandra María. (1990). *Bluestown Mockingbird Mambo*. Houston: Arte Público Press.

Film Index International. (1993–1995). Cambridge, UK: British Film Institute.

Fregoso, Rosa Linda. (1993). *The Bronze Screen: Chicana and Chicano Film Culture*. Minneapolis: University of Minnesota Press, 1993.

Friedman, Lester D. (Ed.). (1991). *Unspeakable Images*. Urbana: University of Illinois Press.

Fullerton, Howard J., Jr. (1995, November). "The 2005 Labor Force: Growing, but Slowly," *Monthly Labor Review, 118*(11), 29–44.

Garcia Berumen, Frank Javier. (1995). *The Chicano/Hispanic Image in American Film*. New York: Vantage.

Garza, Melita. (1992). "Covering Hispanics," *Covering the Community: Newspaper Content Audits*. Reston, VA: American Society of Newspaper Editors, pp. 34–36.

Graham, Allison. (1995). "Teaching Across Race, Class and Gender: Film Course Raises Issues," *Center News, 13*(2), 3, 10 (Center for Research on Women, Memphis State University).

Hadley-Garcia, George. (1993). *Hispanic Hollywood: The Latins in Motion Pictures*. New York: Carol.

Hall, Stuart. (1981). "The Whites of Their Eyes: Racist Ideologies and the Media," in *Silver Linings: Some Strategies for the Eighties*, George Bridges and Rosalind Brunt (Eds.). London: Lawrence & Wishart, pp. 7–23.

Hardy-Fanta, Carol. (1993). *Latina Politics, Latino Politics*. Philadelphia: Temple University Press.

Henry, O. (1907). "The Caballero's Way," in *The Complete Works of O. Henry* (1937). Garden City, NY: Garden City Publishing, pp. 197–206.

Hill, Jane H. (1993). "Hasta La Vista, Baby: Anglo Spanish in the American Southwest," *Critique of Anthropology, 13*(2), 145–176.

Hill, Jane H. (1995). "Junk Spanish, Covert Racism, and the (Leaky) Boundary Between Public and Private Spheres," *Pragmatics, 5*(2), 197–212.

Jarvie, Ian C. (1991). "Stars and Ethnicity: Hollywood and the United States, 1932–51," in *Unspeakable Images*, Lester D. Friedman (Ed.). Urbana: University of Illinois Press, pp. 82–112.

Katz, Ephraim. (1994). *The Film Encyclopedia*. New York: HarperPerennial.

Keller, Gary D. (1994). *Hispanics and United States Film: An Overview and Handbook*. Tempe, AZ: Bilingual Review/Press.

Keller, Gary D. (Ed.). (1985). *Chicano Cinema: Research, Reviews and Resources*. Binghamton, NY: Bilingual Review/Press.

Lichter, S. Robert, and Daniel R. Amundson. (1994, September). *Distorted Reality: Hispanic Characters in TV Entertainment*. Washington, DC: Center for Media and Public Affairs.

Lichter, S. Robert, and Linda S. Lichter. (1988). *Television's Impact on Ethnic and Racial Images: A Study of Howard Beach Adolescents*. New York: American Jewish Committee.

Llano, Todd. (1995, July). "Movie Maze: How Hispanic Films Overcome Obstacles in Hollywood to Get to Market," *Hispanic*, pp. 22–26.

López, Ana M. (1991). "Are All Latins from Manhattan? Hollywood, Ethnography and Cultural Colonialism," in *Unspeakable Images*, Lester D. Friedman (Ed.). Urbana: University of Illinois Press, pp. 277–307.

Massey, Douglas S. (1995, September). *The New Immigration and the Meaning of Ethnicity in the United States.* Population and Development Review *21*(3): 631–653.

Mejías-Rentas, Antonio. (1995, June 15). "Arts and Entertainment," *Hispanic Link Weekly Report, 3*(20), 8.

Mohr, Nicolasa. (1986). *Rituals of Survival: A Woman's Portfolio.* Houston: Arte Público.

Morales, Ed. (1996, July 30). "Brownout: Searching for the Missing Latinos in the Media," *Village Voice*, pp. 25–29.

National Advisory Commission on Civil Disorders. (1968). *Report.* New York: Bantam.

National Council of La Raza. (1994, August). *Out of the Picture: Hispanics in the Media, State of Hispanic America 1994.* Washington, DC: Author.

"The National Entertainment State." (1996, June 3). *The Nation*, pp. 9–21.

Newman, Kathleen. (1992). "Latino Sacrifice in the Discourse of Citizenship: Acting Against the 'Mainstream,'" in *Chicanos and Film: Essays on Chicano Representation and Resistance,* Chon Noriega (Ed.). New York: Garland, pp. 67–82.

Nieto, Sonia. (1992). *Affirming Diversity: The Sociopolitical Context of Multicultural Education.* New York: Longman.

Noriega, Chon. (Ed.). (1992). *Chicanos and Film: Essays on Chicano Representation and Resistance.* New York: Garland.

Noriega, Chon A., and Ana M. López. (Eds.). (1996). *The Ethnic Eye: Latino Media Arts.* Minneapolis: University of Minnesota Press.

Ortiz Cofer, Judith. (1990). *Silent Dancing: A Partial Remembrance of a Puerto Rican Childhood.* Houston: Arte Público.

Pacheco, Patrick. (1993, May 2). "The Woman in Red Changes to Black," *New York Times,* pp. 21, 39.

Petersen, David J. (1995, November-December). "Affirmative Action Not Reflected in Employee Statistics," *Directors Guild Magazine, 20*(5), 14, 16.

Prida, Delores. (1991). *Beautiful Señoritas.* Houston: Arte Público.

Quiroga, Jorge. (1995). *Hispanic Voices: Is the Press Listening?* (Discussion Paper D-18). The Joan Shorenstein Center, John F. Kennedy School of Government, Harvard University.

Reyes, Luis, and Peter Rubie. (1994). *Hispanics in Hollywood: An Encyclopedia of Film and Television.* New York: Garland.

Richard, Alfred Charles. (1993). *Censorship and Hollywood's Hispanic Image: An Interpretive Filmography, 1936–1955.* Westview, CT: Greenwood.

Richmond, Ray. (1996, August 29). "California Radio DJ Fired for Racial Remarks," *The Reuters Wire* [Reuters/Variety].

Rios-Bustamante, Antonio. (1988, January). "Latinos and the Hollywood Film Industry, 1920–1950's," *Americas, 2001, 1*(4), 6–25.

Rios-Bustamante, Antonio. (1992). "Latino Participation in the Hollywood Film Industry, 1911–1945," in *Chicanos and Film: Essays on Chicano Representation and Resistance*, Chon Noriega (Ed.). New York: Garland, pp. 21–32.

Romero, Mary. (1992). *Maid in the U.S.A.* New York: Routledge.

Sánchez-Korrol, Virginia. (1994). "In Search of Unconventional Women: Women in Religious Vocations," in *Barrios and Borderlands: Cultures of Latinos and Latinas in the United States,* Daly Heyck and Denis Lynn (Eds.). New York: Routledge, pp. 140–151.

Sánchez-Korrol, Virginia. (1996). "Survival of Puerto Rican Women in New York Before World War II," in *Historical Perspectives on Puerto Rican Survival in the United States,* Clara E. Rodríguez and Virginia Sánchez-Korrol (Eds.). Princeton, NJ: Markus Wiener, pp. 55–68.

Screen Actors Guild. (1993, June 15). *Employment in Entertainment: The Search for Diversity.* Hollywood, CA: Author.

Screen Actors Guild. (1995). *SAG Performers Employment Statistics: Industry Totals—Ethnicity & Gender, 1991–1995.* Los Angeles: Author.

"Special Report: Latino Viewing of Network TV 1993/94." (1994, November 10). *BBDO Special Reports, 3*(3), 1–8.

Standard Directory of Advertisers. (Annual). New Providence, NJ: National Register Publishing, Reed Reference Publishing.

Subervi-Vélez, Federico, with Charles Ramírez Berg, Patricia Constantakis-Valdés, Chon Noriega, Diana I. Ríos, and Kenton T. Wilkinson. (1994). "Hispanic Oriented Media," in the *Handbook of Hispanic Cultures in the United States: Sociology,* Felix Padilla (Ed.). Houston: Arte Público, pp. 304–357.

Torres, Joseph. (1995, May 8). "Several Advertisers Pull Ads from Stern Show," *Hispanic Link, 13*(19), 1.

Torres, Joseph. (1996, September 9). "Media Report: Small Screen Viewing Habits," *Hispanic Link, 14*(36), 10.

U.S. Bureau of the Census. (1990a). *1990 Census of Population. General Population Characteristics, 1990 CP-1-1* (Table 258). Washington, DC: Author.

U.S. Bureau of the Census. (1990b). *1990 Census of Population and Housing. CP-3-3, Persons of Hispanic Origin in the United States: 1990.* Washington, DC: Author.

Vásquez, Blanca. (1990). "Puerto Ricans and the Media: A Personal Statement," *Centro Bulletin,* 3(1), 5–15 (Centro de Estudios Puertorriquenos, Hunter College).

"When a Newspaper Touches a Nerve." (1996, March 6). [Editorial]. *Chicago Tribune,* p. 12.

Wilson, Clint C. II, and Félix Gutiérrez. (1985). *Minorities and the Media* (1st ed.). Thousand Oaks, CA: Sage.

Wilson, Clint C. II, and Félix Gutiérrez. (1995). *Race, Multiculturalism and the Media* (2nd ed.). Thousand Oaks, CA: Sage.

Woll, Allen L. (1980). *The Latin Image in American Film* (rev. ed.). Latin American Center Publications, University of California, Los Angeles.

Woll, Allen L., and Randall M. Miller. (1987). *Ethnic and Racial Images in American Film and Television: Historical Essays and Bibliography.* New York: Garland.

World Almanac and Book of Facts. (1996). Mahwah, NJ: Author.

About the Book and Editor

What are "Latin looks"? A Latin look may seem at first blush to be something that everyone recognizes—brunette, sensual, expressive, animated, perhaps threatening. But upon reflection, we realize that these are the images that are prevalent in the media, while the reality in Latino communities is of a rich diversity of people and images. This book brings together a selection of the best, the most interesting, and the most analytically sophisticated writing on how Latinos have been portrayed in movies, television, and other media since the early years of the twentieth century and how images have changed over time in response to social and political change. Particular emphasis is given to representations of class, gender, color, race, and the political relationship between the United States and Latin America. Together the essays offer a corrective lens for interpreting how images are created, perpetuated, and manipulated.

Clara Rodríguez is professor of sociology at Fordham University at Lincoln Center.

About the Contributors

The **National Council of La Raza** (NCLR) report was prepared by Lisa Navarrete with Charles Kamasaki. Based in Washington, D.C., and headed by Raul Yzaguirre, the NCLR is the largest constituency-based Hispanic organization in the United States; major areas of interest include policy analysis, advocacy, and legislation.

Jorge Quiroga is an award-winning senior news reporter for WCVB-TV in Boston. He was also the creator, first producer, and host of *Aqui*, a Hispanic public affairs program that first aired in 1974 on WCVB-TV.

S. Robert Lichter is the Founder of the Center for Media and Public Affairs; **Daniel R. Amundson** is its Research Director. The center is a nonpartisan and nonprofit research and educational organization that conducts scientific studies of news and entertainment media.

Chon Noriega is Assistant Professor in the University of California, Los Angeles, Department of Film and Television. He is the author of numerous works that examine ethnicity and the media.

Charles Ramírez Berg is Associate Professor in the Department of Radio-Television-Film at the University of Texas at Austin.

Carlos E. Cortés is Professor Emeritus of History in the Department of History at the University of California, Riverside.

Richie Pérez is currently Director of Community Development and Voter Participation at the Community Service Society in New York City. He is a former member of various activist organizations, including the Young Lords Party and the National Congress for Puerto Rican Rights, as well as a professor of Puerto Rican Studies.

Alberto Sandoval Sánchez is Professor of Spanish in the Department of Spanish and Italian at Mount Holyoke College.

Lillian Jiménez is Acting Executive Director of Media Network, a national media arts center. She has been active in the field of independent film and video for the past twenty years and launched the National Latino Film and Video Festival at El Museo del Barrio in 1981.

Liz Kotz has written on film, video, and visual arts for *Artforum, Art in America,* and other publications. A graduate student in comparative literature at Columbia University, she is completing a dissertation on the obsession with language in 1960s U.S. art.

Linda Williams is Professor of Film Studies and Womens Studies at the University of California, Irvine.

Santiago Nieves is a veteran print and broadcast journalist and media critic who in 1976 founded *Latino Journal,* radio's longest-running Latino news and opinion program. He also still hosts and produces this program, as well as *Talk Back* on WBAI in New York.

Frank Algarin works for the Latino Collaborative, an independent film and video collaborative in New York.

Federico Subervi-Vélez is Associate Professor in the Department of Radio-Television-Film at the University of Texas at Austin.

Patricia Constantakis-Valdés is Director of Media Services at Academic Systems Corporation in Mountain View, California. Her research areas include interactive media and education and ethnic media in the United States.

Diana I. Ríos is Assistant Professor in the Department of Communication and Journalism, University of New Mexico.

Kenton T. Wilkinson is Assistant Professor in the Division of English, Classics, Philosophy, and Communication, University of Texas at San Antonio.

Index